A PROTESTANT LEGACY

A PROTESTANT LEGACY

*Attitudes to Death and Illness
among Older Aberdonians*

RORY WILLIAMS

CLARENDON PRESS . OXFORD
1990

Oxford University Press, Walton Street, Oxford OX2 6DP
Oxford New York Toronto
Delhi Bombay Calcutta Madras Karachi
Petaling Jaya Singapore Hong Kong Tokyo
Nairobi Dar es Salaam Cape Town
Melbourne Auckland
and associated companies in
Berlin Ibadan

Oxford is a trade mark of Oxford University Press

Published in the United States
by Oxford University Press, New York

British Library Cataloguing in Publication Data
Williams, Rory
A Protestant legacy: attitudes to death and illness
among older Aberdonians.
1. Death. Attitudes of society
I. Title
306.9
ISBN 0–19–827736–9

Library of Congress Cataloging in Publication Data
Williams, Rory.
A Protestant legacy: attitudes to death and illness among older
Aberdonians/Rory Williams.
p. cm.
Includes bibliographical references.
1. Aged—Scotland—Aberdeen—Attitudes. 2. Protestants—Scotland—
Aberdeen—Attitudes. 3. Aging—Scotland—Aberdeen—Public opinion.
4. Death—Scotland—Aberdeen—Public opinion. 5. Public opinion—
Scotland—Aberdeen. 6. Health attitudes—Scotland—Aberdeen.
I. Title.
HQ1064.G7W57 1990 89-22776
305.26'09412'35—dc20
ISBN 0–19–827736–9

Typeset by
Jaygee Export Private Limited, India
Printed and bound in
Great Britain by Bookcraft (Bath) Ltd.,
Midsomer Norton, Avon

For Julie

Acknowledgements

My first and chief debt is to the Aberdonians who talked to me, and especially to those who espoused the subject as their own and gave me introductions to others. Having tried to portray their life and way of thinking, my chief sensation is of how much has been left out, and of how impossible it is to do justice to their individual biographies. I can only hope that, whatever these individual deficiencies, they would find this patchwork from their stories a recognizable rendering of the overall colour and pattern of Aberdeen life in their generation. Certainly they helped me to rediscover my own Aberdonian past, and I am grateful.

The genesis of the book goes back some years now. The field-work on which it is based came out of a programme of research on ageing funded by the Medical Research Council and devised in the MRC Medical Sociology Unit in the late 1970s, when it was in Aberdeen. I formulated my own project within this programme under the benevolent, if sceptical, eyes of Raymond Illsley, then Director, and of Rex Taylor, who led the programme, and they alerted a not always willing listener to many snares along the way. Rex and Graeme Ford then conducted the survey side of the programme, allowing me generous access to their results, and refusing anything more than the grateful acknowledgement which I am glad to give them here. In my own fieldwork I had the benefit of advice not only from these three, but also from Mildred Blaxter, Mick Bloor, and Gordon Horobin. Mildred's work opened a number of gates for me. Mick befriended me, and, as always, helped to his own hindrance, even involving himself in the tedious testing described in Appendix 1. Gordon's death in 1987 left me, amongst other things, wishing that I had finished this in time for him to read it. That inconsequential but stubborn feeling is a selfish tribute to the infinite capacity he had for interest in others and their work.

The successive drafts of the analysis which followed would have been impossible without Vye Bruce, Muriel Burnett, Kim Macindoe, Edna McIntyre, Jean Money, Eleanor Rattray, Gill Sinclair, and Jeanette Thorn. I remember their good-humoured help with pleasure. When I eventually mastered the microcomputer and word processor it was Guy Muhlemann who taught and retaught me, and who resolved my recurrent confusions with a patience which continues to astonish me. The work of indexing was shared by Irene Hind, who saved me many hours of labour.

The resultant text has benefited from many readers and critics. The whole, or a large portion, was read by Mildred Blaxter, Mick Bloor, Mike Hepworth, Peter McCaffery, and Sally Macintyre; and individual chapters were read by Bill Bytheway, Jocelyn Cornwell, Sarah Cunningham-Burley, David Field, Graeme Ford, Mary Gilhooly, Teresa McCaffery, Jim McIntosh, Neil McKeganey, John Miller, Emma Shackle, Rex Taylor, Tony Walter, Andrew Wear, and Pat West. They, and Henry Hardy and his advisers at OUP, have all helped me to make the book better than it was. I wish I could have made it as good as it should be; but I have come to the point where I have to say, I have done what I can.

Three people have not entered this chronology of my debts because my debt to them is timeless. My mother and father have given me an enduring example of gracefulness in their age as in their youth. And my wife Julie has sustained us both, in sickness and in health, with her unquenchable zest. Not only that, but in the difficult business of words and social portraiture, she has been my critic throughout, and set me standards of imagination and simplicity which I have not matched, but which I am glad to honour.

March 1989   *R.W.*

Contents

List of Tables

Introduction

The place

Perhaps the shortest way of putting the subject of this book is to say that it attempts to paint a picture of some of the moral and economic resources which Aberdonians turn to when they think about how to cope with physical limitation and loss—with illness, ageing, and death. In the background of this picture are a few of the large themes of contemporary society, and of the past, and the questions which bring these issues into focus are discussed shortly. But in the foreground are the clear-cut particulars of time and place; and I begin here by sketching the context for these particulars, and by giving a brief 'reading' of the visible contemporary city concerned here, in terms of themes which are important in this book.

Of the four chief cities of Scotland, Aberdeen is by a long way furthest north, and it is also, by a lesser margin, furthest east. With its North Sea harbour and sands on the one side, and the undulating hinterland which serves its cattle markets on the other, it inhabits a region of its own, set apart from the rest of Scotland by the rock and heather of the Grampians. There is a consciousness of difference. It is largely from the farming and fishing communities around it that the city's population has, right up to the present day, been built up; and one sign of this can be heard in the dialect, which has sounds, words, and expressions unknown elsewhere in Scotland, let alone in Britain as a whole. In some ways it is a private or a family language; and recognitions based on it are a recurring theme in Aberdonian stories of war and travel. The sahibs of the Raj who once gathered round a newly arrived Aberdonian at the sound of familiar place-names, or the stretcher bearers who recognized and singled out a wounded Aberdeen loon (lad) to take with them before the position was overrun, are typical characters in a perennial drama of North-East solidarity.

There is a strong local consciousness in the North-East of Scotland, therefore, and many aspects of it are thrown into relief by the topics of this book. I have referred to the North-East dialect as one expression of collective identity; but there are other aspects, too, of this shared background, which emerge in what follows. It is significant, for example, that Aberdonians who have not met before can 'place' each other, and discover common acquaintances, in a remarkably short space of time. And so it is no surprise to find, also, that those who are neighbours know a good deal about each other, are careful of their reputations, and in matters of health both contribute to, and answer to, a vigorous and demanding public opinion. There are strong conventions in Aberdeen, as southerners sometimes discover to their cost; yet by the same token, too, there is a strong sense of reciprocal obligation and care.

However, while the farming and fishing ancestry of most Aberdonians remains a unifying factor, contemporary experience at work has brought divisions, and these too enter into discussions of ageing. The range of industry in the city runs from rugged nineteenth century textile factories to the bland shapes of the oil supply vessels in the harbour which was rapidly reorganized for them during the 1970s. North Sea oil has, until the last year or two, saved Aberdeen from the decline and unemployment which has afflicted other Scottish cities, and has given a prosperity to its younger generations which has sustained the sense of post-war boom. The bankers and financiers of Union Street and its adjoining terraces, and the shipwrights, chandlers, engineers, box makers, and chemical firms which crowd the cobbled back streets of the port, and spread southwards over the industrial estate, have been able to add outlets in the oil industry to those in trawling and agriculture. Yet these continuing conditions of relative prosperity have been regarded cautiously. The oil is getting harder to find, and in any case incomers too have taken a substantial share of the proceeds. But also, there is a caution which can be traced in part to memories of the Depression, when up to a fifth of the city's labour force was out of work,[1] a proportion not quite so dramatic as those of Dundee or Glasgow, but one still deeply entrenched in public consciousness, and in the minds of those who are now growing old. And in part too, scepticism of easy times can be traced to experience of the harsher, more exposed conditions of the old core industries of the region—not only the notorious stresses of the fishing, and of the agricultural bothies where older men remember waking to see the walls clothed in ice, but also of the granite industry which shaped the austere lines of the city's streets.

Another aspect of these historic divisions in Aberdonians' industrial experience is reflected in neighbourhood allegiances. The city lies astride two fast-flowing Highland rivers, and while the southern one, the Dee, has formed the port, the northern Don provided the power for a cluster of mills producing paper and textiles, which were for a long time the foundation of villages separate from Aberdeen proper. Their names—Bucksburn, Stoneywood, Woodside—reflect their once rural surroundings, and their populations together with that of the ancient university town, also near the Don, and also no more than a village, have retained a sense of their own identity, even though they have since been flooded by the housing expansion of the port city.

Other divisions in Aberdeen life are portrayed in the structure of the housing, where again there are distinctive local peculiarities which are reflected in accounts of illness and old age. The narrow streets of crowded granite tenements round the port, run by private landlords, belonged to a communal structure of living characteristic of Scottish cities, with shared stairs and lobbies, and a shared drying green, whose cleaning and use were the subject of rigid rotas and public comment. After the First and Second World Wars, the Town, like other Scottish authorities, used the council house legislation to an exceptional degree to reduce the overcrowding and improve facilities; but in other respects they merely exported the tenemental model. There are sporadic outbreaks of tower blocks, but on the whole two, three, or four storey terraces of flats, with shared stairs and greens, dominate, flowing out to the south-west perimeter, as well as to the north and north-west around the Don. All this stands in sharp contrast to the West End, where the majority of the older granite owner-occupied houses are found, with long gardens at the back and tree-lined streets in front.

Above the roofs of all these houses that clothe the hill lines as they sink down to the sea, rise the eaves and ridges of magisterial stone buildings which are as prominent as the church spires—the schools of the older part of Aberdeen, also a frequent focus of solidarity and social distinction among those who are themselves growing old. School and age group are the first characteristics sought by one Aberdonian placing another in order to find common acquaintances. For the most part such questions discriminate the same quarters of the city as have already been distinguished;

but three schools near the centre long had a special social significance—for boys, Robert Gordon's and the Grammar, and for
girls the High School. The latter two were brought into the state
education system in the last quarter of the nineteenth century, but
remained fee-paying, although there were bursaries for poorer
children.. It was only after the Second World War that fees were
abolished, against strong opposition, and the subsequent process
of turning the Grammar into a comprehensive was accompanied
by a similar furore from former pupils.

As one turns from this older area of settlement towards the
suburbs that flow up and over the western ridge of the city,
two newer and more egalitarian kinds of institution, constantly
alluded to in discussions of health, rise amid acres of grass and
parked cars—the two major hospitals, and the offices of the
Regional Council at Woodhill House. For present purposes, the
medical and social services which these institutions respectively
represent contain little that is locally distinctive, and much that is
typical of Britain as a whole. The former Poor Law institution of
Oldmill—an isolated and impressive structure of stone, still on the
fringe of an expanded city—is now Woodend Hospital, which
includes, as so often, the geriatric longstay wing. Explosions of
new glass and concrete are chiefly visible elsewhere—around the
acute specialties in the Aberdeen Royal Infirmary, still known, by
the name of the open land it began to occupy between the wars, as
Foresterhill. These, together with various smaller institutions,
most of which are also in Aberdeen, are teaching hospitals which
serve the whole of the North-East. At the time of this study, their
provision for the problems of those growing old was very much in
the middle of the Scottish range, and approximated to that of Scotland as a whole. Table 1 gives the picture for some relevant specialties. Against the elderly population, the figures for geriatric and
longstay beds, both in the local area and in Scotland, were better,
in so far as they can be compared, than contemporary figures for
England.[2] Thus in the Grampian Health Board, where the death
rate at older ages was a little lower than the Scottish figure and
only a little above the English figure,[3] the provision could be
reckoned as being average to good.

Where curative or rehabilitative medicine fails, however, and
the need is for care of the dying, Aberdeen has until recently been
less well provided. It was only in 1977 that the first unit directed to

Table 1. *Grampian Health Board and Scotland: statistics for selected specialties, 1980*

Specialty	Average available staffed beds per 100,000 population		Discharges per 100,000 population	
	Grampian	Scotland	Grampian	Scotland
Geriatric assessment	47	46	270	265
Geriatric longstay	121	140	95	144
Psychogeriatric	95	53	72	46
SUBTOTAL	263	239	437	455
General medicine	79	87	2,123	2,256
TOTAL	342	326	2,560	2,711

Source: Information Services Division, *Scottish Health Statistics 1980*, Edinburgh: HMSO, 1982, Table 6.4.

care of the dying was opened, and this is a point to which I return. Death itself was more efficiently provided for, among the granite monuments of the city's cemeteries, or the immaculate lawns of the crematorium. The cemeteries, predictably, are features of the Victorian suburbs, while the crematorium is a semi-rural exemplar of the municipal style of the 1970s, answering to a greatly increased demand since its predecessor and original opened in 1937. The final destination of Aberdonians is thus, as will become apparent, a subject for discussion and choice.

For others who elude these destinations, but linger on in a more or less disabled state, the social services from Woodhill House, and more broadly, all services given at home, acquire a vital significance. Statistics for these forms of help provide a similar picture to those for the hospitals (Table 2). Only day centres were not so well provided at the time of this study; otherwise figures for home help and meals on wheels were close to those for Scotland, and in both services Scottish norms were close to those for Britain. Much the same, too, can be said for home nursing[4] and for residential places.[5] On the whole, then, social and medical services for the elderly are reasonably well developed in Aberdeen, and while

Table 2. *Grampian Region, Scotland, and Great Britain: statistics for selected community services, 1980*

Region	Clients per 1,000 aged 65 and over		
	Day centres	Home help	Meals on wheels
Grampian	1.4	7.1	2.0
Scotland	5.1	7.7	2.1
Great Britain	5	9	2

Sources: Grampian and Scotland: Scottish Education Department, *Home care services, day care establishments and day services 1980, Scotland,* Statistical Bulletin, Social Work Services Group, 1981, Tables 3, 5, and 18; figures for clients/places at 31 March 1980. Great Britain: Office of Population Censuses and Surveys, *General household survey 1980,* London: HMSO, 1982, Table 10.41; the table relates to use of the service in the month before interview.

on the whole they do not have the cachet of the maternity services, for which Aberdeen has a national reputation, they partake in some of the pride with which Aberdonians regard all these services.

Woodhill House and the Town, Woodend and Foresterhill, the churches and schools, the West End and the estates, the harbour and the old mill villages, the city, the farming hinterland, and the sea—these, then, are some of the enduring features of the landscape between which Aberdonian lives and Aberdonian talk move in an intricate web. These fixed structures—fixed, that is, in the short term—act to constrain and shape the web. Yet the web is also constantly being rewoven, and the enduring structures themselves have slowly mutated, under the influence of the guiding ideas of the period—ideas whose manifestations in the visible city are less obvious. While local sources, or redirecting channels, can be found for these ideas in the city's churches and schools, in the university, in the *Aberdeen Press & Journal,* in the district and regional councils and party offices, or in North-East literature and song, their provenance is ultimately much wider. But a few important features of the character they take in Aberdonian conversation can be sketched by looking finally at local political and religious institutions.

The present political complexion of Aberdeen has its roots in the agrarian radicalism of the period before the First World War.[6] While the balladry of that time has now become part of the rural nostalgia of the contemporary city, its critique of the powerful was absorbed into the themes of radical protest against the war and the Depression which followed—a strain of North-East thinking which was chronicled in Lewis Grassic Gibbon's trilogy *A Scots Quair*.[7] It is not surprising, therefore, that after the Second World War most of Aberdeen settled into institutionalized support of the Labour Party. The Town—the City Council whose burghal pride is marked by the tower which dominates the port end of Union Street—was controlled by Labour virtually without interruption in the post-war period. And in parliamentary elections the two chief city constituencies reflected a similar balance of forces. While South Aberdeen—which includes the West End—had a moderate Conservative majority in the 1950s, it slid into marginal status during the 1960s and 1970s; and North Aberdeen continued to return some of the biggest Labour majorities in the country.

Aberdonian religion has a still longer continuity with the past. While there was a sustained rearguard action fought against the Reformation, led by the 'Aberdeen doctors' in the medieval village around King's college, the Reformers were eventually successful in gaining overwhelming control of the city's churches. Their strength even in the sixteenth century is attested by the separate foundation, in the port town, of Marischal College in opposition to King's; and while a native Catholic and Episcopalian presence remains to the present day, members of these churches constitute only a small fraction of the city's population. Among the rest, the established Presbyterian Church of Scotland far outstrips other denominations; but this has been so only since the healing of the split between the established church and the Free Church in 1929.

This major division in the Presbyterian Church—the Disruption of 1843—occurred over the role of the gentry in appointing ministers, and was pregnant with the social and political changes of the period. For it was during this period, and the decades following, that the city and its population became industrialized. The effects of this social and religious crisis, and of the later Victorian movements for temperance and self-improvement, are still observable in Aberdonian talk, in ways which are discussed later.

These, then, are some of the aspects of Aberdeen which are picked out when its people talk about the questions addressed in this book. The landmarks and institutions mentioned are not the whole of the place; but as many of its characteristic features are lit up from this, as from any other angle. The perspective taken is one which is both opened up, and limited, by the questions being asked; and it is now time to lay these out in more detail.

The questions

Aberdeen is the prism for this study, but the issues it refracts are of a wider significance. In statistical terms, indeed, the material on which this book is based can only be generalized, with cautions which are noted later, to Aberdonians over sixty; and I refer throughout to 'these Aberdonians', 'Aberdonians of this age group' or, as a shorthand, just to 'Aberdonians', as a way of keeping this in mind. But theoretical inferences can obviously be made to wider populations, forming generalizations based on the comparative literature, or hypotheses awaiting confirmation or modification by other similar studies elsewhere. Much of what is true of Aberdeen can be shown from the literature to be true of other places, much can be suspected to be true of other places subject to testing, and only some things look as if they might be peculiar to the city or to the North-East of Scotland. For each of these characteristics found in Aberdeen, the explanation of it which is given points to social, economic, or religious categories of people elsewhere to whom generalization could be made, and readers can appraise from the references given the extent to which the inference is conjectural, or has support from other literature.

The questions to be asked are therefore critical in assessing the interest of this Aberdeen material. I have said that at its simplest my question concerns the moral and economic resources which people call upon when they consider how to cope with physical limitation and loss; but several constituent questions are rolled up in this formulation. The detailed issues are set out sequentially at the beginning of each chapter following; and here my aim is only to provide, for the general reader more than for the specialist, a sketch of the direction which is taken by the book as a whole.

In order to paint a rapid picture, it is easiest to begin at the end of the journey, and take the story in reverse order. I end by arguing that the way in which contemporary Aberdonians think about medical themes—about death and ageing, health and the doctor—has been profoundly influenced by their past, especially by their economic history under capitalism and by their religious history under Protestantism. In each of these medical aspects of living the mix of influences has of course been different. In old age and in clinical relationships it is chiefly economic factors which have left their mark; in bereavement religious issues have imprinted the main traces; in illness and in dying, economic and religious history have been intertwined. And it is as a gesture towards this tangle of both religious and economic issues that I have entitled the book *A Protestant Legacy*.

These facts are not just about the past, however; they are also the key to the present. In Chapters 7 to 9 I show that the shape of Aberdonian ways of coping today, the pattern of their strengths and weaknesses, reflects the present resources which Aberdonians possess in working experience, in material wealth, and in religion. And it is this present repertoire of resources that carries in it the strengths, limitations, and conflicts of the past.

At the same time, the people I spoke to can be seen, in the course of the book, to be using their own individual creativity with this repertoire. They choose and combine themes from it which they work out, with greater or lesser success, in practice. Selective snapshots revealing some of the detail of this biographical process are given in Chapter 6, which depicts the way ideas about coping are expressed in later behaviour, and the way they are affected by public opinion and by the experience of major physical changes.

At any one time, though, this untidy process of working out how to cope is always unfinished; and so, in each aspect of physical loss which Aberdonians encounter, while they find many coherent themes from the economic and religious aspects of their lives to help them, they are also plagued by typical contradictions between favourite themes, creating dilemmas which they resolve only slowly and with pain. And it is these themes and dilemmas—each set fairly specific to the talk about death, old age, illness, or medical care in which it occurs—which occupy the first five chapters.

So much for the book in bold outline. There are, however, many turns in the road, which are hidden in this swift backward glance; and I now begin afresh from the beginning, picking my way through the route at slightly greater length, and indicating some of the problems on the path.

First, the book starts from various problems of coping; but it is important that the focus is not directly on coping but on conceptions of how to cope. Often, indeed, conception and practice mirror each other. Many of the people I spoke to had already been at close quarters with illness, ageing, dying, or bereavement, and their idea of how to cope reflected their experience as well as projecting their intentions. But some had only a more distant acquaintance with such matters, and their ideas were often correspondingly less detailed or more tentative. Thus conception and practice are woven together to differing degrees in what follows, and how these conceptions fare when confronted with new experiences is of course a question of great interest, and one to which I refer again shortly.

This starting point marks the present endeavour as being in the interpretive tradition of social analysis, which does not merely record behaviour from an external point of view, but seeks to enter into its subjective meaning. Thus the study has much in common with several lines of contemporary thinking about the biographical meaning of health. Sociological research, to which I refer frequently in what follows, has described the lines people draw between normal and abnormal behaviour, the pictures which they acquire of illness and death, and the accounts which they accordingly construct to make sense of their own health. Related psychological work has shown that the cognitive appraisal made of problems like death and illness, and the sense of coherence felt in facing them, are a central feature of coping.[8] A rich anthropological literature has revealed how a culture provides its members with a repertoire of rules, symbols, or explanatory models which guide their perceptions of their body and their identity.[9] And finally a growing historical literature is exploring how these enduring structures of meaning reveal themselves in both biographical and historical events.[10]

All these levels of interpretation are involved in the chapters which follow. However, the first part of the book is concerned mainly with outlining the various patterns of coping which are to be explained. Each chapter of this first part takes one of the hazards of physical decline and loss—illness, ageing, dying, bereavement—and considers Aberdonian ways of coping with it; and an additional chapter in this part deals separately with ways of approaching the doctor, who is the accustomed source of professional help in such contexts, and especially in the context of illness and death.

After a brief initial description of the range of Aberdonian understandings on each topic, the chief analytical task, in each chapter of Part I, is that of revealing patterns of consistency and contradiction in each set of understandings.[11] Contradictions have always been full of potential significance for students of society. They may be the battleground between the conventional order and private choice. They may be the frontier at which the ruling ideas of the ruling class meet the experience of the less fortunate. They may mark the fault line at which the discourse of experts and professionals meets resistance from those who are in their charge. Or they may represent the collision between ideas from different historical layers in the society. All these themes appear at some point in what follows.

At the same time there are some well-known problems about the contradictions which occur in popular talk, and I have tried to take these problems into account. In some situations, for example, it can be argued that people are not sufficiently bound by the consequences of what they are saying to examine its logic. On political subjects, in particular, some writers have concluded that many issues are not of vital everyday concern for members of the public, and so their ideas are fragmentary, in a way which enables contradictions to be cheerfully disregarded.[12] Others have pointed to the general problem, especially evident in dealing with ambiguous phenomena like symptoms, of the way descriptions can shift their meaning as the context changes, with the consequence that contradictions, and patterns of consistency, may be more apparent than real.[13] These are perennial problems of interpretation, and they are exacerbated further by the fact that talk is a highly selective account of experience, dramatized to portray the speaker in an acceptable light.[14] But for all that, there do exist pressing everyday concerns in which consistency matters greatly to people in achieving the practical outcome they desire; and there are situations in which others' criticism of inconsistency is well informed and acute. Health and ageing, for example, are often vital issues, and if people still find it difficult, as no doubt they do, to organize their experiences in an entirely coherent fashion, it is at least often the case that the contradictions in their thinking matter to them. For, if personal hopes or intentions are closely tied to the beliefs concerned, and if two beliefs which are in contradiction necessarily cannot both be realized, the hopes tied to one or the other, or to both, must be frustrated. The search, therefore, in the latter part of each initial chapter, is for patterns among these Aberdonian ideas which are coherent, and for boundary lines which cannot be crossed without contradictions which are painful, imposing personal dilemmas or attracting criticism from others.

Once these contradictions have been isolated, it becomes possible to ask the questions which form the second part of the book. These concern the way in which such contradictions are worked out in practice, and the way they have been shaped in the first place by assumptions, doctrines, and discourses about economy, society, and religion. A bridge to these questions is provided by the conclusion to each chapter in the first part, where I explore a range of contemporary or historical factors which have helped to form Aberdonian ideas about the topic of that chapter. But whereas in the first part the focus is on the thing to be explained, in the second part it is on what principally does the explaining.

Two things which obviously help to explain the way Aberdonians cope at the day to day level are the praise and criticism they get from others, and the threatening or reassuring signals of change which they get from their own bodies. In Chapter 6 I give examples of how Aberdonians build and consolidate opinion in a circle of acquaintances through mutual criticism and persuasion; and I consider how far the views of coping thus entrenched and supported are sustained over time in the particular case of health changes— the commonest source of threatening crises in the short term. Here I describe the relation of belief to practice—how far the ideas concerned here merely reflect behaviour, or merely present the speaker in a socially acceptable light, and how far these ideas express themselves in active attempts to control or manage behaviour. And I also describe the way different beliefs fare in the face of disruptive events.

At a deeper level, though people draw their beliefs not just from the neighbourly comment and physical ups and downs of the moment, but also from their own past experience. A biographical explanation is thus needed, and this may take several forms.

One such way of explaining popular ideas is to see whether they are an expression of certain interests—interests whose requirements follow naturally from the position Aberdonians have occupied in their social structure. Thus according as they have been manual workers or managers, council tenants or house owners, Aberdonians have very different resources and very different ways of defending their interests, and they shape their ideas of how to cope appropriately. For example, managers and house owners easily think in terms of their interests as consumers, and so may insist on choosing for themselves in matters of medical care.

However, this kind of explanation, while valid enough at its own level, does not go nearly far enough. Without engaging unnecessarily in the labyrinthine debates on this subject, it is important to recognize that interests are not disembodied facts which control people. Rather, they are reasons for acting which people argue for, either on behalf of others, or for themselves; and they are formulated within a wider discourse—a conception of the economy, of social structure—which is of its own culture and period, which may compete with other conceptions, and which may not be equally accessible or relevant to all members of society.[15] Part of the task of explanation, therefore, is to look at these very conceptions of economy and society—at notions of honest work and fair reward, for instance—to see what conceptions are available and felt to be relevant to present topics in Aberdeen, and, according to how people place themselves within these schemes, to show something of how they assess their own interests—their own deserts—and those of others, in coping with the problems of physical loss.

Again, from another point of view, too narrow a definition of interests also makes it difficult to explain the relation made by Aberdonians between ways of coping and ideas that are moral, religious, or cosmological. Clearly there is a straightforward sense in which some of these ideas may be adopted because they are consistent with the economic experience or aspirations of one particular group—rich or poor, propertied or propertyless. It is said, for example, that aspiring Aberdonian bank managers can help their business if they are pillars of a prominent kirk. But such explanations are seriously deficient if they do not also recognize that, self-interest aside, cosmological ideas are adopted for their own sake, as a way of making sense of the world.[16] It is in recognition of this that the term interest has been extended to cover the way in which people pursue 'cognitive', 'ideal', or 'religious' interests in discovering, maintaining, and disseminating a particular view of things.[17]

Thus it is not merely that Aberdonian ideas about coping need to be understood in terms of the kind of discourse about economy and society which is available in Aberdeen, but also that they need to be understood in terms of the kinds of cosmology and morality which are available, and which Aberdonians seek to uphold. The logical links between these wider conceptions and Aberdonian attitudes to illness, ageing, death, and the doctor, are explored in the chapters on work, wealth, and religion.

Finally, in the conclusion I consider, in a necessarily brief and limited fashion, two still broader issues which are implicit in the kind of explanation being attempted.

The first of these broader questions asks whether there is a single, dominant set of values which governs Aberdonian discussions about what are, after all, universal predicaments.[18] If this were so, one might be tempted to see Aberdeen as a culture which is solidly cohesive, or else tightly controlled, with little inner dissension or dynamic, and its history would be of little present consequence. But it is not so; and the second question asks how to explain the historical development of conflicting Aberdonian traditions in dealing with these predicaments. In answering these questions, I try to draw together into a single historical view the various perspectives on the past which have opened up from time to time in the preceding chapters. Here I deal more explicitly with the ways in which the economic and religious interests of the past have shaped the cultural capital on which contemporary Aberdonians draw in coping with physical loss.

These, then, are the principal questions with which this study is concerned—daunting questions, to which the answers, even over the space of a book, must necessarily be both tentative and incomplete, but also questions of some interest, which are still very little explored.

Inevitably, the scope of the subject chosen strictly limits the possibility of discussing other related topics. Some of these issues are left aside both because they involve separate questions, and because they require a different kind of data. Asking about the social factors which influence the actual distribution of illness, dependency, or death in old age, for example, involves issues of causation, and also requires a statistical analysis of large numbers as the primary source of evidence. Here, though, we are dealing, not with the distribution and causes of these events, but with the conceptions which enable people to shape plans for coping with the experiences they bring. Naturally the probability of each experience may affect these plans, but I consider this possibility as it arises.

Other questions are bypassed in this study not because they require a different sort of data, but solely because they would have led the argument too far afield. Probably the most significant of these questions, or at any rate the one which I cut out with the most reluctance, concerns the way in which ideas about coping are shaped by ideas about men and women, and about the family. To integrate with present themes the enormous amount of material I was given on the family was, I concluded, beyond the scope of a single book; and while I tried to preserve an account of the economic situation, at least, of men and women, and the way in which this entered their view of coping, I decided in the end that this too would overburden some already long chapters. I can only hope to present this material at another time.

Less radical, but still substantial, omissions include the subject of popular attitudes to public services other than the doctor. Though family relationships are one of the most critical influences on how people expect to cope with ageing, the sort of relationship which they expect to conduct with social workers, home helps, district nurses, health visitors, and organized volunteers can also be important—more important, indeed, at times, than relationships with the doctor. These public resources, however, are often unfamiliar until catastrophe threatens in old age, and they are usually assigned by administrative action, while my concern is to study the resources which people are familiar with at all ages, and which they call upon directly.

Other omissions, finally, are principally a matter of the level of detail which can be attained while addressing the themes which have been chosen. I have tried to deal with a very broad range of themes by choosing a topic which is in other respects quite narrow. But the breadth is at the expense not only of the omissions I have mentioned but also of detail in some evolving fields of study where many particular questions of interest are emerging. An example to which I refer in Chapter 1, is the field of health beliefs. Many issues in this field, especially many concerned with beliefs about the causation and prevention of illness, are passed over in that chapter, partly because, among the old, issues of coping with chronic illness already established must bulk large, and partly because space would not permit the relatively intricate analysis which my material would require on this topic.

These limitations in the scope of this book, therefore, are a consequence of the attempt made to see popular understandings about illness, ageing, and death in a wide explanatory perspective. Equally, there are limitations in the evidence and methods used, together with some corresponding strengths, and I now turn to these.

The methods

Two sources of evidence are used in this study. The first and principal source is a qualitative study of 70 Aberdonians aged 60 and over, belonging to two circles of acquaintances, one situated in the West End and one in a council housing estate to which I have given the pseudonym Mannoch. The second and supplementary source is a random sample survey of 619 Aberdonians aged 60 and over, stratified by age and sex, and drawn from the Primary Care Register of the city. The survey was carried out by colleagues, the qualitative study by myself, as part of a programme of linked studies; and all the materials relate to the period 1978–80. In what follows, the survey is referred to as the Aberdeen Survey, and any material which is not specifically referred to the Aberdeen Survey is drawn from the qualitative study.

Information about the sampling procedures, controls on bias, and questions asked in these two sets of data is given in Appendix 1. Given the primarily interpretive issues of this study, it was appropriate that qualitative material should form the primary evidence. The actual conversation of the people concerned, the way they defined their own practices, and the logical and contextual linkages which they themselves made between topics, are the touchstone against which all other evidence about the structure of their ideas has to be validated. Samples of their conversation can be obtained most accurately by tape-recording open-ended interviews, and this is one method used here; but vital additional materials can be gathered by taking part in, or observing, more informal conversations, behaviour, and events which are written up in field-notes. This, the classic anthropological procedure, is not as easily achieved in the largely private domestic world of chronic illness and ageing in a modern city, as it is in the public world of small-scale societies. But much can still be done to create opportunities for such insights.

Thus I revisited on a more informal basis about half of the people who had already been interviewed, and saw some, who were my chief source of news about others, several times; I went to public events in churches or associations in which they were involved, and I met people casually in the street and participated to some extent in their everyday gossip. All these ways of learning about Aberdonian ideas enabled me to record conversation, observe its practical context, test its consistency against the impressions of others, and note any shifts in positions taken over time.

The Aberdeen Survey was initially of help in checking and confirming the representative character of the qualitative study in the broad terms which are appropriate for this study; but it has also been useful because, while the study's central questions are qualitative, there are various points at which they can be illuminated by other evidence which is quantitative. In what follows the survey evidence is used in many areas where issues of mortality, morbidity, and social class impinge on the argument; and while it is used more sparingly as a source on beliefs and attitudes, there are occasions when it supplies an answer to an essentially quantitative question—when it is important to know how many people think something, as well as the implications to which it leads.

This, then, is the evidence used; but how it is used is also important. In the present study the aim is to discover the logic of ideas about coping, and the way these relate to assumptions about work, property, religion, and so forth. There are many existing ways of doing this kind of analysis, centred on beliefs and values, which cannot be summarized adequately here. But by bearing in mind two extreme alternatives, one can quickly see the aims of the present method. First there is the traditional method of history, and often of the sociology of knowledge, which reveals contrasting doctrines and ideologies by close examination of the logic of historical writings. The standard difficulty here is that of relating these literate views of the period with the practical attitudes of the population as a whole. Then at the other extreme is the traditional method of anthropological analysis. This method at its best has a deep sensitivity to the practical thinking of the population as a whole, but there are situations where the views elicited are so cryptic and fragmentary that they can only be put into a logical order on the assumption that a single coherent culture underlies the utterances of different informants. This assumption of cultural coherence is often reasonable in anthropological field-work, though it may also be debated when it is made; but it is certainly hazardous for ethnographers to adopt it in industrial society, where divergent thinking even in health subjects is easily demonstrated.

The method of analysis used here, therefore, begins from the practical context of popular talk, but at the same time seeks to reveal experience of coherence and conflict between different schools of thought within it. Thus it can be seen as one of a group of methods—one based in this case on qualitative material—which are seeking to understand connections of thought in popular culture.[19] Inevitably these new approaches, while more sensitive and encompassing than most, still retain some danger, for the reader as much as for the analyst, of oversimplifying. Although there is nothing necessary about this, the process of classifying types of ideas can quickly become a way of classifying types of people, and this is misleading. People use ideas: they draw on conflicting assumptions, they reflect on conflicts and attempt to resolve them, they change, they innovate, they reconstruct. Thus to see people working with their ideas is to see them recognizing logical relationships, but not necessarily, and not often, to see them exemplifying in all respects a single coherent type. This is not to say that they ignore logic—on the contrary, I argued earlier that those who violate it in matters essential to them know that they are paying a price—but it is to say that while the ideas available have definite logical patterns, people try to select from them, and remould them, in ways which are always new, always incomplete, and quite often contradictory.

If this caution is borne in mind, the present method is easily understood. I have written elsewhere about the way the analysis of typical arguments has been done,[20] and this is supplemented by the details in Appendix 1. Here it is important only to notice that the method is essentially a cumulative comparison of case studies. It looks first at all the links a person makes on a particular topic such as illness; then compares the types of links made by others; then examines all the links a person makes between two topics—say illness and material resources; again compares the types of links made by others; and so on. All these links are logical, and are revealed by the internal evidence of each person's conversation in its practical context.

There are some points about this use of case studies which it may be helpful to bear in mind. To begin with, the examples of the first part of the book differ somewhat in their form from those in the second. In the first part, their function is to show, in conformity with the questions I discussed earlier, that there is a contradiction between two schools of thought. This is not to say that this initial emphasis on contradictions is an assumption of the questions or method; for if the evidence had shown there to be a single conceptual scheme for coping with the problems concerned here—composed of ideas which had strong mutual implications—the case studies would have been used to show this. But as it happens, Aberdonian ideas about coping were more strongly linked with wider conceptions than with each other, and contradictions at this initial level were therefore frequent. Hence the cases presented are generally used to show that each contradiction is real and significant. It is not merely the result of different people using words in a different way, because here the same person is speaking throughout. Nor is the conflict manufactured by the way in which the analyst has grouped together ideas taken from different contexts, because individuals recognize the contradiction in their own terms. Nor, finally, is it a contradiction which is disregarded, or a merely formal contradiction, due to difficulty in articulating something which is nevertheless felt to be coherent. There were such instances, but again case study reveals how far the contradiction is felt as a personal dilemma. For all these reasons this analysis of individual instances is essential because it is the best evidence that the underlying logical opposition is recognized. And while I have occasionally used other, weaker kinds of evidence—for example, conversation between two well-acquainted people who understand themselves to be opposed on the point in question—my chief reliance, in both analysis and presentation, has been on the evidence of the individual case studies.

Naturally, the argument is based on an analysis of all the relevant cases, and not just on those presented. Relevant instances are those of people who express both the ideas which are found to be contradictory. Some of these people may have resolved the contradiction, for reasons which become apparent in the comparison, and which I try to summarize briefly where appropriate. And similarly, some of the contexts in which the ideas are expressed may vary significantly from those in the case presented, and this too has been noted.

These principles of the method also apply to the second part of the book, but here both the form of the presentations and the form of the accompanying analysis changes as concordant rather than contradictory ideas come to the fore. The aim for the most part is to show that particular views of coping are saturated with implications deriving from economic and religious conceptions and experience. The links are direct, whether through connections which can be reformulated in the shape 'If A then B', or through terms which are partially interchangeable, with many overlapping connotations, as for example the terms 'activity' and 'work' are for many Aberdonians. Hence it is the role of the case studies in these chapters to show that individuals themselves recognize and argue these direct inferences in their own terms. Again, these presentations offer the best evidence that the ideas concerned are genuinely linked—that they are not merely combined from different sources by the analyst on the assumption of cultural consensus, or by the construction of ideal types in the abstract.

It follows that, because they are *par excellence* the evidence revealing logical connection, the case studies used here are theoretical, not merely illustrative.[21] And they have a related theoretical role when, in Chapter 6, I portray the logical manœuvres made in persuasion and counter-persuasion, together with those made in response to health changes.

These are the strengths of the case study method in the present context; but of course the method also has its limitations. No example can be entirely representative, and it is important, as I have noted, to summarize variations among the cases not presented as well. Moreover, it is often objected that the examples chosen for presentation are likely to be those which provide the fullest information, and that this constitutes a bias. However, the sheer number of case studies in this book reduces that risk: the majority of the people I spoke to appear in these analyses, and I have made a deliberate attempt to present the reticent as well as the garrulous.[22] And there is also another, opposite consideration in the present context. If logical connections are only satisfactorily established where they are used and recognized by members of the linguistic community concerned, then those who make the most connections on a given topic necessarily contribute critical evidence on that topic. People link their ideas together to a different extent in different areas of their experience, and it is therefore more truly representative of the thought of a community to portray not only the basic connections perceived by all, but also the connections perceived by those who have thought most about the topic concerned. At the same time, though, it is important to indicate also, for each topic, the broad gradation of complexity in the thought of all those interviewed; and this too I have tried to do.

Three other details, finally, are needed to guide the reader through this qualitative evidence. First, in order to show clearly the links between ideas which are analysed in different chapters, and especially the links between Part I and Part II, I have used not only descriptive references to each idea, but also a system of reference numbers, adopting the notation used for formulae in mathematical texts. This notation numbers typical statements in accordance with the chapter in which they occur, and their position in the series of ideas analysed in that chapter. The relevant statements are listed in the section headed 'Themes and dilemmas' in each chapter of Part I; but an integrated list is also available for reference in Appendix 3.

Secondly, because the material is partly from tape-recordings and partly from field-notes, I have attempted, where this was feasible without undue clumsiness, to mark tape-recorded quotations by giving them initial and final (double) quotation marks. Quotations from field-notes do not have these, though they may have internal quotation marks. Note also that, when quoting Aberdonians, I distinguish omissions (four points) from trailing sentences and pauses (three points).

Finally, because many of the case studies must be highly detailed, I have cloaked identity by changes which are not germane to the argument, and also, where this did not seem feasible, by vagueness. It is idle to pretend that this does not change the 'feel' of the situation, or leave it at times suspended in a neutered atmosphere. That is unsatisfying—to nobody more than to the author, who remembers the people concerned not as cases, but as flesh and blood. But by the same token, I owe them a debt of consideration which is only a small recompense for their confidences.

With this guide to the methods used and questions asked in this study, and with at least some preliminary picture of Aberdeen and Aberdeenshire as it is seen through the eyes of its older inhabitants, I turn to the topics on which their own voice can be heard.

Notes and References

1. H. Mackenzie, *The city of Aberdeen*, Third Statistical Account of Scotland, London: Oliver and Boyd, 1953.
2. In 1980 there were 11.8 beds per 1,000 aged 65 and over in Grampian and 13.3 in Scotland vs. 7.8 in England—see Information Services Division, *Scottish health statistics 1980*, Edinburgh: HMSO, 1982, Table 6.4, adjusted to estimated population aged 65 and over ibid. Table 1.2, and Department of Health and Social Security, *Health and personal social services statistics for England*, London: HMSO, 1982, Table 4.9.
3. In 1980 the death rate was 62.9 per 1,000 aged 65 and over in Grampian vs. 64.3 (Scotland) and 60.2 (England and Wales)—see Information Services Division, *Scottish health statistics 1980*, Table 1.5; Office of Population Censuses and Surveys, *Mortality statistics 1980*, London: HMSO, 1983, Tables 1 & 10.
4. Information Services Division, *Scottish health statistics 1980*, Table 8.13.
5. In 1980 there were 23 residential places per 1,000 aged 65 and over in Grampian vs. 20 (Scotland) and 22 (England)—see Scottish Education Department, *Residential accommodation for the elderly, Scotland 1980*, Statistical Bulletin, Social Work Services Group, 1981, Table 2; Department of Health and Social Security, *Health and personal social services statistics for England*, Tables 1.1, 7.1, and 7.3.
6. I. R. Carter, *Farm life in north-east Scotland 1840–1914*, Edinburgh: Donald, 1979.
7. Lewis Grassic Gibbon, *A Scots quair*, London: Pan Books, 1973.
8. R. S. Lazarus and S. Folkman, *Stress, appraisal and coping*, New York: Springer, 1984; A. Antonovsky, *Unravelling the mystery of health: how people manage stress and stay well*, London: Jossey-Bass, 1987.
9. E.g. A. Kleinman, *Patients and healers in the context of culture*, London: University of California Press, 1980; G. Lewis, *Illness in a Sepik society*, London: Athlone Press, 1975; J. Buxton, *Religion and healing in Mandari*, Oxford University Press, 1973; M. Douglas, *Natural symbols*, London: Pelican, 1973.

10. A good starting place is P. Abrams, *Historical sociology*, Shepton Mallet: Open Books, 1982.
11. In the chapters on dying and bereavement I have varied this procedure to make for easier presentation, bringing some case studies of contradiction into the initial account of the evidence.
12. H. Newby, *The deferential worker*, London: Allen Lane, 1977, ch. 7; M. Mann, 'The social cohesion of liberal democracy', *Amer. Sociol. Rev.* 35 (1970), 423-31; P. Converse, 'The nature of belief systems in mass publics', in D. Apter (ed.), *Ideology and discontent*, New York: Free Press, 1964.
13. See D. Locker, *Symptoms and illness*, London: Tavistock, 1981, who refers to the main sources of this ethnomethodological critique.
14. E. Goffman, *Frame analysis*, London: Penguin, 1975, ch. 13; id., *The presentation of self in everyday life*, New York: Doubleday, 1959.
15. B. Hindess, '"Interests" in political analysis', in J. Law (ed.), *Power, action and belief: a new sociology of knowledge?*, Sociol. Rev. Monographs no. 32, London: Routledge, 1986.
16. P. L. Berger and T. Luckmann, *The social construction of reality*, London: Allen Lane, 1967.
17. J. Habermas, *Knowledge and human interests*, tr. J. J. Shapiro, London: Heinemann, 1972; M. Hill, *A sociology of religion*, London: Heinemann, 1973, chs. 5–6; M. Weber, 'The social psychology of the world religions', in H. H. Gerth and C. W. Mills, *From Max Weber*, London: Kegan Paul, 1947.
18. N. Abercrombie, S. Hill, and B. S. Turner, *The dominant ideology thesis*, London: Allen and Unwin, 1980.
19. For a specially adapted factor analytic approach see W. Stainton-Rogers, 'Accounting for health and illness: a social psychological investigation', Ph.D. thesis, Open University, 1987.
20. R. G. A. Williams, 'Logical analysis as a qualitative method', *Sociol. of Health and Illness*, 3 (1981), 141–87.
21. J. C. Mitchell, 'Case and situation analysis', *Sociol. Rev.* 31 (1983), 187–211.
22. Ignoring illustrative quotations, there are 52 case studies in the course of the book, which are drawn from 43 of the 70 members of the sample. In order to preserve anonymity, I have given a different name on their second appearance to the few who appear more than once.

PART I

Patterns of Coping

1

Illness

'It was the way he would have wantit it,' they said to one another, knowing the man. 'He would not have wantit to be long an invalid-body, not able to step round his parks whenever he had a mind to.'
They spoke too for themselves.

David Kerr Cameron, *Willie Gavin, Crofter Man,* 1980

Introduction

It is usually illness, rather than old age or imminent death, that first gives people experience of narrowing physical boundaries. At first the experience can be dismissed as a temporary deviation from normal life; but when illness becomes chronic it is easy to see it—sometimes quite wrongly—as something more encompassing, as the first step in a downward path, as in some respects an end, and a renunciation. And in this way it is like ageing and the approach of death, even though it may come at a young age, and without threatening life. Hence in looking at how Aberdonians respond to the loss of physical powers, I begin with illness, and I have focused not so much on the minutiae of day-to-day assessments of symptoms as on deeper-seated judgements about the meaning of chronic illness in a biographical context.

Popular talk about the onset of illness is concerned with describing illness, explaining it, and, by these means, suggesting how to cope with it; but at the same time it plays continuously on a few basic assumptions—especially on what people take to be the sources of health, whether moral or mechanical, and on whether, correspondingly, the normal moral life of their society seems to them on balance health-giving or health-destroying. Talking to middle-class Parisians in the 1960s, Claudine Herzlich[1] was given descriptions of health at three quite different levels: a mechanical level, at which health was the simple absence of invasive illness;

a personal level, where health was a reserve of strength and resistance which could be built up by one's own conduct; and a social level, where health was being equal to, in 'equilibrium' with, the demands of social life. But the way these ideas were used revealed underlying presuppositions. To these Parisians the social level of health was only achieved by individuals acting against their society: the social duties of normal metropolitan life were fundamentally stressful, noxious, and health-destroying, and the resistance necessary to cope with them successfully had to be built up at the personal level.

This example of the deeper assumptions underlying health talk is obviously from a quite distinctive cultural setting. As yet very little of the cultural variation in such ideas is mapped, though there are now some comparable British studies. Just as assumptions of this kind appear in the way health is described in Paris, so also they appear in Britain, though somewhat differently. For example, while the British also talk of health as the absence of invasive illness, it is common to contrast illness as a subjective condition with illness as organic disease, perhaps because British doctors are in a position to discount subjective illness and make disease the accepted source of 'real' illness[2]. Another difference is that the British do not always give such prominence to health as a reserve of strength. It is important in ideas about prevention, but some people feel too constrained by their circumstances to engage in prevention, and regard illness primarily as an invasive physical agent.[3] Again, amongst worse-off families, being equal to the demands of daily life seems to be defined in terms of the bare necessities of work and the family's survival, rather than in terms of additional requirements for fulfilment, pleasure, and satisfaction.[4] Much of this material suggests a tendency for British descriptions of health to emphasize the functional or mechanical level, though this may reflect the tendency of British studies of this type to focus on working-class families.

These variations underlie the way health is described; but similar cultural themes also underlie the way health is explained. Popular explanations are aimed at trying to treat illness, to prevent its recurrence, and to justify disabilities; and in each case there are further cultural variations. My discussion of treatment and prevention in this chapter is limited to the role accorded to being active and meeting social obligations, since in chronic illness this dwarfs even such favourite topics as diet.[5] In the Paris study referred to earlier, this social activity was regarded as stressful and destructive to the individual. Yet in an American study, it was found to be fundamental to morale and to a person's sense of self.[6]

By the same token, too, there is a special interest, when talking about chronic illness, in what justifies limitations on activity; and here the confused but critical issue of what part is assigned to mechanical and what to psychosomatic causation in different cultures becomes acute. In the West there is a contemporary penchant for psychologizing illness, which contrasts with the somatic explanations common elsewhere.[7] There is, first, in both popular and academic thinking, an accumulated debris of historical diagnoses such as 'hypochondria' and 'hysteria' which, together with the legacy of Freud, provides a resource for ascribing disabilities to unconscious wishes and conflicts. This kind of explanation stands in opposition to mechanical accounts, and is thus especially popular where there is uncertainty about what mechanical account is appropriate.[8] Less dependent on diagnostic uncertainty, on the other hand, and more susceptible to evidence, are explanations which are not opposed to, but compatible with physical causation. These explanations take various forms. Some see physical and mental causation as combining in the genesis of illness—for example, they may ascribe physical antecedents of a disabling condition, such as muscle tension or endocrine changes, to stresses on the whole integrated system of mind and body.[9] Some, on the contrary, presuppose a physical condition which begins the process, and seek to account for the degree of disability in terms of subconscious responses to the condition, such as the degree of attention given to symptoms by the sufferer.[10] And some again presuppose a physical condition at the start, but suggest that quite often the sufferer makes rational choices between activities to maintain and activities to cut down.[11] The popularity of each of these psychological or social ways of accounting for disability obviously affects the moral position of the disabled quite considerably; and there are indications that, in Britain, the emphasis on rather minimal functional and mechanical descriptions of health is complemented by a popular theory of mind over matter which is freely used to explain everything else.[12]

Finally, the same cultural variation which informs ways of describing or explaining illness also informs ways of coping with it.

Several British and American writers have described people who adopted strategies of 'denying' or 'normalizing' disabilities, and who were thus able to 'pass' as ordinary members of society; and they have contrasted others who adopted an approach which 'disassociated' them from normal society, and which gave them a special, dependent position and a disabled role.[13] Now the choice between these two strategies ought to be especially critical in a society where most behaviour is quickly categorized as either normal or deviant—that is, in societies which are both vigilant and conformist. And this raises the question of how chronic illness is dealt with in societies where conventions on health matters are either poorly established or subject to sustained criticism from dissenters. It was in Paris once again, with its individualist attitudes, that a third approach emerged to chronic illness, existing alongside the first which held on to the normal roles of social life, and the second which accepted a dependent role for the chronic sick. This third approach saw illness as a 'liberator' from social duties which precluded the expression of nonconformist values. There were, it is true, somewhat diverse attitudes which fell under this head. In less interesting instances, illness was still deviance, still dropping out of society, but a deviance which was welcomed rather than feared, and which expressed no other values than the release from existing obligations. In more interesting cases, however, deeper values which were usually eclipsed by the pressures of normal living found expression in illness, especially where importance was placed on contemplation and reflection, or on intense personal relationships.

These styles of coping with chronic illness have historical dimensions which have begun to be appreciated. According to a recent exploration of French history,[14] illness was earlier seen in images of punishment—a natural corruption mimicking moral corruption, a consequence of sin, or, simply, an ineluctable fate; and one would expect such images to pose a threat which reinforced the assumption that most minor illness could and should be disregarded or 'normalized'. It was only in the nineteenth century that the protected, if segregated, role for the sick or disabled, described earlier, became accessible to most people through social legislation. These two older attitudes—one normalizing illness and the other protecting the sick—were then supplemented and opposed in post-war France by movements seeking control for the sick person—movements which tried to enable the sick to express nonconformist values, in the way described earlier, through associations based on self-help. Hence, in the present day, all these three ways of coping with chronic illness are in evidence, although their historical lineages are very different. But much remains to be discovered about the history of coping with illness; and a recent article points out that in Germany, the stoical, 'normalizing' attitude to illness was an Enlightenment attitude, and was opposed by a pietist introspection with older religious roots which suggested, long before the contemporary exaltation of self-understanding and self-help, ways of transposing and revaluing the experience of sickness.[15]

All these examples, from past and present, help to place the way in which the contemporary culture of Aberdeen helps people to shape their thoughts so as to cope with threats to their health.

Concepts of health in Aberdeen

For the most part, Aberdonians thought of health very much along the different dimensions already discussed. From one angle they thought of it as being free from illness or disease; from another they saw it as being a source of strength to resist illness even in situations where illness was irrevocably entrenched; and from yet a third angle they saw it as a capacity to function in accordance with the demands of their daily life, even in situations where they felt ill, or had some acknowledged weakness which impaired their resistance. At the extremes of best and worst health, these three dimensions overlapped; but in the wide range of experience in between they were often separated and contrasted. The way in which this was done has been discussed in detail elsewhere,[16] and in the present context only a few points need to be summarized.

Among these three concepts, the most significant were the strength to resist and the capacity to function. Illness—the subjective experience of symptoms—was firmly devalued if it could not be validated as disease, the organic disruption detectable by eye or by clinical testing; and disease itself was a commonplace which only became serious when the strength to resist or the capacity to function was threatened.

Many things were comprised in the strength to resist. Essentially, strength was the power of recovery, and it was opposed to various kinds of 'weakness'. There was the straightforward kind of weakness which consisted in a total, though temporary, sense of debility, of being easily tired, of having little in reserve. In addition, weakness could be metaphorical, indicating a point of constitutional vulnerability. Such weaknesses could be identified through sequential occurrences of diseases in the same organ, limb, or part of the body—the 'weak chest' was a typical example—or through other suggestions of a chain of causation which linked different episodes of illness together. And as well as these various forms of localized, partial weakness, there was also finally a notion of total and permanent collapse, of a fundamental loss of the power of recovery.

Constitutional weaknesses of these kinds did not, Aberdonians felt, imply that they should curtail their normal activities; and disabilities were not normally justified in these terms. Constitutional weakness could be acknowledged, especially one attributable to heredity or a pattern of past illnesses, but pride was nevertheless taken in functioning normally; or again constitutional strength could be celebrated, especially strength built up by one's own actions, even while disabilities were acknowledged. Thus strength was in many ways a separate and a moral matter, and closely linked to responsibility for generating health and preventing illness.

Prevention through normal living

The central idea expressed by most Aberdonians who thought about coping with illness was that their way of life itself generated health, and they had only to continue its normal round of activities to control or suppress illness:

"Are there things you do to keep yourself healthy?"

"No—just, I'm never off my feet. I'm always going about doing work and helping somebody else. As a rule I'll go to see them, and I still do it yet. I've always been on the go, and that's the thing to keep you going."

—or in the West End:

"We never expected either of them (relatives) to come up out of these illnesses, but they did—out and kept going, you see . . . . Well you see my parents were like that—they were both terrible hard-working, never wanted just to sit down and do nothing.''

All dimensions of health were involved at some point in this commendation of normal living. First, and most commonly, activity was thought to increase, in a general way, one's reserves of strength. Nearly always this renewal of reserves was seen as simultaneously physical and psychological, and it was even more important in rebuilding defences breached by some constitutional weakness than in maintaining an already strong constitution. Secondly, and almost as commonly, normal activity was regarded as helpful for a range of specific diseases and handicaps. Naturally the conditions specified often involved locomotor problems—strokes, arthritis, multiple sclerosis, amputation—or circulatory conditions, and practising the impeded activity in gradual stages was seen as a commonsense remedy. In these respects, the remedial rules followed had parallels in clinical rehabilitation; but though medical advice was often referred to in this context, this advice was also cheerfully flouted when it conflicted with such rules, on the grounds that the rules also helped to maintain general resistance. And finally the psychological element of this resistance was evident in the power of normal activities to help people cope with, and suppress, symptoms for which there was apparently no corresponding disease.

Activity was thus health-generating in that mental 'determination' or focus, associated with ordinary physical tasks, was felt to engage the whole system, to assist in mobilizing defective parts of it, and to draw attention away from feelings which might otherwise engender or aggravate clinical problems, or make them hard to bear. And it was precisely the absence of such a mental focus which made exercises unsatisfactory. Thus while an exercise such as press-ups could be admitted to be effective, as in the case of a man so breathless as to be unable to walk up the hill nearby, it was at the same time self-evident to this man that press-ups were not worth considering:

Wife: "[His brother Alfie the boxer] keeps fit, does the exercises . . . . and he's more fitter than you, isn't he? He can walk up that road . . ."

Husband: [dismissing the subject] "Oh I would be if I'd been the whole winter on press-ups."

In this case the requirements of neighbourhood errands, not the benefits of press-ups, were the appropriate stimulus, and for these the hill could in fact be avoided. Even a man who lately had become an ardent performer of exercises confessed that he would have had nothing to do with them in the past, and it was only by investing them with a record-breaking competitive purpose during a long spell in hospital that he had become enthusiastic about them.

Finally, purpose and focus were not merely generated by the individual, but suggested, sustained, and shaped by a surrounding social circle. This social influence was implied in various ways, the most obvious of which was the identification of beneficial activity with 'work'. I elaborate on this idea in a later chapter, but briefly, co-operative groups like pensioners' clubs, Masonic meetings, church organizations, and so on generated this sense of focus for some; and while for many it was the often solitary business of housekeeping and gardening which was the essence of healthy activity, the ceaseless neighbourly discussion of prices, cleaning rotas, baking recipes, and growing tips performed a vital role in sustaining commitment. Accordingly health was usually felt to be generated by those activities which were an established part of a customary way of life, and activities abstracted from such contexts were seldom seen as a live option.

Thus strength was sustained and rebuilt, specific diseases and disabilities ameliorated, and symptoms in the absence of disease suppressed, by meeting normal social expectations as far as possible, and by the physical demands and focus of attention which these generated. This conception ran parallel with clinical approaches to rehabilitation in a specific minority of cases, but in the majority it was a set of self-sustaining beliefs, which at times overrode explicit medical advice to the contrary.

Moreover, while it was usual for normal living to be seen in this way as something which could help sustain health or mitigate disease, it was also quite common to see it still more categorically as an indispensable condition for health:

"If you sit down to it, well you've had it really, you won't get up. At my age. Or even at 70. Some of them says they're old at 60, oh I canna get up, I have to sit in a chair, and this and this. And I tells them, I says, you should move about, I says, and get out."

In this indispensable role, activity was nearly always related solely to the total strength and resistance of the whole system, and in particular to avoidance of the dreaded state where strength is exhausted, the power of recovery is broken, and the sufferer drifts on in a condition variously described as 'lost', 'finished' or 'done', a 'spent force', 'broken down', and sometimes with 'the mind gone'. This state was held, as in the last quotation, to come upon those who 'sit down to it', and who 'do not go out', who stop 'doing' or 'making', who do not 'keep an interest', and the state was in itself a proof of such past failures and of a present, final incapacity to change their situation.

Once again there were analogies, in these extreme cases, with the psychological business of controlling or suppressing ambiguous symptoms, for which activity was again indispensable:

Q: "You've got no problems now? Not even a grumble?"

A: "No . . . I think when you get to my age, you'll . . . come in at night—I am a worrier anyway—I worry about things. And I think this sometimes gives me a bit of tension, about a lot of things, and I'll sort of magnify things. But then if I get involved in reading or listening or something—I can more or less get rid of it. Now little things happen, I mean I have myself with cancer all over the place, but—well, a lot of people are like that, I mean their minds turn to it."

And another person commented:

I reckon you'll aye have a grummel or two. But it depends on yourself. I visit a woman down the road here, who lets herself be got down—she willna *go oot*. Some people want sympathy. I hate sympathy.

It is apparent that even in these instances where mere symptoms are being dealt with, the emphasis on active resistance to being 'got down', or to the imagined threat of cancer, was not unlike the emphasis on active avoidance of becoming 'lost', or 'finished', or 'done'. The same ultimate threat of personal and social collapse underlay both prescriptions; but, in the case of symptoms unaccompanied by disease, there was an additional assumption that an illness leading to this state of collapse could actually be induced, by failing to maintain social activity and the psychological resistance which went with it.

In all these ways, then, the responsible, purposive maintenance of socially expected activities was thought by some to provide an indispensable basis for health; and where it was not seen as indispensable to health, it was usually seen as one way of improving it. In this sense health was very much morally controlled, and this made acute the question of how limitations on activity were justified.

Explaining restrictions on activity

Aberdonians in the qualitative study had a representative share of disability, on the relatively severe measures commonly applied among the elderly: over a fifth received help from others with looking after their own person, or with domestic tasks which they would normally have done themselves, or they had ceased to use transport independently or to walk out of doors on their own. But although disability at this level was the experience of a minority, some experience of these or lesser restrictions imposed on activity was described by nearly two-thirds of the people I spoke to. Restriction of some kind was thus, in a statistical sense, the normal experience.

However, there was a certain critical point in these constraints which emerged in a number of discussions. At this point restriction became a physical, psychological, and social threat, representing the loss of things essential to that whole unified way of life that was health-generating. Thus constraints on activity were not only indicted for feelings of restlessness, disappointment, resentment, exasperation, disgust, depression, and a sense of being got down, but were also identified, at the extreme, with being 'socially dead', a 'poor thing', with no longer being 'somebody in the community'. The things people did which were critical to this categoric sense of personal and social worth covered a wide range. Some were restricted in duties which they felt were required by conventional expectations within their particular social milieu: they were hampered in their job, in family and other social visiting, or in housekeeping to accustomed standards. Others were restricted in activities which they recognized to be personal choices, and yet which represented a long investment of interest and reputation and a sense of identification which could be very powerful; these interests included occupational skills, voluntary work with local organizations, hill-walking, golf, bowls, gardening, and reading. These latter preferences are perhaps the kind of thing one might have expected West Enders, with their greater material advantages, to emphasize. But in fact, at this basic level of moral survival, West Enders were mostly as conventional as those living in Mannoch in the activities they held on to, and Mannoch too had its minority who held hard to their own long-standing preferences. Thus whatever their social background, Aberdonians had a conception of their normal self built on either conventional performance or personal reputation, and this normal self was at the heart of the problem of disability.

The question thus arises, how far did the impediments to different activities actually limit responsibility for meeting normal social expectations? How far were they something given, involuntary, a brute fact, and how far was the response to them still open to moral assessments?

Of the constraints discussed, purely physical restriction was obviously the likeliest to be seen as something given; yet it was very seldom the case that a person claimed to be categorically unable to do a thing because of a physical condition. Rather the physical condition was argued to make the activity concerned cost too much in extra effort, pain, or expenditure of time, and the argument was most convincing when there was a specific part of the body affected which was also prominent in performing the specific activity, as a bad leg is prominent in walking difficulties. Alternatively, though less frequently, the condition could be argued to present a risk of catastrophe if the activity was not re- stricted; but in these instances the risk had to be clearly linked to a specific current disease diagnosed by a doctor, and the likelihood of serious consequences from the activity concerned had to be endorsed either by the doctor or by previous experience. Finally, restrictions were also occasionally justified on the grounds of depleted strength, of being 'broken down' or 'finished', or of having no energy, of having, in effect, exhausted one's reserves; but these cases were criticized by others for their feeble-mindedness.

The mechanical nature of the approved factors used to explain restricted activity is thus obvious; yet it was also apparent that many other considerations were tacitly involved in declaring one- self incapable. An explanation in terms of a bad limb which caused pain or extra effort, for example, was very acceptable even when it did not account for other cases where restriction would be explicable in the same way, but where the activity was not in fact restricted. Such cases were sometimes explored, but it was not felt that they invalidated the original explanation:

"I never talk about my hands . . . I've learnt to live with it—just drop things sometimes. I canna play the piano, but I think it's an awful *nice* excuse because my hands don't stretch. But I played so badly. There was a girl at Hillside . . . and she was a wonderful pianist . . . I used to feel very humble when I saw her—just a wee stump and a little wee thumb and yet she—it was her left one—she could put in a left hand better than I could on my five fingers."

Similarly a decision that a particular activity was too risky to perform did not mean that all similar activities were too risky to perform:

"They put me on the committee to get to know the people, but I'm sorry to say I wasn't able. Because I felt—I was pouring the tea with one of these big brown teapots, quite strong in the hands, but somebody had their bag on the floor, and I don't know what way I didn't fall."

But earlier the same woman had said:

"I'll be walking outside—I feel it indoors too, but I'm not frightened indoors—but if I am outside, I'm nervous now, I'm beginning to wait for it. I'll be walking along and something goes. Doesn't lock, but I fall to the side of it. I feel there's something slack or something's moved."

Despite her fear, though, she was still 'able' for walking outside; but she was 'not able' for committee work, though the physical risk was identical.

These explanations for a restriction in terms of mechanical problems were thus proffered not as complete accounts, but as supplying what was, in terms of social expectations, one necessary condition for deciding that an activity should be restricted—that there were other non-mechanical, non-necessary factors in the decision was taken for granted, and these other factors at times supplied the only essential reason why one activity was given up rather than another. Thus choice was seen to be involved in responding to physical limitation; and hence *a fortiori* it was seen to be involved in responding to psychological threat.

This tacit element of choice meant that attitudes to responsibility could go either of two ways. Either mechanical explanations of disability entirely exempted the disabled from being responsible for restrictions of their activity, or moral explanations could be reinvoked to make them partly responsible for not preventing, or not overcoming, the restriction. This issue was acute with those activities which were felt to lie at the core of the person's moral self, and which were considered indispensable to health. Limitation in these activities could imply a spiral of decline in health and a loss of self. Thus the issue of how to respond to limitation was critical.

Coping with restriction

There were a number of different ways of dealing with limitations on activity, which were only occasionally related to the severity of the impairment.

The first common strategy was the familiar one of making special efforts, and using all manner of tricks and devices, to go on living normally, or as near normally as made no difference. This response was commoner where the level of impairment was relatively favourable.

Under this heading of struggling to continue normally I include a number of different tactics. First is the attempt to deal with the psychological threat of illness by shutting the threat out of one's mind. In Aberdeen, this was an approach used with a variety of minor conditions—undiagnosed symptoms, ordinary depression or anxiety, conditions for which surgery was optional, ulcers; but it was also used with some more serious problems—arthritis, heart conditions, and multiple sclerosis. It was generally seen as an admirable response, consistent with the use of normal activity to suppress ambiguous symptoms and hold at bay chronic conditions which were thought to be untreatable; and it was sometimes thought admirable even when it was known to have made a treatable condition worse.

For the most part, though, putting up a struggle did not mean ignoring the threat of illness, but recognizing it squarely, and refusing to give up, or to 'lie' (or 'sit') down to it. The usual threat in these instances was restriction of activity, and it was overcome by 'determination' which either reduced, without eliminating, the restriction, or enabled a continued performance of the restricted activity in spite of the lesser standard achieved, by putting a bold face on a performance which was only a little below conventional standards. The problems involved were usually not very severe, and were amenable to this kind of management—stomach ulcers, varicose veins, breathlessness, eye problems, or the residual problems and risks left by earlier back trouble. By a discreet use of commonplace devices pain and difficulty could be controlled, and active pursuits such as golfing, hiking, or gardening could be continued almost as usual. But some potentially more serious problems, too—amputation, blindness, and severe arthritis—were also handled with real ingenuity so as to enable activities of this order to be continued.

In all these ways, then, the threat posed by illness could be answered by a reassertion of normal living. But this was not always possible; and there were conditions, on the whole more seriously restrictive, where Aberdonians had found, to their dismay, that this favourite response not only failed them, but actually made things worse. To succeed, determination sometimes had to change its meaning:

Wife: "I lay in my bed for a year last year, aye, up and doon, aye forced mysel' tae walk and forced mysel' tae walk. But I found mysel' aye walkin' against the wall. But I didna understand fit [what] it was . . . . and it wis the eye doctor that told me it was hardening o' the arteries. But once I knew what it was I tried to control it you see. Oh, I got some awful wallops for a start . . . . but I hinna fell for a long time now, hiven't I nae?"

Husband: "Touch wood—fa's [where's] your stick . . . .?"

Q: "So now that you know about it can you control it?"

Wife: "I control it, I control it, I just . . ."

Q: "Now how do you do that?"

Wife: "Just—determination."

Husband: "Nae jumpin' up quick or naething like that, takin' her time."

Wife: "I dinna jump up quick . . . . if I was doin' too much, I mean, if I was fleein' around and daein' [doing] a' thing as I used tae dae, I wid just collapse, just collapse, it's hopeless."

This was one of the peculiar dilemmas of a determined approach. The difficulty was particularly evident in activities restricted not so much because of their risks, as in the case just quoted, but because of a stable local defect: back problems, a weak leg, arthritic knees, arthritic hip. These were restrictions which in most respects were felt to be reducible or containable by dealing with them in an attacking spirit; but they could also be made worse at times by a delayed reaction following excessive activity:

"I suppose now, you know, I'm a bit stupid about this. I still find myself tugging about furniture and things, and I know damned fine I'm going to have a sore back after it—and I still keep doing it, you see. I think we've all a tendency to do that; when you're fine, you know, you do things and you know damned fine you're going to suffer for it afterwards. But you still keep doing it. Isn't that a peculiar thing? I think it's because you don't want to give in to not being able to do things—I think that's what it is."

Experiences like these could become sufficiently repeated and disabling to pose a new threat, to which the responses varied markedly.

The most positive reaction, though it was that of a minority, was to search for new activities and interests, or to increase involvement in activities previously neglected, and to reorder values and preferences so that the new interests appeared as a positive gain amid the other losses imposed by illness. The activities concerned were very varied. Some were necessarily capable of being done alone, when confined to the house: listening to 'talking books' on tape when sight failed, knitting, crocheting work and embroidery, painting and reading. Purely sociable alternatives were, nevertheless, also often feasible. Club life, or involvement in certain voluntary organizations, could provide its own self-contained world; and so could cruises or package holidays, since people who met on holiday became correspondents with whom further holidays or excursions were planned. Some who were more sedentary, on the other hand, recommended a more intensive cultivation of old friendships. And finally a third type of alternative—variously solitary or social according to circumstances—was offered by meditation, prayer, or involvement in a church community.

Sometimes these alternative activities were sought out in spite of an unresolved sense that, in the normal terms of the person's past history and of Aberdeen life, they remained eccentric and odd; but in many cases they expressed a transmutation of earlier values. Where human abilities failed, a 'great faith' could help people to search for alternatives; and while prayer offered them a continuing possibility of recovering, through a 'miracle', what they had given up, they learned at the same time to look for blessings in other places, because the answer to prayer might be other than what was asked for:

"I have a great belief in prayer for everything. Prayers are not always answered, you see; I know, if they're not answered, well to me it's answered too. Not supposed to be answered. You know what I mean?—a kind o' mix up . . . . That's my belief. It's nae a'body's [everybody's], but still."

More is said about this kind of transmutation in the chapter on religion; for present purposes, it is enough to note that this response to chronic illness involved an acceptance of restriction, together with a reorientation of interests and purposes to which a positive value was given.

Contrasted with this positive kind of acceptance, though, and by far the commonest response to restriction, was a containment of negative feelings, with a sense that nothing could compensate for what was lost, and that what replaced it was only a way of passing time. In terms of standard measures of disability, the restrictions faced in these cases did not appear to be any worse than where the more positive response just discussed was made; and there was a similar range of fears for the future. The difference lay rather in the immutable sense of loss stoically borne. Other activities of a sort perforce took up the day, but they were devalued. Clubs and societies associated with particular disabling diseases tended to be viewed in this light, and other less formal gatherings of people who had some similarity of misfortune took place *faute de mieux* in pubs or around public walks and gardens, especially during the daytime. And apart from such activities, response was limited to a sheer maintenance of residual activity and of defences against depression and resentment. This attempt to 'manage', or to 'carry on' with what was left, or to 'content yourself' by putting away frustrated wishes, was a way of dealing with the downward spiral implied when activities felt to be indispensable to health and to one's moral self were restricted. Thus there loomed alongside the stoicism a sense that in this situation the 'I' who once had been was 'lost' or 'finished'.

Finally, there was also a third response to chronic restriction. This response, again that of a minority, treated the loss of an activity as welcome, or at any rate as not regrettable, because the time for it or the desire for it had passed. The levels of restriction in these instances were again similar to that evident in the other two types of response. At a relatively slight level of restriction, such welcome sacrifices could be presented as legitimate preferences. Work was one of these activities whose loss through ill health was sometimes not regrettable, in one case because pleasanter alternatives had opened up, but in two other cases because a rest had been well earned. Giving up the piano, as in a case already cited, or giving up tennis or swimming at a certain age, might be done with relief or without regret. But there were more striking and, to most Aberdonians, more suspect instances, too, in which confinement to bed or to the home, far from being frustrating, brought freedom from cares. In one case this restful state had been known to be temporary; but for some of the more elderly women the peace was not an interlude—it was the thankful giving up of tasks or social activities with which they no longer wished to keep on struggling, accompanied by the decision that they were 'done' and deserved a rest. In these instances, illness and restriction had virtually lost their negative valuation altogether, and no effort of resistance or adaptation was required.

These varying responses to restriction can now be brought together with the strategies described earlier for preventing and mitigating illness, in order to see how far they form a consistent whole.

Themes and dilemmas

The ideas which have been discussed so far were expressed in varying combinations, and people made an effort to be coherent and engaged in heart-searching about contradictions. In order to summarize the patterns of coherence, and to point to the dividing lines of contradiction, I have simplified the material discussed into a number of typical autobiographical descriptions of the sort which act as premises or assumptions when Aberdonians consider how to cope with illness. In doing so, I have used terms standardized to represent the distinctions of the preceding analysis; and I summarize further by grouping the various premises under five broad captions. These are as follows:

1.1 *Illness as controlled by normal living*
(a) If I keep up my normal activity, I help myself to prevent or cope with illness, and/or
(b) If I do not keep up my normal activity, I make my condition worse.
1.2 *Illness as a continuous struggle*
Even if I am partly restricted, I do not stop struggling to perform my normal activities.
1.3 *Illness as an alternative way of life*
If I am seriously restricted by illness, I develop alternative interests which offer positive rewards.
1.4 *Illness as a loss to be endured*
(a) If I am seriously restricted by illness, I am finished, and/or
(b) If I am seriously restricted by illness, I forget about my past interests, and/or
(c) If I am seriously restricted by illness, I pass the time with distasteful alternatives.
1.5 *Illness as a release from effort*
If I am restricted by illness, I give some things up with relief.

A small number of coherent patterns were formed from these premisses. The first was a combination of ordinary illness as controlled by normal living (1.1) with serious illness as a loss to be endured (1.4). This pattern resembles some of the central ideas in the view of illness 'as a destroyer' which was depicted by Claudine Herzlich in her Paris study. There is the same emphasis on banishing illness through assiduous performance of normal responsibilities, together with a sense of helplessness, loss of self, and passive abandonment when illness breaks through these defences. But since I am not dealing here with the additional notions about the doctor's role which are involved in 'illness as a destroyer', I call this pattern 'illness as exile'. Exile here indicates the estrangement from oneself and from normal living which is the other side of the coin from the Aberdonian emphasis on moral control over health. In this view the possibility of self-estrangement is recognized from the start, and between controllable and uncontrollable conditions there is a catastrophic turning point when the claim to be normal can no longer be felt to hold.

The second coherent pattern formed out of the premisses listed earlier was a combination of ordinary illness as controlled by normal living (1.1) with serious illness as a continuous struggle (1.2). Again, there is a resemblance between this pattern and some constituents of the view of 'illness as an occupation' described in Paris; but two important differences should also be noted. First, Aberdonians with this optimistic view shared notions about the health-giving properties of their customary way of life with those who saw 'illness as exile', and they too emphasized the value of ignoring minor illness and continuing with that way of life regardless. There was little sense here of a protected position for the chronically ill which parallels the social duties of an occupation, other than in the context of hospital care.

Secondly, the pattern here is narrower in other respects and does not include recourse to alternative activities; for the present pattern could come into conflict, as I show later, with an attempt to develop alternatives. Thus I call this pattern 'illness as a test of achievement', for it is centred on normality, like 'illness as exile', but it refuses to contemplate the possibility that normal living cannot be sustained, or virtually sustained, by heroic effort.

Since these two patterns of thinking share the idea that illness is controlled by normal living (1.1), the contrast between them rests in the opposition between the determination to struggle on at all costs (1.2), and the decision that the losses imposed by illness must simply be accepted and endured (1.4). In the instances where both these opposed ideas were endorsed, they generated considerable conflict. David Vincent, for example, had had arthritis for nearly thirty years, and his strategy had been to try to continue living normally (1.1). But increasing disability had made this more and more of a struggle (1.2). He now had difficulty walking any distance, and though the widowed brother with whom he lived took him most places by car, he had had to give up golf, at which he had excelled. By this time the housework would also have fallen wholly on his brother, but for the services of a home help.

In his embattled resistance to these increasing constraints, David Vincent took as his model an experience of his brother Sandy in the war. Severely wounded, Sandy had been thought inoperable.

"And do you know what saved him? The nurse took him in her arms and said"—this with whispered ferocity—"stick it! keep breathing! So he kept breathing. And he's still breathing. It was an order—and those men were accustomed to obey orders."

This was the example that David applied in dealing with his own increased pain:

"I just have to thole it, you see, and the first severe pain dies away, you see, if ye just thole it . . . . Fight through it, and keep something in your mind to look forward to . . . . Be like Sandy—keep breathing."

Nevertheless, for all this effort, there were times when he swung towards the alternative of giving up his aspiration to keep living as normally as possible, and envisaged circumstances in which he could successfully suppress it:

I wish I was old, then I wouldn't get so exasperated. There's something to be said for being old—no, I mean it,

—this to his niece, who reacted to this statement with an incredulous and somewhat worried smile—

I'm not old, in my mind, and it gets me so frustrated and exasperated; but if you're old you accept it . . . . When they gave me cortisone . . . . I felt so much better. I went out on the golf course at Hazlehead, but I could only play two holes and then I had to give up, and the tears were dashing down my cheeks, whether from the pain or the frustration, I couldn't say.

The alternative to these moments of acute disappointment, his picture of old age as a time of acceptance, was not accompanied by any idea of fresh interests or alternative activities; it was, it turned out, a picture of the ancient in the chimney corner, all passion spent, and its principal attraction was that, with desire put away, frustration would also be put away. Such contrary images of 'contenting yourself' (1.4) thus sometimes haunted those who had committed themselves to fighting on against increasing odds; and from the other side of the divide, too, those who embodied these images had to distance themselves from their own previous struggles. A younger man than David Vincent, for example, who had prided himself on having done 'the same job as a fit man', in spite of losing an arm in the war, was content now to 'brak the time' with little more than sardonic observation of men on social security in a local bar:

"At a certain age in your life ye're stopped at rinnin' anyway, y'know, ye dinna rin aboot the same. I was aboot 25/26 year aul fin [when] this happened. So it's passed—the rinnin' bit o' my life's passed, y'know."

This conflict between resignation and resistance, then, was what divided those who saw illness as exile and those who saw it as a test of achievement. There was also, however, a third coherent combination of ideas which contrasted with both these views, and which linked the notion of illness as a loss to be endured (1.4) with illness as (in some respects) a release from effort (1.5). This pattern of ideas was expressed by relatively few people, for whom the release from obligation sanctioned by old age or hospital treatment was actually pleasant in some ways, although in other respects the curtailment of their aspirations in order to achieve contentment had run a little against the grain. This way of thinking was not unlike the view of those Parisians who saw illness 'as a liberator', as a time for solitary contemplation; but it must be said that nothing more serious than day-dreaming was involved here, and solitariness was not implied: the emphasis was simply on resting and release from demands. It is more accurate, therefore, to see this pattern of thought as an instance of disengagement in old age, with the uneasy mixture of voluntary and involuntary elements contained in that term; and I have named it 'illness as disengagement'.

People who expressed this view shared with those who saw illness as exile some of the emphasis on unavoidable restriction and containment of feelings (1.4); and the conflict between these views centred on the tension between the sense that the consequent release from normal tasks was pleasant (1.5), and the rule otherwise generally propounded by Aberdonians, that one should keep doing one's normal tasks and so control illness (1.1). Alice Bruce had a stomach problem which gave her occasional attacks of nausea, and some problems with the circulation in her legs, and she felt that she had 'broken down' (1.4). On the one hand, since she did not go out so much, she felt lonelier; but on the other hand she argued that at her age people 'deserve some peace' (1.5), and fought a determined rearguard action against the rota for cleaning the common paths, hall, and stairways. She slept late in the morning, when she was not on the rota, arousing some neighbourly comment on these grounds alone, and when she was on the rota stipulated that she would sleep late nevertheless on Sundays, when the stairs were, she said, little used. Further, she held out for the view that the council should be responsible for keeping paths clear of snow. In regard to all these tasks, she maintained that they 'shouldn't make old people do all that—they're not fit for it' and against her son's view that she should 'do more' she argued that after a morning's cleaning, 'you feel like just sitting in your chair'.

With all her sense that she deserved a rest, however, Alice Bruce had sufficient humour to like and be liked by her neighbours, and sufficient sensitivity to respect their moral discipline. Indeed she had to recognize that they were in fact mostly older than herself; and hence at times she swung round to their way of looking at illness. When a neighbour cleared the path which she had left as a reproach to the council sweepers, she was apologetic and complimentary, and she was proud of the labour she herself had once put in to blacking the fireplace 'in the old days'. Hence it was intelligible that she should, in a private conversation, suddenly contradict a comment which agreed with her own view of the cleaning rota, and endorse instead the conventional view of its beneficial effect (1.1):

Yes—but it gives you a nudge, and makes you keep going.

Others, too, felt this ambivalence between self-reproach and a sense of deserving to take it easy; and only where the activity given up could be represented as minor and as an accepted matter of preference, could the privilege of age be welcomed without felt inconsistency by people who saw normal tasks as obligatory.

Finally, one further idea—the notion of illness as an alternative way of life with positive rewards—is particularly interesting because, although it made good sense by itself, it tended, in any combination with other ideas, to generate contradictions. Yet in spite of this tendency, the search for alternative activities was seldom undertaken as the sole tenet in dealing with illness. It was combined most successfully with the theme of struggle (1.2) and with reinterpretations of normal living (1.1), and it clashed most violently with the view of illness as a loss to be endured (1.4). However, even in the most successful of these combinations, the problem was that, given the Aberdonian emphasis on sustaining normality, the search for alternatives was only justified where normal activity was unquestionably restricted by the illness. Since the constraint imposed by the illness was, as I indicated earlier, seldom absolute, ambiguity often lurked in the possibility that, with sufficient resolution, the restriction could in fact be resisted. In this uncertainty, the opinion of others, reassuring or upsetting, was often especially important. Christine Taylor was a business woman who had retired when a health problem had interrupted her work. The problem—a diagnosis of kidney disease—was only temporarily restrictive in the short term, but it threatened trouble in the future, and she decided to retire and take up hill walking—something which she enjoyed, and which she felt was also good for her health. In her own opinion this was not merely a positive alternative (1.3), but it still constituted normal, active living (1.1):

"I'm not a person—I don't think anyway—to knuckle under an illness or anything; I don't feel that I should just not pursue as normal a life as possible, in spite of this and in spite of other things."

Correspondingly, she contrasted her own approach with the way her uncle had responded to retirement:

"When he retired, I don't remember him doing anything other than sitting reading his papers, something like that. I don't think he had any activity whatsoever. He never cleaned his own shoes or anything—you know his wife always did this."

Yet in spite of this activist account of herself, the fact that she had retired when her contemporaries were still working, and had taken up an alternative which could be construed as a mere hobby, gave the occasion for a different view of herself as having reneged on the normal tasks which sustain health; and this view was given credibility by the rapid onset of further health problems:

"I retired reasonably early—I was only 56, you see—and a lot of my friends and relations said 'Oh, you can't be serious.' I had the kidney trouble, that was the first thing, and then the stomach operation and then back trouble:

and this has all more or less been since I retired. But it would have happened anyway, whether I retired or not. People say, 'Oh you shouldn't have retired so young!' But that had nothing to do with the fact that I had this; at least I choose not to think so."

The uncertainty in this last sentence, as in the first quotation given, underlines the force which public definitions of normality could bring to bear in Aberdeen when people attempted to construct an alternative way of life in response to illness. It was the normal way—whether that was a job during working years, or some other activity in retirement—which conduced to health and maintained resistance, and those who stepped outside it had to convince themselves and those around them that their alternative had the same moral and salutary value. Hence, for Christine Taylor, an ambivalence remained:

"I've no regrets at all about retiring—none. Only the *odd* time, and again I've got pressures from other people, younger friends. They say you shouldn't be retired; you're not doing anything, you know, and you ought to be working. Take a part-time job or something. One solicitor friend of mine particularly—'Oh you're wasting your life, you ought to be working!' He's *always* at me about this, but on the few occasions when I've felt myself bored . . . let's face it, often, quite often bored, I've thought well . . . I'd be all right in the office, and keep myself occupied and speaking with people."

It could be difficult, then, to establish an alternative activity, taken up because of illness, as having the same validity and beneficence as what was previously normal.

The case studies which have been given thus reveal lines of consistency, and boundaries marked by contradiction, in Aberdonian thinking about how to cope with illness; and other examples which illustrate these points are also described in later chapters. But it is important to emphasize again, as these studies of inner conflict make clear, that people cannot regularly be typified as exponents of a single coherent pattern of coping. Nearly two-fifths of these Aberdonians did combine their ideas coherently, mainly along the most popular lines of seeing illness as exile or as a test of achievement; but around a fifth recognized conflicts in themselves over these matters, and the remainder expressed only a single fundamental idea. These last people, who had only the one idea, were fairly equally divided between seeing illness as controllable by normal living, as a continuous struggle, or as a loss to be endured; and for the most part these were ideas which could consistently develop in either of two directions. Those who simply emphasized normal living (1.1), for example, had often been relatively insulated from ill health; and if they were to cope with serious illness, consistency could point them either towards the fatalism of seeing illness as loss (1.4), or towards the optimism of continuous struggle (1.2). Those who simply emphasized endurance of loss (1.4), similarly, were silent on whether they felt a responsibility for maintaining resistance (1.1); and again, if faced with the suggestion that they should, they could consistently move either towards accepting the responsibility or towards regarding it as unreasonably burdensome (1.5).

While consistency mattered to these Aberdonians, therefore, and their repertoire of ideas about coping with illness permitted only a few consistent combinations, their thought represented a very varied exploration of these limits. Some held to one simple guideline, some attempted a more sensitive elaboration; some stuck to accepted consistencies, some sought for a resolution of contraries. More enduring, therefore, than these personal explorations or ways of thinking were the moral boundaries between which all Aberdonians moved in responding to illness. The moral repertoire which they thus exploited had its own definite features, and it is now time to bring together what has emerged about it.

Conclusion

At the beginning of this chapter I suggested that in describing, explaining, and coping with illness, people draw on deeper assumptions about the moral and mechanical sources of health, and about the health-giving or health-destroying nature of their society. Much has now emerged about the assumptions which Aberdonians make in these respects.

Among the several dimensions which run through Aberdonian descriptions of chronic illness—the symptoms, the disease, constitutional strength, capacity for the demands of daily life—the major part is played by the latter two dimensions, strength to resist, and capacity for tasks. In many ways these two notions fit into schemes of understanding which are complementary but opposed. Constitutional strength is something one must be at least partly responsible for; it depends to some extent on both mind and body, on creating and sustaining the union of purpose and activity in the social life of Aberdeen. Incapacity for tasks, on the other hand, must be exempt from responsibility or blame; it is presented as a mechanical matter, and elements of choice which are tacitly acknowledged to be present remain inexplicit.

Constitutional strength, then, is in Aberdeen easily interpreted as a moral matter, even though there is felt to be a strong element of heredity and past illness experiences in it as well. The integration of mental purpose and physical activity which is held to sustain it is at the heart of ideas about the willing and acting self; and it is for this reason that the self-created union of mind and body in daily purposes is a moral attribute. Correspondingly, the obverse of this moral element is the idea that a breakdown of resistance originates not only from loss of activity but also from failures of will or attention. These negative assumptions, which may imply that a sick person has an unconscious wish for illness or pays undue attention to symptoms, are only occasionally canvassed; but they form a threat and a moral sanction of disproportionate significance, and are the ultimate weapon either for keeping oneself in hand or for criticizing others. They are examples of popular theories of psychosomatic causation which do attribute moral responsibility, and these correspond in a broad way with clinical theories which supposedly do not attribute moral responsibility, with the considerable risk that, in any communication between clinicians and laity, the two may become confounded.

It is the same sanctions, too, which ensure that many Aberdonians, while emphasizing how active they are in maintaining their powers of resistance, refer also to limits on their activity which are, for mechanical reasons, out of their control; but these two ideas are only sustainable together by distinguishing implicitly between levels of activity—the core activities which maintain the moral person's resistance, and the peripheral activities which are limited by mere mechanical failure. The point where this distinction is drawn is significant: it is one of those places where one can see some settling for the barest necessities, while others require much more. Some hold on to core activities which are merely conventional and universal in Aberdeen life, others fight to keep interests which are a matter of long-standing personal preference. Whatever the reason for this difference, though, it does not seem, at this fundamental level of personal worth and social survival, to be related to material advantages, in the way broader expectations of health can be. Only when Aberdonians came to describe their expectations, not of disabling illness, but of a normal healthy retirement, did people in the West End have more optimistic expectations than those in Mannoch—a subject dealt with in the next chapter and Chapter 8.

Two concepts of health, then, intertwine in Aberdonian talk, one emphasizing moral, and one mechanical, explanations. According to the moral account, the normal way of life in Aberdeen is health-giving, and people are responsible for the essential 'core' activity which preserves their normal self. But the very strength of this view makes it imperative to avoid hypochondria, and to show that any restriction on activity is peripheral, and can be given a mechanical explanation.

It is apparent from what has been said so far that both the moral and the mechanical explanations of illness make for a certain conformity in Aberdonian attitudes; and when it comes to coping with chronic illness, and the very divergent ways in which this is attempted, much is again explained by the particular balance struck between conformity and creative innovation in Aberdonian culture. The conformity is evident not only in a tendency to view common activities, such as housekeeping, as normal for everyone, but also in a tendency to view the individual preferences a person has previously stood for as normal for that person. Both tendencies perhaps reflect a society in which personal and biographical characterizations are for the most part easily available through long-standing networks of acquaintanceship, so that in addition to what is generally expected, there are certain things individually expected of each person as part of their established character. In either case, failure to meet these expectations carries a stigma of abnormality. However, innovation remains possible within limits, and is reflected in the capacity of some people to adapt and redefine their core activity, so that the moral self which depends upon it is not endangered.

The logic of conformity is directly reflected in two of the three coherent patterns of thought which Aberdonians drew on in coping with chronic illness. Put starkly, those who saw illness as a test of achievement believed they could maintain their normal way of life against all odds by sheer moral effort; while those who saw illness

as exile believed that effort notwithstanding, there were circumstances in which they would not be able to maintain their normal
way of life, and that their essential moral self would in that case
be lost. In the latter, more pessimistic, instances, the illness conditions involved were on the whole more restrictive and threatening
than in the former, more optimistic examples, though this was by
no means always the case. And relatively severe problems were
also involved in the third coherent pattern of response—illness as a
legitimate disengagement—which likewise reflected something of
the same logic, though in an indirect fashion. Those who saw
illness in this way sometimes pleaded age or the status of being a
patient as a justification for their passivity, but some were beyond
bothering about normal behaviour and wished merely to give up
and rest. To this extent, their way of dealing with chronic illness
was merely a negation of the conventional norm and, as emerges
in Chapter 6, an acceptance of deviancy.

The pressure to conform was thus strong in Aberdeen, and
as a consequence of this pressure, attempts to innovate, to develop
an alternative way of life in illness and an alternative expression of
the sick person's sense of worth, were often hedged with contradiction. The effort to find new interests partly depended on the
extent to which people saw their values, needs, and preferences
as malleable, and—still more important—on the extent to which
they felt it consistent with themselves and what they stood for
in the eyes of others that their values should be malleable. There
was a certain gloomy dignity in refusing to like what others
disliked and what one had never liked before. Yet some were
able to alter focus and find new rewards, to retain their sense of
worth, and even at times to reconcile their abnormal situation
with a continued avowal of the values of normality and moral
struggle. In this creative effort religion was an important resource,
in a way which I describe further in the chapter on that subject.

In historical terms, though, so far as one can speak of these
as yet, Aberdeen appears, in regard to illness, as a somewhat
conservative society where boundaries are quite strongly marked.
The tradition of dissent, and the ambivalence between the active
and the contemplative life, which enables the French at times
to see illness as a liberator, and personal autonomy and alternative styles of life as a legitimate response, is virtually absent.
But at the same time older Aberdonians have a confidence in the

health-giving character of their way of life which contrasts sharply with the metropolitan disillusion of Paris. Perhaps this is partly for the very reason that they are older,[17] and belong to a small city still integrated with its maritime and rural hinterland. Perhaps, too, Aberdonian attitudes have something to do with Scotland's Calvinist past. These are all themes which need further exploration, and which reappear later in this book.

Notes and References

1. C. Herzlich, *Health and illness,* tr. H. D. Graham, London: Academic Press, 1973.
2. R. G. A. Williams, 'Concepts of health: an analysis of lay logic', *Sociology,* 17 (1983), 185–204; D. Locker, *Symptoms and illness,* London: Tavistock, 1981; D. Field, 'The social definition of illness', in D. Tuckett (ed.), *An introduction to medical sociology,* London: Tavistock, 1976.
3. R. Pill and N. C. H. Stott, 'Concepts of illness causation and responsibility: some preliminary data from a sample of working-class mothers', *Soc. Sci. and Med.* 16 (1982), 43–52; eid., 'Choice or chance: further evidence on ideas of illness and responsibility for health', *Soc. Sci. and Med.* 20 (1985), 981–91.
4. M. Calnan, *Health and illness,* London: Tavistock, 1987, ch. 2; M. Blaxter and E. Paterson, *Mothers and daughters: a three-generational study of health attitudes and behaviour,* London: Heinemann, 1982, ch. 4.; but see also A. d'Houtaud and M. G. Field, 'The image of health: variations in perceptions by social class in a French population', *Sociol. of Health and Illness,* 6 (1984), 30–60.
5. I have discussed diet in R. G. A. Williams, 'The salt of the earth: ideas linking diet, exercise and virtue among elderly Aberdonians', in A. Murcott (ed.), *The sociology of food and eating,* London: Gower, 1983.
6. K. Charmaz, 'Loss of self: a fundamental form of suffering in the chronically ill', *Sociology of Health and Illness,* 5 (1983), 168–95.
7. G. M. White, 'The role of cultural explanations in "somatisation" and "psychologisation" ', *Soc. Sci. and Med.* 16 (1982), 1519–30; C. Currer, 'Concepts of mental well- and ill-being; the case of Pathan mothers in Britain', in C. Currer and M. Stacey (eds.), *Concepts of health, illness and disease,* Leamington: Berg, 1986.
8. See e.g., B. Inglis, *The book of the back,* London: Ebury Press, 1978, ch. 6.
9. R. Totman, *Social causes of illness,* London: Souvenir Press, 1980; E. T. Cassell, *The healer's art,* London: Pelican, 1978.

10. G. Waddell, C. J. Main, E. W. Morris, and I. C. M. Gray, 'Chronic low back pain, psychologic distress, and illness behaviour', *Spine*, 9 (1984), 209–13.
11. R. G. A. Williams, 'Theories and measurement in disability', *Epidemiol. and Community Health*, 33 (1979), 32–47.
12. Blaxter and Paterson, *Mothers and daughters*, ch. 4.
13. These ideas go back to F. Davis, *Passage through crisis*, Indianapolis: Bobbs-Merrill, 1963.
14. C. Herzlich and J. Pierret, *Malades d'hier, malades d'aujourd'hui*, Paris: Payot, 1984
15. J. Geyer-Kordesch, 'Cultural habits of illness: the Enlightened and the Pious in eighteenth century Germany', in R. Porter (ed.), *Patients and practitioners*, Cambridge University Press, 1985. Herzlich and Pierret also recognize that this is a very old strand in Christian piety, though their emphasis is on illness as a consequence of sin and an occasion for penitence.
16. Williams, 'Concepts of health'.
17. Activism is also being urged upon the elderly in France: see X. Gaullier, 'Economic crisis and old age policies in France', *Ageing and Society*, 2 (1982), 165–82.

2

Old age

We must prepare ourselves, my friends, against old age; and as it is advancing, endeavour by our diligence to mitigate and correct the natural infirmities that attend it . . . That silly doltishness, that is imputed to old age, will be found only in persons of weak and abject spirits.

Cicero, *On Old Age,* from the translation printed by R. Urie in Glasgow, 1751

Introduction

Old age both encompasses illness and points more insistently towards death. But while it includes both these and other connotations of decline, and poses the question of how to respond, it can have many more positive associations as well, suggesting a picture of a whole stage of life with its own duties and rewards. From such materials each society carves its own image of age, and its own model of response; and to clarify these is especially important in our society, where not only life expectancy at older ages, but also the proportion of older people in the population has reached unprecedented levels.

This task of elucidating our ideas about old age has proved to be surprisingly difficult. In the 1960s, attempts to define popular ideas about ageing tended to assume that there was a single agreed conception; and a good deal of contradictory work resulted, some of which portrayed old age as a time of maintained activity and some as a time of passive disengagement. This work can perhaps best be understood now as an imperfect reflection of several different sets of popular prescriptions and experiences relating to ageing. And it is this variety and conflict which now poses a challenge to understanding and explanation.

One recent approach to explanation has focused on old age as a stigma.[1] Both active and passive approaches to ageing spring, it is argued, from the continued existence of a negative stereotype of what it is to be old. In the face of this stereotype some respond resignedly, accepting for themselves the passive and helpless role which it implies; but at the same time others respond with strategies of avoidance, presenting themselves as active, and attributing real old age to others. In this way, both active and passive attitudes to ageing can be seen to spring from the same origin.

A different and more optimistic line of explanation, on the other hand, has focused on situations where there seems to be increased solidarity among the old.[2] Stimulated by the growth of retirement villages in the United States during the 1960s, this argument has suggested that with the increasing independence of generations in the family, some older people are turning to their peers for support, and are beginning to constitute local enclaves and 'subcultures', promoting beliefs and values and a way of living of their own, which are partially distinct from that of other older people and of the population as a whole. Critics of this notion from the more pessimistic tradition have pointed out that since a stigma attaches to old age, membership of many groups or communities of the old is regarded with ambivalence and avoided by most of those who are putative candidates for it. These groups have therefore to be seen as associations of the stigmatized, and they are not sub-cultures, in that the shared values which are peculiar to them are imposed by the world outside. Hence where a subculture of the aged really exists, it must be identified not with a stigmatized image of age, but with some other image suggestive of certain positive shared values generated from within.

There are at least two possible sources of such solidarity for the old in our society. The first relates to the new values which may attach to retirement. In some societies, economic roles are set aside in favour of positive tasks of healing, counselling, ritual observance, piety, or pilgrimage; but though there have in the past been some indications of such ideas in parts of Europe, they seem to be more strongly expressed in other traditions.[3] In the contemporary West, retirement, when it is given a positive purpose, seems rather to be prized for the power it affords of individual choice in the use of leisure;[4] but whether this purpose is capable of generating a group consciousness among older people as a whole, especially one which can sustain a supportive subculture with its own partially distinct values, remains in question.

A second source of solidarity is implicit in the claim that certain groups of the elderly belong to a particular generation. A generation can become a moral or a political force, in which special experiences of youth, and special values and idioms, are preserved as badges of membership.[5] Theoretical interest has been expressed in generational consciousness among the elderly;[6] however, references to it in empirical studies have often remained tantalizingly inexplicit and underdeveloped.

Finally, a third and more comprehensive line of explanation has sought to relate the new ideas about ageing to historical change. As yet the main attention in this tradition has been concentrated on the ideas expressed in public policy;[7] and the relation of such official notions to popular thinking is uncertain. It is obvious that on the whole the public image of old age has benefited from the improvements in life expectancy achieved by capitalism. But there are also interesting indications that public statements have promoted negative views of retirement when capitalist industry needs to draw on its reserve army of labour, and positive views when there is high unemployment. Furthermore, even where retirement is promoted as a new style of life, it is argued that the unequal distribution of the necessary skills has limited it to a few.

These historical aspects of public attitudes to ageing are important, but they do not have as long a history as private attitudes. In Britain, for example, old age only emerged as an issue for central government in the late nineteenth century, and it was viewed then in straightforward negative terms as a social problem.[8] But in personal views of ageing the stock of ideas which has come down to us is more complex and more deeply rooted in the past. One tradition goes back to the sequential schemes of the Middle Ages, the varying Ages of Man of which Jacques provides an example in *As You Like It*, in which a distinction is often made between a 'green' old age and the last stage of withering. But in addition there has also been a long European counter-tradition, based on classical sources, in which the distinction has been rather between the honoured and the despised old, the honoured retaining their powers and faculties through wealth and moral effort, and the despised losing theirs through poverty and moral weakness.[9] The relation of contemporary ideas of ageing to these pre-industrial notions has been little explored; but obviously it is a relation which needs to be charted in any account of contemporary developments in terms of economic change.

All these varying positive and negative images of age and generation appear in various ways in the thinking of Aberdonians, and I now consider how this occurs.

Concepts of age in Aberdeen

Nearly all Aberdonians had something to say about old age; indeed they had a bewildering variety of evaluations and prescriptions related to getting older, which only begin to appear orderly once it is recognized that the terms 'old' or 'older', and their equivalents, indicated different ideas in different contexts. The word 'old' was very sensitive to context, and the first task is to distinguish the main contextual meanings which were involved.

The inter-war generation

The generational meaning of age was clearly marked. By 1980 most Aberdonian survivors of the First World War were over eighty, and many survivors of the Second World War were beginning to enter their sixties; but the generational consciousness of both these groups was similar in kind and it usually differentiated all older people as a whole from the experience of the 'young' who grew up after the Second World War. About a quarter of those interviewed, diffused through all social classes, made an explicit connection between this generational consciousness and some aspect of their morale, daily activity, or health. Probably for many more, however, the consciousness was implicit; in talking about conclusions from war experiences, for instance, few bothered to underline the obvious fact that in contrasting themselves with those who had not been servicemen they were contrasting themselves with those born after them.

There were two main aspects of the past to which people related their generational notions: its economic austerity and its sterner morality. While the hardships of pensioners in the past were acknowledged to be greater than those of pensioners now, the burdens of the young in the past—the poverty and wartime hazards which those I spoke to had themselves experienced—were for them still more strikingly contrasted with youth's present prosperity. The lessons which people drew from these earlier deprivations were those of hard work, courage, effort and activity, an ability to be satisfied with little, and the thrift to make a little go a long way. The hard work was felt, as might be expected from the last chapter, to conduce towards health, and to fortify in illness, although it could also make the adjustment to retirement more difficult. The thrift made it possible to accept the limitations of a reduced income with equanimity, and tended to express itself in domesticity. There was little experience of the kind of sociability, now seen as commonplace among the young, which involved groups of unrelated people sharing in conspicuous consumption:

"I've been very fortunate inasmuch as I don't belong to an age that finds it necessary to eat or drink out, or anything like that. Well, when we were young, one didn't. I mean, I used to have a friend in for sherry or something like that . . . . but I've never been out much for meals at all. We have an occasional pub lunch. We had the other day, on Saturday, with Jeannie and myself and a couple of friends and then back here for coffee. It was the highlight . . . [laughing] . . . not very exciting, but, you know . . ."

This home-centred life—all the more valued for having been forcibly deferred, in some cases, by war—was at the same time seen to make for strong marriages in which material distractions were not allowed to compete for attention: the car did not come first, the wife did not 'go her own way' too much. But the attachment to home, and the associated habit of penny-pinching, could also, it was recognized, work against people after bereavement, making them unwilling to spend on the transport and the outside entertainments which would maintain friendships.

These domestic features of economic austerity were accompanied additionally by a public morality supported by strong social sanctions. The sanctions, imposed by parents, older neighbours, police, and landlords, were on petty theft, vandalism, noise, or on failure to do one's share in the common task of cleaning which has always, as I noted earlier, been a major feature of Scottish tenement flats, whether catering for working-class or for middle-class tenants. The morality sanctioned was thus at these outer limits a neighbourly morality; and its inner rationale was also often expressed in neighbourly terms of 'spreading a helping hand', of a place which was 'more of a community', in which I was called to witness that my own mother, by virtue of her generation, 'wouldn't have let any-body go without help, would she?' This communal spirit was also, finally, sometimes accompanied by, or related to, a perception of coevals as people brought up with a firmer religious belief than the present generation:

"Well, the young folk winna bother with the kirk. The older folk—well, we were brought up wi' the kirk, and of course, naturally, I suppose it's just, I would say, the natural thing for ye tae still stick tae yer own beliefs."

Out of a wide range of past experience, then, people selected a few major contrasts to express a sense of difference from the young. Fortitude and effort in confronting difficulties, domestic thrift in dealing with meagre rewards, a strongly sanctioned neigh-bourly ethic, and, for some, faithful religious belief, constituted the ideal identity of their generation. Within this generation, how-ever, age in the sense of a particular historical experience was secondary to ageing as a present process, in which certain phases were distinguished.

Stages of ageing

There are many gradual changes in appearance, in abilities and pre-ferences, which can serve to define an individual as older than pre-viously, but few have the categoric quality which sorts people into an age-specific group. There were no surprises about the changes which Aberdonians used to group people as old: the main such events were retirement, illness, and the death of contemporaries.

Retirement was usually the earliest of these events to be asso-ciated with ideas of being 'old'. Ageing was in some cases grounds for retirement, in other cases one of retirement's consequences. As grounds for retirement, feeling old implied loss of physical strength, increasing slowness in organizing tasks, or, in risk-taking occupations, a loss of 'guts'. But feeling old could also be a conse-quence of retirement when stopping work was involuntary—when employers had taken the initiative to retire someone in advance of, or even in accordance with, the national age norm, or when illness had made the decision inevitable. Nor was it earners alone who became old in these senses in the course of becoming retired: retire-ment was also referred to, by transference, as a phase of life for wives who might have stayed at home most of their lives, but who experienced crucial changes when their husbands finished their working lives; and retirement was also referred to metaphorically by women widowed early, as a stage when they had launched their children and no longer felt responsible for them. All these situations were thus linked by analogy as a first phase of ageing.

Perceptions of a second stage of ageing were not always immediate for those newly retired. Especially in the case of involuntary retirement, feeling old could at first be an absolute and undifferentiated state; but with time further distinctions began to be made. Many of these distinctions related to illness, some indirectly: in Mannoch (the council estate) for example, the retired might feel old, but not old enough to join the clubs which advertised themselves as being for pensioners or for the over-sixties; despite such official claims, these were saddled with associations of decrepitude and immobility, and the age seen as appropriate for joining them was placed somewhere in the seventies. They were seen, in short, as clubs for people at an older, ill stage.

Two-thirds of the Aberdonians I spoke to discussed the connection between ageing and illness, and of these the great majority saw poor health as ultimately an almost inevitable consequence of growing old. The dimension of health singled out in this connection was only occasionally the experience of increasing symptoms or handicaps; more usually it was that of failing strength and resistance. Mechanical metaphors—the body's works go, the body runs down—were paralleled by images of the blood: the blood is thin, or there is not enough of it, leaving one vulnerable to the cold, for example, or to dizziness. 'Auld age disna come itsel' (alone)' as the proverb had it: localized weaknesses, generally losing energy or 'spirit', getting thin, becoming 'waur of the wear', or finally 'just dane' (done) were its accompaniments.

It was, then, a commonplace that age aggravated the burden of disease or weakened resistance to it; and although there were also times when people were concerned to deny one of these propositions, the belief that age brought illness was sufficiently entrenched to make it possible, eventually, to make illness the grounds for seeing oneself as 'really' old:

"Although I'm not old, this [threatening symptom] has given me certain food for thought. I lay awake last night, for example: I'd scarcely any sleep at all and this [symptom] was worrying me, I mean it was bothering me physically. And then, of course, in the small hours of the morning my mind starts chattering and wondering what's going to happen. Everything's much worse during the night when you can't sleep, so I had a pretty bad night . . . . I don't feel like an elderly gentleman, but then when this starts bothering me (again I say during the night) that's when I begin to think I'm getting older."

Or more succinctly:

Well, you're not as old as Mrs Ronald, surely?
Oh, no—it's when you're ill, really, that's when you feel old.

It was to forestall this inference that people fought hard to avoid adopting the characteristic props of the 'auld wifie'—in particular the stick:

"I'm told to use my stick, but I don't. It's just vanity. I don't want people to say, 'That's an auld wifie.' I've young ideas. I like things nice. I don't like to be old-fashioned. I just don't want to feel old. I'll never say I'm old really. No. It's what the doctor says, he says, use the stick, will ye? I says, ach, I'll be like an auld wifie. He says, well, you'll maybe be going to get a lot of falls if you winna use a stick. I says, well, my husband's here at night to carry me. He's awfa' good."

Thus, the public signalling of infirmity, springing from a loss of mental resistance to the idea of being old, a resistance which in turn was undermined by a general loss of strength with a consequent increase in symptoms and handicaps—this was true old age. However, this ultimate old age was not inevitable; besides describing methods of counteracting or preventing it, discussed later, people were very conscious that there was an alternative outcome: death.

Nearly half the people I spoke to linked age in a particular way with dying, and of these two-thirds linked it, amongst other things, with an expected time of dying. First, reasons were given for isolating a certain chronological age, or range of ages, as the likely time for death, either on Biblical authority ('three score years and ten'), or by analogy with the death of people—normally kin—with whom an identification was felt. Those who were most specific in this respect were nearly all men, and their estimates, naturally more pessimistic than those of women, were also pessimistic in the absolute, centring around 70 or earlier. Only once was a more accurate and generous estimate made, based on statistics relating to men over 60, recognizing that on average such older Scottish men have always enjoyed, throughout the last hundred years, the probability of a somewhat longer lifespan. Only once, too, was the probability of death felt to be conditional upon current illness; rather, the view was expressed that illness was actually an alternative to being 'taken suddenly'. Thus, the typical age assigned to death seems to have been more influenced by examples of such sudden deaths concluding the early part of old age than by a mere averaging of deaths at all ages, including those following longer illnesses.

These estimates of the likely age for death had two important ramifications. First, alongside those who discussed these quasi-statistical expectations, there were others who voiced moral expectations, and the two easily became confounded. These moral conceptions, clustered round the twin ideas that people ought to die only when old, and that they ought to die before they were too old, are discussed in the next two chapters.

In addition, though, the experience of others dying, which seems to lie at the foundation of the pessimistic statistical estimates made, itself defined a new stage of life. To live on at this point was to pass into a time of life when friends and relatives of the same generation were dead, and one was left as 'the last of the race—not a nice feeling', as in the following conversation, which took place between a couple who had numerous children and grandchildren alive:

Wife: "Practically a' wir [our] folk are deid. The amount o' folk that's died since we came to the town, it's been terrible."

Husband: "Och, well, I suppose it's just the fact we're getting older wirselves, and wir friends are getting older, and that's that. Coming tae that stage."

Wife: "Just tae that stage, as you say."

It was a stage when, in an evocative phrase which is quoted in a later chapter, 'the doors close'.

The second stage of ageing was, then, specified as the fate of those who were not taken suddenly, and defined by the inevitability of other people's deaths and by the probability of illness as an accepted feature of life. The sense of there being a time to die was, however, not incompatible with prescriptions for maintaining strength so as to keep the last age at bay, and these ways of dealing with this and earlier stages of life form the next topic to be discussed.

Prescriptions for ageing

A few people were content to define the stages of old age without going on to advocate any particular way of dealing with them; but most people had a good deal to say about the behaviour appropriate to each stage. Whatever their disagreements, retirement—the first stage of ageing—carried for Aberdonians an obligation to be active; and they seldom expressed, in the context of early old age, the idea that standards could now be relaxed. This idea has already emerged as something which mitigated the seriousness of illness or disability, but it tended to be ambiguous. Relaxation from the demands of work could be delighted in when it was understood that standards in other activities were raised; but without that implied compensation, and without adequate health reasons for its absence, the idea of relaxation kept running into contradiction with the activist tenor of most nostrums for retirement.

However, within the general obligation to remain active there was also divergence. First there was the optimistic response: for some (most of whom were in the West End) retirement was properly a liberation from constraint and an upsurge of activity. It was extolled as a time for husband and wife to have time together, to see their children, to make loving improvements to house and garden, to practise arts and skills, to travel, see friends, and play golf; and the activity was expected to be a matter of preference, so that criticisms were readily made of people who were merely energetic in filling time because there was time now vacant, as in the following two comments, made independently:

"I've got the feeling within myself that that's an admission of, well, you've got to *do* something, you must *do* something. And I don't want just to do *any*thing. I want to do something that I like and not just take up an activity because I think I ought to do so . . . . That to me is an admission of defeat, if I were to do that."

"Oh, we were talking about what the old people do—well, it's all sort of keeping up with the Joneses, and I can't be bothered with that. I know what it is, they try so hard to be with it; you know, they try to bring all their current affairs up to date to prove that their brains are still working, and they do the crossword puzzle every day to keep it active, and all this sort of thing you see—which I think is rather sad."

To become obsessive, as others did, about cleaning the house, to go to group activities which were dull in themselves, for the company, to become over-competitive in petty sports, these were failings—a slide towards defeat and genuine old age—in this middle-class view of retirement, because they represented an absence of the spontaneous pleasures which should be ready to spring up when work was laid aside. Such interests were represented as inner resources, and thus as claims for distinctiveness, though it was also recognized, as I show later, that external resources such as schooling, occupational skills, or house ownership had been necessary to their realization.

Opposed to this view, however, was the equally common sentiment that retirement, far from offering a release, constituted a threat to maintaining the purposes and social relationships which might fend off old age proper. Across a wide range of occupations retirement meant a loss of company, a loss of identity in the eyes of other people, or, in the case of a married woman, a husband who obstructed the running of the household without making a corresponding contribution to it. Co-operative involvement at work was missed, and co-operative involvement at home was not a compelling or easily negotiated idea. These were not sectional views, but pervasive, and voiced as if they expressed a common fate, whether in Mannoch or in the West End.

Nor was the loss of work the only setback; for generational antagonism also acquired significance in this phase of ageing. The problem lay not so much with the next generation—that of the sons and daughters in middle life—as with the generation after that. It was encounters with this age group, in impersonal settings not tamed by prior personal ties of acquaintanceship, in which people were shaken by a lack of respect for age. In part, this was recognized as a perennial problem not just for people over 60, but for everyone who was older than this young age group and their juniors. But those over 60, and especially women, often felt themselves least able to cope; and it was also felt to be a problem exacerbated by social change:

1st Neighbour: "The children seemed to be different. Some of them are very destructive . . . . I think they're left too much on their own, and they just go to please themselves."

2nd Neighbour: "Their mothers working, that's just it."

1st Neighbour: "I mean, if you wis telling their mothers, they wouldn't hae believed it. Not her boy, you see . . . ."

2nd Neighbour: "Yes, but we try not to bother with them because . . ."

1st Neighbour: "Because . . ."

2nd Neighbour: "For, well, they just, they wouldna leave us."

1st Neighbour: "We might have to go through something else with them any time. You never know what they might do, you know."

2nd Neighbour: "Oh, and they say, if you check them, they say some terrible language to you. They don't care. They just don't care a hair. Oh, the language you get, and I says, oh, don't speak to them, don't speak to them."

1st Neighbour: "Ye're better just to ignore them . . . . Of course, we're old fashioned . . . [with mock solemnity] . . . Well, this lady here's 21, I'm 22 . . . [guffaws] . . . . No, but long ago we were frightened if we saw a policeman."

Similarly, two teachers recollected their own teachers:

1st Teacher: "I wouldn't have given her a wrong *look*."

2nd Teacher: "Oh, no, never."

1st Teacher: "She'd only to *look* and they'd just . . ."

2nd Teacher: "Get miserable, the way I did when my father looked at me."

1st Teacher: "I know, my father never spoke, he just looked round the side of his paper, if that was necessary . . . . There were no vandals then. There was no beating up the teacher in class."

2nd Teacher: "You had respect for teachers, you see."

1st Teacher: "You had respect for others."

2nd Teacher: "Anybody older you had to respect."

This sense of a rising generation borne on a current of secular change, to whom one's own ties of family and friendship no longer penetrated in any depth, and for whom one appeared simply 'geriatric', interfering, or undeserving of respect, was thus felt as commonly as the threat of retirement.

The hazards posed by such generational conflicts, and by retirement, were countered by a belief in cultivating social connections, or in developing an activity to replace the former full-time occupation. Activities were indeed themselves a way of keeping up social connections—at this time of life doing things with people was important even if their presence was not enjoyed:

I'm expected to do a lot, and I'm not a do-gooder . . . . I've decided that I don't like people . . . . but it's dangerous. At my age it's dangerous to ignore your friends.

The risk of neglecting present acquaintanceships was in the increasing difficulty of making new friends at this time of life;

hence, existing connections were conserved and activities shared with them were intensified. Here the generational problem re-appeared, and there was a division of opinion about whether, at this time of life, it was better to mix with those of the same age or to strengthen ties also with those who were younger. Those who valued the company of mixed ages relied heavily on relationships specifically with young children, in the belief that 'there's a great affinity between old folks and children', and that 'the more you mix with young people the less likely you are to get old'. Others, who argued that 'the generations don't mix', and who consequently preferred, sometimes regretfully, the society of their peers, were referring to the young adolescent and adult generation; and even those in favour of mixing the generations had some trouble with this relationship.

The way in which activities and social relationships were combined also varied. People in the West End aimed to cultivate a variety of individual relationships, each centring on a different activity, while those in Mannoch, when they thought about it, thought in terms of a collective solution, a 'community centre'. One was a retired man who had himself tried to start a community centre—a 'place where people could meet and do things casually', this being a feature distinguishing the idea from clubs for the truly old. In conception, the 'community centre' was imagined to embrace all ages and 'all sorts of interests . . . . sewing and making things and bowls . . . . That's the sort of thing you need to get every member of the community active or involved.' But, in practice, with the exception of the church, such collective organizations were lacking in the area, and they proved hard to form in any way which genuinely cut across all ages.

Social integration, then, and active involvement with others was consciously to be sought to repair whatever damage was inflicted by the transition into early old age. Retirement, ushering in this earlier stage, was for some a liberation into such involvement; while for others it constituted a threat to such involvement, as did the generational conflict to which people felt themselves, at times, to be liable. These threats were met by individualistic strategies or, less successfully in present instances, through strategies which were collective.

This summary of the way early old age was seen is not the whole story, for preparation was not only aimed at deferring late old age but at responding to the alternative possibility of death, about which more is said in the next chapter. But if death did not come, what then?

Those who envisaged being left with chronic illness settling in and much of their acquaintance gone, saw the old people's club, sheltered or 'health' housing, the old people's home, and the geriatric ward looming as images of the life which remained; and ways of escaping, confronting, or reconciling oneself to, such a life became critical. The strongest tendency, in the context of this stage of life, was towards an accepted passivity: the belief that people at this point deserved help and pity, and that they could only give in to their limitations gracefully, finding what company they could with other 'poor bodies,' or 'waiting patiently for their call' until they 'earned their rest'. Significantly, this was not a response commended by many people as their own present philosophy, although, as emerged earlier, there was a small group of women who veered towards this position, not without continuing ambivalence, on the grounds that their strength was done; rather, it was a response felt appropriate to the real old age which had not yet arrived, and might yet be escaped, and a role in which other, truly old, people were cast:

". . . . people that I've maybe felt sorry for, people that aren't so fit as I am, although they're maybe not much older. There's a deaf old body . . . . I went and saw her yesterday when I was feeling nice and holy."

It was also sometimes felt to be the role of extreme age in the past, the past of the fishing people who used to be 'great on the Bible' and who, reading there that they had three score years and ten, sat down when they got to that age and waited:

Grandfather had his clay pipe sticking out here, had those big boxes of matches, and just lit match after match. He had a mark this side of his face from the smoke.

These prototypical figures waited 'until they fell out of bed at 93, and that's how they died'. But the classic embodiments of this role were felt to be the residents of old people's homes: it was a situation known from visiting institutionalized relatives, and from remarking on how their preferences seemed to have changed from rejecting the institution to accepting it. Such examples helped to make a passive acceptance expected and legitimated in real old age; but it was still mostly from an external point of view. For themselves and those closest to them many people of this cast of thought retained the belief that in spite of illness and chronological years they themselves were still not 'really' old; at most it was as if this old age was a shadow of the known person, unattended to in the day, and only significant in the darkness:

"I sometimes—I look at him when he's sleeping, and I think, 'Gosh, you're getting old.' Especially with this chest, because his mouth's not closed during the night, you see. I sometimes stand over him and just look, you know: and his mouth's open and he's maybe lying on his back if he's snoring, and his hair's grey . . . . I just hope he doesn't do the same with me . . . (laughing) . . . Because I don't tell him. And I just think, 'Oh, Edward,' you know, 'What a shame, poor Edward' with this breathing. And he's so nice and so gay and so good, you know, a lovely kind person. It makes me sad. Then in the morning he comes down all dressed up with his fancy tie and his nice suit on . . . ."

Old age proper was thus always in some way external to the person, and even where it was envisaged as a possible personal future, death provided an alternative possibility.

Nevertheless, though many accepted that it was legitimate for the very old to sink into passivity, there remained some who were convinced that resistance in some form was always possible. The most vigorous recommendations for staving off second stage of old age were essentially versions of the recommendations discussed earlier for preserving resistance against illness. Vigour was sustained by keeping up normal interests and activities, decay was courted by sitting down and doing nothing. Only rarely, and mostly in the middle class, was preventive use of medical screening advocated: just as moral ideas predominated in controlling illness, so the same ideas were extended, by convinced moralists, to the task of defeating true old age. But in addition there were subtler strategies. First, a few people took the bull by the horns, and while still in early old age joined a club that others perceived as being for 'auld wifies', seeing in this an opportunity for 'work' and 'interest' which was not to be despised. These people could accept cheerfully that they themselves were thus turned into 'auld wifies' in many respects, but by giving help and taking positions of responsibility they kept a sense of active involvement: they were old to friends and relatives outside, but not within the club, and even after relinquishing office through illness could retain involvement through their centrality in the gossip chain. Alternatively, another escape from any final lapse into passivity even in extreme age was suggested by a few people who extended their belief in controlled resistance to, and positive acceptance of, illness, into that stage of old age where 'the body runs down' or the mind weakens:

"You see, I don't think it matters if you get old, I don't think it matters if your brain isn't that good; I think you've got to accept it—I mean, you can fight it up to a point, but you've got to accept it at the same time, haven't you?"

Such an acceptance was not passive—it was not 'waiting for the ferryman', an attitude vigorously rejected—rather it was another form of the search for alternative interests.

The varied range of prescriptions for coping with early and late old age has now been described, and important differences have emerged between the expected passivity of the later period and the expected activity of the earlier, and between those liberated and those threatened by retirement. Next the way in which these prescriptions are linked together needs examination, so that patterns of consistency and fault-lines of contradiction can be discerned.

Themes and dilemmas

The premisses underlying the accounts of ageing just described can be summarized under five heads:

2.1 *Early old age as a liberation*
   As I am (we are) retired, I am free to follow my interests.
2.2 *Early old age as a setback*
   (*a*) As I am (we are) retired, my interests and social connections are reduced, and/or
   (*b*) If I encounter the younger generation, I may have trouble.
2.3 *Early old age as a repairing of defences*
   (*a*) As I am (we are) retired, I keep my interests going, and/or
   (*b*) As I am (we are) retired, I keep up my social connections.

I have given these typical statements an alternative 'we' form, as a reminder that women who had not worked themselves could still think of 'retirement' as a situation which they shared with their husband or contemporaries. Finally the second stage of old age was typified thus:

2.4 *Late old age as resistable*
   If I keep active, I will always keep real old age at bay.
2.5 *Late old age as a surrender*
   If I become really old, I may legitimately give up my activities.

While many people made comments which reflected only one of these types of prescription, almost as many combined two or more types of prescription together.

As with views about illness, there were relatively few ways of combining these various premises into a reliably coherent pattern, and there were certain combinations which generated contradictions. Unlike views about illness, however, views about ageing overlapped sufficiently to offer at least one area of common agreement: the importance of actively repairing defences in early old age (2.3), an idea compatible with all coherent perspectives. In this respect everybody could be an activist. Nevertheless, in other respects, three distinct patterns of ideas do emerge.

The first coherent pattern was the most optimistic, viewing ageing *as a resurgence*. Early old age was a new stage, a release into fresh interests, a recovery of skills long neglected, a predominantly pleasurable time in which to strengthen habits of activity and social connections which might protect against the advance of old age proper. The really old, who lined the walls of residential institutions, were in this case those who had not established this protective way of life and held to it. This pattern of thinking was thus one which combined early old age as a liberation (2.1), with early old age as a repairing of defences (2.3), and/or late old age as resistable (2.4).

The second coherent pattern viewed ageing, by contrast, as a *siege*. This pattern shared with that just described the belief that defences could be sufficiently soundly built to keep at bay the advance of old age proper; but it differed in that already in early old age one's social position was under attack, whether because the relationships created by work were not ultimately replaceable, or because generational loyalties and attitudes were bearing one steadily into a position opposed to, or devalued by, the growing generations. The difficulties could be coped with, however, and again the problematic stage of becoming truly old could be avoided. This pattern of ideas, then, combined early old age as a setback (2.2), with early old age as a repairing of defences (2.3), and/or late old age as resistable (2.4).

These two patterns shared common ground in repairing defences in retirement (2.3), and in resisting late old age (2.4), and they were not discriminable in those cases where people restricted themselves to expressing only these two types of idea. Hence any contradiction felt between these two patterns had to centre on the opposition between a liberated and a constrained view of early old age; and there were two cases in which such a contradiction was apparent—both the people concerned being predictably marginal to the typical middle-class location of the liberated view. The first was a man who had been shift foreman in a textile factory, and who had relatives in managerial positions elsewhere. He began on the subject of his retirement with the words, 'But we shoved off to America and really saw life'—and immediately warming to a favourite theme added, 'I'll tell ye some o' the places we were in . . .' Then after a catalogue of sights worth seeing and places which he 'greatly respected' it emerged that when his wife had visited America a second time (at her son's expense) he had chosen to stay at home. Nevertheless he was 'quite content and happy—I'd always something to do, you know'. And, in fact, he continually set himself tasks on the structure of the house, explaining:

"I'm more content when I'm doing something, and I do some jobs you wouldna believe—and I wisna qualified to do either—but I do them quite successful."

Many of these feats would not have been possible earlier when he was working, as a typical comment on one of them testified:

"I says, well, this is going to take a long time, but I've got a long time to do it."

Retirement, then, as he presented it in this part of his conversation, had released both time for the jobs he wished to do at home, and time for seeing life (2.1)—even though seeing it once, it turned out, was enough.

A rather different line of thought appeared, however, when in answer to the question 'Were you looking forward to retiring?' he hesitated, then confessed, 'Well, no. Actually, no,'—and asked further whether he missed the works, he replied, 'Yes and no'. He explained that twice since he stopped work they had wanted him back to resolve some problem:

"I dinna want tae boast or blaw, I winna tell ye the reason why that man was efter me, but I could easily enough."

This sense of recognized worth which his work had brought him had no counterpart in the activities of his retirement, and his self-respect remained centred in the occupation he had given up:

"I'm proud tae say that our family was really productive—because out o' my relatives, three was staff . . . . We all started off at Richards, they landed up in three different works, and every one o' the three is staff."

It was for this reason that he had not been able to look forward to stopping work and could not deny that he missed it (2.2); but he also, from another perspective, wished to say that he did not miss it, because he had made good use of his new freedom (2.1). The contradiction between the two views of retirement remained, and on the nature of the decision to retire he could only say:

"Ach, it's like a' that thing—it comes and goes."

The other case in which a conflict was felt between retirement as a liberation and as a constraint was that of Ann Forbes, the wife of an officer in the District Council. The women in middle-class families could sometimes be in a marginal position in their view of retirement because any increase in their freedom depended in various ways on their husband's reactions. In the present instance, asked about her husband's retirement, Ann Forbes said that initially she had looked forward to it very much: they were going to spend a lot of time golfing together, and they were going to visit their son in Troon, whom she missed. Her personal pleasure in this freedom to be together was also accompanied by an altruistic pleasure in her husband's own freedom:

"I felt, well, he's worked 48 years; all those years that I've been a mother and housewife I could please myself. If it was a fine day I could go round the links while he had to be at the office. I mean, you've got to think of all these years where you could please yourself, so I felt that, now he's retired, that he could please himself."

Thus far, retirement was all opportunity (2.1): they entered for a few golfing competitions, and the son was visited in Troon. But soon it began to emerge that the husband's liberation was becoming the wife's constraint. A keen football coach, he soon spent most of the week coaching and attending matches and socializing after-wards. Having been to Troon a few times he 'lost interest' and now went only rarely; and he was seldom free to go golfing. Her reaction was to say, 'Well, now, I'm not going to sit at home any more—I'll find my own golfing partners.' But she remained both disappointed

by her husband's use of his freedom and also less free herself than
before (2.2)—because, for instance, he was under her feet on
weekday mornings:

"It's just not as we thought it might be. I don't know, the wife is terribly
disturbed, that's what I feel. Before, I could be out by ten o'clock in the
morning with the housework done, the lunch organized. I could choose
my own programmes on the radio. And if I felt like doing nothing I did
nothing; if I felt like writing letters I sat down and wrote letters. I can't do
that now. It's useless unless you're doing things *together*."

This promise of togetherness, she now recognized, had permitted
her to see his freedom both as deserved and as synonymous with
her freedom; the collapse of this togetherness, and the separate
pattern of living which followed, left her divided between a continued belief that retirement should be liberation for him, and a
reluctance to accept that it should not be for her:

"He should please himself and I should try to fit in but I must admit that
sometimes there's a niggle of resentment, and I can't help it no matter
how much I try."

An expectation of release in early old age could thus come into
sharp conflict with a perception of constraint, but it was also
relatively easy to avoid such conflicts while holding elements of
both views—and in such cases the flexibility of ideas about ageing
was apparent. The obvious resolution which offered itself was
to distinguish the particular aspects of early old age for which
each view held good. In such resolutions this stage of life was
characteristically a gain in regard to stopping work and turning to
neglected interests—provided suitable resources were available—
but a loss in regard to the ability to control conflicts with young
people casually encountered, or in regard to the wider acquaintanceship available through work. Thus it was only when one of
these aspects on its own was the subject of both these contrary
expectations—when work had been both a pride and a burden to
the worker, or both a cause of separation and a source of freedom
to the spouse—that contradiction was inevitable.

Two patterns of thinking about old age, and the potentiality of
conflict between them, have now been discussed; a third pattern,
however, was more frequent than either, which viewed ageing *as a
delayed capitulation*. This pattern shared with previous patterns
the belief in early old age as a time for an active strengthening of

defences, and shared also with one of them an acceptance that this stage was inaugurated by various attacks on an accustomed way of life; but it included an ultimate pessimism about late old age, a conviction that in the end, for those who lived long enough, it was necessary and legitimate to lay down one's arms and accept the care of others. Ageing thus viewed as a delayed capitulation, then, combined early old age as a setback (2.2), and/or early old age as a repairing of defences (2.3), with late old age as a surrender (2.5).

This view was hard to square with either of the other views already considered. Obviously there was a fundamental conflict between surrendering to late old age (2.5) and resisting it (2.4), especially for those who expected to blossom in retirement (2.1). The contradiction was evident on three occasions when somebody pondered on these differing perspectives. The two people whose comments I describe were women poised, appropriately, between early and late old age. The first of these, Sheila Denny, had formed her notion of real old age partly form visits to a relative in a denominational home:

"When I first went I was told 'We're only here till the Lord sends for us.' So am I, I suppose, but Heaven help me!—that's not the way to talk."

The unacceptable aspect of this approach lay precisely in the fact that 'to me they're just sitting around waiting to die'; and in this context she plainly would have preferred a more vigorous attitude which could belie the lable of 'old folks' (2.4). This responsibility for an active attitude was also accepted personally. She chided herself:

"I'm wasting time. On terribly cold days I wouldn't work, I wouldn't do anything, and I kept saying to myself, 'Ah, don't waste time.' Still feel it's sinful."

And this urge to keep doing was of a piece with her remembered sense of liberation in early old age. Retirement had been an opportunity to renew her social life, to entertain her friends, to get to know her neighbours, and her work in the social services had been thankfully laid aside. But alongside this activism she expressed an uneasy sense that real old age might eventually be inescapable, that it could be 'awfully sad'; and she also had an increasing feeling that many of the activities she had taken up in retirement were in any case too troublesome, or too pointless:

"I used to go for long walks, to kind of pass the time. Then I started this church work. And when I stopped it, I never missed it. It was just a time when you needed something."

"[Home baking]—that's one thing I've stopped doing. I get so overexcited about it and think things won't be right and things won't be ready and I get worked up and upset."

It was of a piece with her sense of the reasonableness and legitimacy of a gradual withdrawal from these former activities (2.5), that having expressed a forcible rejection of the passivity of the 'old folks', she shifted abruptly to a contrary position:

"They're well fed, well looked after; of course, they're maybe happy enough—and what are we to judge? [And later] Of course we maybe pity some of these old folkies and they're maybe quite happy."

Then she switched back again:

"Some of them—but not all."

And the dilemma between fighting and giving up was shortly summed up thus:

"I always remember what my friend Sandra said—never wish too hard for anything because by the time you get it you don't want it. And it's very, very true."

This dilemma between resistance and surrender was, finally, expressed, in my last example, as another problem of the wife in retirement. The wife in this case, while joking wryly that she and her husband were 'twa old pensioners, and proper cracked up', had fought a tremendous battle against her illnesses. This militancy similarly caused both of them to reject, except as a joke, the status of old people in care (2.4):

"They winted tae gae's [wanted to give us] a sheltered house. Well, we dae wint [don't want] a sheltered house. Fit we wint [what we want] is a hoose that we can sort up wirsel' [ourselves]."

But in order thus to 'sort up' the house she had to rely on her husband's help, for she had stopped doing the main part of the household tasks on doctor's instructions:

"I said [to the doctor] 'Could I get home?' I says, 'my pain's all gone now.' He says, 'Aye, if ye promise tae behave yersel' an' nae hurry aboot.' And I says, 'Oh, but I'll dae that.' So I've just done that since. So I retired."

This legitimate 'retirement' associated with being an 'old pensioner and proper cracked up' (2.5) did not, however, prove sustainable, because the house was not kept to her standards. Her husband was no cook:

"He was mairrit [married] forty year afore he kent the wye tae bile [way to boil] tatties. He wis nivver a helper. I hid a boy and a girl, and they both cried night and day an' he never once nursed them—nivver . . . . It wis aye my biggest disappointment my daughter wint to Australia. Ken, I aye thinks, well, if I hid my daughter, wid have helped ye mair than fit [what] the lad did, y'ken. 'Cause he saw his father daein' naethin', even his claes [clothes] lyin' a' o'er the place—and he just did the same."

The example of a nephew who had learnt better ways with his own wife then introduced one of several duels:

Wife: "He [the nephew] 'll cook and wash the dishes an' a'thing, an' think naething aboot it, but—nae him [the husband]. And he could easy dae it."

Husband: "I'm nae able now."

Wife: "Ye're nae able!—but he disna *dae* it, he disna' dae it."

Husband: "I'm a poor thing. Just nae able. I taxis ye here and I taxis ye there—fit [what] mair dae ye want?"

Wife: "Oh, there's naethin' in sittin' drivin' a car."

Husband: "Oh, no?"

Then the wife launched out on a new tack:

Wife: "If we hidna the car, you widna be able to walk aboot some."

But with this observation peace, born out of a mutual recognition of each other's difficulties, suddenly descended:

Husband: "No, I quite agree. I dinna argue aboot that."

Wife: "Neither can I."

Determined as this wife was, then, to keep the house going and resist becoming an old person in care, she had to reconcile with this determination the advisability, explained by her doctor, of 'retiring' from actually doing the main part of the household tasks; but this reconciliation was only achievable if she could maintain control over the tasks and the standards to which they were done, while others helped out in much of their actual performance. Since, however, this condition was never achieved, she remained caught between her principle of resistance to becoming an old person and her acceptance of the need for 'retirement'; hence the bitterness and frustration engendered by her inability to secure appropriate help. Recognizing finally that her husband had some excuse in his own health, she turned in conclusion to her son:

"When he takes a wife, he takes a wife, he forgets his mother. And I mean I know that, and I understand it, and it hurts me, but . . . I never say anything. I just say it wis my misfortune my daughter wint to Australia."

The dilemmas thus portrayed reveal, then, that there could not easily be a legitimate surrender in the last phase for those who had previously put their faith in resistance; and since resistance harmonized with the optimistic view of retirement as a liberation, it is no surprise to find, in such cases as Sheila Denny's, that surrender was incompatible with both. If, as occasionally happened, the surrender of the very old was accepted by people with either of these optimistic views, it was only by making a sharp distinction between 'us' and 'them', in such a way that true old age would never come to 'us'. And this tactic reaffirmed rather than resolved the division of views.

Three distinct schemes of ageing have now been plotted, each internally coherent, which at once supply and limit the stock of ideas on which Aberdonians draw. It is between these possibilities that those searching for coherence have to choose, if they are not to innovate. It now remains to put together these schemes of ageing with the generational ideas which are partially distinct from them, and to consider them in their historical context.

Conclusion

Aberdonian attitudes to old age have given substance to the problem with which this chapter started: not only is there a great variety of ideas on this subject, but there are important contradictions between some of them which are recognized and felt, in certain situations, as personal dilemmas. Indeed the ideas which are held in common—essentially the obligation to build defences and maintain activity in early old age—are less numerous than those which are disputed; and to that extent there is little basis for viewing old age as being subject to expectations which are culturally agreed.

Earlier a number of explanations were rehearsed, each of which sought to account for some aspect of this variety and conflict. The first explanation saw activity and apathy as offensive and defensive responses to a negative stereotype of age. The second explanation, by contrast, presupposed a new growth of solidarity and of positive notions of age amongst the retired. And the third explanation saw both positive and negative views of age as the product of historical developments in the economy. These explanations are in some respects supported, but in other respects shown to be too limited, by the picture which has emerged of Aberdonian culture.

Explanations which are related to negative stereotypes of age have greater force in regard to the late rather than the early stage of ageing, as Aberdonians distinguished them. Late age was certainly stigmatized by many older people themselves, in the sense that it was seen as a passive, pitied state, the outcome of living beyond the normal time to die. And the way in which it was viewed from an external point of view, attributed to others and denied for oneself, 'they' being passive and 'I' being still active, also reflects a general characteristic of stigma. To this extent, late age was indeed viewed as the kind of discreditable identity which is regarded as abnormal and suitable for a degree of segregation and special treatment. But recognizing this does not itself make clear why late age was sometimes viewed as an unlucky outcome which could not be helped, and sometimes in an opposed fashion as a moral failure, a symptom of insufficient self-discipline in preventive activity. The question raised by this opposition was whether late age was within or beyond moral control, and the origin of this dispute lies elsewhere.

How much, then, can be explained by the increasing solidarity amongst some groups of older people, and by positive notions of age which go with this? Certainly positive notions of retirement, and a degree of generational solidarity, were apparent in Aberdeen. However, these two positive themes were in no way related.

Optimistic notions of retirement certainly did conflict with more defensive notions, creating felt contradictions; and it is also true that this optimism was mainly characteristic of a limited group of people with a particular middle-class style of life, and that the interests and skills from which the optimism derived were shared with others of a like background. But this was no age-based sub-culture: those with whom interests were shared were not necessarily

of the same age, and the basis of acquaintanceship was very individualistic. Other acquaintances of the same age and background
remained unconvinced about the liberating effects of retirement,
and became the unrepentant butts of the optimists' disapproval.
Optimism about retirement was in fact a basis for division rather
than for solidarity amongst older members of the middle class;
there was an element of individual distinctiveness, even of one-
upmanship, about it. Furthermore, this conception of the proper
way of growing old was again limited to one phase of ageing—the
early phase—and the sources of these attitudes to early old age
seemed to reside more in past careers than in present membership
of an age-related group or subculture.

By contrast, the other positive notion which characterized people
by age—that of generation—was in essence a unifying one. Although generational differences were brought to the forefront by
only a proportion of older Aberdonians, they were defined in such a
way as to include attributes common to all, and they were expressed
in a similar form and with similar frequency across classes. In that
sense, this generation had the basis for a unified consciousness
of certain distinctive values—respect for neighbourliness, for
authority, for perseverance and thrift; and it was this positive
generational consciousness, more than the stigmatizing character
of age, which, in their own account, lay behind the conflicts and
defeats which this generation had experienced with the young.
Entitled now themselves, within this perspective, to respect, and
to the exercise of authority in defence of these values, they found
their claims to control overturned, especially by the young adolescent and adult generation with whom their ties were weakest. It
was the struggle for control, then, in which the stigmatizing value
of the term 'old' was only one possible weapon, and one matched
by counter-offensives discrediting the 'young', that had inflicted
many of the wounds of age; and it was this same struggle which
had engendered a sense of generational unity. But although this
generational consciousness was quite often expressed, and expressed
in terms applicable to everyone, whether or not everyone expressed
it, it was not to the forefront of most people's minds, nor did it
banish the moral divisions which were based on success in ageing.
And to the extent that it reflected a certain solidarity among older
people, the origins of that solidarity still remain to be considered.

What, then, is it that has shaped the generational consciousness of older Aberdonians? What has given them their conflicting views of retirement? What has made some think that late age is morally controllable, while others disagree? It is these questions about origins which the third sort of explanation, that in terms of political and economic change , seeks to address. I have indicated that in addition to change in public conceptions of old age, embedded in policy documents, this type of explanation needs to assess change in private conceptions, expressed in oral and literary sources. Historical research in this area is only at an early stage, but some limited comparisons with what has emerged in Aberdeen can be made which may have a suggestive value.

Certainly the generational consciousness of older people today has historical roots. It is not necessary to suppose that this now ageing generation has always emphasized its present distinctive values since the formative period of youth. Other ideological allegiances must then have seemed more salient, for the bitterness of the period between the wars in the North-East of Scotland, and the aftermath of the General Strike, portrayed in the trilogy of Lewis Grassic Gibbon,[10] should not be underestimated. But these were themes echoed, in 1980, only in the conversations of a few hardened campaigners, and these felt, in regard to the younger generation, like the rest. It seems, therefore, that it was only as a new generation arose after them that some consciousness of unity was formed around the particular pattern of values which is now emphasized. We can probably relate some of this change to the relative impoverishment, since the war, of those above retirement age compared with those below—an impoverishment which has recently been documented from public statistics.[11] This would not be the first time that generational competition has muted class divisions between contemporaries.[12] But in addition the British experience also owes something to the unity engendered by defence and victory in the war. For among the old in France, the experience of war time occupation has continued to bequeathe divisions between former collaborators and former members of the Resistance, despite the explosion of generational conflict in 1968.[13]

However, if the war, and the unequal benefits of the post-war boom, help to explain the generational solidarity of older Aberdonians, it is necessary to go further back to explain their moral disagreements on the subject of ageing. Comparisons need to be made, however, tentatively, between the ideas of ageing revealed here and those of the pre-industrial past; and it is in regard to pre-industrial conceptions that the task is of course especially difficult.[14] But the question is an interesting one, and deserves a preliminary consideration against such evidence as is currently to hand.

The best-known schemes of ageing in pre-industrial Europe are, I indicated earlier, those presenting the Ages of Man as a natural, indeed inevitable, phenomenon. In their acceptance of inevitability, their assumption of steady decline from a point in mid-life, their ordering of *senectus* and *senium*, of the grave or mature elder and the crooked or decrepit ancient,[15] such schemes have several points of similarity with the scheme which I have entitled 'age as a delayed capitulation'. This contemporary Aberdonian scheme, no less than its predecessor, views the endpoint of ageing as inevitable, as not subject to moral control; it assumes no less that ageing is, after working life, a process of steady decline; and it likewise orders this decline in terms of two stages, that of retirement—a setback, but still a time of activity—and that of late age—a time of legitimate dependence, typified in the 'auld wifie'.

However, the pre-industrial legacy also includes, as I noted earlier, a tradition of thought which sought for moral or technical control over ageing. The classical enthusiasms of the eighteenth-century élite turned to Cicero's moral exhortation against the conventional pessimism of his time; and already there were similar hopes based on scientific ideas. Freedom from poverty was, in this tradition, recognized as a precondition of the moral enterprise;[16] but that granted, continued self-discipline in activity could delay or prevent the advent of the last, despised state, and provide consolations for the loss of the powers of middle life. Again there are several points of similarity between this moral tradition and one of the Aberdonian schemes of ageing—that entitled 'ageing as a siege'. Moral control is emphasized much more than medical control: there is the same insistence that activity can prevent the advent of late age, and the same attempt to repair the breaches made by early old age with new interests and associations. Indeed some Aberdonians go further, as I have shown, and regard retirement as a liberation; and this indication of greater optimism is also paralleled by the absence of any contemporary Aberdonian reference to poverty as a major constraint on moral control of ageing. Where there are differences between these past and present conceptions, therefore, they suggest a greater contemporary confidence in the moral approach.

What changes there are have occurred, however, only within strong cultural continuities. In most respects greater prosperity has merely diffused the former élite view more videly, and though the view of retirement as a liberation appears to be new, this too is probably not as new as it seems—but I leave discussion of this to Chapter 8. In fact the greatest change is simply in where retirement is placed on these relatively unchanging schemes of ageing. Even at the beginning of this century, retirement was associated with the last phase of ageing—the deserved rest.[17] There was too little security for the industrial workforce in Poor Law pensions,[18] and for smallholders in contracts with heirs,[19] to make it worth stopping work until actual incapacity set in. In fact retirement only lost these connotations of breakdown and enforced rest, and only became associated with the 'green' phase of old age, when pension age was lowered between the wars,[20] and when, after 1945, pensions became a right governed by chronological age alone.[21] And of course this change in the place of retirement was also aided by the rise in life expectancy at older ages during this century.

This, then, is one switch, within otherwise constant schemes of ageing, which, like the current generational consciousness of older people, does reflect political and economic developments in the present century. But history also tells a neglected story of cultural continuity in these attitudes, and we owe our principal dilemma—whether age is morally controllable—to a centuries-old European debate.

Notes and References

1. S. H. Matthews, *The social world of old women*, London: Sage, 1979; C. Russell, *The ageing experience*, Sydney: Allen and Unwin, 1981.
2. A. M. Rose, 'The subculture of the ageing', in A. M. Rose and W. A. Peterson, *Older people and their social world*, Philadelphia: Davis, 1965; I. Rosow, *Social integration of the aged*, New York: Free Press, 1967; A. Hochschild, *The unexpected community: portrait of an old age subculture*, Berkeley: University of California Press, 1973.
3. For examples see P. T. Amoss and S. Harrell (eds.), *Other ways of growing old*, Stanford University Press, 1981.
4. A. Fontana, *The last frontier*, London: Sage, 1977.
5. K. Mannheim, 'The problem of generations', in K. Mannheim and D. Kecskemeti, *Essays on the sociology of knowledge*, London: Routledge, 1952.
6. V. L. Bengtson and N. E. Cutler, 'Generations and inter-generational relations', in R. H. Binstock and E. Shanas (eds.), *Handbook of ageing and the social sciences*, New York: Van Nostrand Rheinhold, 1976.
7. The best British study is C. Phillipson, *Capitalism and the construction of old age*, London: Macmillan, 1982.
8. S. Macintyre, 'Old age as a social problem', in R. Dingwall and C. Heath (eds.), *Health care and health knowledge*, London: Croom Helm, 1977.
9. P. N. Stearns, *Old age in European society*, London: Croom Helm, 1976, ch. 1; D. G. Troyansky, 'Old age in the rural family of enlightened Provence', in P. N. Stearns (ed.), *Old age in pre-industrial society*, New York: Holmes and Meier, 1982.
10. Lewis Grassic Gibbon, *A Scots quair*, London: Pan Books, 1973.
11. D. Thomson, 'The decline of social welfare: falling state support for the elderly since Victorian times', *Ageing and Society*, 4 (1984), 451–82.
12. A. Foner, 'Age stratification and conflict in political life', *Amer. Sociol. Rev.* 39 (1974), 187–96.
13. J. Keith-Ross, *Old people, new lives: community creation in a retirement residence*, University of Chicago Press, 1977.

14. Apart from the fact that historians have to rely on literary sources in the hope that these reflect the attitudes of the period, in the absence of a specifically Scottish history of old age it is not easy to know whether the attitudes of the period elsewhere in Europe were also Scottish attitudes.

15. D. Herlihy, 'Growing old in the Quattrocento', in P. N. Stearns (ed.), *Old age in pre-industrial society*, New York: Holmes and Meier, 1982; S. R. Smith, 'Growing old in an age of transition', ibid.

16. Cicero's view that a collapse into helpless old age could be averted by activity and moral character was explicitly restricted to the well-to-do ('On old age', p. 216, in *Selected Works*, tr. Michael Grant, London: Penguin, 1960).

17. Stearns, *Old age in European society*, ch. 2; see also Lloyd-George's speech at the Second Reading of the Old Age Pensions Bill, *Hansard* (15 June 1908).

18. Pensions were only a supplement to other income, of which the chief came from earnings: Thomson, 'The decline of social welfare', p. 466.

19. J. Goody (ed.), *Family and inheritance: rural society in Western Europe 1200–1800*, Cambridge University Press, 1978, pp. 28 f. Compare B. J. O'Neill, *Social inequality in a Portuguese hamlet*, Cambridge University Press, 1987; C. M. Arensberg and S. T. Kimball, *Family and community in Ireland*, Harvard University Press, 1940, ch. 7.

20. S. Riddle, 'Age, obsolescence and unemployment—older men in the British industrial system 1920–1939: a research note', *Ageing and Society*, 4 (1984), 517–24.

21. See Thomson, 'The decline of social welfare', p. 468, for the proportions of elderly receiving pensions before 1945.

3

Dying

Death itself was as gently approached and prepared for:
  'Old Gordon is nae verra weel, I doot.'
Or:
  'Willie is a gey puir cratur, I hear.'
  In such announcements there was a studied avoidance of anything that might come near to the categorical, a concern that kept open a man's option on life even as he slipped out of it.

David Kerr Cameron, *Willie Gavin, Crofter Man*, 1980

Introduction

Death is the prototypic form of physical loss, both for the dying and for the bereaved, and poses most acutely the problem of transcending the body. That attitudes of the living to the dead vary according to culture has long been apparent from the work of anthropologists; but historical work has now made it possible to trace also some of the corresponding modes of dying, and to see something of the sequence which all these attitudes have taken in Europe.

Most influential has been the research of Philippe Ariès, who has discerned four main stages in the journey from medieval to modern experience.[1] The earliest of these, 'tamed death', is distinguished by the immersion of the dying person in the collective life, and by a lively sense of the existence of evil and of the necessity for collective ritual defence against it. It is these collective defences, and the reconstitution and sanctification of the community beyond the grave which they achieve, that constitute the 'taming' of death. In the second stage, originating in the late Middle Ages, the individual becomes more sharply conscious of self, and a corresponding change occurs towards notions of a personal afterlife; but the consciousness of threat, and the communal ritual, remain entrenched.

In the third stage, however, these latter conceptions begin to shift. As, with the Enlightenment, the hope of technological control increases, so suffering is gradually transformed from an aspect of sin and evil into a residual aspect of as yet uncontrolled nature; while at the same time the ritual of death is domesticated to accord with the affectionate sensibilities of the nuclear family. And in due course, as all these shifts reach their culmination in the sentimental death of the nineteenth century, the fourth stage, the 'reversal' of the twentieth, begins to emerge, in which society, no longer able to tolerate what is beyond its control, removes the remains of autonomy from the dying, segregates death, and excludes it as far as possible from the rituals of social life.

Ariès, then, perceives two chief sets of forces in this evolution: first is the progress of self-awareness, collective in the early Middle Ages, increasingly individualist in the late medieval and early modern phases, and primarily familial since the Enlightenment—modifications which bring corresponding shifts in notions of the afterlife; and second is the progress of aspirations to technical control, which eventually replace ritual defences, and transform in the process the understanding of suffering.

A number of criticisms can be made of this picture. The evidence is necessarily uneven, and that for the early Middle Ages necessarily the weakest. Norbert Elias has argued, in conformity with his own thesis on the development of manners, that the medieval period was, rather, characterized by wide extremes in attitudes to death;[2] and he sees the shift towards self-control, imposed first by courtly and then by bourgeois society, as embracing a corresponding shift of self-awareness towards privacy and censorship, in death as in other matters. At the same time neither author pays much attention to contemporary movements which are seeking to redefine the nature of a good death;[3] Ariès, for example, sees them as the largely unavailing efforts of a few interested professionals.

However, on the other side, there is little so far to challenge, and much to confirm, the suggestion that a transition occurred in attitudes to death in the wake of the Enlightenment—a transition reflecting the period's scepticism of evil and endorsement of familial affection;[4] and there is much to support, too, the idea that the early twentieth century extended these conceptions into medical control of dying, and into censorship of its unpalatable realities.[5]

There is, therefore, a useful basis in these accounts for interpreting the movement of contemporary thought in regard to death, although new developments must be considered more closely. The value of the approach lies in its awareness that a culture is always in motion, and the delineation of periods when a particular view was uppermost must not be seen in too absolute a fashion. Ariès speaks of 'survivals' of such views in later periods, as if two or three different strata of the cultural past can coexist at one time;[6] and McManners notes that a 'new' view is not necessarily one which has had no previous adherents, but one which has not hitherto been formulated and propagated successfully.[7] Once a view is formulated and handed down, though, a new force comes into being; and to that extent the process of cultural development is cumulative, barring interruptions. Thus contemporary beliefs about dying can be examined, and are examined in this chapter, as a repository of varying 'strata' within a certain logic of development.

Contemporary evidence on the principal beliefs and attitudes which have been involved in this historical evolution is uneven. The two primary issues are contained, as I have noted already, in the varying forms of self-awareness with which death is faced on the one hand, and in the varying forms of technical control over the time and manner of death on the other hand. Some topics under these heads, which bulked large in the past, barely feature in contemporary research: whether they are overlooked in the researcher's assumptions or ignored in popular thought is unclear. What, for instance, has happened to the kind of self-awareness implied by the notion of preparing for death, so central in certain periods? By what assumptions has the contemporary ideal of a quick death overcome the horror, once general, of death sudden and unforeseen? How has the contrast of a 'natural' with an 'adventitious' death come to be sustainable? These are all matters on which there is very little contemporary evidence, and which this chapter seeks to explore.

However, on two aspects of these primary issues there is today a great deal of discussion. One is the question of whether and how the dying learn of their condition; and the other is the related question of what medical control is exercised over the timing of an individual patient's death. I have gone into these issues at greater length elsewhere,[8] but it is worth briefly summarizing the evidence on each of these matters in turn.

The question whether doctors tell the truth to their dying patients, or whether people wish to know such truths, is a subject on which passions run high, not least because of the general disadvantage suffered by patients in extracting information of any sort from many hospital hierarchies; and there is a tendency, in consequence, to simplify the record by saying, for example, that 'studies of lay people have had a consistent finding: they wish to be told'.[9] The evidence is, however, more complex than this, for several different preferences are in question.

The first question concerns preferences about being told an apparently threatening diagnosis, without the subject of the prognosis being raised: in practice, of course, the diagnosis in this research is cancer. The evidence on this question varies considerably in both Britain and North America, and suggests that, certainly in Britain, preferences about being told a diagnosis depend on what is believed to be the associated prognosis, and on preferences about being told this prognosis.

This second question, about whether people wish to know their prognosis, has been relatively neglected; but it is both critical and complex. The evidence on this issue from the 1950s and 1960s—which is North American—is again variable, and shows differing groups of patients as being only marginally favourable to disclosure, with large dissenting minorities, while healthy people were rather more favourable. By the late 1970s, however, research from North America was suggesting that the overwhelming majority of people, with or without cancer, wished to know a good deal about the prognosis, especially in the younger generation. This evidence was not without its ambiguities, but despite these it seems that by this period North Americans generally wished to know if they were dying, in a way which was much more explicit than the relatively tentative developments in Britain.

If, as this evidence suggests, a greater change has occurred in the North American than in the European countries in attitudes to learning a fatal prognosis, the change is one which corresponds with what seems to have been happening to the attitudes of doctors. In the 1950s the usual practice in both Britain and the USA was to avoid telling even the diagnosis in cases of cancer. And a cautious policy continues in many hospitals and general practices in Britain, although innovations in hospice and nursing care have encouraged openness with patients who wish it. Significantly, the emphasis of recent British studies has been on the complexity of communication in this area, and on the problems which sympathy and affection can create for members of the family as well as for doctors. In the USA, though, studies have suggested a positive revolution in doctors' attitudes such that it is actually the rule to tell, with exceptions not often made. Much of the pressure for this change seems to have come from outside the medical profession, in the form of malpractice suits and other public scrutinies of informed consent, an aspect of law which has been little used in Britain, and similar issues have bulked large in the increasing tendency to devise Natural Death Directives to prevent heroic measures being taken in a terminal illness.

Thus a change, radical in the USA, much more cautious in Britain, seems to have been occurring in attitudes to knowing and telling a fatal prognosis—a subject central to the first of our historical themes, the dying person's self-awareness. And a connection has emerged between this subject and the second historical theme outlined earlier—technical control of the timing of death.

The modern history of arguments for euthanasia can be said to begin in the latter part of the nineteenth century, but it was only in the 1930s that evidence showed British opinion to be strongly in favour of statements permitting doctors deliberately to take life, while American opinion long remained unfavourable even to statements which were relatively ambiguous. Only by the late 1970s did American views appear to be approximating to the British, but even then there remained some puzzling inconsistencies, and it is probably unsafe to conclude that majority approval in the USA covered much more than permitting the omission of extraordinary means for saving life, and the use of pain-relieving drugs at risk to life.

These changes in public opinion about legislation may or may not be an accurate reflection of personal beliefs and preferences on these subjects—that is one question which the present study can address. Still more important, though, is the question of what has brought about these changes, whether in personal wishes or in opinions about the law in this area. Obviously some of the preferences currently expressed reflect religious or rationalist beliefs, or alternatively conservative or liberal views of law; but others reflect the way medical care is organized, and the alternatives it offers. Here the main influences have been the growth of

life-saving technology in this century on the one hand, and latterly
the new alternatives pioneered by the hospice movement on the
other. Thus in Aberdeen, it is the teaching hospitals which have
hitherto been the scene of most deaths. A National Health Service
unit on hospice principles was opened in 1977;[10] but at the time of
the present study the unit was small (22 beds). Aberdonians
seldom referred to it, and then only negatively as a new place
where, so it was said, people were sent to die.[11] Thus the impact
of the hospice movement on Aberdonian attitudes to death was
at the time of this study somewhat limited, at least in terms of
direct experience.

Controversy continues, then, about these two major practical
questions—control of the timing of death, and awareness of its
imminence; and while there are grounds for inferring that beliefs
about them have been subject to important historical changes,
much remains to be learned about the present structure of lay
thinking on these issues. More especially, there is much to learn
about notions of preparation, and about the ideal timing of death,
which form the background to contemporary ideas about awareness
and control.

In what follows, I begin by considering these background concepts
and beliefs, as they emerge in Aberdonian talk.

Natural death and prepared death in Aberdeen

Ideas about the biographical timing of death took a number of
forms in Aberdeen, and were alluded to by over two-thirds of
those I met. Half of these allusions did not imply much more than
factual suppositions about the likely timing of death in old age,
which were discussed in the last chapter. But half went further,
bringing, as I noted in that discussion, a number of moral expectations to bear.

One of these moral expectations was the idea that there is a
natural time to die. This idea was directly connected with age, in
the notion that one should die when old but not too old; and it
was also alluded to indirectly, in references to the necessity and
appropriateness of death, of older generations going before the
younger and making way for them, and so on. The expectation was
one of acceptance:

"When you get older you just have to live from day to day. When you're young you think what'll we do next year?—but when you're old there may be no next year. You don't worry about it."

"It wouldn't trouble me at all. I'd be ready to go and that's the main thing. It'll make room for somebody else when I'm gone."

Chances of individual longevity, calculated on the basis of heredity, were not necessarily to be welcomed, as in the following conversation between a mother and a daughter:

Daughter: "We're a long-lived family—there's three of them over 90."

Mother: "Not another 20 years of this. Not unless they can get better with these monkey organs."

Daughter: "They're making advances all the time."

Mother: "They won't be in time for me."

Similarly, too credulous a reliance on longevity could be punished. A man who had emphasized his family's powers of survival, and the hard work with which he had reinforced these powers in himself, was subsequently shaken by apparently life-threatening symptoms. Although he cloaked this reversal with an air of elaborate unconcern, indicating that whether the test results were good or bad was of no importance, and that death was natural at his age, he was not allowed to escape. His wife interjected:

Oh he was gey [very] feared when it first happened, he was gey feared.

The husband was visibly stung by this, and rose vigorously:

That's something you'll never find me. There's nothing for a man to be afraid of, we all have to dee.

And a fierce duel followed, he insisting on his calm acceptance of his fate, she repeating with cackles her description of his dismay. There were of course a few who openly admitted to hoping they would live as long as possible, but this wish to die at the same time succinctly acknowledged the countervailing wish not to become truly old:

Q: "Let me ask you about your awareness of getting older" . . .

A: "I'm not getting older."

Q: "You're not getting older?"

A: "I don't want to be an old old person . . . but I don't want to die."

There's a saying, tired of living and scared of dying—that's me.

It was against this continued fear of dying, then, and against the urge to live on, Tithonus-like, that norms of a natural lifespan opposed themselves.

However the idea of a natural term was opposed not only to living too long, but also to dying too soon. This was particularly so for those who were bereaved by deaths which were felt to be premature, as I describe in the next chapter; but the moral expectation of survival was also apparent in the way people referred to a heredity or a health history which was a poor risk. These were only considered retrospectively, as a history of actual survival which showed that a health risk could be overcome by the right response. Hence bad survival risks were assessed only as the alternative outcome to taking care, keeping up strength through good living, and preserving an appropriate attitude, and premature death could argue some failure in this regard. This was a bias, therefore, which presented premature death in particular as controllable, not necessarily in the case of cancer, admittedly, but certainly in the case of, for example, life-threatening heart or chest conditions.

Nevertheless, strong as was this notion of a natural time to die, there was in Aberdeen an alternative way of contemplating the long-term expectation of death: the notion of an individual destiny, of 'your time'. The notion of 'your time' was independent of age-based expectations; and thus it became available as a way of understanding the death of the young as well as the unexpected survival of the old. Also, this destined time was opposed to the notion of controllability—invoked in retrospect it could release from guilt those who felt responsible for not controlling events, invoked in prospect it could relieve the agony of decision over a dangerous operation:

I ken if it's not your time then you won't go; and if it is your time there's nothing you can do.

At the same time the working of destiny was not usually seen in these cases as prescribing or permitting apathy: efforts to assess probabilities or to control the situation were no less thorough, and the appointed time was invoked only in recognition that however thorough the prepared defences, forces beyond human control or prediction would combine with those within human control or prediction to achieve an unknown conclusion which was in some sense already written. For those who thought in this way, therefore, this view was not fatalism, for fatalism implied first and foremost a refusal to act. On the few occasions when inaction was connected with the idea of an appointed time, the connection was imputed by those opposed to the idea, as in the caricature of those immobile ancients who, having passed the expected age of death, were said, in words referred to earlier, to be 'only here till the Lord sends for us', and to be 'patiently waiting for their call'. When adopted as a personal conviction, however, the idea of a due time was not fatalistic but preparatory or consolatory; and in either sense the assurance that the dying person was, or had been, 'ready', confirmed the appropriateness of the appointed time. Readiness was thus a recognition—it could not itself determine the time. I was told of a macabre scene in which an older invalid sister had tried to persuade a younger to join her in taking an overdose, enumerating the members of the family who were, she said, all waiting for them; to which the younger, according to her account, replied:

Well maybe, Chrissie, but you canna go before your time, and it's not my time yet.

When's your time then?

I don't know, Chrissie, but I'll wait for it to come.

The time therefore could not be chosen, and was in principle unknowable; that it came appropriately was essentially providential, or at any rate foreordained, and for those who wished to die well, as for Gloucester in the last act of *King Lear*, ripeness was all.

This ripeness or readiness was thus appropriate to the notion of 'your time', though it was not necessarily tied to it. It was accomplished in two ways: prospectively, by spiritual preparation for one's own death; and retrospectively, by reviewing the life of those who had died—a subject considered in the next chapter. Spiritual preparation was in principle a requirement at any time of life:

Wife: "Well of course we should always be prepared, this is the thing—we should always be. There's another question."

Husband: "It all depends. Preparation spiritually—but then you need preparation for your family too. Another thing that should be done beforehand is all your will and affairs all sorted out beforehand—but how many people do that?"

Wife: "There's always a reticence in dealing with that. They think that it's a foreboding, that it hastens it on, but it doesn't. A cousin of Hamish's lost his mother and his sister within a very short time and sadly he went himself within a couple of years, the same trouble. But I always remember what he said: when he was left alone he said he was going to prepare, have everything in order, prepare for going and continue living. And he did so, and forgot about it; did all his preparations, forgot about it and then went on living."

But although one should always be ready, some aspects of this preparation were certainly easier with the time available after retirement:

"Another thing I think is important: the sins of omission and the sins of commission. Now I don't know how many times we've mentioned to each other, we must write to so-and-so, we haven't done it and we're due a letter. I think that these are things to which one should [turn]—I mean after you retire you have more time to think."

Similarly, in another case, an appropriate detachment from possessions could be made easier by the contraction of income in later life, and the need to sell things:

"It's a bit sad sometimes—you get terribly fond of them—but then you see I got over that; you get over that because you realize when you get older that you don't own anything in life, and that you're borrowing it. You see everything is borrowed—you own nothing."

Hence, in another person's eyes, age became also a time to give away:

"To begin with I thought 'Oh heavens, to do away with that!'—but you give up all that, and then you sit down and have a think to yourself and say 'Well look, what's the use of having possessions?' I always think there's a time to accumulate stuff and there's a time to give it away."

"And that time would be—when?"

"Well just as you get on in years, I think . . . . You find, you know, that when you're not using things as you get on in years, if there's things you're not using, you're better to give them to people who *can* use them. I'm not what you would call a hoarder. Some people do, you know—well my neighbour was like that . . . . After she died, you just have no idea what she'd hoarded, and her brother was nearly in tears. And I thought 'Now . . .'—you see I'd watched all this—and I thought 'Let that be a lesson to you; don't you hoard any stuff to make all this work for people that will be tidying up after you.' "

The idea of preparation could, therefore, merge in this way with the idea that death was to be predicted in old age, but it was also a wider idea relevant to death at any age; and again the practices that prepared a person spiritually for death were not in any case relevant solely to death, but also to the normal conduct of spiritual life. The practice of prayer, for instance, was another person's preparation both as a routine and in the face of various kinds of challenge, only one of which was the possibility of dying. Thus spiritual or moral preparedness was an end in itself; but it was also stimulated by the prospect of dying, and could be reinforced by the statistical link between death and old age.

This idea of death as an individual destiny requiring an inner readiness, then, was not wholly opposed to the idea of old age being the natural time to die; but it led to opposed implications in certain cases. Both ideas were compatible when death came at the 'natural' age; but they were incompatible when death came markedly before or after such an age. The doctrine of a natural term made prolonged survival unnatural, and dying young unjust; that of individual destiny made prolonged survival a test of patience— or an excuse for pious inactivity, according to one's point of view—and it made dying young part of the workings of providence. The conflict between these doctrines was particularly sharp in regard to premature loss, as I show in the next chapter on bereavement; but it was also related to ideas about what constituted dying well at any age, and I now turn to these.

Good and bad ways of dying

How do people come to be defined as dying in the first place? Aberdonian definitions took three basic forms. First, there was dying as defined by the doctor—on the one hand by a prediction of varying exactitude, and on the other hand by a diagnosis such as cancer and (formerly) TB which was assumed to imply a steady and fatal decline. In this definition, although examples of medical error were recounted, the likelihood of such error was not rated highly, and the socially recognized state of dying was typically confirmed by the event of death. But these typical features were not in harmony in the other forms of dying which exercised Aberdonians. First there was the situation where somebody died before they were recognized to be dying, so that the recognition had to be reconstructed retrospectively; and second there was the situation where somebody recognized as effectively dying failed in fact to die.

These three sorts of dying had a definite relation to ideals about good and bad deaths. To die 'the proper way' was on the one hand to go quickly, easily, quietly, and unconsciously. However, there was also a potential clash here with another imperative, that the dying should be cared for, looked after, among 'people, light and warmth', and that they should have been reunited with brothers, sisters, parents, children, even cousins, before going. Too quick a death might be, proverbially, 'good for the one that's gone but bad for those left behind'. Thus reunion was defined as being in the interests of the living rather than the dying, and in meetings between them it was a particular virtue in the dying, gratefully remembered, when they showed an interest in the doings of those who had come to see them.

There were, then, two broad ideals of dying well: going as quickly and unconsciously as possible; and going only after an affectionate reunion with kin. In defining good deaths these two ideals were, at the extreme, incompatible, and the interests of the dying were perceived as at variance with the interests of the bereaved. However, in defining bad deaths both ideals had similar implications, for both were often threatened by the same situation.

This threat to both ideals arose from the third sort of dying, when people lived on who were considered as good as dead, and who were thought likely to be better off dead. This judgement was made when either the ideal rapid transition from life to death was arrested, or the ideal affectionate relationship with kin was distorted. A disturbance in the ideal relationship with kin was typically symbolized in the image of being a 'burden', a 'nuisance', a 'baby' with no 'dignity'. An arrested transition, on the other hand, was typically symbolized in the idea of being a 'vegetable', fed artificially, just existing. It was a confusion in the orders of being which place man as a life form superior to the other orders; it was a barely sensate condition, in which the quality of life was so altered that 'life' was a questionable description; or it was a condition where there was no sensation but of pain, where the dying person was afflicted, suffering, and with no pleasures. Naturally such violations of both ideals tended to occur in the same instances: cases in which somebody had become not only 'afflicted', or a 'vegetable', but also a 'burden to others', were only too well known; and both ideals agreed in defining such a situation as an outrage. This I call 'arrested' or 'delayed' death.

At the most general level, therefore, there were three sorts of dying—two good in different ways, but at the limit incompatible, and one bad in every way. Ways of dealing with this bad sort of death form the central issue of the next section.

Controlling the time of death

It follows from the ideals about the timing of death which have been discussed, that in so far as control of the timing is possible and permissible, it will be advocated in order to bring the experience of dying into closer accord with the ideal. Unexpected deaths can of course only raise such questions of control retrospectively, and I return to this issue in dealing with bereavement; prospectively, though, control can be an issue both in predicted deaths and in 'arrested' deaths.

In this section, and in the next, data are drawn both from the Aberdeen Survey and from the qualitative study. In the qualitative study, the data on the questions following are generally confined to that half of the sample which was visited more than once, since these were issues which were more easily discussed on a closer acquaintance.

In the Aberdeen Survey, a question was asked about predicted deaths; but in the qualitative study people talked about both predicted and 'arrested' deaths, and were especially concerned, as it turned out, with the latter. These differences in the situations envisaged were sharply reflected in attitudes towards attempted control. The Aberdeen Survey question ran:

Suppose you had a serious illness and the doctor thought you were going to die. Some people would prefer the doctor to fight on at all costs, some would prefer him to stop and let nature take its course and some would prefer him to help them on their way. Which would you prefer for yourself?

In the answers to this question 19% chose to be helped on, while 33% chose to let nature take its course, and 37% to fight on, 11% remaining undecided. Thus the least popular option was to be helped on; and it should be noted also that since the various meanings which this term might carry were not spelt out, 'helping on' may not necessarily have been seen to imply the use of drugs which are specifically lethal, but might have been thought by some to include anything down to the use of pain-relieving doses which carry an increased risk of death as part of their alleviatory effect—a procedure which, in medical ethics, is normally seen as sharply distinct from euthanasia.

In this context, then, preferences for euthanasia were not much in evidence. But when the subject of prolonging or shortening life was discussed in the qualitative study, the focus shifted rapidly from predicted deaths to include 'arrested' deaths; and in this context most of those who commented could envisage situations in which they would wish to be helped on, the language and examples used being for the most part explicitly concerned with deliberate taking of life. This intention to take life was evident in several ways—in descriptions of the appropriate response as 'suicide', 'euthanasia', or the taking of a 'lethal dose'; as an act of 'murder' or 'killing' at law; or as an act of 'putting away' people in the fashion of a sick animal. And it was evident in the result of the act being immediate death, 'getting it over with', 'finishing it', as well as in the implication that death was not otherwise expected. The language was generally plain, therefore. It was, however, in terms of contemporary medical ethics, seldom discriminating. Alternatives such as stopping or withholding treatment or relieving pain at higher levels of risk were seldom distinguished; and in a few cases they seemed actually to be confounded with deliberately ending life. Thus in these extreme instances which focused especially on 'arrested' death, extreme and undifferentiated actions were envisaged which were seldom thought of when death was predicted by the doctor in the ordinary course of events.

Not surprisingly, in view of this generally undifferentiated response, discussions of the problem of 'arrested' death were complicated by special considerations.

First was the problem of agency—of who should bring the situation to an end. Three people argued firmly and coherently for suicide as a way out. They chose this way on the grounds that doctors should not be asked to take life; and one added that it would be necessary to conceal the intentional nature of the act from family members, not only before, but also after, the event. The great majority, however, of those who considered these measures, assumed, in so far as they had considered the problem of agency at all, that doctors would do what was necessary. In one case, a sense of repugnance was actually made the reason why the doctor, rather than anyone else, should do the task. A man had been instructed, he said, to dose his dying father with what he believed to be laudanum. It had a bad taste, and the patient would not take it from his wife, so the son had to 'force-feed' him on alternate days, and the father would be unconscious for a day and then 'kick up' for the second day. When he died, the doctor said, according to the account given, that he should have had the dose every day, and he would have died sooner; but, said the son with some bitterness:

They shouldn't make the relatives do it. You can't do it, knowing it's going to kill them.

This man had already indicated his support in such cases for measures which would shorten life; and when asked whether his difficulty in carrying out these measures qualified his view that it was the doctor's task he replied simply, 'They do those things anyway'. Thus problems of repugnance on the doctor's side were often not anticipated; but in addition some people apparently expected neither to state in advance the conditions in which doctors should make such decisions, nor, as emerges shortly, to know when such decisions were being taken. It was sometimes argued that doctors should 'keep their own judgement', and only in two cases were they spontaneously expected to seek the patient's or the relatives' consent.

The second complication in dealing with arrested death was that even when the decision was not left entirely to the doctor, it did not always prove easy to match general criteria to particular cases. General indications offered included being bedridden, incontinent, fed, or unable to speak; but confronted with an actual known case a closer intimacy could make the decision seem suddenly more complicated. One man and his wife began unequivocally:

Husband: "If there's no hope at all tae live a . . . well fit [what] is it they often say, if ye're just a cabbage or something you know—"

Wife: "A vegetable."

Husband: "—A vegetable; now if you come tae that stage, I say the doctor should . . ."

Wife: "Be allowed to put you away."

Husband: "Be allowed to do it, if you were agreeable. That's fit [what] I say."

The example of a cat was then given which got old and used to lie whimpering all night; and this cat they did duly put away. Then the example of a close relative of the husband was introduced by the wife:

Wife: "Well ye can tak Kenny's brother in Fife just now."

Husband: "Oh well he's not, he's not quite so bad, no no he hasn't come to that yet."

Wife: "Now what pleasure can Eddie be getting out o' life?"

Husband: "Ah well but I . . . "

Wife: "Even his own daughter says Dad would be better away."

Husband: "He hasn't come to that stage."

Wife: "And she's quite right."

Husband: "He's certainly likely to be bedridden. His hip went wrong, and they put it in a pin or something. That was a' right, he was beginning to get out wi' the zimmer and that, but he was never right. And one evening, he'd been turning to pick up a cup, and that hip went again. So they had to rush him intae hospital and he lay quite a while there without anything being done to it, and then . . ."

Wife: "Aye, they put in a plastic joint."

Husband: "A plastic joint; and unfortunately whatever it was they did come adrift and had to be done again. Well . . ."

Wife: "But he canna walk."

Husband: "It's agony for him tae walk, and he canna walk on his own yet."

Wife: "He canna even hold the zimmer."

Husband: "No, he hasna got the strength."

Wife: "Now can you see that anybody . . ."

Husband: "Ah but, no, I don't . . ."

Wife: ". . . [like that] is having much pleasure in life?"

Husband: "No, no; but I don't think he's come tae the helpless state yet."

Wife: "Apart fae [from the fact] that [the daughter] is being killed?"

Husband: "Ah well, but I wouldna say he's come tae that stage. Now you see that's just where ye canna think o' it, when there's two opinions."

In this instance, then, two contrary judgements were ultimately derived from a single principle of euthanasia agreed initially by both parties, and it seems evident that the reason for the husband's resistance to his wife's judgement in this case was the fact that his own brother was concerned.

A similar disjunction between particular judgements also occurred not in this case between two different people but in the same person on two different occasions: again both judgements were derived from a principle, sustained and indeed reinforced over time, concerned with circumstances in which death should be allowed to occur. The man concerned, William Ure, talked about the question first at a time when he was due for an investigation to check the possibility of melanoma. He had been 'under a little bit of tension':

"You know, you think shall I write and say don't keep me alive because I don't want to live."

"Is that something you . . .?"

"Oh definitely. In fact I've read the bits that you write to say don't keep me alive, because I don't see any point—my family can live without me. I would hate to be kept alive, I definitely would, so if there's anything there—and I'm to get that clear before I go in—I don't want to. You know, I want to live, I want to live, but . . ."

"Yes. what would you do? Have you done anything with your GP, or . . .?"

"No, but it's been on my mind a lot, and I have a thing somewhere that says do not keep me alive, and I just wrote 'me too'. It's somewhere, I don't know if it's in my papers to go to the hospital or not, if I have to go in."

It is already apparent in this extract that some ambivalence was involved in moving from a general principle, stated very definitely, against being 'kept alive', to the particular decision of applying, attesting, or making known this preference in the actual situation. William Ure had cut the statements concerned out of a magazine— one requesting no radium treatment in the event of cancer, the other requesting no resuscitation in the event of brain damage— but his manner of signing them was, as he was obviously aware, not valid, and it emerged also that none of his family knew about them. However he left them in a drawer with other papers such as his medical card, and said that his daughter, who had a key to his house, would have found them when looking for the card. However, the immediate possibility of melanoma receded shortly afterwards: the test results proved negative, and three months later, looking through his drawers, he found the statements again:

I saw them yesterday and thought, shall I tear them up? But I'm sure I didn't.

Q: Why did you think of tearing them up? Did you feel you would want to make the decision afresh?

A: Yes I'd want to make it afresh. I don't know, I was sort of depressed before I went into hospital.

His specific decision against radium treatment or resuscitation was thus later reassessed as marginal, seen as perhaps the outcome of depression, distrusted as a possible misjudgement. However, notwithstanding this difficulty over particulars, he again, on my next visit, expressed his general principle, and indeed formulated it more strongly, in answer to a question about deliberate intervention:

I would be in favour that. A prick—if you had unendurable pain and no hope, what's the point? That's Jesus Christ all over again.

These are two extended examples of people who became ambivalent over specifics, while also stating simultaneously a general preference for deliberately ending life. In the time span of this study there were no other examples of people coming to face practical applications of their convictions after stating such a preference, but there were accounts from people who recalled such situations in the past. The details of these accounts naturally cannot be checked, but what is important is the way the past has been interpreted.

In these retrospective examples, an unresolved conflict between mercy killing and guilt at taking life becomes explicit. The first instance was the man mentioned earlier, who had experienced his own repugnance at being called upon to administer something he believed to be lethal to his father. The second and third of these situations were war experiences described by ex-servicemen. Both arose in the context of an initial argument in favour of euthanasia—for example:

"If there's without any doubt no chance of life and that person is suffering, they should be helped. But that is provided the person can't possibly live in his suffering. Because I have seen people suffering, and in some cases doctors try to keep a person alive for nothing, and the man suffers agony."

Then, in both cases, the problem arose. The man just quoted, who was in a medical corps, continued:

"But I have seen a doctor . . . I'd given a man an injection of morphia who was very, very badly [hurt]—his bowels were gone—and as there was absolutely no chance of the man surviving very long, and he was in agony, he said to give him morphia. I said I'd already given him, and he said well give him another. But I said, look it will kill him. And he said, well would you like to see your own friend suffer like that? I couldn't do it, but he did."

There was admiration for this doctor, but the doctor's suggestion that friendship would provide an impulse adequate to overcome the inhibition proved false:

"Another case—a great friend of mine—was admitted with a rather large hole of shrapnel, and he was in great pain, I should say in pain for at least an hour, and he asked me to give him morphine. He'd already had an injection of morphine—the doctor had given him when he first came in, and he asked me to give him more. I couldn't. And then he said, well for old times' sake will you shoot me? And I . . . I just couldn't . . . couldn't do it. Although it would have been a mercy. But I just didn't believe in taking a person's life."

Thus both principles, that of putting people out of their suffering, and that of not taking life, continued unresolved:

"I still don't know whether . . . well I feel I did the right thing by not doing it, because it would have been on my conscience; but at the same time the man died in agony, even with the morphine."

Finally the last instance of this type came from civilian life, like the first-mentioned of the four. A woman described the death of her father over forty years earlier, and said that because 'his heart wouldna brak', the doctor agreed with the family to give him the 'mercy cup'. A small white tablet was broken into a glass of water and mixed, and the daughter, as the one who had spent longest looking after her father, was deputed to give it to him:

I said, 'Will you take a suppy o' this, father?' He said, 'What is it, quine [girl]?' I said, 'It's something that'll maybe help you.' And he just took one mouthful and said, 'Ach quine, that was awfu' bitter.'

After this her father lay back and closed his eyes, and, according to the story, the doctor counted two minutes and said, "All over": and at this point in her recollection the daughter suddenly began to cry unrestrainedly. Then, after a pause, recovering herself, she explained that at this moment there was a 'flash' outside, though the weather was clear, and one of the family blurted out, 'Maybe we did wrong?' However the doctor reassured them, and the story ended on this note of exoneration. This was a dramatic account whose relation to the events of forty years ago must remain entirely speculative; what is evident, though, is the same complex, of approval for euthanasia contending with guilt, as occurs in all these instances—a theme underlined by the fact that when this story-teller first began she broke off abruptly before she came to the 'mercy cup' and questioned me closely about who I was, only returning to the story when she had recovered her confidence some time later.

A number of problems, then, surrounded the Aberdonian tendency, when someone was 'as good as dead' yet could not die, to shift towards deliberate intervention to end life. There was the continued conflict provided by beliefs in the sanctity of life; there was the difficulty of moving from general principles to particular judgements; and there was the problem of defining who, in realistic circumstances, would make the decision and act. Tied up with this last problem were Aberdonian attitudes to knowing the truth about a fatal prognosis, and I now consider this aspect of their ideas about dying.

Knowing the truth

When people talk about someone knowing that death is approaching, what 'knowing' means is not always easy to define. In the Aberdeen Survey the question ran:

If you were going to die, do you think you would want to be told?

The source of the information was, in context, implied to be the doctor, and so the knowledge concerned was necessarily either about a medical prediction of death, or possibly about a diagnosis assumed to amount to the same thing. In order to reflect the qualifications often underlying answers to this question, respondents graded their preferences by probability as follows:

definitely not	17%
probably not	13%
might and might not	13%
probably	19%
certainly	38%

In the qualitative study most people expressed preferences either for knowing or for not knowing, and many opposed the two categorically; but there was also a group who held qualified preferences in accordance with varied conditions. These qualified preferences probably correspond to those of survey respondents who said they might or might not want to be told; certainly amongst the rest there was a marginal overall preponderance of wishes to know over wishes not to know which was very similar in both studies, the wish to know being commoner in the middle class.

However, if knowing was the commoner preference, there was nevertheless a strong inclination, when the roles were reversed, not to tell. This silence was something taken for granted in a way that preferences for knowledge or ignorance were not: the usual expression was '*of course* we didn't tell him'. Where silence was felt to need explanation, it was on the lines that one 'should not worry the dying' but allow them to 'go quietly'; and where there were extra aspects of the situation which would contribute to the worry, such as leaving a young widow to bring up small children, the interdict on speaking was only intensified. The only qualification which was discussed here occurred in the case of a man who came to his own conclusions about his situation from the nature of the hospital investigations, but who found that his wife and daughters would not listen to what he had to tell them. It was agreed by other relatives that in this case 'they should have received it'; but even the relatives who did 'receive' his account acknowledged the difficulty of doing so:

He said to me, 'I always thought you'd go before me and now I'm going before you.' I—what could you say—I said, 'Ye're nae awa' yet.'

Clearly, while these attitudes to telling were consistent with the minority preference for ignorance, they were potentially in conflict with the majority preference for knowing. The conflict was indeed reconcilable for some in one of two different ways: by distinguishing certain types of personality—often very cloudily defined—who should not be told, or by asserting that one would know without being told. The latter belief was asserted prospectively by several middle-class men, in the form that anyone of average intelligence would know eventually by analysing what was happening to him; hence for these men the question of being told was a question only about whether they preferred to know early. However the belief in self-generated knowledge was also commonly inferred, at the time or in retrospect, from indirect comments of the person who had died:

"I remember when my husband was very ill, I think he knew he was dying—I did, but of course it was never mentioned, but there was such a lot of nurses I knew it—he says well my brother was in here, my two brothers were in here, and your mam was in here, and now it's my turn. And I knew then he knew."

Such inferences belonged also to the commonplaces of funerals, and I heard them made on such an occasion by people who had themselves expressed at other times a wish not to be told about their situation if they were dying, and made in the case of a death which had in any case been only a risk and not an expectation when it happened. In the second of these instances three of us were talking, and one said:

Kathleen knew. She said she didn't know if she'd get over the operation. I said 'Of course you will.' But she said 'I don't know if I might die.' I said 'Get away with you.' But the last time she had tea with me, when she went she kissed me on the cheek.

The narrator said she had been very surprised, but had said nothing and had drawn her own conclusions. I noted at the time:

I found myself wondering about this account. The words didn't sound very like Kathleen. It may just have been the solemn intonation. Mrs Hastie seemed to share these doubts as she said 'Oh I don't know, she was saying to me I'll be out again in a month.'

In such retrospective accounts there was, it seems, a combining of two assumptions: that a proper sensibility on the part of friends to the feelings of the dying required silence, and at the same time that a proper sensibility on the part of the dying to the feelings of their friends required a recognition of the significance of their last meetings together.

Such resolutions between the need for knowledge and the need not to say the awful thing were not always, however, possible: while there was usually some room for rewriting history, people did not necessarily wish to fudge the evidence. Louisa Ross had for many months afterwards remained sharply divided about not having told her husband the prognosis:

"I really was bothered, because I thought I'd let him down, you know, because we never had kept anything from each other."

But at the same time she maintained the opposing conviction which had led her to act in this way:

"I did the right thing as far as he was concerned, because I knew that to have left me to fend for myself the way things were would have worried him no end."

And she did not make use of the usual reconciling formula even when friends urged it:

"I'm positive that he really didn't have any idea. I'm so sure of that. But this friend of mine who's a very forthright person said 'Oh that's ridiculous, Louisa, Bob was a very intelligent man, he must have known he was going to die.' And I said, 'Well but Iris, one only dies once, how does one know?' "

In the result this conflict, after continuing for two years after the death, was resolved only by a freak event: she had a dream, in which her husband told her that he had not known, but also that this had been the right thing to do. This message was effective, evidently, because it did not run counter, as did the argument that he had known all along, to the facts as she understood them.

In this case, then, the concealment from the dying man of diagnosis and prognosis was presented as clear-cut, as was also the conflicting preference of husband and wife for shared knowledge; but both the preference for knowledge and the amount of information given could also be partial, could shade off in a way which made it hard to determine whether what was told did or did not match with what knowledge was desired. In the case referred to earlier, where a risky operation proved fatal, different views of the patient's knowledge of this risk were, I have indicated, held by her circle; and it is possible to compare these views with my notes of numerous conversations with her over the preceding year and a half.

Before any question of the operation or of any major change in her health, Kathleen Leslie answered a general question about knowing the probabilities of dying in a qualified way: that she would not like it, but that it might help, if you knew to the day, with deciding how to spend everything. The question evidently made an impression, and in this instance may itself have helped to crystallize and fix the answer, because a year later, after the question of the operation had arisen, she told someone else of this conversation:

Do you know what he asked me? Would I like to know I was going to die?
I said I would and I wouldna, that was the answer he got. Yes and no. Yes
because you could plan everything out, and no because I wouldna like to
go to bed at night and know I wouldna wake up in the morning. I wouldna
like that: nae the morn.

If her wish for knowledge in the short term was qualified, however,
she had been definite a week earlier about her wish to know the
long-term risks attaching to the operation:

The specialist sees me in three weeks, and I'll ask him what would he say,
is it fifty-fifty or what? Only I had a friend die this year after an operation—
and that gives you a wee thochty [thought].

But although the risk of dying was present in her mind on this
occasion, the actual encounter with the doctor yielded a different
sort of information:

The doctor came in and said 'Do you want to have it?' I said 'What are
your percentages?' He said 75 per cent. Well I'll be one of the 75 per cent.
Then he found out about my previous operation and that more or less
fixed it. He says, if you've had that, it's only 20 per cent.

The percentages given here were, it emerged, success rates: the
risks of harm were not discussed, but implicit attention was paid to
them, because the doctor said he would not do the operation at
present, though he would do it if the condition got worse. Hence
danger, more than merely a failure to improve, could be understood to be present for the 80% who were not successes, though
the nature of this danger was not made explicit, except in so far as
the doctor remarked that Mrs Leslie was 'not so young', and that it
was a major operation.

  The question whether this information constituted telling Kathleen
Leslie what she wanted to know became acute six months later.
The condition did get worse, and the doctor, after a brief examination, announced that he would operate: the presumption was thus
against further discussion being necessary, though a conversation
did follow which, as recalled by Kathleen, was at best elliptical:

I said, 'Dinna forget now, I'm an auld wifie.' He said, 'Oh you're not too
old.' I thought, 'Changed days', and nearly said it. I was 'too old' six
months ago.

After this she reverted on several occasions, in the next three
weeks before the operation, to the question, had she made a correct

interpretation of the doctors' thinking? The version she produced on each occasion was as follows: that the doctors had not been sure six months ago whether her condition would improve or get worse, and the low chance of success was therefore not worth taking then; but following her deterioration it was worth taking now. All this was coherent with her previous accounts and clearly constituted an adequate explanation; yet in her repeated testing of it there was apparent a dissatisfaction with some aspect of it which was a source of tension. It seemed evident to myself and others, not least from our own sense of aspects which we were unwilling to mention, that it was what the explanation excluded, rather than what it included, that was the problem: that is, the extent of the undiscussed danger which had prevented the doctors from operating on the earlier occasion, and which was glanced at in the reference to being too old. Both the doctors and Kathleen's own circle had avoided talking about this; and although she had shown more than once, by referring to her friend's death, that she knew there was a risk of dying, the question remains whether she had been prevented from knowing what she wished to know about the extent of this risk.

My own conclusion is suggested by the earliest material which I have cited: that Kathleen had from the beginning wished only to know enough about her chances of dying to make long-term plans, and not so much as to know her fate accurately in the short-term; and this conclusion is supported by another statement seven months before her death:

Of course there's a risk attached to every operation but you dinna think aboot that.

Hence the tension which emerged on occasions in her last few weeks derived from her resolutely not thinking about the extent of risk, in accordance with her own lights. When she died, however, it emerged that she had in fact made plans in her last months for the disposal of all her possessions. Thus she wished both to know and not to know; and had arguably been told what she wished to know, and not told the rest.

This history underlines the complexity of what counts as knowing and as not being told in such situations. It is a complexity which is not captured even by such descriptions as 'suspecting the truth'[12] or 'mutual pretence'[13] which have been coined to characterize similar interactions in cancer wards. Something less than pretence was involved here, for there was only a vagueness of definition in regard to the risk; and something more than suspicion was involved, for Kathleen Leslie had antecedent preferences, potentially conflicting, for the degree of definition to be achieved.

Because of this complexity, one should not underestimate the extent to which a delicate resolution is achievable between the need to know bad news, and the need not to speak it. In Aberdeen these needs were most acutely in danger of conflict among members of the middle class, for it was members of the middle class who most frequently wished to know if they were dying, while at the same time the general ethic of not telling remained, if in attenuated form. In Mannoch, the estate, however, the assumptions against knowing and against telling both were more pronounced, and were consistent with one another. From this perspective, both knowing and telling meant worry, and 'awful feeling', misery, and there was no offsetting advantage in it. Also there was a subtler version of this view, that those who did not give up hope would live a longer as well as a happier coda to their lives. That ignorance was not only bliss, but also functional, was argued by a skilled engineering worker on the basis of an engaging analogy. His brother and he shared a motorbike, but while he himself always came home on it without trouble, his brother found that it frequently broke down:

"He was always paying attention to the engine, you see, so he knew when something was wrong, but I would ride on just the same and never came to harm."

So when, at the end of a series of recent tests, the doctor asked this man if he had any questions,

"I said I didn't think so. He kept on asking me. But I wouldn't want to know."

This difference of emphasis between middle-class and working-class attitudes to knowing and to telling news of impending death is interesting—although it is no more than a tendency—and its significance is considered in Chapter 8. But first it is time to draw together the reasoning which connects this question of knowing with attitudes to intervention, with ideals of a good death, and with notions of the proper time of life for death to come.

Themes and dilemmas

In every aspect of dying discussed so far in this chapter, certain opposed premisses have already been revealed by case studies and other evidence. First, as regards the biographical timing of death, there was the division between those who saw death as natural and right at a certain age, and those who saw the time of death as an individual destiny requiring an attitude of readiness at any age. These were not the only long-term expectations held about the time of dying. I referred earlier to other, weaker formulations which were based merely on the estimated probability of death, and which were compatible with most other ideas. I return to these later, but meanwhile the most important point of conflict here arose, in the special cases of premature and overdue death, between the notions of a natural death and of a prepared death, whose assumptions can be summarized in the following premisses:

3.1 *Natural death*
   We ought to die when, and only when, we are old and not too old.

3.2 *Prepared death*
(a) We only die when our time has come, and/or
(b) We ought to be ready when we die.

The reference to 'we' in these formulations is a reminder that the assumptions are held not only for oneself but for those near to one; and thus they affect attitudes both to dying and to bereavement.

   Next, a second opposition emerged between two forms of good death:

3.3 *A quick death*
   If we die quickly, we die the proper way.

3.4 *Death after reunion*
   When people are dying, those close to them must spend time with them before they die.

Again this opposition emerged only in the special circumstances of a death so sudden that no opportunity for farewells arose.

   These four premisses related in various ways to the issue of knowledge about one's condition, where again opposed assumptions were revealed:

3.5 *Death aware*
    If I am dying, I wish to know it.
3.6 *Silence about death*
(*a*) If I am dying, I do not wish to know it, and/or
(*b*) One should not tell people if they are dying.

And many of these notions bore on the conflict felt about arrested transitions:

3.7 *Euthanasia*
    If I am a burden, or if I am in pain or virtually unconscious, and have no pleasure, I wish to be helped to die.
3.8 *The sanctity of life*
    Nobody should take a person's life.

I have noted that these oppositions too could be resolved, or at any rate blurred, in various ways: the wish for awareness could be partial, or it could be regarded as impractical for certain sorts of people; and knowing could be regarded as automatic, and independent of telling. Similarly, the principle of the sanctity of life could be qualified to leave suicide as an option, or to except doctors as professionals trained to decide on and administer a lethal dose; while the principle of euthanasia, in its turn, could meet unforeseen qualifications in its application.

In what follows, I leave aside all these qualifications in order to underline the basic structure of these ideas. As before, there were only a few consistent ways of combining premises from these four opposed sets.

The first of these consistent patterns can be termed *ritual dying*, in that it was oriented towards the symbolic significance of the event. This pattern combined a value on achieving a readiness for death (3.2) with an emphasis on the reunion of the dying with those close to them (3.4); and it connected these notions with the expectation that the dying should be fully aware of their state (3.5), and with an affirmation of the sanctity of life (3.8).

These ideas hung together mainly through two internal links. The first was the view that, to be willing to know one was dying, it was necessary to be prepared for death:

"I think, if I had a terminal illness like cancer, I would want to know . . . . Quite honestly I wouldn't worry when I died. I'm quite prepared to. I admit I wouldn't worry now if I died tomorrow. Does that sound awful?

Because I'm not afraid of death in the slightest bit. I think you go on to something better than this. Well I hope so anyway."

or again:

A: "I would like to know, yes. Of course I'm ready for it. I'm just . . . I don't know, I've just made my peace and would go at any time."

Q: "Is this something that you would say recently, or is it something that all your life . . .?"

A: "Well in the past few years. The past few years, I just feel that I could face my maker, and reply."

This was one connection of ideas expressed by a number of religious people. And a second connection was expressed in the idea that if the time of death was appointed by God, it should not be anticipated by man. Ideas of a destined time to die were often, as I have shown, implicit in preparing for death; and where this sense of destiny was present, people could not choose for themselves the time of their death. Hence, in an example already given, suicide was ruled out.

This, then, was the first coherent pattern of ideas about dying. Next, at the opposite extreme from this way of thinking, was another consistent pattern which can be characterized broadly as *disregarded dying*—as a pattern which excluded as far as possible the relevance of dying to the concerns of life. It combined the moral expectation of a natural death in old age (3.1) with the ideal of a quick death (3.3) and the wish to die unawares (3.6); and with these assumptions it also became necessary to avoid practical decisions about the timing of death, thus effectively excluding euthanasia (3.7), even though some people who thought this way also had strong feelings about states worse than death.

Again these ideas were linked internally. The principal link, expressed by several people, was the notion that it was best to know nothing about what was happening, and therefore it was best to die quickly. This was the same implication as that which gave a sense of rightness to death during sleep. Without such a rapid passing, the possibility of remaining in ignorance was felt to become with time increasingly fragile, for reasons already discussed. Given sufficient intelligence people were expected in time to draw their own conclusions, and this was needless misery. Nothing useful could be done with this knowledge, and it might take away hope. Thus to die unaware, the only sure way was to die quickly.

These ideas tended to go with the expectation that death would occur naturally at a ripe, though not too ripe, age, if only because this belief did not require one to think about death or to know when it was actually imminent. But it has to be added, perhaps surprisingly, that the alternative belief—that one should be prepared for death at any age—did not strictly require one to have this alarming knowledge either. While those who wished to know a fatal prognosis certainly wished it because they were prepared, it did not follow that those who were prepared necessarily wished to know. Preparedness was ideally, as I indicated earlier, a lifelong state, and so it was at times felt to be consistent with not wishing to know when death was near, if knowing was too unpleasant.

This argument made possible a third, *transitional pattern,* falling between 'ritual dying' and 'disregarded dying'. In this pattern a lifelong state of preparedness (3.2) could be combined with an attempt to minimize awareness of dying in every other way. It could be combined, that is, with a quick death (3.3), and with ignorance of what was happening (3.6), thus again effectively excluding euthanasia (3.7).

There was a symmetry about these three ways of thinking which was absent in one important respect from the fourth and last. All these first three ways expected either a natural death (3.1) or a prepared death (3.2); but I have indicated that it was possible to adopt much weaker versions of these expectations. Some people said merely that death at a particular age was probable, and avoided further implicit assumptions about the justice of receiving a natural term of life; and similarly, some believed in preparing for death without necessarily supposing that its timing was predestined. These weakened assumptions were important because either could be combined with the remaining premises not only along the lines already indicated, but also in a new way which can be described as *controlled dying.* Here the ordering of one's own fate was paramount, including the claim to be given some control over the time of one's death (3.7); and this required a full knowledge of one's fate (3.5). In this scheme a quick death (3.3) might be desirable, but it was not the only kind of good death, and the scheme was quite consistent also with a value on reunion before death (3.4).

The internal link which was crucial to this pattern was the notion that in order to control one's own life, including, at the extreme, one's own death, it was necessary to have full information about one's condition. From examples already given it has been apparent that several people wished to know enough to plan what to spend and what to bequeath, and to think out the fulfilments and pleasures which they could still hope to achieve. And in addition there were a few cases, one of which has been described, where the logic of planning against being given extraordinary life-saving treatments, or of planning for suicide or euthanasia, plainly indicated a requirement to know the truth.

It follows of course from this view that one cannot wish to make such plans and at the same time wish, if conscious, not to know one's condition. Thus those who wished to remain ignorant could not consistently wish for euthanasia, and one person who did express both preferences acknowledged that they were contradictory, in the sense that satisfying both was 'legally impossible'. What was more remarkable, though, was that most of those who wished to remain ignorant did also express a wish for euthanasia without recognizing any such contradiction, and without adding any qualifications that would resolve it. Even if one supposes, for example, that by implication some wished euthanasia to be carried out only if they were unconscious— which ignores those who used pain as a criterion—they still had no notion of documenting their wish that this should happen. It seemed at times that in expressing a wish that, in extreme circumstances, they would be 'helped on', some Aberdonians were expressing no more than a conviction that certain situations they had known of were worse than death, and that the quicker such situations were ended the better. In these instances, at the same time, little thought had been taken about the practical means of resolving a problem which most people hoped never to face themselves.

There was thus a tendency towards contradiction in these attitudes to dying, and on this subject it is especially necessary to beware of supposing that individuals exemplify one coherent pattern of thought. Nearly all the Aberdonians who discussed dying had more than one conviction to express about it, and contradiction was as frequent as coherence. The commonest coherent pattern of thought was the minority pattern I have described as 'controlled dying'; but commoner still was the incoherent combination of 'disregarded dying' (and the transitional pattern which is like it) with a wish to see cases of arrested dying somehow despatched by undocumented medical intervention. Meanwhile 'ritual dying', distinguished especially by its value on preparation and 'your time', and only a little less common than these competitors, was sometimes expressed coherently, and sometimes opposed by a drift towards other ideas.

All these patterns of consistency, and some of the typical inconsistencies in their use, can now be compared with the historical picture described earlier.

Conclusion

In the introduction to this chapter I described how it is possible to understand the separate streams of contemporary thought about dying as 'strata' deposited by a long process of cultural change. Thus the strata observed today are themselves relevant to the interpretation of how the process occurred, though they are of course only a small part of the evidence. It remains now to consider how Aberdonian views of dying fit into the broad outline of the historical interpretations at present available.

Within this broad outline, what I have called 'ritual dying' can be traced back a long way, though it appears in the present instance in a form in which many of the characteristic rigours of medieval and Counter-Reformation Catholic practice are excluded. Thus the preparation for death which is advocated here has lost the final urgency which informed earlier Catholicism; nor does it require awareness of dying, though it may be confirmed and completed by such awareness. In Protestant countries this change was a logical outcome of the Puritan rejection of deathbed repentances, entailing that preparation was a lifetime business dependent on marks of conversion.[14] While this did not of itself mean that it was good to go suddenly and without warning, it nevertheless assuaged the fear of such a death, and opened the way for it to become accepted as the ideal when the time came; and I have noted a transitional compromise of this kind in the thinking of some Aberdonian Protestants. Thus the Protestant version of ritual dying proved more easily compatible than Catholic Counter-Reformation practice with the evolution towards what I have called 'disregarded dying'.[15] But though it has been easily compromised, it is still very much alive—a point to which I return shortly.

If 'ritual dying' is the oldest pattern to survive in contemporary Scotland, 'disregarded dying', still the dominant pattern, seems to have developed slowly out of the Europe of the Enlightenment. The crucial shift was that of a new familial consciousness, which began to place a value on the considerate deception of the dying, and thus on death unawares and unforeseen.[16] But an important consequence of this change was that knowledge and control of the situation around the deathbed passed to medicine; and it was in this context that popular ideals of heroic medicine developed, and early death became an event which was 'adventitious' and senseless. The moral and religious protest against these 'senseless' events has been referred to the Judaeo-Christian tradition;[17] and Aberdonian material quoted in the next chapter and Chapter 9 suggests similarly that there is a connection with Old Testament assumptions equating righteousness and long life. But it seems unlikely that this emphasis could have achieved its present unqualified character against the facts of pre-industrial life expectancy—before the fall in the death rate from the last quarter of the nineteenth century, and the subsequent concentration of death and acquaintance with death in older age groups. Thus it was only when hopes of a natural term of life, formerly discounted, were increasingly made real in experience, that heroic medicine acquired its popular basis, and the pattern of 'disregarded dying' was completed.

It is as a historical reaction to heroic medicine and the life-saving ethic that the pattern I have described as 'controlled dying' is best understood. The issue was initially formulated in an extreme form by British pressure groups in favour of euthanasia, for it was in 1936 that the United Kingdom Parliament discussed and rejected its first Voluntary Euthanasia Bill.[18] At this stage the argument advanced concerned people who were going to die anyway, and was essentially a matter of controlling their pain in situations where there was a risk or certainty of death from the drug to be used. This argument is, as I have noted, much more restricted than that advanced by the Aberdonians of the present study, which mainly concerned people who were 'as good as dead' but still living on, and involved direct killing even when they were not necessarily in pain. These extensions reflect a change in the nature of the debate between 1936 and 1969, when a second Voluntary Euthanasia Bill including these provisions was considered and rejected.[19] Both Bills, however, required, as many Aberdonians did not, the documented preference and, except in cases of unconsciousness or dementia, the full awareness of the person who would die. That such a requirement presented considerable problems was made evident in the late 1950s and early 1960s, when the reluctance of doctors to divulge fatal prognoses was demonstrated in several studies; and I have argued earlier that this reluctance corresponded also to complex ambiguities in lay attitudes, which are still evident in Aberdeen.

In America the reaction against medical heroism has been more recent and in many ways a complementary opposite to that in Britain—less radical in the matter of euthanasia, more radical in the matter of awareness. I said earlier that in America common approval is only definitely evident for more limited ways of controlling death—the use of painkillers even at risk of shortening life, and the avoidance of extraordinary means of prolonging life.[20] But once the issue of medical control was raised, the belief in asserting consumer sovereignty over the doctor made full information a necessity. By comparison, British attitudes to information remain ambiguous, and British hospice doctors tend to regard American demands for knowledge as excessively suspicious and lacking in trust.[21]

A resolution to this pattern of complementary but contradictory positions only began to emerge with the British hospice movement. Hospice care, at the time of this study, had arrived too recently in Aberdeen to make an impact on popular attitudes. But elsewhere this movement sought a resolution at two levels. It sought technical control without taking life; and it sought open communication without imposing it. What is interesting is that in both these resolutions—not only in encouraging awareness, as I noted earlier, but also, and more fundamentally, in resisting deliberate intervention to end life—the leaders of this movement have been reproducing afresh the characteristic emphases of ritual dying. And this is no accident, as a recent biography of Cicely Saunders makes clear.[22]

In all these ways, then, contemporary attitudes to dying appear as historical strata laid down by a culture in motion. All these strata are exemplified in Aberdonian attitudes, though the chief source of these attitudes still lies in the pattern of disregard formed in the late nineteenth and early twentieth centuries. But new movements may take root in any of these historical layers, and in Britain the newest movement—hospice care—has sprung from the oldest layer of all.

Notes and References

1. P. Ariès, *The hour of our death*, tr. H. Weaver, London: Allen Lane, 1981.
2. N. Elias, *The loneliness of the dying*, tr. E. Jephcott, Oxford: Blackwell, 1985; but for a contrary view which consults ethnographic evidence on European peasant societies as well as historical evidence see M. Vovelle, *La mort et l'Occident de 1300 à nos jours*, Paris: Gallimard, 1983.
3. L. H. Lofland, *The craft of dying: the modern face of death*, London: Sage, 1978.
4. D. E. Stannard, *The Puritan way of death*, Oxford University Press, 1977; J. McManners, *Death and the Enlightenment*, Oxford University Press, 1981; L. Stone, *The family, sex and marriage in England 1500–1800*, London: Weidenfeld and Nicolson, 1977.
5. Some of the classic sources of a large literature are: G. Gorer, *Death, grief and mourning in contemporary Britain*, London: Cresset Press, 1965; B. G. Glaser and A. L. Strauss, *Awareness of dying*, Chicago: Aldine, 1965; D. Sudnow, *Passing on: the social organisation of dying*, Englewood Cliffs: Prentice Hall, 1967.
6. Ariès, *The hour of our death*, pp. 19 f., 590–1.
7. McManners, *Death and the Enlightenment*, pp. 458 f.
8. R. G. A. Williams, 'Awareness and control of dying: some paradoxical trends in public opinion', *Sociology of Health and Illness*, 11.3 (1989), 202–12.
9. R. M. Veatch and E. Tai, 'Talking about death: patterns of lay and professional change', in R. C. Fox (ed.), *The social meaning of death*, Annals of the American Academy of Political and Social Science, 1980, p. 33.
10. J. Askham, *Report of a pilot study on the choice of place of care for patients in the later stages of cancer*, Institute of Medical Sociology, Aberdeen, 1981.
11. Patients and relatives at the unit in 1980 often admitted to similar initial attitudes, though more than half were converted by their experience: see Askham, *Report of a pilot study*, p. 34.

12. J. McIntosh, *Communication and awareness in a cancer ward*, London: Croom Helm, 1977.
13. Glaser and Strauss, *Awareness of dying*.
14. Stannard, *The Puritan way of Death*.
15. McManners, *Death and the Enlightenment*, ch. 8, documents the continuing antipathy to dying suddenly even among deists and atheists of 18th century France, and Ariès, *The hour of our death*, pp. 562–3 argues that 'it was only in the early 20th century, after the First World War, that priests began to be called after the dying person was unconscious. This, according to Ariès, contributed to the Second Vatican Council's decision to reconstitute unction in its original form as a sacrament for the sick, given now also to the old.
16. Ariès, *The hour of our Death*, p. 587.
17. T. Parsons, R. C. Fox, and V. M. Lidz, 'The "gift of life", and its reciprocation', *Social Research*, 39 (1972), 367–415.
18. G. Williams, *The sanctity of life and the criminal law*, London: Faber, 1958, ch. 8.
19. For a résumé of this bill see Church Information Office, *On dying well; an Anglican contribution to the debate on euthanasia*, 1974.
20. It may be relevant that formulations of this kind emerged from a number of statements made by Pius XII during 1957, and, at least to this degree, resistance against life-saving treatments certainly had majority approval in the USA by the 1970s: Pius XII, 'Allocution on ordinary and extraordinary means', *Acta Apostolicae Sedis*, 24 November 1957; Pius XII, 'Religious and moral aspects of pain prevention in medical practice', Address of 24 February 1957, *Irish Ecclesiastical Record*, 88 (1957), 193–209.
21. See e.g. R. Lamerton's review of R. Veatch, *Death, dying and the biological revolution*, in *J. Med. Ethics*, 3 (1977), 194–5.
22. S. du Boulay, *Cicely Saunders: the founder of the modern hospice movement*, London: Hodder and Stoughton, 1984.

4

Bereavement

The bodies of men after death return to dust, and see corruption; but their souls (which neither die nor sleep), having an immortal subsistence, immediately return to God who gave them.

> *The Westminster Confession* (approved by the General Assembly 1647, and ratified and established by Acts of Parliament 1649 and 1690, as the public and avowed confession of the Church of Scotland)

Introduction

It is a common theme in social imagery that every ending is a death; and by the same token every ending is also a grief. But even if grief is a prototypical experience, we still understand very little about how people in different cultures help one another to manage it. What bereavement shares with lesser endings is the contradiction between orientations towards the past and towards the future, and the necessity of working through this conflict.[1] When these issues were first raised at the turn of the century, this work was thought to be accomplished in the performance of rites of passage; and mourning rites were given detailed study along these lines by Robert Hertz.[2] Today, though, we have lost many of these institutions, and it is not clear whether anything has replaced them.

Hertz's work makes a good starting point for understanding this problem. His studies convinced him that the loss of a person was the loss of a whole set of relationships involving that person, and the necessity of adapting to new relationships created a tension of allegiances which could not be tolerated. Therefore it was necessary to separate the two sets of relationships by an interval in which a task of bridging or reconciling could be carried out. Hertz spelt out this transition in terms of three elements which, he found, underwent exactly parallel transformations: first, the body of the dead person was reduced to something definitely non-corporeal, to bones or ashes; second, and concurrently, the soul was shown to be separated from the body and from living society, and was incorporated in the world of the dead; and thirdly, when these things were finally effected, the mourners, having held till then a transitional status, had achieved a release from their past attachments and had become incorporated, in their turn, in a reconstructed set of relationships.

These formulations have successfully made sense of death practices in a wide range of pre-industrial societies; and it is only with modern Western industrial societies that their validity comes in doubt. The problem lies in what is apparently a drastic shrinkage of accustomed ritual in these societies since the time when Hertz and van Gennep wrote. One attempt at a solution to this problem suggests that the growth of a new ritual of 'civil' religion has been overlooked in the decline of the old rituals of supernatural religion;[3] but in the accounts given, the content of this new ritual appears more exiguous and bland than the remains of the old. Others view the decline of mourning ritual as a perhaps temporary pathology of repression;[4] but it is not easy to see how one can make this kind of diagnosis testable. One formulation states that in those cultures where appropriate rituals are performed, the main burden of grief is time-limited in a way which it is not elsewhere. This does have the merit of being testable; and there is some crosscultural evidence for such a view.[5] But this formulation necessarily leaves open the possibility that rituals of transition at death are not universal, not even in the sense of being a universal need which is occasionally repressed; and this recognition again leaves open the explanation of what is happening in the industrial West.

Another way of looking at the problem is to consider the history of Western death practices, to see by what stages the change has occurred, and what has happened in the process to Hertz's three elements—the body, the soul, and the mourner—and to their supposed correspondence. In Ariès's work there are certainly successive correspondences of a sort in the ritual expression of Hertz's three elements.[6] In the early Middle Ages, collective burial round the church is matched by the notion of a collective resting place of the souls of the dead, awaiting the resurrection, and this corresponds to a communal rite of mourning. From the late Middle Ages the individual soul in purgatory matches individualized tombs and individual bequeathal of legacies for masses. The garden cemeteries conceived by the Enlightenment and built in the nineteenth century correspond with the concept of a family reunion in the world beyond and with the practice of grave-visiting. And cremation seems to correspond with the simultaneous end of soul and body and with the abolition of mourning ritual. I have stated these symmetries too simply, but my aim is to bring out their shape in the context of Hertz's formulation.

There remains, however, the problem of explaining the European transition through these successive stages. Perhaps the strongest explanatory feature is that invoked for the transition to the melancholy style of the nineteenth century—the development of the domesticated nuclear family. But there is an obscurity about the reasons for the twentieth-century suppression of mourning which is particularly important for a contemporary study. One can point to the centuries-long intensification of self-control and personal delicacy in Europe,[7] and to the similarly slow shift from ritualized group behaviour to impersonal market dealing,[8] but these gradual processes seem inadequate to account for the abruptness and the exact timing of this phenomenon.

If we are looking for something specific to this century, one leading contender must be the demographic explanation. Death now occurs mostly among the old, this argument runs, and therefore amongst those now considered to be least needed for the work of society. In so far as they are devalued, and only too easily replaced, their death has little symbolic significance, and thus there is no need to assert spiritual survival, or to take any prolonged care of their body.

However, there is a problem with this somewhat disillusioned view as well. For the geography of the change is puzzling. It seemed to Ariès that it was originally in some way an 'Anglo-Saxon' thing. It might have been a Protestant one but for evidence such as Gorer's that traditional mourning had been especially long-lived in Presbyterian Scotland.[9] A Scottish study may thus be strategically placed to cast some light on this problem. At the same time the date of the decline of mourning has prompted another author to consider the neglected effect of war, and especially the First World War, on this aspect of things.[10] These are all possibilities which need evaluation with the aid of further evidence; and both the archaeological strata of thought discerned by Ariès, and the explanation for their evolution, are reconsidered at the end of this chapter in the light of Aberdonian attitudes to mourning.

Mourning in Aberdeen

The Aberdonians I met were conscious that much had changed during their lifetime in the customary way of dealing with a death. First there was an old style of mourning, more prevalent in their youth than now, which included, besides grave-visiting and the keeping of death dates, the wearing of dark colours for a period after the funeral, and abstention for a period of months from the same sort of leisure activities as were proscribed on the Scottish Sunday. This was a Lowland pattern, to be distinguished from customs encountered in Highland areas. Native Aberdonians who had visited the Highlands noted the peculiarity of the wake, were shocked by the heavy consumption of whisky there, but were impressed by the carrying of the coffin on foot and the insistence on all clothes being dark-coloured; while an émigré Gael differed only in remembering the Highland funeral not with disapproval but with nostalgia as being 'like a marriage—many of them too far gone to hold the coffin'. The old Aberdonian way was not at all like this, agreeing only in the wearing of black. According to local recollections, it was originally a stronger version of the pattern found to be surviving in Lowland Scotland by Gorer in 1963, when over a third of those he surveyed were still accepting limitations of dress and activity after a death, though normally only for short periods of between a week and a month. But even for those who still followed the old style, such restrictions were no longer expected in Aberdeen in 1980; rather the old way was outwardly marked only by burial and by keeping up the grave.

The opportunity for an alternative to the old style was provided by the Aberdeen crematorium, the first version of which opened in 1937. Cremation removes the necessity of keeping up a grave, but it still offers a number of choices which include an inscription in the book of remembrance at the crematorium, which can be viewed on the anniversary of the death; visits to the garden of remembrance where ashes are scattered; and the leaving of wreaths or flowers in the chapel on occasions such as Christmas, Easter, or the anniversaries of birth and death. But there is no general expectation that any of these options should be taken up, and they often are not.

Public expectations which are common to both these ways of dealing with a death are therefore few, and they cluster around the time of the funeral, after which no standard progression of mourning is now assumed. Instead, there is a range of choice about how to cope with a bereavement, which varies between memorial observances of different kinds on the one hand, and the strict resumption of the appearance of normality on the other; and the choice made is assumed to last into an indefinite future.

In this situation it may be illuminating to look not so much at the behaviour which is prescribed after a death, as at the meanings which are cast on the event in talk. There are indeed many details of behaviour after a death, even in this very restrained milieu, which a more extended observational study could bring out; but in general, sorrow in Aberdeen is a private matter, and much of its shape is expressed only in intimate conversation.

Reflections on a death focused mainly on two things—the situation of the dead, and the situation of the bereaved; and I describe the ideas held about each in turn.

The situation of the dead

Not surprisingly, the condition of the dead depended initially on beliefs about whether or not there was some sort of life after death; but the range of positions taken on this issue was narrow. First there was an undifferentiated denial of any form of life after death. Occasionally this denial countered a clearly stated range of beliefs typified, for example, by the idea of reunion with kin, and was tied to a clear assertion that these beliefs were impossible because death is the end of consciousness, or because the only immortality lay in effects of the influence exerted on others during one's lifetime:

"Sometimes I think that memories of people are what lives on. In a way, what we are is the result of everybody else having been what they are; and I have been formed by my parents, and I am the continuation."

Here consciousness and feeling in the dead were denied, while their formative role was accepted. But more often the denial was simply an inability to make sense of what was assumed to be asserted by others, whose content was as vague as the phrase 'life after death' itself.

A similar undifferentiated vagueness also sometimes appeared in the accounts of those who did assert a life after death; but generally the beliefs involved were more specific. The usual conception was a reunion with kin, in a better place. In its simplest form the reunion was only after death, and was 'waited for' during the period of separation by the dead and, often, by the living; but in a more elaborate form the reunion was also anticipated by communication from the dead to the living, in a dream, or by a sense of their presence, or by contact of varying casualness through a medium. Resort to a medium rarely denoted a distinctively spiritualist adherence, and could merely be regarded as one kind of link with the dead efficacious in, for instance, a particular crisis. But an emphasis on the dead as spirit, in explicit opposition to body, emerged in several comments on relations with dead kin; and this emphasis sometimes seemed to represent a reaction against imagery based on the corpse. For example, symbolism such as that of a Catholic priest, who claimed that 'If you come back to the church, your father's body will rest easier', struck even a lapsed Catholic as incongruous. Hence a sharp separation between spirit and body, and an emphasis on the spirit, seemed to underlie these ideas of ultimate reunion with, and present communication from, dead kin.

This other-worldly order in terms of kinship tended to overbear any alternative order in terms of judgement. Judgement implied hell, and it was not obvious who should be consigned to hell. It was not, for instance, easy, in a society of many denominations and much intermarriage, to see hell as the fate of those outside one's own church, for then close relatives might be condemned. A few Aberdonians solved the problem by thinking of hell as a place for extreme crimes only, arguing that without it 'people could do any-thing'. And a few glanced very obliquely at ideas of graduated punishment and purification—only to reject them as obviously

'Catholic'. Hence in the virtual absence of ways to harmonize the loyalties of kinship with belief in judgement, it became necessary to reject judgement altogether—a need accentuated also by personal anxiety deriving from memories of hellfire preaching in childhood. And this rejection produced variously a world of the dead exclusively organized around kinship, or a world of the dead with no clear attributes, or finally no world of the dead at all:

"I don't want to believe in an afterlife because it would bring back all my fears of judgement and not having done my duty."

The main division, then, in Aberdonian thinking about the other world, was between this interpretation of it in terms of family reunion, and the sceptical denial of any life beyond the grave. Not surprisingly, this was an opposition which did not always give rise to any positive internal dilemma; sometimes it gave issue merely to a question, for which no immediate pressures required even a guessed answer:

I'll tell you this, my mother never came back to me in my dreams. Although me and Mum were so close she's never come back to me in my dreams after she died. You hear folk say when something was going to happen Uncle Bob came and stood at the foot of the bed and said this and that. But mother never came back. If we go somewhere I dinna ken where we go.

"I don't know if there's an afterlife or not. I've gone to the Spiritualist Church with friends occasionally. I've had messages, but the messages don't convince you somehow because they're always about the past, and they never tell you anything about the other side."

However the opposition became unequivocal in dialogue between those who held the different views firmly. When a conversation with a convinced spiritualist was interrupted, the following exchange took place:

RW: "We were talking about spiritualism. Do you have any beliefs that . . .?"
Arrival: "We are in *complete* disagreement."
Spiritualist: "Yes, Fiona—she's not having any the noo of these ghosts coming back."
Arrival: "I don't think there's anything. I think immortality is what you've left behind, yourself, your influence on other people. That to me is immortality and I don't believe in any other."
Spiritualist: "Your mother's listening to you right now."
Arrival: "She didn't either."
Spiritualist: "No, no."

Arrival: "She said to me a week before she died, 'It's time I was away—you see I think it *is* the end.' And I was just getting the house dusted, and I said, 'I agree.'"

Spiritualist: "Oh we agree to differ. It'll be a pleasant surprise, Fiona, when they're all waiting for you."

Arrival: "Oh I don't know. I think there are people I don't want to see again."

Only once was an attempt made to bridge this chasm of contradiction between death as the end of consciousness and death as reunion with kin, but it was so tentative that I was unable to get the nature of the attempt clear.

These ideas about the fate of the mind, spirit, or consciousness of the dead were accompanied also by varying attitudes to the body. On the one hand a sacred aura could be felt to surround both the body itself and its last resting place; and it was felt that the body should end in an identified and symbolic place, usually with kin. Such a burial place, whether for the body or for ashes, provided the focus for what was felt vaguely to be a 'religious' ritual of grave-visiting; the remains were themselves essentially sacred, and horseplay with the gravestones reported in the papers shocked because it suggested that in that case nothing was sacred. On the whole such ideas were connected with burial rather than cremation; but cremation might itself be useful because it actually allowed access to a symbolic resting place, when, for example, the family plot was far away, or there was not enough space in it for another burial.

Other views of how to deal with the dead differed, however, by rejecting burial or the cult of grave-visiting and by giving priority to the interests of the living. These interests were conceived as those either of kin or of the community at large. The aim of saving close kin, usually children, expense and work, even at times of saving them the embarrassment of talking about the practicalities of a parent's death, was the reason why some people made their own detailed plans for their funerals; and some also justified on these grounds their choice of what was seen as the present trend away from a laying out at home, and towards the 'rest room' or funeral parlour. And while a deference to close kin could give some public tolerance to displays of grief, the interests of the family were generally assumed to be in the curtailment rather than the elaboration of funerary effort; and the interests of the wider community were likewise argued mainly in the direction of restricting the degree of attention paid to the corpse. Cremation was in this context singled out as a positive value, not merely a special tactic, since it saved the ground otherwise needed for big cemeteries, and expunged dreaded diseases like TB which might otherwise 'come up out of the ground'. Similarly donating one's body to medicine was argued as a possible communal use for an otherwise valueless article, though it was also felt that an old body might be too useless even for this purpose. In so far as it was useful, the act of giving it represented, to this way of thinking, gratitude to the institution of medicine or altruism towards the society of the living.

The opposition between these two approaches to the body was felt unequivocally, and I quote examples later in which this opposition was tied up with other notions. However, while the two views tended to be associated with burial and cremation, the association was blurred by other considerations and circumstances such as those I have described; and the essential distinction remained as one between a 'religious' way of thinking which commemorated the particular identity and resting place of the corpse, and an altruistic way of thinking, a consideration for others, which demanded the corpse's efficient and rapid disposal.

The situation of the dead was thus defined in terms of two separate sets of ideas concerning the body and the soul respectively; and I consider the relation between these twin aspects shortly.

The situation of the bereaved

The experience of bereavement was described by Aberdonians in terms of a single overwhelming tension between the replaceable and irreplaceable aspects of loss. Thus on the one hand there was the loss of a person, which was in principle not calculable nor replaceable; while on the other hand there were secondary losses of whole sectors of social connections and of resources for social participation which were eminently calculable and desirable, though difficult, to replace.

Amongst these calculable secondary losses, poverty after the loss of a father, the scattering of brothers and sisters after the loss of a mother, the ending of connections with a place of origin after the death of parents, grandparents, or siblings are common themes which were all represented; but the typical case on which thoughts naturally centred in this age group was marital bereavement, and specifically, for obvious reasons of frequency, widowhood. A feature of twentieth-century demography has been the increasing preponderance of widows, and the increasing rarity of widowers, following marital bereavement. Hence while widowers certainly suffered secondary losses of social connections, such as those, for example, which had depended on hospitality in the home, and their situation was in many ways the lonelier for its rarity, popular wisdom focused on the secondary losses of widows.

Primarily, widows were felt to lose not only their husbands but, in one eloquent phrase, 'married society' as well. Like all familiar facts, this was not always an easy phenomenon to explain. Many couples continued to invite widows, and some relationships with couples were sustained, but new acquaintanceships made between widows and couples did not seem to 'take', and many old acquaintanceships fell off:

"I always think fin [when] the man seems tae go the connections seems tae—tae break. I find that wi' a lot o' people, you know. Same with your friends. When one of the partners goes, it just seems to break up, you know?"

"You find that with friends?"

"Yes, aye. You know the wife's left on her own. Well the couples don't come to the house because there's not a man there, and the other way about."

"Yes I've heard people say something like that."

"And I think it's a shame—because that's when they need ye."

A stigma was felt which was at times almost metaphysical: widows were 'hard to place'; at a dance or social event 'you want a balance,' and where 'it used to be six or four, now it's five or three, and you feel the gap'. The ceremonial impropriety of odd numbers in social gatherings has of course a long European history; but the issues here were in fact more than ceremonial. Relationships between a widow and a couple were felt to be resented by the wife: one widow was careful to answer invitations from husbands by saying, 'I'll wait for your wife to ring.' It was not only monogamous but also financial proprieties which were involved—another widow stated the case with forthright precision:

"The women resent their men spending money on you; and the men don't like it when you pay your way."

"Is it the paying thing then?"

"Oh but the women don't want you to take their men away. It all comes down to the demon sex in the end. And the men all think a widow's desperate for it—they make a dead set. Some of them are of course."

With very old friends the difficulty could be surmounted, but it was sufficiently present to become an institutionalized joke, in which wives would allude to their husband's harem. Similarly with childless couples too, according to some, relations were easier— perhaps because the presence of children underlined an orientation towards the future rather than towards contemporaries and the past. In one sense of course widows as mothers themselves had such an orientation; but in this respect too they could feel disabled. It was assumed by one widow that her grandchildren over from New Zealand would spend longer with the other side of the family, where the grandparental couple was still intact, than with her, 'because I can't offer them a grandfather'. Thus the institutional primacy of marriage penetrated into many remote corners, and widows could be at a disadvantage in any of them.

Despite the apparent softening of sexual divisions in British society over the last century, then, despite the weakening of mourning restrictions, despite the redress attempted by many friendly couples, and despite the fact that these widows were over 60 years old, there remained an unmistakable assumption in society as they perceived it that a widow did not fit in, was in that sense stigmatized, and was moreover sexually dangerous; and with this partial exclusion from married society went a loss of the attributes assumed of the married: command over resources, shared activities, a shared table. Fear of debt was accompanied by a sense of vulnerability to fraud and an unwillingness to fight for one's preferences against, for instance, council housing allocators; activities felt to require a companion, like holidays, evenings out, joint leisure pastimes, even shopping in the city centre, were given up; and the daily structure of shared meals collapsed, making 'eating sensibly' not a routine but a task to be borne in mind.

These secondary losses were common to many; but there was also the aspect of bereavement which was unique to each person— the relationship which was gone, and the time of life in which it had flourished. Aberdonians do not like to 'greet' (weep), and they had few words for such matters; and one who did weep, and subsequently found words to express the cause, was only able to do so through the oblique imagery of misfortune inherited from Scottish folk belief—and even this was an accident, and a continuing source of surprise:

"I never cried . . . never cried at all. And even at the funeral I never cried. And it wasn't until I found a piece of wood, a chip from a tree—is this deviating? We had a rowan tree which is supposed to be very lucky, and I had planted it. We were great folk for walks in the woods, my father as well was with us at this time, came home with this rowan tree and we planted it. But we planted it too near the house you see. As it grew, it grew away, the roots were going under the house, and oh, the rowan tree was about this fat, you know, it wasn't a slender rowan tree at all. And everybody that came said you should get rid of that rowan tree, and my mother always said, 'No, no, it's not lucky to get rid of a rowan tree.' And just about a fortnight before she died we had to get this gardener in because the garden was getting in an awful mess and I couldn't cope with it all. And he said, 'Oh for a start, that tree's coming down,' you see, and she agreed. And it was lying there, this great big rowan tree, and unknown to me she'd kept a chip of the tree, and written on it in pencil was 'Jeannie's tree, cut down on such and such a date.' And it was in a box—and I came across that in this box—and then I cried. Funny things isn't it how . . . the things you do when you're young. And I just cried, and cried, and cried."

There was unconscious eloquence in this recognition of intrinsic loss; and it was the rowan tree, which in Scottish folklore wards off evil from the house, that released it, unbidden and unforeseen, coincidentally echoing, in its life and its death, the child's vision of its mother.

For the most part, though, the uniqueness of loss was expressed in a number of brief, almost ritual phrases whose hackneyed character could nevertheless belie an intensity of inarticulate feeling: 'never the same after', 'nae life for me then', 'canna forget it', 'a long, long time to get over it'. Similarly it was symbolic of this uniqueness of the loss that people had for a time felt also a wish to resist substitutes, to be alone, to avoid other company.

That this irreplaceability should be affirmed was however so much a premiss of familial affection and loyalty that it only needed saying in certain contexts which were themselves significant—those, for the most part, where an opposed statement was about to follow. There were various of these oppositions, but the usual contrast was with the need nevertheless to make a new life, to have the company of other relationships, to replace what was replaceable. The irretrievable nature of the loss was expressed, in fact, precisely because it was threatened by the concomitant necessity of assessing and retrieving as much of the loss as possible. Such opportunities for restoring secondary losses were, it is true, never felt to be more than partial, and were often severely lacking. The most complete strategy was remarriage; however remarriage after bereavement rather than divorce was distinguished as a lesser kind of marriage, merely companionship, not the same as the relationship from which one's family sprang. Otherwise a shift towards the society of other widows, an effort to sustain such relationships with couples as remained possible, or a move towards joining organized groups were the only options commonly seen to be available. There was a sense that more help was needed, but little idea of what form it could take; and eventually the loss, remaining for the most part unredeemed, was merely dulled by time.

Limited as these ameliorative options were, however, all could be felt to stand in opposition to what was intrinsic and unique in the loss of bereavement, even the dulling effect of time:

" 'It'll pass' or 'Time will heal'—never say that to anybody who's recently bereaved. It's silly, you don't *want* to believe that, it's just no use. Yet it does [pass], it's true."

Initially, then, the need to reconstruct was inevitably in conflict with loyalty to the dead; but for most, the conflict eventually subsided. Perhaps this conflict is in some degree universal soon after a death; but it is actually distinct from the basic conflict involved in grief—the clash between the wish for the past and the fact of the present. In addition to this conflict between wish and fact, Aberdonians felt a conflict between the wish for the past and a responsibility for the future. For example, Andrew Tait had found himself, for some months after his wife's sudden death, obsessively looking at head scarves, looking, as he began to realize, for the scarf which his wife wore; he had thought he was going mad, felt that 'if there was a hole, you'd crawl away into it'. But at the same time he had felt that 'you can't go on doing that or you'll cut yourself off; told himself that he must take up social life again—a responsibility made more urgent by the fact that, with some of his friends who 'didn't know what to say', it was he who had to make the first move.

This confusion and ambivalence in the months following bereavement, between loyalty to the dead and the need to take the initiative in restoring social life, was paralleled again in the months before bereavement in the case of Ann Nicol. She guessed, and events confirmed, that her husband had not long to live; and the recognition precipitated a conflict between her present reliance on him and her anxiety for the future—her sense that she must make her own preparations to manage the reordering of social life which would soon be needed. First was the question of money, the expectation of 'a big drop', the knowledge of never having had to cope on a low budget; and this was followed in due course by the expectation of collapses in the fabric of family and friendship. This anticipation of social loss, and the sense of a pressing need to advance to meet it, had accordingly led her to start behaving in some ways as if her husband was already dead:

"I suppose if ye're on your own you just have tae manage, have ye . . . . I think ye get a kind o' warnin' beforehand and ye just kind o' start being that extra careful, you know. I've noticed that this last year."

"You've started being extra careful?"

"Aye. Just in different things, you know."

"What sort of things do you mean?"

"Well it's hard to explain really, it's eh, hard to explain. We don't go out the same, and things like that. More a recluse."

Then the difficulty, increasingly evident in this quotation, of anticipating what should not be anticipated, diverted the conversation into euphemism:

"You mean you're sort of preparing yourself?"

"I think so. Like *I* could be away first, that's it, I mean I could get knocked down by a bus you know."

This paradoxical conclusion was evidently an escape from the unacceptable fact that it was her husband's loss for which she was preparing. On the one hand was the sense that her concern should be for her husband, while on the other hand was the knowledge shared by women of their ultimate fate as widows, so markedly defined by secondary losses:

"People that we meet—we used to go to the club, you know—ladies, they used to speak about it, used to say 'Well I used to have friends that came to the house, but after my husband died they stopped coming, because there isn't a man in the house,' you know . . . . But ye'll hear that, and eh, conversation at work and that, I hear them saying. I think it wis kind o'—well it scared me, you know. People dinna realize they're saying it, do they?"

In both these cases, then, loyalty to the dying or the dead was felt to be in conflict with an opposite pressure to make an effort towards adapting to, or reconstructing, a new social position—a pressure which is especially strong when the process of reconstruction is not dictated by custom, but is a matter for individual responsibility.

It may be, then, that individual responsibility for choice helps to generate or exacerbate the conflict between past and future soon after a death; but while in Aberdeen the conflict usually subsided in time as the past was laid to rest, there were also cases where the past still troubled the present, and these pose additional questions. What was most noticeable about these aggravated instances was the belief, already discussed, that death was morally appropriate only to old age—a belief which had been breached by the premature death of someone close. Periods of three years, six years, even fifteen years had been insufficient in some cases to achieve a reconciliation between these opposing understandings, and in one case the resulting conflict had been passed on to the next generation and was still present in attenuated form fifty years later. The precipitating event in this last instance was the death of Jessie Thomson's mother in middle age:

"I'm not a member of a church; I was brought up very much within the church and attended everything that could be attended in the church, until the war. And then after we came back from the war—I just never picked up the threads again . . . . My father influenced me that way because my mother had an exploratory operation a while before she died, but he wasn't told that she wouldn't live for long after that. And he'd been to church on the Sunday, and it was a very well known minister at that time and he was a very good preacher, and his sermon was 'They shall not hurt or destroy on my holy mountain.' And my mother had been ill that weekend; and he came home from church, and he just felt, well, everything's going to be all right, and this sermon was to *him*. And she died the next day. And he just thought, you know . . . his faith sort of left him. You know you begin to see how . . . how hypocritical everyone is—not *everyone* in church but—how they were dressed, and—you begin to get more cynical. How so and so had on a new hat, and such and such had on the same old coat. It was a West End church that we were brought up in. I don't know, I just sort of lost . . . not faith, I don't know if I ever had faith. But occasionally I feel I want to go to church, and occasionally I'll go alone."

Here the continuing conflict centred on the church; indeed religious adherence was several times identified in this way with the expectation of a natural term of life, and although there seem to be few grounds for this identification in Christian, rather than specifically Old Testament, theology, its validity was taken for granted:

Mrs Gilbert then began talking about her son-in-law's death and she flushed and tears came into her eyes. Her daughter always went to the church and the Guild, and so did she, and it makes you think why did it happen to her? It turned the daughter very bitter. The minister only came to see her once, after all she'd done for the church. Well she never went again. Now the new minister's come to see her but she said she's found something to fill her life with working for the Red Cross and that'll do her now.

Similarly Maureen Baikie commented, apropos the deaths of her sisters:

I have a friend who says she's been helped by going to church. But then I think if she's so mean and she goes to church why does God help her? Then I think of my sister who'd give anything to anyone. She once gave away her husband's new shirt to a jumble sale. She went to church. I used to say, oh don't speak to me about church. And then she died so young. They all died so young.

Maureen Baikie was vulnerable partly because she was divided between belief and scepticism in regard to other-worldly consolations. Nevertheless a more committed scepticism than hers was not necessarily a defence against expectations of a normal span of life, nor against the wider expectation of freedom from suffering with which it was connected. James Dearness had 'never been convinced of anything' about life after death, despite a normal religious upbringing. When his wife was taken into hospital she was put in the same ward as a neighbour in her sixties, but 'the neighbour came out and my wife didn't—she was the young one, and the old one survived'. As he spoke he suddenly became hoarse and looked away:

"After she went I felt a bit . . . bitter, I must admit, selfishly so perhaps— because she was a very good type of woman, was very popular, was just . . . very good. And then she was *stricken* with this thing, which was *ghastly,* and . . . what a shame, that she suffered, that length of time, and she was a very good person. That was . . . I was bitter shall I say."

Then he collected himself and gradually reasserted his scepticism and the role of chance:

"Yes, that was wrong. I feel it was a temporary thing, you know, but . . . I just . . . never will . . . I don't know."
"You felt in a way . . . I mean, that you'd been cheated?"

"No, because I'd rather . . . that's life, it doesn't go to a pattern at all. I mean that's just silly, to think in that way."

All these examples, then, reveal the power and tenacity of beliefs in a this-worldly justice of nature or providence, and their specific manifestation in the claims of good people to a natural span of life.

Nevertheless, for all their strength and stubbornness, these were not universal beliefs, nor were they universally expressed by those who had been bereaved by an untimely death. A further eleven people, for instance, had lost husbands or wives through deaths occurring before the age of 60: most of these expressed their grief, but indicated at the same time that it was in the past, and none referred to the injustice of dying so young. Thus the practical and moral expectation of a natural span, while the commonest of all precepts on the timing of death, emerged as only one distinctive view of it, and a view notably liable to contradiction, conflict, and unresolved mourning.

Moreover, just as belief in a natural term of life contrasted in the last chapter with notions of preparing for an appointed time, so another view of premature death was voiced by Aberdonians which depended on the notion that such readiness had been accomplished. The readiness of the dead for the death which had overtaken them could be perceived in two senses. Understood in one sense, it followed from the fulfilment before death of personal hopes or aims, and consolation could be drawn from the fact that even when dying prematurely, a person could say 'I've had a damned good life'. Understood in a second sense, however, readiness betokened not so much a personal fulfilment as the renewal of relationships with others in explicitly Christian terms—a brother's enemy was ready to die when they had been reconciled, a mother was ready to die after the resolution of a family tragedy. This retrospective view could also include, as an added consolation, the idea that death was natural in old age; but for those who died before their natural term, and for those who mourned them, the notion of destiny and of readiness was the only thing capable of providing alleviation. Andrew Tait, haunted by the suggestion that if he had watched for signs of his wife's vulnerability, and had helped her to live prudently, she would have lived her term, countered the problem by a shift towards the notion of destiny:

The doctor understood this guilt thing—if I'd seen the signs, if I'd stopped her in time. But when your time's up, it's up, I'm a great believer in that.

Even when you're born, you're a day nearer. If you're going to go, all the medicine in the world canna stop you.

Similarly, Nancy Paterson, shaken by her husband's early death, had to cope in addition with her mother's sense of its unnaturalness:

"It broke her heart when Sam died of course. I had to tell her just about a day or two before he died. She kept saying 'You know it should have been me; it's not fair.' There you are, that's just . . ."

"Yes of course. That would not be a help to you."

"No. You had to keep saying it's not a case of that. We can't arrange these things, they just happen."

Her own resolution of the problem, however, went beyond this bare sense that expectations of this-worldly justice were irrelevant:

"I have an awful lot of faith—well I think I have anyway, it's kept me going—and I have absolute faith that one day this is all going to just pass, and I'm going to be with him again."

And correspondingly, reviewing her husband's life, she became convinced that the timing of his death had its own kind of sense:

"Fortunately, I always look back with great gratitude, that I met Sam when I was just turned 18; you see we were married when I was 23 and a half. Well counting that time, about 5 years, along with the fact we'd 19 years of marriage, I had quite a long time of happiness, you know—25 years all told, and that's quite a lot you see. And then I had the girls which again gave me a stake, you know, something of him. And that I think was what kept me going . . . You see after Sam died, I thought, well he's just got all his wishes fulfilled really. I mean, he had the girls, and he had his home and he had made a success of his job and he really had done extremely well, you know, in the while he had."

In this way, then, a sense that a fulfilment had been achieved which made even an early death acceptable, and a conviction that death was to be seen not in this-worldly but in other-worldly terms, enabled her to set aside the sense of injustice pressed on her by her mother's view of the natural order governing the time of dying.

There was thus a specific cultural context in which unresolved contradictions of grief were expressed—a context characterized on the one hand by a sense of the dead having had an unfulfilled claim to a natural span of life, and on the other hand by a sense that the bereaved had sole responsibility for reconstructing their lives.

These ideas about mourning must now be considered in relation to those concerning the soul and body of the dead, in order to see their overall pattern.

Themes and dilemmas

The chief ways in which these Aberdonians thought about the dead and the experience of grief can be typified in six ideas which, simplified as they are in the following formulation, help to point up underlying patterns of consistency and contradiction. In the description already given, one pair of opposed ideas has emerged in each of the three main aspects of death; and the first of these relates to life after death, or—though Aberdonians seldom use this term—to the state of the soul. On the soul's condition the two chief ideas, mutually opposed, were these:

4.1 *Reunion*
When we die, we are at once united with our family in the next world.

4.2 *Annihilation*
When we die, nothing of us lives on except in others' memories.

At the same time, two principal oppositions emerged concerning the way in which the body should be dealt with:

4.3 *The sanctity of the body*
It is a religious act to visit the grave and keep it up.

4.4 *The interests of the living*
The body should be disposed of so as to minimize problems for the living.

Finally, grief itself was the subject of two contrary conceptions:

4.5 *The uniqueness of loss*
The person who has died is unique and irreplaceable.

4.6 *The need for replacement*
Grief must be got over and a new life begun.

The way in which these six ideas combined was affected not only by explicit forms of logical relationship, but also by one significant absence of relationship which is peculiar to the present topic, and which concerns grief and the need to replace a loss.

The need for replacement was in some way an impotent idea, expressed only in one context—the context already described, in which it acted as a counterweight to the opposed idea that the loss was unique and irreplaceable. The need to make a new life was not linked, as it might plausibly have been, to rapid disposal of the corpse, nor to lack of belief in an afterlife. Nor was the theme of replacing loss an acceptable one on its own, without a concomitant expression of the loss's irreplaceability. These are important facts, which signal, not the callousness or stoicism of contemporary attitudes to the dead, but on the contrary their naked emphasis on loss, and their inability to create a symbolic framework and a time structure for its subsequent healing.

In the absence, then, of any cultural framework to give shape and confirmation to the idea of replacing a loss, the patterns of thought available to Aberdonians were effectively built from the other five ideas which I have outlined; and amongst these, for the first time in the topics dealt with in this book, no wholly coherent pattern emerges. This is to put the case strongly, for, on the subject of the dead, thoughts tend necessarily to be somewhat cloudy and speculative; but within the limitations of this sort of topic, in which the practical choices entailed are few, and opposing alternatives do not always need to be well defined, the evidence is that while there were three almost coherent patterns into which ideas about the dead could be fitted, each pattern involved some degree of felt inconsistency at some point.

The first of these near-coherent patterns which Aberdonians drew on in thinking about the dead represented what they thought of as the old order. It included the reunion of the dead person with kin in the next world (4.1), and the sanctity of the body and the grave (4.3), with an emphasis on the irreplaceability of the loss (4.5). What marked these ideas out as having some consonance with each other was the way in which a belief in the ultimate reunion of the family, and the act of tending the grave, could both be felt to imply a continuing relationship of fidelity to the person who had died. A partial example has already been given in Nancy Paterson's story of how the hope of reunion sustained her memories of her husband, as well as reconciling her to his loss; and future reunion easily turned, as I noted earlier, into present communion: 'I was very happy with my husband,' another woman told me, 'And he's still with me. I have lots of friends, but he is *the* friend.' This husband's faith in life after death certified his wife's faith in it, and it was in this context that she spoke of his continuing presence. Similarly the keeping of his grave, which was planted with flowers and maintained with regular visits, was spoken of in the same breath as her regular meetings with her daughter, as evidence of family loyalty as it ought to be, and as it was not in the case of some of her friends. Thus fidelity was expressed in caring for the grave, and endorsed by future hopes, and from this point of view there was sufficient harmony in this way of thinking to suggest the basis at least for a coherent pattern.

Nevertheless, some people felt there to be an anomaly in thus joining the spiritual meaning of future reunion or present communion with such attention to the buried body. Reunion was not conceived as a gradual process like the body's decay, but as something which happened immediately. Indeed, amongst the evidences of communication from dead relatives which tended to confirm a belief in reunion, one lay in the appearance of dead relatives to the dying:

"There was an awful bonny smile on her face, and she jist waved like this. She says, 'I'm comin' Dod'—that was to my father, she aye called him Dod, George was his name. I'm comin' Dod, jist as though she hid seen him, with the smile over her face."

Hence in cases like this, where reunion seemed imminent as the last moments approached, and where reunion was in any case defined as the final state of the dead, there was no reason to interpose any progression of stages in the experience of the soul, and certainly no reason to see this experience as in any way tied to treatment of the body after death. In fact the old pattern of mourning had confused body and spirit, so some felt, in a way which was grotesque—a conclusion well exemplified in the following conversation:

1st friend: "I was scared stiff of being buried alive. I was terrified of that. It was with these little brothers, and you know you were always up to the cemetery."

2nd friend: "You knew about cemeteries, yes."

1st friend: "Every Sunday, to put down the flowers, and I always hated going away and leaving them. You always felt they were there. Mother had a wire cross into which she put lavender and white sweet peas, and carried it up in tartan, and when you'd put flowers on the grave off you went for a walk. That's gone out of date. Though I remember a child not long ago saying to me 'Went down to see Daddy yesterday.' 'Oh? And where does Daddy live?'—'Doon in Trinity cemetery.'"

2nd friend: "I think that's a wee bitty macabre, for children."

In rejecting this emphasis on the grave as 'out-of-date', the chief speaker in this conversation was reasserting the immediate spiritual contact of those who die with their kin, as exemplified in a later remark that 'We don't get disturbed or morbid about it, but I do believe that your people come.' And while it was quite possible for some to accept both emphases without felt inconsistency—to assent to this immediate spiritual transition, and still to treat the body left behind in the grave as a symbol of ultimate family reunion—this was evidently felt by others to have sinister and irrational implications.

The same sharp distinction between spirit and body, which thus gave rise to these problems with the old pattern of mourning, was responsible also for the coherent core of two new patterns. The first of these patterns combined the familiar emphases on reunion of the newly dead with their kin (4.1) and the uniqueness of the person lost (4.5) with the rapid disposal of the body in the interests of the living (4.4). The soul being gone to those on the other side, and the body thus done with, the fate of the body was the subject of the purely secular considerations mentioned earlier—not taking up land with cemeteries, not leaving relatives with unnecessary work and unpleasant duties. The interests of the close family were not indeed conceived of in wholly utilitarian terms. For example, they also required a strong show of support at the funeral. But where the funeral was Catholic, and carried additional overtones of doubtful doctrines about the soul, the pragmatic view was reasserted, and the ceremonies of mourners around the body were tersely disjoined from the fate of the soul. 'The dead's awa', I was firmly told by a reluctant Protestant attender, evidently pre-empting enquiry, 'The funeral's for them that's left.' And in another case, symbolism at a Catholic funeral—or suspected symbolism—which did not seem to relate purely to the feelings of the mourners, was regarded with scandalized embarrassment:

Black from head to foot, and dark glasses as well. It was like a Mafia funeral. I thought maybe the glasses were because they'd been crying, but they took them off in church—and you couldna *ask*.

Protestants were thus sometimes uneasy with Catholic funerals, and the unease was directed at anything apparently superfluous to the practical needs of the living, and especially at any notion that the funerary rites around the body had a relation to the state of the soul.

It is obvious that very little had to be changed in this complex of ideas to create the other new pattern which was available to Aberdonians—one in which the expectation of reunion with kin at death (4.1) was replaced by the belief that death was the end of consciousness (4.2). People in either of these two camps could agree that after death the body had no further function or personal significance, and should be dealt with as was required by the interests of the living; and people in either camp could nevertheless join in expressing, despite their need to get over it, the loss of the person, and the continuing ache of a particular affection. Divided in their view of the soul, they could share every other aspect of mourning.

However, just as there was a dissonant element in the old pattern of mourning, so also in these two new patterns there was something that jarred, though in a different place. The two new patterns had in common both a determined pragmatism about disposal of the body (4.4), and a sensibility towards the unique aspect of personal loss (4.5); and these two sentiments did not always combine happily. It was certainly easy enough to espouse both attitudes when taking different perspectives—to be pragmatic about one's own funeral arrangements while expressing personal feeling about the death of someone else. In such instances there was an emotional continuity, whether or not there was a logical inconsistency, in that both attitudes expressed the same care for others—in the one case sparing trouble to survivors, in the other case conserving a relationship from the past. But sometimes people felt the force of practical and personal considerations in the same context, and this was uncomfortable. Penelope Taylor, for example, was pragmatic in some respects: she saw the body as simply something left over, and had never taken an interest in her parents' grave; indeed the arrival of 'religious' relatives who 'had to go to my mother's grave and arrange some flowers' severely embarrassed her.

"I couldn't tell them I didn't know where my mother and father's grave was, because I mean they were very religious."

A hasty subterfuge gave her time to find the man at the Lodge who kept the book, and the embarrassment was passed off. But although she did not think that the grave was a proper focus for reverence, she still disliked the impersonal, routine character of cremation, and, more than that, the concealment of this character beneath a veneer of ritual:

"I don't want to be cremated. I don't know why. Yes, I *can* tell you why. It's not that I . . . the body's finished with anyway, but the crematorium is to me far too false. I won't go to a funeral there. I just won't go. I've only been twice and, I don't know, there's something awfully false about it. So Americanized with piped music, and you've got to hurry out and you've got to shake hands with the poor person at the door, and the other lot are waiting to get in, and they can't—you've got to get out quick so the next lot can come in."

Here, then, was the centralized, mass institution of the crematorium, certainly the most practical way of dealing with the useless physical remains, apparently destroying the unique, personal nature of loss, while pretending not to. Perhaps, for Penelope Taylor, there might have been a resolution of the problem, which could combine her dismissive attitude to the body with an expression of her personal character as a passionate fisherwoman and naturalist, but this was precluded by other practicalities of environmental health:

"I don't want any fuss . . . . I would like to be put in a plain box, and I would like a hole dug beside the river somewhere, and some heather on top. But you can't do that, seemingly."

There was, in fact, no way out of the impasse: the body could not be efficiently got rid of, at the same time as the uniqueness of the person was preserved. And the same conflict reappeared, with altered particulars, in the comments of James Unwin. In this case cremation was assumed, and the symbolism of identity was focused on where the ashes were to be buried:

"We lost our first baby during the war, and we put his ashes down in Banff; and at that time I was certain I was going to have the girls put my ashes there."

In this way he had sought to preserve and underline a unique family tie; but he also admired his brother's conviction that the right thing was to consider the living, and this had changed his view of what was possible in the way of expressing personal history:

"He was so organized it was unbelievable. He had everything ready for his son so that he wouldn't have any work in burying him. I'm in between. I put [in] a copy of my will that I'd like to be put down beside Mum and Nigel; but I've even changed my mind about that. I've a feeling they wouldn't give you your own ashes . . . . I'm not sure I'll do that now, I'm not *greatly* religious, you know I haven't *great* beliefs."

Thus personal recognition was tied up with the 'religious' way of treating the body, and James Unwin had grown less religious in this respect in proportion as he paid more attention to the practical interests of the living; for in the practical way of treating the body unknown operators could not be trusted to distinguish one person's ashes from another's.

There was a tension, therefore, in the 'new' patterns of mourning, between the new pragmatism about the body and the continued wish to express personal history and a personal affection. And there was a tension in the 'old' pattern of mourning between the undiminished sacral attitude to the body and the belief that the spirit of the dead was gone and already reunited with its own in the other world. It is worth repeating that the difference between 'old' and 'new' was not reducible to the difference between burial and cremation, though various aspects of cremation could be construed as being impersonal compared with burial. The essential difference between 'old' and 'new' lay in the understanding in which cremation was used—whether it was treated as eliminating the sacral element felt to be present in burial, or as preceding some continuing symbolic ritual with the ashes. But this said, there is a historical shift suggested in Aberdonian patterns of mourning which, with certain constants in beliefs about the soul and about the irreplaceability of personal loss, turns in part on the introduction of cremation. This wider historical picture, and the light which Aberdonian patterns of mourning cast on it, must now be considered.

Conclusion

In the introduction I referred to Hertz's insight that in dealing with a death, ideas about the body, the soul, and the mourner will tend to correspond; and I sketched several successive sets of correspondences which can be marked out in the historical record of mourning in Europe. It is of a piece with this picture that in contemporary Aberdonian patterns of mourning, too, ideas cluster round the body, the spirit, and the process of grief. There is an old pattern, uniting a grave cult, a belief in family reunion after death, and an emphasis on fidelity to the person lost, and Aberdonians themselves recognize that they are caught in a historical succession from this old pattern to something new.

However, the picture of Aberdonian mourning which has emerged does not fit with the picture drawn in the introduction in one important respect: we do not find a straightforwardly repressed or rationalistic new pattern, emphasizing cremation, a belief in annihilation, and replacement of the dead. This is firstly because any emphasis on the swift replacement of the dead continues to be unacceptable; and even the acknowledged need for gradual replacement is not part of a coherent framework of thought, and its acknowledgement generates tensions with the need to express continuing affection. And the second reason is that cremation is felt to be quite compatible with a belief in reunion after death, as well as with a belief in annihilation.

These two facts are difficult to square with the demographic explanation for changes in mourning. Certainly the experience of grief has become more concentrated in older age groups during this century, but the dead are not thereby accepted as replaceable. Their death may seldom be significant for society as a whole, but among the chief mourners family affection continues to be deeply felt, and it is universally accepted that the dead are, or should be, irreplaceable. Similarly the trend to cremation does not depend on indifference to the spiritual survival of the dead. On the contrary, the body is often devalued in order to emphasize the spirit. These characteristics of the new mourning patterns, together with their peculiar 'Anglo-Saxon' geography, noted in the introduction to this chapter, point back to Reformation and Enlightenment themes.

To understand the effect of the Reformation, we have to understand the old set of correspondences in mourning. In medieval Europe, the slow purgation of the soul corresponded to the slow dissolution of the body. The purified soul was freeing itself from the sinful flesh; and both notions were caught up in the diminishing sequence of requiem masses which were usually timed to emphasize the day of the funeral, the first month, and the first year. It is a rhythm of interlocking conceptions whose presence in northern Britain in former centuries is attested by the Lykewake Dirge.[11] In this rhythm, the sequential stages achieved by the soul, and the accompanying and supporting prayer of the mourners, mark gradually evolving correspondences between the situation of the dead and of the bereaved which are still evident in the peasant cultures of Catholic and Orthodox Europe.[12]

The process of change which has overtaken these conceptions in many areas began with Luther's attack on the sale of indulgences for the souls in Purgatory. As it met resistance, so the Reformers' attack broadened to include the theological conception which was being exploited—the doctrine of the soul's gradual purgation. Puritan writers entirely reconstructed the doctrine of the soul, insisting rigorously that no such period of purgation could take place, for 'the faithful depart straightways into glory'. But this done, consequences immediately followed, both for the treatment of the body and for the pattern of mourning, which produced an entirely new set of correspondences. In the first place, the body ceased to have any continuing significance, and became an object to be discarded as simply and quickly as possible; and in the second place the mourning pattern of 'month's minds' and 'year's minds' which had been built round prayers for the dead became redundant.[13]

Some Puritans did not shrink from these consequences for the body and the mourner of their doctrine of the soul; and for a period in mid-seventeenth-century England a set of correspondences emerged which in essential features strikingly resembled and indeed exceeded the new patterns which I have described in contemporary Aberdeen. For the immediate transition of the soul was paralleled by the immediate disposal of the body 'without any Ceremony', and by subsequent neglect of the grave; and at the same time black dress, displays of grief, memorial services, and (lest they be reminiscent of memorial services) even funeral sermons were forbidden.[14]

This remarkable anticipation of contemporary attitudes thus linked soul, body, and mourner in an immediate transition; but this completed logic was perhaps fully realized only amongst the most fervent, and for the bulk of the population a compromise had to be reached with inherited attitudes. In particular, concessions were made by the Puritans to those aspects of mourning ceremony, centred on the body and the cortège, which symbolized rank and authority, and which they deemed to have no religious connotation of prayer for the dead. The survival of such ceremony is attested by the undiminished expense of most funerals in the seventeenth century, including that of the Lord Protector himself.[15]

Deprived of its relationship to the fate of the soul, therefore, the activity of the mourner became centred on secular symbolism and on the body; and as the acceptability of grief was enhanced by the late eighteenth-century trend towards sensibility and domestic affection, so the focus of the mourner on the body and the grave intensified. Everywhere cemeteries—a new notion—were created and beautified as places of melancholy meditation, and the romantic style of mourning was born.

What caused this body-centred style of mourning to give way in its turn to newer, more austere styles is still unclear; but a number of indications point to the body itself—the body when it reasserted its obtrusive and unavoidable evidence of corruption—as the source of offence. And the corruption of the body seems to have been a cause of offence especially to the Protestant view of death, with its instant transition of the soul to a spiritualized other world.

Much of this later part of the picture remains to be filled in and, no doubt, corrected as more is learnt; but some things are documented. For example, cremation proposals—the radical solution to bodily decay—made little impact against clear-cut Catholic resistance in France and Italy; but they were taken up in Britain by medical reformers in response to the grave scandals of the 1840s, and met with a mixture of assent and dissent from Protestant divines.[16] The British flirtation with spiritualism—a spirit divorced from the body—was particularly strong around the time of the cataclysmic death scenes of the First World War; and it was at this time also that mourning conventions began to collapse.[17] And it is in the Protestant countries of Europe that cremation has now taken hold, while in Catholic countries, despite an informal relaxation of the rule against cremation, there remains a near total resistance in practice.[18]

One can only speculate about the meanings which connect these facts, but the material of this chapter suggests something like this. We have seen that when modernizing Aberdonians rejected the old body-centred style of mourning, they were indeed trying to safeguard their view of the soul, with its instant transition to the other world or to nothingness. They were anxious not to confuse the flesh and the spirit, the decay of the body and the fate of the person; for such linkages had uneasy connotations of apparently magical or 'Catholic' thinking. This was not indeed how the old style of mourning seemed to its practitioners, for they saw the grave cult only as an expression of that same immediate spiritual reunion of the family that is also endorsed in some of the new styles of mourning. But their bodily symbolism for this spiritual event is now at risk of seeming odd and inappropriate, because the body has again come to be seen, after the lessons taught by congested city graveyards and by modern battlefields, as something essentially worthless and corrupt. 'The modern soul has seen too many real corpses stark against the walls of Europe,' says a dry contemporary comment on a Victorian poet's death symbolism.[19] And while Catholicism could easily accommodate this vile flesh, because it was always what the purified soul had to escape, Protestantism had to get rid of it, because it could no longer serve to image the immediate passage of the soul to its felicity. So the body was again expelled, as it was in the time of the Puritans, from the sphere of Protestant religious concern, and was defined as something to be dealt with according to the practical needs of the living.

If this picture is anywhere near the truth, the significance of the changes which are occurring in styles of mourning is that they are consequences unfolding from Reformation changes in ideas about the soul; and this possibility is perhaps surprising, for it has been obscured by two things. First, it was not at first sight obvious how such changes could have led to the baroque mourning of the Victorians. Here the developments in family sentiment emphasized by Ariès clearly played a part; but more recent researches on the Puritans help to explain how, in addition, baroque mourning was created by a shift of the mourner's symbolic focus from the soul towards the body.

Second, another factor which has helped to obscure the evolving implications of the Reformation is the geography of the way in which baroque mourning has receded in the twentieth century. Chief amongst these geographical anomalies has been the long retention of the older mourning pattern in Presbyterian Scotland. The problem of Scotland is, however, perhaps not so great. It has been evident from this study of Aberdeen that the old pattern of mourning is going, and characteristically Protestant views of the soul are indeed one source—in alliance with secularism—of its felt contradictions. But the history of the past century and a half shows that these contradictions are only clearly felt where the scandal of bodily decay becomes overpowering, and in peace time such problems have been associated chiefly with the breakdown of burial practices in the context of dense urban growth. Thus within the Protestant countries that have taken up cremation the geographical pattern of its adoption is likely to vary; and in Britain it is clearly associated with urban density (Table 3). Scotland is amongst the most sparsely populated areas of Britain, and Gorer's study,

Table 3. *Percentage of deaths cremated by regional density of population, Great Britain, 1984*

Regional density	Deaths cremated (%)			N deaths
	Mean	Minimum	Maximum	
Conurbations	74.5	69.2	88.9	167,170
Regions outside conurbations:				
high density[a]	71.0	63.2	74.2	197,214
medium density[b]	63.3	51.9	70.9	143,678
low density[c]	53.1	50.1	54.9	119,249

[a] South-East, Yorkshire and Humberside, North-West (>3 persons per hectare).
[b] South-West, East Anglia, East Midlands, West Midlands.
[c] North, Wales, Scotland (<1.4 persons per hectare).

Sources: (for numbers of cremations) *Pharos International* (Summer 1986), pp.41 f.; (for numbers of deaths) OPCS, *Population and vital statistics 1984*, London: HMSO, 1986, Table 4.1, and Registrar-General (Scotland), *Annual Report 1984*, Edinburgh: HMSO, 1985, Table Bl.2; (for population densities) Census 1981, *Key statistics for local authorities*, London: HMSO, 1984, Table 1.

which revealed Scotland's traditionalism, was not done in any of Scotland's few major conurbations. Thus in contemporary Aberdeen, too, with its substantial country-born population, the old attitude to the body remains as one stratum of popular thought, though a contrary devaluation of the body is now gaining ground.

Whether the new Protestant and secularist views of death have reshaped, or can reshape, the needs of the bereaved is doubtful. Any view which represents changes at death as immediate certainly tends to bring needs for replacement into conflict with feelings of loss; and this must be the more so when feelings of loss continue to be endorsed by the ethic of family affection. Such conflicts are heightened, moreover, where the common contemporary belief in a right to a natural term of life is contradicted by a death which is premature. This moral claim to life has a relation to Protestantism, but so has the opposite and consoling belief in death at an appointed time, and the task of disentangling these relationships must await the later chapter on religion. But certainly there appears to be a distinctive cultural context here in which the wounds of grief are slow to heal. Whether this is because the understandings involved create an impasse for grief, or because the ambivalence of grief seizes upon this cultural clothing, cannot here be determined. But it remains a characteristic problem of our time, and it helps to explain the renewed interest, from a psychotherapeutic point of view, in ritual forms which prescribe a slower transition. Whether psychotherapeutic world views are capable of imparting the same force and credence to these ritual forms as is imparted by the older religious traditions remains, however, at best uncertain.

Notes and References

1. P. Marris, *Loss and change*, London, Routledge, 1974; C. M. Parkes, 'Psychosocial transitions', *Soc. Sci. and Med.* 5 (1971), 101–15.
2. A. van Gennep, *Rites of passage*, tr. M. B. Vizedom and G. L. Caffee, Chicago University Press, 1960; R. Hertz, *Death and the right hand*, tr. R. & C. Needham, Aberdeen University Press, 1960.
3. R. Huntington and P. Metcalf, *Celebrations of death: the anthropology of mortuary rituals*, Cambridge University Press, 1979.
4. L. Pincus, *Death and the family*, London: Faber, 1976; G. Gorer, *Death, grief and mourning in contemporary Britain*, London: Cresset Press, 1965.
5. P. C. Rosenblatt, R. P. Walsh, and D. A. Jackson, *Grief and mourning in cross-cultural perspective*, New Haven: Human Relations Area Files Press, 1976.
6. P. Ariès, *The hour of our death*, tr. H. Weaver, London: Allen Lane, 1981.
7. N. Elias, *The loneliness of the dying*, tr. E. Jephcott, Oxford: Blackwell, 1985.
8. M. Douglas, *Natural symbols*, London: Pelican, 1973.
9. Ariès, *The hour of our death*, p. 594; Gorer, *Death, grief and mourning*.
10. D. Cannadine, 'War and death, grief and mourning in modern Britain', in J. Whaley (ed.), *Mirrors of mortality: studies in the social history of death*, London: Europa, 1981.
11. This composition, which is part of the corpus of British folk-song, and is in a dialect marked by northern English and lowland Scottish vocabulary, takes the form of an antiphonal ritual, in which the mourners at the wake instruct the dead on the journey now to be accomplished. For a version see A. Quiller-Couch (ed.), *The Oxford book of English verse*, 2nd edn., Oxford University Press, 1939, no. 391.
12. J. de Pina Cabral, *Sons of Adam, daughters of Eve*, Oxford University Press, 1986; L. M. Danforth, *The death rituals of rural Greece*, Princeton University Press, 1982; S. Ott, *The circle of mountains*, Oxford University Press, 1981; W. A. Douglas,

Death in Murelaga, London: University of Washington Press, 1969.

13. T. Becon, *The sicke man's salve*, Edinburgh: Thomas Vautroullier, 1584, pp.142, 129 f.; for the background to this popular work of the 16th century see N. L. Beatty, *The craft of dying*, New Haven: Yale University Press, 1970.

14. D. E. Stannard, *The Puritan way of death*, Oxford University Press, 1977, ch. 5.

15. C. Gittings, *Death, burial and the individual in early modern England*, London: Croom Helm, 1984.

16. J. Morley, *Death, heaven and the Victorians*, London: Studio Vista, 1971.

17. Cannadine, 'War and death, grief and mourning'.

18. M. Vovelle, *La mort et l'Occident de 1300 à nos jours*, Paris: Gallimard, 1983, p. 700.

19. F. L. Lucas (ed.), *Tennyson: poetry and prose*, Oxford University Press, 1947, 'Introduction', p. ix.

5

The doctor

She was loath tae sen for the doctor till's unless it was rale
serious . . . So it was aa the waur faan he did come: Dad said
that Dickson was the only man he didna like aboot the place.

David Ogston, *White Stone Country: Growing up in
Buchan*, 1986

Introduction

For all the forms of physical loss which have been described there is
a corresponding aspect of medicine—helping the disabled, caring
for the very old, easing death, counselling the bereaved. In this
sense, the topics of this book are all medical. However, in their
lifelong contact with medicine, Aberdonians had learnt to call on
doctors not so much for these broader needs, as to get treatment for
a specific episode. Hence, accounts of this relationship were less
concerned with the special help which the doctor could give when
these broader needs were felt, than with the politics of encounters
between doctors and patients in ordinary circumstances. In these
encounters, the ideas people had about chronic illness, ageing, and
death entered only obliquely, disrupting or facilitating a relationship which otherwise ran on its own well-established lines. What the
politics of this relationship were, and how they were helped or
hindered by Aberdonian ideas about physical limitation or loss, is
the subject of this chapter.

Evidence from a number of sources suggests that in recent years a
historical change has been taking place in popular attitudes to the
doctor—one in which criticism has been becoming more frequent
and vocal.[1] The change accompanies observations of generational
differences in such attitudes, with the younger generation being
more willing than the older to find fault;[2] and it also accompanies
class differences[3] of a kind which in France have led to the identification of the new criticism with the ideas of the 'new middle classes'

and the political impetus provided by the events of May 1968.[4] Similarly, in Britain a major study of general practice was obliged to take account of the way in which 'during the 1970s the demands of the young, of women, of lower status occupations, and of ethnic minorities for recognition became more strident and their criticisms of those they saw as responsible for their subordination became more outspoken'.[5] Such critical approaches have, in turn, been connected with the search for alternative, less hierarchical forms of relationship with the doctor or, more radically, with the search for alternative forms of medicine.[6]

These trends are interesting not least because they have been paralleled by a similar post-war shift in academic analyses of the doctor/patient relationship. From the idea that there was a single kind of relationship conventionally approved, in which the doctor and the patient played harmonious and complementary parts,[7] there first gradually developed a notion that there were varying relationships, with parts for the patient ranging from the wholly passive to the actively collaborative—a still conventional and harmonious variation depending on the nature of the illness.[8] It was only after this recognition of a plurality of approved relationships that the possibility of conflict was mooted between the authoritative doctor and the active patient,[9] and encounters between the two came to be seen as struggles for control, and for possession of the knowledge on which control depended.[10] It seemed, however, that doctors nevertheless kept control, and there were seen to be at least two kinds of advantage which they possessed in this struggle—first, structural advantages such as their professional monopoly,[11] and second, advantages in the consultation such as their control over clinical routines.[12]

Hence by a further step the medical profession came to be seen, in some of the more radical critiques of capitalism or industrialism, as having expropriated the sick person's capacity for self-determination and self-knowledge; and in attempting to account for, and to rouse opposition to, this assumed expropriation, these critiques went beyond existing explanations to suggest that patients had themselves been duped by an ideology of medical expertise.[13] Alternatively, and more pessimistically, if they were not expressly duped, they were seen to be rendered inarticulate, helpless, and passive by the sheer power of the 'clinical gaze'[14] and its 'object-orientated medical cosmology'.[15] And there remains some substance in this pessimism, for even moves towards 'democratic' or 'patient-centred' medicine have been shown to occur in a context and a manner which tends to extend the doctor's, rather than the patient's, knowledge and control.[16]

Yet even with this sobering message, the hope is that patients, the 'acting subjects', can find ways of regaining a measure of control. It may be that doctors preserve their moral dominance of the consultation not so much by their scientific knowledge, as by their skill in playing off the conflicting moral demands which enmesh both doctor and patient. Among the conflicts which are especially relevant here are the double binds which require the doctor to be both policeman and negotiator, and the patient to be both compliant and self-regulating.[17] Doctors learn by experience how to switch between these roles; the question here is whether patients can learn to defend their position with equal skill.

Does this relationship during and following consultation affect the way in which people reason before consulting? Again there has been a shift of both academic and popular ideas on this connection. According to earlier academic interpretations, there was a conventional rule that, just as the sick should obey medical orders, so they should also consult promptly in the first place. But this ignored the problems associated with defining when sickness was present. Complaints by general practitioners in the 1960s about the high proportion of trivial conditions brought to them[18] highlighted some of the potential contradictions which this rule too might imply. One such possible 'double bind' was outlined by Bloor and Horobin:[19] those who obeyed medical orders would presumably depend also on the doctor's judgement to decide when they were sick; and conversely those who used their own judgement about when they were sick would presumably think it sensible to use their own judgement about medical orders. This suggestion was not tested empirically, but it did a valuable service in pointing out that the rules for how to behave before consulting might well be incompatible with the rules for how to behave afterwards. One example may in fact be hidden in the consulting practices endorsed by the older generation: the evidence given earlier suggests that older people are more submissive once they are in the consultation, yet other evidence suggests that their rule is to consult, not promptly, but as little as possible.[20]

It appears, then, from all this evidence, that if there are indeed good patients who, having consulted, submit wholly to the doctor because they have been convinced by medical ideology, or rendered helpless by medical knowledge, it is amongst the older generation that they will most frequently be found. But whether their decisions before consulting are informed by the same submissive attitude, or by some other conflicting point of view, is unclear. These considerations lend to the present study of older Aberdonians a particular interest.

Before looking at the Aberdeen material a caution must be noted on some of the notorious difficulties of eliciting, and of interpreting, negative views about doctors. In observed consultations very little conflict is usually noticeable,[21] yet the subsequent response of patients varies in such a way that sometimes nearly all appear satisfied, while at other times many appear critical. Criticism seems to be most free when people speak at home or in the company of other patients, not in hospital or surgery or in the company of those associated with doctors, and when they control the conversation themselves and can tell stories, rather than when they are subjected to an organized questionnaire.[22] Thus the circumstances of the present study made it easy for criticism to emerge in a way which would doubtless be less apparent in a medical setting, or in response to other methods of enquiry. These considerations need to be borne in mind in making sense of the Aberdonian views which follow.

Deciding to consult in Aberdeen

When they were ill, and wanted professional help, this generation of Aberdonians seldom thought in terms of practitioners who were outside orthodox medicine. When they did think in such terms, it was primarily the osteopath whom they considered as an alternative, for back problems; otherwise they remembered recourse to alternative medicine as something done in the days when they had to pay for the doctor. Then they might have sought out one of the women who knew traditional cures—a warmed stocking round a sore throat, a porridge poultice for pleurisy, even raw meat on a cancer so that the cancer 'ate the meat'; but those who continued to prefer such help out of disbelief in the doctor, now that the doctor was free, were 'queer people'.

The fact that few alternatives were envisaged to orthodox medicine did not mean, however, that recourse to the doctor was automatic, least of all by way of prevention. Preserving health was, as we have seen, a concern, but it was seldom one in which the doctor was expected to play a part. Such notions as the regular 'MOT' test were only mooted rarely whether by professional members of the middle class, or by politically articulate members of the working class. But even leaving aside the issue of prevention, recourse to the doctor was subject to heavy qualifications.

Even after the onset of symptoms, there still remained as many arguments for delay as for consultation. Some of these arguments arose from the reasoning used in the interpretation of symptoms—a subject too complex to pursue in this book. Some, again, reflected the historical experience of this generation before the National Health Service, an experience which, in one view, had instilled a continuing reluctance to consult. But there was also a tendency, whether derived from this experience or from a wider morality, to declare allegiance to a fixed principle of 'not bothering the doctor', of not being 'one of those that go easily to the doctor', of going 'only if it's absolutely necessary', of 'carrying on in your own way'—a belief in getting oneself better, and a corresponding tendency, on arriving in a doctor's surgery without spectacular symptoms, to feel embarrassed.

It was a reflection of this moral dimension in people's reluctance to consult that in remembered clashes over such decisions between the sick person and the doctor or the other members of the family, emphasis was heavily on the resistance of the sufferer to calling in the doctor. Indeed, in working-class families the process of consultation was often presented as a ritual drama in which a key relative—the relative always in present examples a woman, though the sick person might be either sex—had to overcome the sufferer's resistance either by forcefulness or by trickery. Wives and daughters phoned the surgery without the knowledge of ailing mothers, fathers, or husbands, sometimes beseeching the doctor to represent the visit as a casual afterthought while passing by; and the drama was sometimes played out into the consultation itself. Ellen Neil's battles were with her husband:

"I says till him, 'Now we'll phone for the doctor.' 'Oh no, no, wait, ye can't dae that, ye can't.' I says, 'Ye can,' but oh he widna hear o't. He's gettin' worse y'see, and I says oh I'll phone my daughter. So I phoned. I says that her dad wis really ill, he can't lift his arms or nothing. So she says, *'I'll* phone.' I says, 'Aye, you phone right away, he won't let me.' She says, *'You* don't ask him.' *She* phoned . . . . We sent for the doctor till him, you know this, my daughter and me, this is God's truth, you know what he said to the doctor? He says, 'Who sent for you?' And I says, 'I did,' I says, 'and your daughter.' 'Well, there's nothing wrong with me, I don't know why they sent' . . . . What an affront! I says, in front o' the doctor I was so mad, I dinna often, I says, 'Well, you devil, you could die and I won't send for the doctor.' So Dr Andrews just laughed."

Correspondingly, when the woman concerned in such duels failed to circumvent this resistance, as happened in another case, apologies were in order :

"Dr Moulton said to him, 'Why on earth didn't you phone?' You know the poor devils are worked hard. And I said, 'I am deeply sorry but he wouldn't allow me to send for you three days ago, and even though you were to give me a telling off I wid agree with you, because—well, it was Saturday afternoon, but he thought he wid fight it on his own."

In such cases, however, where delay incurred the censure of the doctor, or even of other outsiders, it no longer seemed so meritorious to any but the hardiest; for it opened the way to an alternative interpretation of reluctance as the product of unreasonable fear. With those who were too slow to consult, the charge could be made of being afraid to know the worst, of having apprehensions or misgivings, of being 'funny', or in a peculiar state of mind— charges as seriously stigmatizing as the 'panic' attributed to those who called in the doctor too quickly, or for symptoms uncorroborated by the medical diagnosis. Thus while the role of the reluctant patient was initially at any rate a creditable role to adopt, judgement had to be exercised to prevent it from turning suddenly, at a certain point, into a discreditable one.

So difficult was this balance, in fact, that one can see the ritual struggle between relatives, referred to earlier, as a social form for dramatizing and resolving the problem. The strict asymmetry of these struggles, with the sick person espousing delay and the nurse espousing realism, was so noticeable as to suggest that the conflict was itself institutionalized, and that an adversarial type of bargaining, on the analogy of the trade unions or law courts, was being used to achieve a negotiated result. But the adversarial analogy is itself insufficient; for on that model one might expect it to be the sick person who argued for being relieved of obligations, and the nurse who argued against incurring more of them. In fact, though, the reverse was true: it seemed that the sick person argued against being relieved of obligations and the nurse for incurring them, suggesting that what was being bargained about here was not the self-interest of both, but their altruism. Hence an appropriate model for what was going on here seems to be that of gift exchange,[23] and the bargaining associated therewith which establishes degrees of credit and of mutual trust.

The struggle between relatives can thus be seen as an institution which regulated the credit due to the nurse and to the patient for their response to a given condition; but for the most part it was not consciously seen in this way by Aberdonians. If the reluctant patient and the assiduous nurse were both heroes of a conventional drama, both nevertheless played their roles for the most part as if the other was the villain. The Neils were quoted earlier as a particularly robust example:

RW: "You were saying that you don't like going to the doctor?"

Mrs Neil: "He disna like bothering the doctor. I think he's scared at the doctor, I will say that. Ye are a bit scared tae go sometimes."

Mr Neil: "No, I'll tell ye one thing—"

Mrs Neil: "Scared tae hear more than you want tae hear . . . ."

RW: [redressing] "*I* never want to call the doctor."

Mr Neil: "Oh I don't like that, I don't like that. I don't like sitting up there by myself, I'd raether—I don't like them comin' here either, tae tell ye the truth."

RW: "Why not coming here?"

Mr Neil: "I don't—well, I think it's just a, it's just a *fallacy*. I don't *like* doctors anyway. Well I don't dislike them but—"

Mrs Neil: "Ye've naught them [needed them] now, dinna say ye don't like them, because ye naught a doctor that last time . . . . It's stupid. If you need a doctor why not send for him?"

Both parties here were so convinced of their respective views that the alternative was 'stupid', a 'fallacy'; and yet it was also possible, even with this sharply opposed couple, for a sudden shift to occur, in which the husband, without deserting his own argument, could simultaneously acknowledge the validity of his wife's:

Mrs Neil: "One time the doctor says tae me . . . . that was a young doctor that was with them, he was very good, now he says tae me . . . . never be so long in sending, it's a lot more work. Now that last time you was ill, the doctor had a lot of comin' back and fore here. He came, and Dr Finzean came once."

Mr Neil: "Yes, I suppose it's a sensible way of lookin' at it as well, you know."

Thus for a moment both ways of looking at it were seen to be sensible, and an element of hidden consensus appeared.

Where these moments of consensus did appear, they confirmed the picture of an orderly ritual underlying the conflict, and enabling a mutually creditable bargain to be struck. But this picture has to be considered cautiously. While in some cases agreement was the outcome of the conflict, in other cases it was not. The debate between relatives about consulting habits could merely escalate, inflaming other well-established areas of conflict. And a person living alone, without regular opportunities to talk things over, could face a real dilemma over whether it was delay, or calling the doctor, which was unreasonable. One man who lived alone in a garden basement had a heart attack during the night: having tried to ring the doctor early in the evening and failed to get him he did not ring again:

"I sat up the whole night. I toyed with the idea of sending for the Samaritans, because I really thought I was going to die. I figured, will I send for the Samaritans? I thought no. I'll send for the police? No."

He explained that he was too breathless to go up the stairs and open the door. Whoever came would have to break the door down and 'I don't like waking people at night. I'd only do it if it was a matter of life and death.' Was it a matter of life and death? Reminded of his remark that he had really thought he was going to die, he switched back and confirmed it. Thus on the one hand he thought he was going to die, which would justify his waking people at night; and on the other hand he did not feel justified in waking people at night, because he would only do this if it was a matter of life and death. He commented wryly that 'you don't think straight when you're gasping your heart out.' The result of this unresolved dilemma was that in the present attack he delayed till the morning before calling the doctor, and then for the future he installed an electrical system which would open the front door from his sitting room. This example suggests that where one person, as here, had to play both the reluctant patient and the sensible nurse, the result was indeed a plain contradiction and an oscillation between appropriate courses of action.

When people were deciding to consult, therefore, the obligations to delay and to be realistic were genuinely opposed even though the opposition could in favourable circumstances be resolved. At the same time delay was emphasized not only for this reason, but also because of fears of hypochondria. Such fears lent even to confessedly unwise stoicism a meritorious aspect; and similarly the drama of resistance and persuasion can also be seen as a way in which symptoms were certified, independently of any subjective tendencies in the sufferer, as suitable for the doctor. Lay criticisms of overhastiness were the main threat; and though there was also a potential for medical criticism, it seems that in so far as such criticism was reflected in lay talk, it was usually in the indirect form of conflict about the diagnosis. In a small number of cases, a diagnosis had been offered which was less serious or more psychological than expected, and the arguments rehearsed against this verdict perhaps acquired some added impetus as a rejection of an indirect imputation of self-deception. But in general, anxieties about hypochondria were worked out in the way illness was coped with at home, and before the court of lay opinion, and they do not seem to have owed much to the overt censure of doctors after consultation, even if they played a covert role in some diagnostic disputes.

The decision to consult was, however, only the starting point of a sequence of dealings with the doctor which involved other points of conflict, also vividly reflected in lay talk; and I now turn to these issues.

Compliance and autonomy

The question of whether to obey the doctor, and the question of how some control could be preserved after the doctor had been consulted, occasioned almost universal comment. And while people in the West End and in Mannoch differed markedly in the degree of control they sought, and in the degree of compliance they professed, tension proliferated between doctor and patient over these issues in either area notwithstanding.

In both the middle-class quarter and the Mannoch estate, compliance with the doctor's orders was accepted as reasonable enough; but compliance as a principle was seldom insisted on except among working-class Aberdonians. It was among some members of this circle that pride was taken in being a 'good patient', in 'doing your part'; and correspondingly it was amongst these Aberdonians that support was declared for the disciplining of bad patients, and that disapproval was voiced against breaking the rules of hospital hygiene, or of 'wasting the hospital's time' by going against advice. Such attitudes reflected not merely an inhibition against making a nuisance of oneself to others, but also the accompanying conviction that compliance was 'only sensible' and 'for your own good'. These general prescriptions were reinforced by references to particular cases where the doctor's advice was either automatically obeyed or rashly disobeyed, with appropriate consequences; and allied notions were also expressed, that it was silly to wish to know exactly what was wrong, or to wish to choose, when a GP retired, among the other GPs in the practice. Such arguments went a good deal further than was conceded by nearly all of those middle-class Aberdonians who thought compliance reasonable. Their judgements were particular: they tried out a suggestion and saw if it worked, or gave way to a suggestion when neglecting it had not worked. In this as in other respects, their strategy was to seek knowledge and control for themselves.

This search for knowledge and control was indeed a predominantly middle-class characteristic, though it was not confined to the West End, and overall was as common as the principle of obedience. It was expressed in the wish to know the diagnosis and prognosis, or to have a say in treatment; but it was even more clearly expressed in the desire to choose, in the first place, the doctor who drew these inferences and made these recommendations. In this way of thinking, when a GP retired, the right to choose a successor was claimed as a matter of course; the advice of medical acquaintances might have been sought in picking a good GP initially, and a good GP, once picked, could be a reason for not moving away. But more important than access to GPs was access to specialists in general, and to the specialists of the teaching hospital in particular. Specialist referrals were not seen as being determined solely by the GP; they were asked for, sometimes insisted upon, and occasionally steered towards a particular consultant with whom there was a personal connection through family, friends, or neighbours. The adviser was thus to be chosen carefully; but the advice too was, irrespective of the adviser chosen, a matter for discussion. Treatment was not to be accepted unquestioningly: these people wanted to weigh the risks and the gains for themselves, and hence they sought an adequate explanation of what was wrong and of what could be expected in the future.

For all the difference between this search for control and the ethic of compliance, however, conflict between doctor and patient remained, as I have indicated, a widely shared experience. In this context conflict did not necessarily imply open opposition, still less florid quarrelling; indeed, such manifestations were remarkable, in the accounts given, for their absence. Rather, what was implied was simply a recognition by patients that, at the time of consulting, their view and the doctor's disagreed, and it was often doubtful whether the doctors for their part had ever known that this was the case. Such silences on the patients' part were not necessarily because they believed, then or subsequently, that they were in the wrong, but because, even when they believed that they were in the right, they frequently felt it wise to keep their own counsel. 'I said nothing, because I ken that doctors like to *know*,' as it was once put; or, in another's words, 'I'm frightened to ask any more because he'd—he, och, I don't know, he gets scunnered of me [fed up with me] asking things sometimes.' For such patients, consultation was an intense but unspoken struggle between the doctor's advice and their own convictions.

Such conflicts of judgement could be interpreted in two ways. First the doctor's judgement could be vindicated in spite of all. In the light of subsequent events, some wished they had listened, saw they had done the wrong thing; or even without such proofs, they viewed their actions as mere rebelliousness or evasion:

The doctor said, 'Are you taking all your pills?' and I said yes. He said, '*All* of them?' I telt a lee [told a lie]—I said yes.

These last words were accompanied by a schoolgirl gesture of guilt, hand clapped over mouth; and the sequel was morally inevitable:

He listened with his stethoscope, and I suppose he knew.

Even without such remorse, however, disobedience could be a tacit acknowledgement that medical orders were in fact authorita- tive. Positively zestful accounts were given of beer, stout, and bottles of whisky smuggled into hospital, even, in special circumstances, of strings of sausages brought in to cook, of which the point lay in the outrageousness of the attempt and in the narrow escape from detection. And a similar kind of licensed jesting could take place face to face with the doctor, dissipating the tension between the acknowledged legitimacy of authority and the inborn deviance of human nature.

However it was also as common, indeed slightly commoner, especially amongst the middle class, to interpret conflicts of judgement as a sign, not that the patient was delinquent, but that the doctor was wrong. And even when the doctor was acknowledged to be right on a particular occasion, there was often a feeling that the patient's argument was right in general. The main basis for the way patients argued in these instances lay in the beliefs already portrayed in previous chapters, especially those about illness.

Amongst these beliefs, far the most prominent in medical encounters was the conviction that health could be built up by normal living (1.1), together with its extension in the principle of continuous struggle against illness (1.2). These assumptions were a powerful ally to the doctor in some situations, and as powerful an enemy in others. As a symbol of determination, such convictions fitted easily into the picture of the good patient, becoming a necessary feature of doing one's part for the doctor and being an example to others. And these militant themes were just as popular with those patients who preferred to take control for themselves. Obviously such beliefs ensured a most satisfactory response with any condition where the doctor advised activity and effort. But disagreement was correspondingly profound when the doctor advised restraint, caution, and self-control. For example, a man whose only health nostrum was to be 'aye active . . . . aye oot' flouted advice to stay quietly at home after a bad accident:

"The doctor kicked up a row for gan [going] back tae work. He kicked up a row and he says, 'Ye've enough trouble wi' yer leg an' that.' I says, 'Aye, well I'm gan. I've got to start some wye [way], so I'm gan tae dee it [do it].' 'Well, well,' he says, 'It's a waste o' time speakin' tae you,' he says."

The mirror image of these responses was visible with the smaller group of people who saw illness as a loss to be endured (1.4) or as a release from effort (1.5). Here advice from the doctor to take care permitted obedience to become the idiom in which apathy was expressed. A once recalcitrant patient who was unwillingly convinced, by the worsening of her condition, that she had entered a new phase of chronic health problems, now took the resigned view that 'I suppose you have to expect it as you get older', and adopted an attitude of total submission, leaving everything in the doctor's hands 'just like in an aeroplane—it's all in the pilot's hands'. On the other hand advice demanding more active co-operation from such patients fell on deaf ears. Urged by her doctor to walk out for her groceries every day, a woman who felt that at her age her daughter should do it described bitterly an acquaintance's experience of a similar geriatric activism:

When her daughter was on holiday they took her into a home, and they made her do things. Walking, taking her elbow. They just do it. It's wrong.

These various ideas about how to cope with illness were the most important factor in whether patients welcomed or rejected the doctor's advice; but at times, too, the reaction to these encounters was also coloured by ideas about old age and dying. Instructtions were ignored by some because they involved actions symbolic of the stigmatized 'auld wifie'—examples are given later—and they were dismissed by others because they were felt to be hopelessly optimistic about the chances of throwing off true old age. Similarly, as we have seen, criticism was voiced over the way deaths were managed, and a follow-up appointment was stoically ignored in case it would imply too much eagerness to cling on to life at an age when death was natural.

Finally, disagreements with the doctor also arose from lay assessments of professional practice. These judgements were of two kinds—those which accused a doctor of pursuing professional interests rather than the patient's interests, and those which claimed to detect mistakes in diagnosis or treatment. In the latter case one obvious source of information was the doctors themselves. By comparing earlier and later diagnoses of a long-running problem by different doctors, it was often easy to see where something had been missed; and further, sharp observations of doctors' behaviour at the time gave clues to hesitations, changes of mind, or ill-concealed manifestations of alarm. But lay beliefs too played a substantial part in the critical arguments put forward, especially those concerned with the causation of illness.

In all these ways, disagreement springing from lay beliefs, often passed over in silence at the time, was a major feature of

Aberdonian stories about the doctor. And whether they spoke about their reactions to advice or the process of seeking help, even this older and arguably rather traditional generation of Aberdonians displayed little of the consensus necessary to identify a single harmonious contract between doctor and patient. But nor was it possible, for all that, to choose at will from the range of approaches talked about; for the demands of consistency restricted the options to certain patterns, and these must now be elucidated.

Themes and dilemmas

The key premisses about doctors which I have pointed out in Aberdonian talk can be rendered as follows:

5.1 *Obligatory delay in consulting*
   If I have symptoms, I don't go easily to the doctor.
5.2 *Realism in consulting*
   If I have symptoms, I am not afraid to know the truth.
5.3 *Control of decisions*
   When I consult the doctor, I want to make my own decisions.
5.4 *Obedience to orders*
   When I consult, I ought to take the doctor's advice.
5.5 *Expectation of disagreement*
   When I consult, I don't always agree with the doctor's opinion.

Plainly, these premisses could not all be held together without some inconsistencies being felt.

   The first and commonest consistent pattern of ideas combined any of three premisses: realism in consulting (5.2), control of the decisions (5.3), and an expectation of disagreement (5.5). Such a view—essentially one of the *doctor as a collaborator*—is not at all the deferent one usually attributed to this generation. However, a coherent pattern of a more deferent kind, viewing the *doctor as authority*, was also available. This view combined realism in consulting (5.2) with obedience to doctors (5.4); but it was rarely expressed as one consistent view. It was rare especially because, as I noted earlier, in accounts of the decision to consult, Aberdonians felt it important to establish that they did not go to the doctor easily even when realism would require it. On the whole, it was only after they arrived in the consulting room—if then—that they became concerned to show themselves as good patients.

There were two points of conflict between these alternative views of the doctor as collaborator and as authority. One conflict centred on whether obedience could be combined with autonomy; and the other centred on whether people felt guilty about disagreements with the doctor.

It seems obvious that obedience and autonomy would be felt to conflict, and there were some examples of this. Mary McLachlan said at first, on the subject of doctors, that if people were trying to help you, to go against them was just not fair; and she added to this self-denying view comments on how hard doctors worked and how wrong it was to blame the hospital when things went badly. One month later, however, she had a slight stroke, and in the aftermath she overturned this precept. Starting with the remark that she was not very satisfied with her doctor, who had taken two hours to arrive, she went on to say that it was time something was done about her blood pressure, to get to the cause of the problem: she was going to see to it that she got specialist attention, and, if necessary, she would pay for it. Her previous docility suddenly seemed to her childish, and she expressed this in, paradoxically, the idiom of children:

When you're big, you get no sympathy. When you're big you have to see to it yourself.

Thus it was not so much that she rejected the connection she had previously made between the help or sympathy of doctors and obedience to their orders, as that she now saw no real help and sympathy as being in fact present in the doctor's dealings with adults. Even six months later she was saying that doctors put people off with this and that, and she had advised a friend who was put off in this way to go and say something *must* be done. Her former picture of the hard-working doctor was now subtly transformed into the doctor who had no time to be thorough; she felt free to disagree with his diagnosis, and she repeated the idea that the only solution would be to go private. Thus from believing that doctors did try to help, and should therefore be obeyed, she had moved to the belief that doctors did not try to help, and that one therefore had to see to it oneself. It was in fact rare to ground the wish for control in a disillusioning experience of this kind, but certainly in such a case autonomy and obedience were seen as incompatible.

However, although in this and another case, and in general terms, autonomy and obedience might seem to be conflicting principles, they were in practice often capable of resolution. People might take the initiative in what they saw as their own sphere of control, but accept orders wherever the doctor claimed authority. They might take action to keep up morale, but give way on bio-medical matters. Or they might go so far as to hint at a past diagnosis and treatment in order to 'give the doctor a line' on a present condition and its treatment, but shelve their suggestion philosophically when the doctor took a different view. And more thorough-going than any such division of spheres between a specific obedience and a residual autonomy was the actual identification of autonomy with obedience. This identification was rare—there was only one example of it here—but it was possible where the rationale which lay behind medical instructions was so eagerly absorbed that it became in effect the spontaneous rationale of the patient's behaviour. Thus recovery became as much the patient's achievement as the doctor's, and as much the doctor's as the patient's—a reciprocity summed up in the present instance, when the patient returned for his first post-operative outpatient appointment, by the following exchange:

Doctor: Hallo, wonderboy, you're looking fit.

Patient: [wagging his finger] That's *your* fault.

While such courtesies do not always reflect a genuinely co-operative effort,[24] in this case the patient was both reintroduced as an example to other less satisfactory inmates of his former ward, and cited as 'a great advertisement for the hospital' by friends at home; and at the same time he portrayed himself as a man converted by his doctors to the vigorous regimen which had secured his recovery.

Obedience to doctor's orders did not always, therefore, conflict in principle with a wish for autonomy; it was more apt to founder instead on the rocks of emerging disagreements. Those who believed in obeying orders felt guilty about disagreements, in a way which those who sought for control did not. Some of the disputes involved have been described already: for instance, the woman who, in Chapter 2, would not follow the doctor's advice to use a stick for fear of being seen as an 'auld wifie'. She and another woman both argued the same way, yet both also expressed a belief in compliance. One emphasized the effort she had expended in losing a stone in weight on medical instructions; and the other represented herself as 'leaving it to the doctor' even in decisions with which she was eagerly concerned. With the first of these women, the tension between approved compliance and actual disagreement resulted in an oscillation between choices. Having ignored the GP's advice to use a stick before her operation, she did begin to use it afterwards, her belief in obedience having been reinforced by the hospital stay; but she continued to hesitate over the decision:

"Oh, I'm afraid they'll say there goes an auld wifie with a stick"—"It's nae a broomstick," put in her husband—"But I wouldn't like to—oh I hardly dare say it—I've never had a fall."

Eventually she resolved the problem by deciding on a compromise: she would follow her doctor's advice for three-quarters of the prescribed year, and then when she went on holiday to Jersey— where presumably appearances would be more important—she would abandon it. Thus in this instance the conflict led to a see-saw between choices. In the other instance, the woman concerned was led into a running battle with her husband, who took the doctor's part, broadening the attack to argue that his wife had also overborne the doctor's advice in securing an early discharge. To this second accusation, implying that she was a headstrong patient in a general way, she was highly sensitive, arguing 'You don't do me credit', and emphasizing, in repeated accounts of this and other issues, her readiness for whatever decision was made. But although she rejected the charge of wilfulness in general, and could have removed the suspicion of it altogether by using her stick, she would not use it—and accepted that she was wrong:

"It wis my attitude. I did get some falls too. It wis my ain fault."

There were six such cases of conflict between a belief in obedience to, and an actual dissent from, the doctor's orders. All the doubts and disagreements concerned sprang from other lay conceptions which have already been discussed—in the two cases just described, from stigmatizing conceptions of old age, in three cases from ideas about controlling illness, and in one case from ideas about the management of a relative's death. In nearly all these instances the outcome in terms of behaviour was at best highly equivocal.

These were far from being the only instances, however, in which good patients found themselves in disagreement with doctor's orders because of entrenched beliefs of their own—indeed there were only a few good patients who did not bring up any such disagreement; and it is worth asking why the contradiction was not still more frequently felt. The answer lies, for the most part, in what was said earlier about the cheerful recognition of deviance. Many people felt they ought to obey the doctor, but did not expect always to do everything they ought to do, and indeed expected at times to enjoy not doing it. Then again, obedience was occasionally urged on somebody else while its application to the speaker was mysteriously missed. Alternatively, with those that were conscientious, the disagreement which threatened obedience was on rare occasions pushed back to the borders of conscious recognition. After five months of apparently fruitless investigations, a man who at first left questions to the doctors finally found himself asking 'the reason for a' this':

Wife: "Oh he wis fair browned off."

Husband: "Oh I wis a bitty browned off wi' it. An' then ye wis always wondering, now what is it going tae be this time."

RW: "Was it anxious-making?"

Wife: "No it wisna anxious. We werena anxious."

Husband: "Oh no, no, no, but then there's a' this . . ."

Wife: "It wis at the back o' oor mind."

Husband: "The subconscious mind, we were workin', eh, wondering. Oh many a sleepless night I've had, but—not thinking aboot anything o' that—but just something keeping me off my sleep, you see, just that something."

This suppressed worry had thus gradually given way to a questioning, 'browned-off' attitude which, for the conscientiously obedient, was itself difficult to admit; and only Mary McLachlan appeared to resolve the conflict between the duty of compliance and the fact of dissent, by making compliance conditional on the doctor's intentions. But even in her case, as we have seen, the conflict remained implicit.

In general, then, those who approved obedience and yet disagreed with doctor's orders remained untroubled only when they were not very serious about their obedience, or more lenient on themselves than on others. Those who were indeed serious, and who applied the principle of obedience to themselves, found disagreements of this kind a recurring problem—and, as I have said, such disagreements were common.

Dissent did not, however, present this kind of problem to those who sought autonomy. Where patients both sought control over an issue, and also disagreed about it with the doctor, they simply regarded the doctor as mistaken, and resented attempts to enforce the medical view. The only exceptions to this pattern were themselves illuminating. They occurred when two patients, following their own line, got worse, and received a drubbing from doctor and relatives. One acknowledged he was wrong on this point, but complained that he had not been given enough information to evaluate the doctor's advice; and the other conceded the 'fairness' of obeying the doctor on this point henceforward, because he had given everyone 'a fright', but he continued to think the doctor's warning mistaken and the link with his deterioration fortuitous.

Disagreement, therefore, even disagreement in which the patient had to concede, was quite reconcilable with a continued search for control, and so with a collaborative approach; but it was irreconcilable with conscientious obedience, and so with treating the doctor as the authority. Hence when disagreements occurred, as with strong lay convictions they were apt to, attempts to reconcile these two views of the doctor became impossible.

There remained, though, a third view which, again coherent in itself, was in some measure incompatible with both these preceding approaches. This view, while not common, was distinctive, and offered an awkward but logical possibility which has generally been overlooked: a view of the doctor *as enemy*. An attitude of this kind combined delay in consulting (5.1), with an expectation of disagreement (5.5). It represented a situation where conventional reluctance to consult was so extreme that it became difficult to accept help, and even more difficult to accept advice, or where the help and advice expected was unacceptable anyway, so that consultation was out of the question. Thus in effect this way of thinking became a policy of general hostility to medicine.

A typical example was Elsie Burr, who lived alone and had suffered from breathlessness for four years. In an earlier episode, years previously, an X-ray had shown a 'shadow' on the lung, and the doctor had diagnosed bronchitis; but impressed by the 'shadow', and conscious of having been a heavy smoker both before and since this earlier episode, Miss Burr did not accept that it was bronchitis, and when the breathlessness recurred, would not consult. She was not sure enough of her suspicion that it was cancer to speak clearly about it; she merely hinted darkly, and she had no close family to insist that the problem should be faced and tested. Also, another important deterrent was a brother who had had cancer, and after being 'experimented' upon by the hospital, died, she believed, sooner than necessary. Miss Burr concluded that it was as well not to go to the hospital, but just 'pine away', and thus perhaps survive a little longer. The reaction of her neighbours to these reflections was incredulous—but she regarded this tolerantly as inevitable. Thus against conventional beliefs in the efficacy of doctor's orders, and in going to the doctor in good time, she argued that treatments for cancer did more harm than good, and therefore, when she thought there was a possibility of cancer, did not go to the doctor at all. And with this conclusion she knowingly forfeited the approval of others. As a 'bad patient', she reflected, as in a mirror, the logic of 'good' patients.

This view of the doctor as enemy could not of course be reconciled with seeing the doctor as authority because it assumed disagreement, and disagreement, as we have seen, undermined obedience to the doctor's orders. But nor could it be reconciled with seeing the doctor as a collaborator, for while disagreements were natural to this view, delay in consulting was not.

There were various instances of this tension between delay and the wish to keep personal control, and these argue against the suggestions in the literature, mentioned in the introduction to this chapter, that those who use their own judgement will be inclined to wait before consulting. A simple example was consulting for a lump in the breast: a self-determined couple assumed that immediate information was needed about the nature of the lump in order to take effective decisions, and this made the delay of an acquaintance seem, in comparison with their own response, merely to be sticking one's head in the sand. Similarly, in the night-long dilemma of the heart-attack victim described earlier, his usual insistence on planning his own life was asserted in his subsequent acquisition of an electrical system for opening the door, rather than in his counteracting inclination at the time to wait till morning for fear of making a fuss. And again, in a third case, a wish for control was asserted in the account of the first symptoms, and consultation followed as a matter of course:

"I diagnosed myself before I went to the doctor. I said, 'I'll give you one of two options. It's either the liver or more likely I think a peptic ulcer from the symptoms I have' . . . . And he said, 'Well, okay, I'll examine you.' And he said, 'Yes, I think your diagnosis is quite right.'"

And yet when the specialist appointment came, the fear of appearing overhasty and hypochondriacal asserted itself in opposition:

"'Up on the couch,' he says, 'How are you feeling?' I says, 'Well, I feel very much a cheat.' He says, 'Why's that?' I says, 'Well, frankly, lying here, taking up your time. I feel so much better, you know, I feel almost back to normal apart from spasmodic discomfort, which I just treat myself.'"

Here there was reluctance to see the doctor only when most of the relevant information had already been obtained, and personal control had thereby been asserted. In all these cases, then, the search for control was incompatible with reluctance to consult. Only in one case was such reluctance made consistent with self-reliance, and even the person concerned found it a little paradoxical. This was a man who insisted above all things on 'independence', and who on this basis took the initiative in asking to see a specialist about his leg ulcers, and wished to know about his condition and to make his own arrangements. But on the same basis, he tended to view aggravations of his condition as under his control, and would not in these circumstances trouble the doctor:

"I never call out the doctor unless absolutely necessary."

"Now with your leg, for instance, when you have these—"

"Well, I don't do much about it. I get myself better, and if I see it's not going to get better I go and ask the doctor for something for it . . . ."

"So how long would you take before you did that?"

"Oh quite a long time. I suffer on. I, I rather overdo it sometimes."

"Yes. You've obviously had it longer than a week from time to time?"

"Yes."

"How long?"

"Oh maybe a fortnight I might struggle on, and then if I see no betterment I would go to the doctor after that."

"Yes. If you went straight away do you think the [medication] would help?"

"Probably."

"I see, yes. But you sort of feel it would be—?"

"Well I think it will get better on its own if you're patient and, eh—be sensible about it. Because after all when I'm talking about my leg I know perfectly well as I said to you that I've brought it on myself by rather overdoing things, you see."

"Mmm. So you blame—?"

"I sound all bent and twisted don't I? [Laughs] Not really, no. I know I've a lot of trouble to really blame on myself, shall I put it that way. A lot of the trouble with my leg has been entirely my own fault."

"Yes—so that makes you hesitate to go and?—"

"Yes, well I know."

This uncompromising self-reliance thus asserted not only the need to demand a specialist, and thus to control the quality of the treatment, but also the need to delay, and thus to discipline oneself for causing the problem. However, to delay a fortnight in this case did not betoken any great isolationism, and in the remaining instances which I have discussed conventional pressures to delay were distinctly in tension with attempts to keep control.

Accordingly, when people expected to disagree with the doctor and also tried to avoid consulting, they found it difficult to treat the doctor even as an equal collaborator, let alone as an expert authority; and they were indeed seeing the doctor as an enemy. Such hostility was not, in this Aberdonian generation, part of any elaborated critique of the medical profession based on a preference for alternative ways of healing. Rather, it represented a sceptical stoicism—sceptical towards medicine, stoical towards illness, and always the reverse image of the prompt and obedient 'good patient'. Those who held this reverse image of the appropriate response to doctors were usually aware that other Aberdonians might react forcefully against it; and their expectation of this reaction, together with the precise way in which they reversed the ideal of medical authority, marked out their view as an abandonment of convention which was itself shaped by the logic of that convention.

There were three coherent patterns, then, into which Aberdonian ideas about doctors could be shaped, and two of these were mirror images of one another—the two rationales of the 'good' and the 'bad' patient, the doctor as authority and the doctor as enemy, the positive and its negative, the rule and its antitype. But besides these, and opposed to both, there was also a notion of collaboration, not chary of disagreement, and asserting the ultimate autonomy of the patient— and this was in fact much more common. In the conclusion I consider how the ideas which formed these patterns compare with our present knowledge of relationships between doctors and patients.

Conclusion

At the beginning of this chapter I outlined some of the changes which have occurred in the post-war period in conceptions of the doctor/patient relationship: a picture of a single ideal contract has given way to one in which even this original ideal can subject the patient to uncomfortable double binds; and, in addition, other emerging ideals of patient autonomy have created further potential for contradictions. But in this contemporary picture, it nevertheless seemed clear that the place of older Aberdonians should be at the most conventional and deferent end of the scale of change.

It is plain from the evidence which has followed, though, that these older Aberdonians do not fit their expected place in the existing picture at all well. They recognize more than one valid way of approaching the doctor; and they experience many of the same conflicts and double binds as their juniors. Morever how far these Aberdonians were especially 'medicalized', and regarded their own knowledge as doubtful or worthless, is much in question.

There were two major problems in the relationship between doctor and patient in Aberdeen. There was a problem in harmonizing the conventional Aberdonian principle of delaying consultation with the realism demanded in obeying or collaborating with the doctor; and there was also a recurrent conflict in harmonizing obedience with disagreements arising from personal beliefs and experience. These two problems were distinct. Those who delayed consulting did not do so because they believed in using their own personal judgement, as the work discussed in the introduction to this chapter suggested they might; on the contrary, when people insisted on their own judgement, they wanted good information, and so consulted early. Thus the problem of delay and the problem of obedience can be summarized separately.

Delaying consultation is in Aberdeen not so much an expression of a duty to the doctor, as of a duty to exclude the charge of hypochondria before the court of family and associates; and it is a principle which works well enough provided that there is somebody close at hand to express the opposing principle of realistic need to consult. In these circumstances a bargain can be negotiated in a sort of ritual combat within the family, and a coherent course of consultation and advice can follow. But if there is nobody to take the opposing role, or if either party will not bargain in the (apparently unconscious) fashion which leads to a successful outcome, then there can be serious difficulty in making the transition to accepting help, and this attitude can freeze into one of entrenched hostility to medicine.

As for the convention of medical authority, the problem here is not one of internal incoherence; nor is it primarily a problem with the apparently conflicting principle of autonomy. The need for autonomy can be opposed to medical authority, but there are also many specific ways of reconciling them. Rather, the problem lies in the way people following these two principles react to emerging disagreements; and it is here that acceptance of medical authority leaves the dutiful in a hopeless double bind. For they cannot simply lay aside the convictions derived from their own culture and experience. It is a conflict which the conscientious few acknowledge, expressing it in oscillating choices or running arguments; but it is also a conflict which the shameless majority elude altogether, by making obedience more and more a mere front—something commended to others rather than to oneself, or something cut down to size by indulging in covert pranks. Clearly, though, none of these tactics is an effective way of dealing with the double bind; for, crucially, all undermine patients' chance of sustaining and defending their judgement of events when they meet the doctor.

Turning now to the question of whether these Aberdonians had absorbed a belief in medical expertise and a distrust in their own judgement, it is obvious that the conclusions just drawn pose serious difficulties for such an inference. The two problems which have been identified in relationships with the doctor both reveal a considerable capacity for inner resistance to medical control, based on judgements derived from beliefs which at other times were a powerful ally of medicine. Lay theories of hypochondria lay behind the principle of delayed consultation. And moral convictions about illness, ageing, and death governed the majority of the disagreements which led to covert resistance. The most that can be said for the view that older Aberdonians were 'medicalized' is that obedience, when it was professed, was a working-class maxim, and thus may reflect a (frequently nominal) acceptance of medical control based upon the different positions of the doctor and the working-class patient in the social hierarchy—a subject further explored in Chapter 8. And it is also true that, even amongst those who liked to use their own judgement, orthodox medicine was much more readily accepted than alternative medicine; indeed the kind of control which Aberdonians sought was likely to make them consult orthodox medicine promptly, and the wish for control could at times be accommodated with obedience to doctor's orders. But with these qualifications stated, these Aberdonians had in no sense given up their own convictions or acquired an overall deference to experts; they held hard to their point of view, and it led them into frequent disagreement with, and even obstinate hostility towards, the doctor.

Rather than finding the basis for medical control in beliefs about the doctor's expertise, therefore, even in this reputedly well-disposed generation, a stronger case can be made for finding it in the moral dilemmas of patients and in the courtesies of the consultation. Some of the ideas detailed here are significant, not because they represent an uncritical submissiveness, but because they create contradictory moral imperatives by which the patient's account can be subverted. Patients have to be good communicators if they are to convince themselves and others that they do not go to the doctor for every little thing, and yet that they are not scared to face the truth; or that they obey doctor's orders, and yet that they know how to fight illness and old age for themselves. But even where patients can successfully avoid inconsistency—the best examples in Aberdeen being the full-blooded consumerists who believed in making their own decisions—there remain tight limits in the rules of consultation as this generation understands them. Just as the doctor behaves as if the patient were generically competent,[25] so the patient, with a like courtesy, behaves as if the doctor typically possessed ideal qualities: 'I ken that doctors like to know.' And being bound by this convention of gentility, the Aberdonian patient of this generation is further bound by the assumption that there are few alternatives to orthodox medicine, and by the various monopolistic practices that, everywhere in Britain, make escape from unsatisfactory relationships difficult.

What distinguishes this generation from its successors, then, is not its greater faith in the medical profession—there is too much private criticism, struggle for autonomy, disagreement, deviance, and downright avoidance to argue that; rather, it is a greater tendency, in spite of these private views, to fear the charge of hypochondria, to believe in obeying orders, and, in answers to formal questions or in meetings on medical ground, to maintain the courtesies towards professionals who are in any case considered to be almost the sole recourse.

Why, then, should this generation be especially susceptible to these moral dilemmas, and especially deferent to these ceremonial forms? The evidence given earlier, together with historical considerations, offers some hypotheses.

First, the moral dilemmas arise partly because the NHS inherited somewhat separate clinical relationships for rich and poor. Those born in families who were able to pay were previously accustomed to consumer choice, and the NHS continued to give many opportunities to exercise consumer choice, in ways which I discuss further in Chapter 8. Those born in poorer families, meanwhile, were previously accustomed to gratitude for voluntary or charitable provision, to sparing use of insured services provided under strict control by friendly societies of their peers, or to ill-afforded expense. The NHS removed these restrictions, but not the habit of sanctioning those felt to be prone to malingering or hypochondria; and care continued to be given or received on paternalistic assumptions which place these patients in a characteristic double bind.

Secondly, habits of deference are also illuminated by the fact that all the members of this generation were brought up in a complex structure of private medicine—a structure mitigated certainly by varying levels of medical insurance, and by extensive charitable and voluntary provision, but in either event using doctors who also had private practices. This was a system characterized by private contract, gentility in forms of address, and deference to clinical expertise.[26] These characteristics were again inherited by the NHS; and so throughout their medical careers, all of this generation have been accustomed to ceremonial forms expressing clinical authority; and this is congruent with the respect for authority which is, as we have seen, part of the way they conceive their generational identity.

For all these reasons, therefore, doctors under the NHS continue to command this generation's deference in public and medical settings. But it is also intelligible that in private they are neither passive nor uncritical; on the contrary, partly because the diversity of ideal doctor/patient relationships makes for mismatched expectations, partly because their respect for authority and fear of hypochondria generate moral dilemmas, disagreement, disappointment, and frustration are commonplace. It is this distinction between public and private attitudes towards the doctor which is thus sharpest among the old. They do not have the younger generation's general antagonism to ceremonial forms expressive of hierarchy, nor their uncomplicated endorsement of private judgement, nor are they so conscious of, or courted by, new forms of alternative medicine; and it is these developments which enable their juniors to be less diffident about taking their private frustrations into the public and medical arena.

Notes and References

1. C. Herzlich and J. Pierret, *Malades d'heir, malades d'aujour-d'hui*, Paris: Payot, 1984, chs. 11–12; M. Jefferys and H. Sachs, *Rethinking general practice*, London: Tavistock, 1983, chs. 15–16; A. Cartwright and R. Anderson, *General practice revisited*, London: Tavistock, 1981.

2. D. Tuckett, M. Boulton, C. Olson, and A. Williams, *Meetings between experts: an approach to sharing ideas in medical consultations*, London: Tavistock, 1985, ch. 9; S. Halpern, 'What the public thinks of the NHS', *Health and Soc. Servs. J.* (6 June 1985), 703–4; M. Blaxter and E. Paterson, *Mothers and daughters: a three-generational study of health attitudes and behaviour*, London: Heinemann, 1982, ch. 14; J. Cornwell, *Hard-earned lives: accounts of health and illness from East London*, London: Tavistock, 1984, pp. 182–7; Jefferys and Sachs, *Rethinking general practice*; Cartwright and Anderson, *General practice revisited*, ch. 8.

3. Tuckett *et al.*, *Meetings between experts*, pp. 107 f.; Jefferys and Sachs, *Rethinking general practice*.

4. Herzlich, *Malades d'hier*, pp. 252, 277, 282.

5. Jefferys and Sachs, *Rethinking general practice*, p. 21.

6. Herzlich and Pierret, *Malades d'hier*, chs. 11–12.

7. T. Parsons, *The social system*, London: Routledge, 1951, ch. 10.

8. T. Szasz and M. H. Hollender, 'A contribution to the philosophy of medicine', *Arch. Intern. Med.* 97 (1956), 585–92.

9. E. Freidson, *Profession of medicine*, New York: Dodd, Mead and Co., 1971, ch. 14.

10. G. Stimson and B. Webb, *Going to see the doctor*, London: Routledge, 1975.

11. E. Freidson, *Professional dominance*, New York: Atherton, 1970.

12. M. J. Bloor, 'Professional autonomy and client exclusion: a study in ENT clinics', in M. Wadsworth and D. Robinson (eds.), *Studies in everyday medical life*, London: Martin Robertson, 1976; Stimson and Webb, *Going to see the doctor*.

13. H. Waitzkin, 'Medicine, superstructure and micropolitics', *Soc. Sci. and Med.* 13A (1979), 601–9; I. Illich, *Limits to medicine*, London: Penguin, 1977.

14. M. Foucault, *The birth of the clinic*, London: Tavistock, 1973.
15. N. D. Jewson, 'The disappearance of the sick man from medical cosmology 1770–1870', *Sociology*, 10 (1976), 225–44.
16. D. Silverman, *Communication and medical practice*, London: Sage, 1987; D. Armstrong, *The political anatomy of the body*, Cambridge University Press, 1983.
17. Silverman, *Communication and medical practice*, chs. 8–10.
18. A. Cartwright, *Patients and their doctors*, London: Routledge, 1967, ch. 4.
19. M. J. Bloor and G. W. Horobin, 'Conflict and conflict resolution in doctor/patient interactions,' in C. Cox and A. Mead (eds.), *A sociology of medical practice*, London: Collier-Macmillan, 1975.
20. Blaxter and Paterson, *Mothers and daughters*.
21. M. Calnan, 'Clinical uncertainty: is it a problem in the doctor-patient relationship,' *Sociol. Health and Illness*, 6 (1984), 74–85; P. M. Strong, *The ceremonial order of the clinic*, London: Routledge, 1979; Jefferys and Sachs, *Rethinking general practice*, pp. 288–91; Tuckett *et al.*, *Meetings between experts*, ch. 6; Stimson and Webb, *Going to see the doctor*, ch. 3.
22. Stimson and Webb, *Going to see the doctor*, ch. 5.
23. D. Robinson, *The process of becoming ill*, London: Routledge, 1971.
24. Similar congratulatory forms are a routine feature of successful surgery on infants— see Silverman, *Communication and medical practice*, ch. 3.
25. See Strong, *The ceremonial order of the clinic*.
26. This is Strong's argument, from a mimeo which is summarized and supported in Silverman, *Communication and medical practice*, ch. 5.

PART II
Formative Influences

6

Moral persuasion and physical experience

Where, or how, she obtained the information which formed
the subject of her gossip it would often have been vain to
inquire; but on this you might rely that, in matters of domestic
history in the neighbourhood, and particularly if the subject
approached the borders of scandal, Meg was certain to be
informed.

William Alexander, *Johnny Gibb of Gushetneuk*, 1884

Introduction

We have now seen something of how older Aberdonians think
when coping with medical aspects of their life. We have seen their
certainties and their dilemmas. But what are the vital influences
that shape these inner resources, with their strengths and their
flaws? Some of the influences derive from past experience, and I
deal with these in the chapters following. But some are continuously
at work in everyday life, and they are the concern of this chapter.
Most prominent among them are, on the one hand, the continuous
persuasive effort of Aberdonian public opinion, and on the other,
the harsh necessities of physical change.

Public opinion is formed by the interaction of people's attitudes,
while physical change typically affects their behaviour. Therefore
a study of public opinion and physical change inevitably raises
questions about the relation between attitudes and behaviour. Up
till now, attitudes and behaviour, thinking and practice, have been
closely interwoven in Aberdonian accounts of how to cope. In this
chapter, though, we have to consider a fundamental question
about such accounts: how far are the attitudes which I have described merely a surface phenomenon, simply justifying behaviour,
or alternatively denying it in order to present an acceptable picture

of the person speaking; and how far are they the arguments of people who, after discussing their situation with others, are shaping their practice in as rational a process as possible?

The exchanges which form public opinion are embedded in the informal life of gossip and acquaintanceship, and, as I noted in the introduction to this book, the best accounts of them have usually come from anthropologists who participate in a public village society. The private commentaries of urban acquaintanceship are not so easily observed; and illness, ageing, and death are among the areas of life in which they have been least observed. Among the exceptions are several studies, mostly in America, of homes or housing arrangements where the elderly live together, or of centres where they meet by day.[1] But in the wider community outside such centres, comment passes around unseen networks of acquaintanceship whose structure can be very variable.[2] There are indications of the importance of advice and support from such networks in coronary heart disease and in pregnancy,[3] and also immediately after a death,[4] but in general very little is known about the praise and criticism given to those who are coping in the long term with the threat of death, ageing, or illness, and it has been suggested that in some of these areas moral guidance from others can be so contradictory, or so ineffective, as to constitute a state of virtual 'normlessness'.[5] A study which opens a window, however small, into this relatively private sphere of social relationships can thus help to fill a considerable gap.

If these processes of moral persuasion are strong among older Aberdonians, there should be a degree of consistency in their attitudes and coping behaviour over time. Any kind of attitude may be relevant. Public opinion does not only enforce norms; it also acts as a witness to the preferences which people express in areas where choice is legitimate. Thus in either case people become committed to their views by public discussion, and the evidence shows that when once committed in this way they are more likely to be consistent in their attitude over time, and to accompany their attitude with appropriate behaviour.[6]

This picture of the way public opinion works presupposes, of course, not only that attitudes agree with behaviour, but also that behaviour flows from attitudes in a relatively rational way. It presupposes that attitudes give rise to intentions, and intentions to behaviour,[7] a formula which in recent years has had a number of reasonably successful applications in the health field.[8] In this case, public opinion, by affecting attitudes, affects behaviour too. However there is also another, less rational way in which attitudes can agree with behaviour, and this occurs when people adopt attitudes in order to make sense of their behaviour retrospectively, by attributing appropriate motives to it after the event.[9] Again there are examples in the health field,[10] but such retrospective glosses are commonest in situations where people accept their behaviour as voluntary, but have forgotten their initial attitude or did not set much store by it in the first place.[11] In this event, public opinion affects, not the behaviour, but merely the interpretation put on it.

In both of these cases attitudes and behaviour—whether rational or irrational—are at least consistent. However this is not always so, for the whole subject of attitudes is also bedevilled by numerous notorious problems of inconsistency; and these are often connected with the way in which new events and experiences are handled— the second topic of this chapter. These responses to new events may also be rational or irrational, but before I consider this let us see what sorts of problems there are.

The first problem is that attitudes themselves can be somewhat volatile. This is not perhaps so surprising, especially in the long term, for certain phases of life are especially liable to experiment and change, and in the health field it has been shown that attitudes to health prevention in middle age can bear little relation to those held in childhood.[12] It is reasonable to suppose that with increasing age such changes may slow down.

Secondly, though, the existing academic literature also provides a remarkable catalogue of inconsistency not only between attitudes over time, but also between attitudes and behaviour;[13] and the applications of this literature in health education have often produced similar anomalies.[14] Some of the blame may attach to defects of method, and suggestions have been made on the one hand for improving the measures used in experiments,[15] and on the other for more thorough naturalistic observation of social life[16]—this second approach being the one attempted here.

In fact, though, all these types of inconsistency can easily occur in ordinary experience, and they can occur in the course of thinking and acting perfectly rationally. Our attitudes themselves can conflict, as earlier chapters have shown, whether because of new experiences in the recent past or because of unresolved contradictions in the culture; and in this situation behaviour which expresses one attitude necessarily conflicts with another attitude. Similarly an action may answer to a corresponding attitude at the moment when it is carried out, but not to an attitude expressed a month before; and this may be an entirely rational process if, in the meantime, an event has occurred which contradicts a belief essential to the earlier attitude. It would be quite natural to be struggling with contradictory beliefs and behaviour in these circumstances, and such contradictions can only be ignored by those who have exceptionally powerful beliefs and strong social support.[17]

Thus new experiences can bring inconsistencies between attitudes and behaviour which are part of a quite rational process. But they can also bring inconsistencies which remain stubbornly irrational. Events can affect behaviour directly without much mediation through conscious attitudes and intentions, and behaviour can grow into a habit which controls subsequent behaviour, even when social norms and personal attitudes and intentions are opposed to it. In the health field the examples of smoking, drugs, and alcohol are a perpetual reminder of this. Even among young schoolchildren, the great majority of regular smokers believe the habit is bad for them and should be stopped.[18] And with drinking and drugs likewise, previous behaviour has an independent influence on present behaviour, and this, in the case of hard drugs, can be clearly contrary to intentions.[19] In the present context such examples may be relevant to behaviour which is restricted by the onset of disability. We have to ask, for instance, whether habits thus engendered can persist even when physical constraints are eased, despite intentions to the contrary. This would be an example of an event producing conflicts between behaviour and attitude which are irrational.

There are many questions to be asked, therefore, about the process through which the attitudes of Aberdonians affect their behaviour, or their behaviour their attitudes, as they cope from day to day; and these questions bear, as we have seen, on larger issues concerned with their responses to moral persuasion and physical experience. On the one hand are the issues related to public opinion; what judgements do Aberdonians agree on, and how effectively do they collaborate to co-opt private attitudes and behaviour? On the other hand are the issues related to physical events: do they compel behavioural changes which give rise to a change in attitudes, or are they appraised in a rational process where attitudes direct, or redirect, behaviour? These forces of social control on the one hand, and of physical change on the other, impinging on people who are trying, often unsuccessfully, to shape their consciousness and their behaviour to deal coherently with both, become sharply apparent when one listens to older Aberdonians commenting on one another, and sees them responding to their situation over a period of time.

Public opinion in Aberdeen

There were two networks of acquaintances down which gossip and comment travelled in the present study, one in the West End and one on the Mannoch estate, of which the estate network was more connected, and the West End one more fragmentary, comprising a loose federation of small social circles. I begin by considering who made the appraisals in each network, and who attracted them; then I review how far the appraisals corresponded with my experience; thirdly, I describe which attitudes attracted appraisal, and which were treated as private, and what standards were agreed in appraising them; and finally I discuss how far praise and blame were relayed back to their subjects, and what effects this may have had.

In both Mannoch and the West End, the people who were pivotal to many lines of acquaintanceship were naturally in the thick of the flow of comment, both contributing liberally to the flow themselves, and as liberally attracting comment on their own actions. There was a small bias here due to my research procedures, which meant that members of the organizations for the retired where I began had slightly more chance than others of airing their views to me as time went on.[20] But this aside, those most frequently commenting and commented upon were unmistakably among the social entrepreneurs of each locality, sometimes competing with one another for leadership in their circle, sometimes forming alliances to bring a waverer into line. Nearly all of these entrepreneurs were women, and the few men who also played this active part had equally active wives—a feminine bias which is general in organizations for older people, though common enough in many local organizations and networks of any age range.[21] But although it was mainly women who linked the varied channels of acquaintanceship, they depended also upon a larger and less vocal constituency which included people from both sexes. Members of this constituency led a less active social life, but were connected by direct acquaintanceship to one or two of the leading figures, and they contributed an opinion on local stories, or attracted notice themselves, now and again. In addition, though, each network also included two other groups. One of these was largely made up of a few husbands who, though known to members of the network, took part in very few of their doings, and were more interested in other acquaintances of their own; and the other group included people of both sexes who were genuinely isolated—a fact which enabled the study to reach the antisocial as well as the gregarious. The distinctive contribution of these latter groups was not so much to comment as to be commented upon; and while much of this comment was unfavourable there were also, in addition to the bad examples thus furnished for censure, good examples made the more impressive by a general ignorance of the detailed situation of the person concerned. Catriona Macpherson, for instance, was warmly commended by three people as being 'aye cheery', though it was said that, compared with certain others who were given to 'moaning', she really had something to complain about; but apart from the fact that she walked very slowly with two sticks nobody knew what was wrong with her, nor yet with the housebound husband she looked after. This ignorance was intelligible in that her conversation with her neighbours (and for much of the time with me) was confined to brief but hearty expressions of good will and optimism; and apart from this she spoke regularly to no one but her husband (infrequently, as he was very deaf), and her home help (who came twice a week). Her remaining friends and sisters all lived over forty miles away, and of her neighbours she merely said that, while they were 'very nice', 'we don't run in and out of each other's houses—it's better that way'. Thus it was not so much in spite of, but because of, this isolation, that she played an important, because uncomplicated, role in the mythology of the network as somebody who was coping well and who ought to be emulated.

This, then, was the kind of structure through which moral criticism made itself felt; but if it was to be effective the content of that criticism had to be well informed. In the West End and Mannoch alike, with certain exceptions, it was. Because it took time for people to trust me with comments, those I heard concerned 37 people interviewed mainly in the first half of the field-work, and I recorded an average of two comments on each. These particular comments concerned attitudes to health, ageing, or death; and in the text of my own conversations with the people concerned there was material to justify the comments made in four-fifths of the instances. In many of the remainder there was no indication either way (occasionally because the comment was vague anyway), and only in a small proportion of instances was the text of my conversations and the commentary of others apparently at odds. In three of these instances the inaccuracy was undoubtedly in my own version, revealing facts and sentiments unavowed to me; in four instances there was a history of divided opinion which made it plausible that the people concerned and their critics would supply differing versions; and in the remaining instance it was unclear whether my version or the critic's was at fault.

This very substantial agreement between what people said to me and what others said they said reflects the fact that most of them had certain well-known and well-rehearsed ideas which they were as happy to impart to me as to their friends. But did they have other ideas which were less well known? Sometimes it was apparent that people had certain areas where they guarded their privacy from their friends, though they might speak to me as a stranger, and that they likewise had areas of privacy which they guarded either from strangers or from both. In the latter case I could realize that people were cautious in some respect without necessarily being able to identify what topics they felt cautious about; but more often I was given a fairly clear idea about topics which people did not wish to be mentioned elsewhere, and it is possible to see how these topics compared with the topics which attracted the comments of others.

Of the various aspects of physical loss so far discussed, death relatively often gave rise to thoughts which were indicated as private in some regard; and death, correspondingly, was a subject on which other people's thoughts were seldom widely known—or seldom, at least, commented upon. This does not mean that death was, in any generalized sense, a taboo subject—on the contrary, there were several occasions on which I heard it discussed freely between neighbours, friends, or relatives—but unlike illness and ageing, which formed part of the daily grist, it was not discussed frequently; and there were situations, and relationships, in which it was difficult to discuss it at all. The chief situation, as I showed earlier, was when somebody was personally threatened by death or bereavement; but even outside this context, discussion of personal preferences was not always easy between husband and wife or between parents and children. It may be that, given this occasional reserve between close relatives, talk was also restricted with friends of the family lest what one relative felt should be accidentally disclosed to another. But whatever the explanation, ideas about death were much less subject to popular criticism than ideas about doctors, health, and ageing.

Of these latter subjects, attitudes to the doctor and attitudes to ageing were not treated as private, but they attracted less comment from other people than attitudes to health. This was despite the fact that health, like death, was a subject on which people quite often sought a degree of privacy. This combination of public interest and personal discretion was in fact a sign that attitudes to health were the main focus of popular criticism and thus of informal social control. This was apparent first in the fact that attempts at secrecy about responses to illness were sometimes designed to evade criticism, though they did not always succeed in doing so. Mrs Sinclair's initial belief that she had cancer was carefully concealed from her neighbours and acquaintances even after she had been operated on for what had turned out to be an unproblematic cyst, though the neighbours proved to be well able to put two and two together on their own. But in addition, concealment was sometimes intended, not to conceal, but rather to display the required self-control. Illness was partly treated as a private topic because, however vigorously other people's illnesses were discussed, to speak about one's own at any length was itself to display the wrong attitude:

Everyone has to listen to her tell about her illnesses and her new drug and I don't know what a'. Now I might tell friends, but she tells everyone. You just get tired out listening. Yap, yap, yap.

Thus the sick had a communicatory task of considerable difficulty: they had to secure credit for their attitude to illness in the public estimation, while at the same time saying very little about it. And it was no wonder that with these constraints the task of accounting for oneself to others was occasionally too much:

People ask me how I am; I just say fine, fine. Dr Cowie used to say to me, no use asking you how you are, you're fine, aren't you? But people aren't interested, you can't explain. I hate explanations.

Attempts to treat illness as private, therefore, signalled the highly constraining power of public opinion in this regard.

What, though, was the content of the judgements made about others on the subject of health? And, considering the diverse attitudes to illness recorded in Chapter 1, how far were these judgements agreed? Despite the variety of personal views, it was not difficult for commentators to trade on large areas of agreement. In the commonly accepted formula, praise was lavished on the active—those who maintained the view that illness could be controlled by normal living (1.1), and on those who, when this failed, nevertheless kept up a continuous struggle against the illness (1.2); and similarly it was awarded to those who resisted through their activity the advance of real old age and the legitimate surrender which it offered (2.4). This common currency of praise was the outcome of an alliance between the two major views of illness, the one optimistically viewing all illness as controllable (1.1) or at least resistable (1.2), and the other pessimistically viewing minor illness as controllable (1.1) and major illness as beyond the pale (1.4).

Nevertheless, this coalition of views was not omnipotent. Those who sought to cope with severe restriction positively, and to make an alternative way of life (1.3), formed one potentially disaffected group who sometimes tried to broaden the views of proponents of normal living, and to work upon their concept of what was normal. And a number of other people did not believe they could meet these standards of normality anyway, and relapsed into one of the views condemned: a view of illness as a loss to be endured (1.4)—exasperatingly false or miserably true to optimists and pessimists respectively, or a view of illness as a release from effort (1.5)—offensive to both. These condemnatory judgements were mostly accepted by those who came out worst from them, but they did not go entirely unchallenged. It is true that, since they emanated from an alliance of the social entrepreneurs at the pivotal points of the network, they represented the governing consensus; but a challenge sometimes came from those isolates who, though unable to raise a constituency of their own, were sufficiently articulate and unconvinced to frame an opposing point of view. In this opposing interpretation things were turned upside down: it was folly in others to believe that health could be sustained by normal living, silly of them to resist real old age, and, as I indicated earlier, senseless of them to consult or listen to a doctor. Thus there was occasional resistance to the commonly agreed criteria for praise and blame, and even amongst those who accepted the criteria there were some who still provoked a reaction by doing the wrong thing. There was, in fact, a process of persuasion and counter-persuasion at work to which I now turn.

For appraisals to persuade, they not only need to be accurate in their facts and agreed in their evaluations, but they also need to be communicated to their subjects. It is not of course necessarily required that a particular conversation should be relayed back, but only that, by whatever means, the subject should be aware that appraisals of a particular kind are likely to be made; and one way in which this is learnt is by making them oneself in the company of others.

In these Aberdeen networks, most people shared appraisals on these subjects and thus knew the pattern they commonly took; but knowledge of how one is oneself seen adds specific persuasive force. In Aberdeen it seemed to be particularly the case with praise that evidence of its being relayed back in this way was lacking. This does not mean that praise was not in fact relayed back, but only that people did not demonstrate knowledge of being commended in the same way as they demonstrated knowledge of being criticized. No doubt such demonstrations were subject to a code of modesty, and certainly there were occasions when I passed on compliments which were discounted as civility, or indeed carefully tested for ambiguities. But whatever the case with compliments, criticism was certainly likely to be cited by those criticized. Indeed it was as likely to be cited as it was to be passed over—cited not in the sense that it was necessarily attributed to the particular person whom I had heard uttering it, though some was, but in the sense that its utterance was known and taken into account in what was said. And in extreme cases, criticism was not only known and attributed, but there was an explicit history of attack and defence, of persuasive expeditions and dissuasive stratagems.

There were examples of these long-running histories both in the West End and in Mannoch. In the West End, for instance, Lilian Eadie, who lived on her own in a large house with no family near and only two regular visitors, had for years been a matter of concern to Margaret Gordon, the most active visitor. Lilian was perfectly clear how she stood in Margaret's estimation as regards attitudes to illness. When Lilian questioned the usefulness of doctors, Margaret exclaimed 'Rubbish!' and called the GP. When Lilian said she was finished with keeping house, Margaret arrived in a car to take her shopping. But Lilian's description of Margaret's views, while factually correct, was charged with wholly opposed connotations. '*She's* not going to be old,' was one summary, and then, gently debunking, 'I didn't think *I* was going to be old.' And there were also counter-attacks:

Margaret comes in and says 'Oh my back is so painful, I've been cleaning this and cleaning that,' and I say you can't go on like that. I say to Edwina [her other visitor] you'll have to stop her. I say what'll you do when it comes to you—because it comes to all of us.

But at the same time Margaret was, in some ways, a being from another world, the sort of person who 'goes out and about', and 'knows many people up and down', and 'looks marvellous'—all attributes in which Lilian felt herself to be painfully lacking. And so the relationship persisted in its delicate stalemate, Margaret always hoping to persuade, Lilian reaping news of Margaret's world and at the same time countering persuasion, until each could predict the other's moves with certainty, as Margaret did when considering plans for a thorough spring-clean:

Lilian would say, don't *do* it [Margaret here waves a languid hand], don't *do* it.

The only difference about such long-running duels in Mannoch was that they tended, because of the more localized and unified character of the network of acquaintanceship, to be played out before a larger audience. Bella Nairn, for example, well known in the locality as 'Big Bella', had made a number of efforts to reform Ivy Johnston, who had, in her view, declined sadly in her attitude to her health in the past decade. The charge was that Ivy went greeting on (complaining), and would not take part in things, although invited to gatherings at the community centre and the Citadel, and—the clinching argument—that she was pleased to be visited by Bella when she was not well, but did not visit Bella when Bella was not well. In her zeal to demonstrate her point, Bella then asked me, when I called on Ivy, to convey Bella's good wishes, and to say that she could not visit her because she was (truthfully enough) unwell. In response to this message Ivy at once showed recognition of how in general Bella viewed her: she said that Bella used to call in on a Saturday morning and take her by the arm (she mimed an energetic sweeping movement) to the shops—but she had stopped calling, and Ivy supposed it was because she, Ivy, had not been up to return the visits. And she said that she would have to go and do so. I was to say that it couldn't be tomorrow, but when she could make her way up. When this was reported to her, Bella remained sceptical, and remarked 'She'll no come, you'll see.' Nor did she. Ivy remained in her house, spending her time, in her own rueful words, in 'raising my voice all the time, complaining', while Bella declared to her many acquaintances that she would visit Ivy no longer, not having any more spirit for hearing her 'girning on'.

This, however, perhaps needless to say, was not the end of the story: the fascination of opposites continued to draw Bella to her perverse acquaintance, and after some months in which she deputed somebody else to visit her, taking care that this should be known as a mark of displeasure, she 'broke the ice' by calling on Ivy and having a 'good row', telling her that 'I think little of you and less of your son' because the one had not visited, nor had the other been deputed to visit, to enquire after Bella's health. Ivy's response— 'Oh, I'm to blame, I'm to blame'—reflected the extent to which she had herself absorbed Bella's judgements; but in her continuing lamented inability to do right by them she was, although a failure in terms of persuasion, a most satisfactory warning to others and a corroboration of the rightness of those judgements. The saga was laughed over by Bella's acquaintance, men and women alike, and the conclusion drawn invariably favoured her side: she was 'gae-aheid', and, though it was acknowledged that she could be 'abrupt' and some did not like her, it was said that nobody would go out of their way to help you more; indeed if anyone did not like Bella Nairn they should be knocked on the head.

It is in these extreme examples, then, that the workings of public criticism through the gossip network are most clearly revealed; and it is here that the parts taken by social entrepreneurs on the one hand, and by social isolates on the other, can be seen being played out before an audience assembled by the entrepreneurs— assembled, not indeed for that purpose, but as a byproduct of their general social energy. And it is plain that the praise or blame circulating around this network is much concerned with health attitudes, and is, in the case of blame, soon picked up and given recognition by the person concerned. But public opinion, although a powerful force in maintaining the boundaries of acceptable thinking, also emerges as a fairly blunt instrument. Being the product of an alliance between the two most compatible, though still partly conflicting, ways of thinking about illness, it elides fine distinctions and tends towards a rather broad separation of the good and the bad.

Bearing in mind these characteristics of Aberdonian public opinion in matters of health, it is now possible to see how far individual Aberdonians became committed by it to attitudes which they maintained over time, expressed in behaviour, and tried to vindicate against the vicissitudes of physical change.

Sustaining views of illness over time

In order to study the operation of these ideas and rules of behaviour over time, the material recorded from each person's conversation on this topic of illness was first mapped to show consistencies and contradictions, and then distinguished by the dates at which it was recorded. Also, the material was divided into simple expressions of attitude and intention, accounts of behaviour (usually of course with attitudinal overtones), and accounts of illness events. In this way, a list was made of all instances suggesting a confirmation or contradiction of earlier attitudes by later attitudes or behaviour, with account being taken of intervening events. These instances were then examined and classified as 'adequate' or 'marginal' examples of consistency or contradiction, using procedures which are more fully explained in Appendix 2. The resulting picture of stability and change is relatively short-term, but not trivial: the time which elapsed between earlier and later accounts varied from one month to fourteen months, with an average of five months.

It was only possible, because of time constraints, to revisit about half the sample (31 cases), and so these were nearly all drawn from those interviewed in the first half of the sequence. This group of cases varies quite similarly to the total sample in age, sex, marital status, and social class, though, as with the group who made appraising comments, it has a higher proportion of people who were members of clubs.[22]

The material on illness thus provided was summarized in a large number of premises which, in the cases revisited, permitted some 62 comparisons of earlier and later expressions, drawn from 26 cases out of the 31,[23] these comparisons comprising nearly a third of all the feasible comparisons on all topics. Taking these comparisons, I first consider the stability of attitudes over time on their own, and then I show what happened when some relevant behaviour, or an intrusive event, took place between the earlier and later interviews. An 'intrusive event', in the sense intended, is something happening to the person concerned which was not an expected aspect of the routine described at an earlier interview. A 'behaviour', however, might be routine or otherwise, provided that it was subsequent to the earlier interview.

Stability of attitudes on their own

There were 22 comparisons available between earlier and later attitudes with no relevant behaviour or intrusive event referred to as intervening. These 22 comparisons were drawn from 15 out of the 31 cases. Out of the 22 comparisons involved here, all showed consistency (one of these cases being a marginal example). None of the comparisons suggested adequate or even marginal examples of a contradiction. Most of these instances involved similar judgements being passed on past events or behaviour, or similar generalities, though some also involved judgements on events which had happened to other people since the earlier interview.

Was this consistency a product of the method—and in particular of my presence as an interviewer? Although earlier attitudes could not be recast in retrospect to suit later attitudes, people might remember something of what they said on an earlier occasion and formulate later attitudes to be consistent with it. There were, certainly, instances when people did recall a small piece of an early conversation for many months; and there were instances when I recalled an earlier comment in order to probe it further. But these instances were noted as such, and they were not a feature of the continuities recorded here. Rather, the present continuities reflected the much more common instances when the same stories were retold and the same beliefs reaffirmed in evident ignorance that they had been told to me once before, as indeed they had been told to other acquaintances to whom I spoke. Thus people sought to remain consistent with these favourite judgements, to which they were committed not just with me but with their acquaintances as well.

As far as pure judgements go, then, undisturbed by the need to act, consistency was the rule among these cases.

Behaviour in the absence of events

There were 23 comparisons of earlier and later attitudes, which involved relevant intervening behaviour, but no relevant intrusive event. These comparisons were drawn from 13 cases out of the 31.

The procedure for determining consistency and contradiction in these instances is similar to that described in Appendix 2; but additional judgements have to be made about how far the intervening behaviour confirms or contradicts initial attitudes. Here an important feature of the procedure is to have the behaviour described, so far as possible, in the actor's own terms. Since my information about what people did usually came from the people themselves, this presents little problem; but in two instances I use descriptions by others of what the people in question told them.

Again the majority of these comparisons indicated consistency (18 adequate examples), although some contradictions also emerged (3 adequate, 2 marginal). Only one of these contradictions was a straightforward case of voluntary behaviour which nevertheless contradicted a consistent earlier attitude—a case which is of course anything but straightforward theoretically, and of considerable interest. The remaining contradictions (2 adequate, 2 marginal) all involved behaviour related to attitudes which were already contradictory at the earlier interview; thus in this last case a relevant response was bound to confirm one of these earlier attitudes and deny the other. Typical examples were the women who were torn between the view of illness as a release (1.5) and that of illness as controllable by normal living (1.1). I described earlier how one of these, Ivy Johnston, failed to keep to her commitment—which she accepted as a normal obligation—to visit her sick friend. This was also an obligation which would get her walking, and this she recognized as a help to her health. But her failure to meet it was only too consistent with her other, opposed conviction, expressed at the outset, that she had lost her health, lost her spirit, could not go on fighting, and at her age needed to lie down and be at peace. Such antecedent contradictions of attitude were thus an important source of later contradictory behaviour.

Turning now to the behaviour which was consistent, it has to be borne in mind that although the attitudes are recorded prospectively, the recording of behaviour necessarily had a retrospective element. I only occasionally witnessed the actions concerned, and on the whole people spoke about selected examples of their recent doings as part of their subsequent account of their intervening experiences. The recording of relevant behaviour is thus unlikely to have been complete, and it may reflect a tendency, in expressing later attitudes, to recall only recent behaviour which was consistent with them. To the extent that this is so, the consistency of the later behaviour which people recalled with the earlier attitudes which I recorded may reflect in part the consistency of attitudes themselves over time. Nevertheless, the material does permit us to explore some of the ways in which different attitudes can be exemplified in behaviour.

The range of attitudes which were later expressed in behaviour was wide, including instances of all the main premises expressed in Aberdonian talk about illness. The idea that illness could be controlled by normal living (1.1), for example, and the view of illness as a continuous struggle (1.2), were often expressed, as I noted in Chapter 1, in a way which identified some key activity—housework, helping others, walking, golfing, and so on—as essential to the person concerned; and later conversations featured news of these activities, or, as with the social entrepreneurs described earlier, accounts of chiding, encouraging, or coaxing others to take part in them. Similarly aids or adaptations considered to be too obviously abnormal had sometimes been suggested in the interim, and rejected. By contrast, those who saw illness as a loss to be endured (1.4) continued to be inactive in significant ways, as when they were offered opportunities to go out, and were given encouragement to do so, but refused, or said it would be of no use. With those who tried to construct illness as an alternative way of life (1.3), on the other hand, the behavioural pattern indicated was more complex. First, it required controlled determination, and a careful observation of limits. This was a theme which, in early conversations, husband and wife—like the couple quoted on this subject in Chapter 1—often orchestrated together; and later conversations confirmed this pattern of collaborative admonition. Combined with this control, though, was the effort made to establish alternative activities, and later accounts gave news of these and of the often complicated arrangements made to organize them, or to get lifts to the place where they occurred. The only view, in fact, which was not always easy to identify specifically in later behaviour was that which saw illness as a release from a burdensome activity (1.5); and this problem of identification arose partly because activities can only be seen to be given up when an occasion for taking part in them arises. With optional activities such occasions need never arise, and so it was only where activities were conventionally required that, as with Ivy Johnston, their omission is in itself a significant piece of behaviour.

It is obvious from this description that these forms of behaviour had a number of common features. They were wholly within the voluntary control of the person concerned; they took place in a continuous context of discussion and comment by others; and they did not involve any responses to unexpected events. Most of these actions were initiatives anyway; and although some were responses to events, these were events which at the earlier interview were confidently expected (for example, continuing recovery after an operation), or already familiar (like repeated examples of a neighbour's behaviour). Thus whether the action was a response to such routine occurrences, or an initiative taken in dealing with familiar health conditions, nearly all these kinds of wholly voluntary behaviour accorded with attitudes expressed earlier.

The one case where, in spite of the absence of external events, behaviour which was apparently voluntary contradicted consistent pre-existing attitudes, deserves, therefore, some detailed consideration. This was the nearest instance here found to the critical case where the logic of evaluation fails to lead to the appropriate behaviour;[24] though it is not in fact so critical a case as this, because I do not have complete evidence of the behaviour intended after the earlier evaluation of the situation. The case concerns Ellen Robb, who developed a paralysis which she was told by her doctor was nervous in origin, the result of a narrow escape from a fire in which a relative died. For a period she was unable to undress or to get up from her bed without help. By practising walking, however, she got to the stage of being able to move about inside the house and manage looking after herself and her indoor household tasks normally; but, I noted,

She says, 'I just can't go out of that front door. I've been down the stairs, but then my legs fail me. They just won't let me go out.'

At the same time she recognized that this confinement to the house was itself contributing to her problem, thus creating a vicious circle. She contrasted a friend who liked to be on his own at times:

Now I *love* company—but of course *he* goes down the town. When you're stuck in the house your thoughts dam up until you almost explode, and that's why I like to have someone to talk to. I've nobody to talk to.

Notwithstanding this comment, she had in fact some nearby friends who called, who were constantly inviting her to come and see them, and who offered lifts to make this easier. Therefore since she clearly wished passionately for company she must have wished to go and see them—though she did not say this in so many words.

When I revisited Mrs Robb a month and a half later her diagnosis of her situation, and her wish to get out of the house, was if anything clearer still. The subject came up spontaneously in a long sequence of thought about old age whose gist I noted as follows:

People say the sixties are the happiest times of their lives. Don't believe it. Your forties are the happiest time. After that it gets faster and faster, it almost leaps ahead, and you don't know where the time has gone. The doors close. They've sold my cousin's house [following her death]. Another door closed. So you haven't anyone to talk to, and it all goes round in your mind, and new people come in, and you don't like them, or they don't like you, and you stay inside, and you get to thinking all the more about it and—that's what's wrong with *me*!

Nevertheless, in spite of recognizing this baneful effect of staying inside, she had in fact done so throughout the intervening period, and repeated her account of her legs giving way suddenly. So I asked how far she had applied her method of practising walking inside the house to walking outside the house. I noted her response as follows:

Mrs Robb: I wouldn't like people to see me.

Q: Which people?

Mrs Robb: The people in the street out in front; they're always going up and down there.

Q: Why not try the lane behind then?

Mrs Robb: Oh, that goes round on a twist—and the people next door go up and down.

However, the lane was broad and level, even if it had a gentle curve, and in the course of four hours spent with Mrs Robb, nobody went up or down it, for, as she explained, all her neighbours were at work. Hence it was difficult to understand these opposing considerations as reasons for not practising walking, when she wanted so much to go out. Thus the exact nature of her collapses, and of her failure to practise out of doors as she had successfully done indoors, remained essentially obscure in so far as her expressed reasoning was concerned; and this may be a case of habitual behaviour—habitual, that is, since her involuntary response to the events of the fire—having a direct influence on subsequent behaviour without the mediation of any conscious attitudes.

All the other cases reviewed in this section, however, make good sense as a process of conscious reasoning, expressing itself later in voluntary behaviour where appropriate.

Intrusive events

Intervening events which were intrusive—disrupting routine expectations—were involved in 20 comparisons of earlier and later attitudes and behaviour, and these instances featured 14 out of the 31 cases. Interestingly, contradictions between earlier and later responses were more frequent when such events had occurred—10 comparisons showing contradiction (2 marginal), and 10 showing consistency (1 marginal).

In interpreting these figures, it is again necessary to remember that the events concerned here, though they followed the initial recording of attitudes, were described retrospectively. Hence this result too could reflect in some degree the way in which popular accounts of illness are constructed; and it is true that not only were most of the contradictions I observed between earlier and later attitudes accounted for by the occurrence of relevant events, but also all the instances where contradictory attitudes were expressed at my first encounter with people were also accounted for in this way. Thus events certainly play a vital role in justifying the development of contradictory attitudes in retrospect. However, in so far as I have relatively complete reports of the major health events, cross-checked with acquaintances and retold and probed on more than one occasion, there is also support for the more far-reaching suggestion that some of these events actually generated contradictions.

If intrusive events were indeed connected with contradictions, therefore, how exactly did this occur? One possibility is that the very intrusiveness of the event, its unexpected and disruptive quality, produced changes in daily routine, and this produced contradictions in accustomed patterns of thought. That is, the event acted initially on behaviour, and the changed behaviour was then accounted for in readjusted ideas. And certainly, all these events were unexpected and disruptive, and most were long-drawn-out processes evolving over several months. But this is not an accurate enough explanation, for while many of these events occasioned contradictions, as many met with entirely consistent responses, including some of the most long-drawn-out and disruptive among them.

A second possibility is that contradictions were produced by those events which were not only disruptive but also severely threatening. Deterioration and recovery, for example, were both at times highly disruptive, but only deterioration was disruptive and threatening. But this is still insufficient as an explanation, for some contradictions were occasioned not by deterioration but by improvement, and some responses to severe deterioration were wholly consistent.

Explanations of this kind, therefore, which look to the direct effect of events on behaviour, and to a simple reactive effect of changed behaviour on beliefs, do not meet the case. Rather, in order to account for all the instances of contradiction and consistency collected here, it is necessary to focus on the relation between the event and the ideas of the person concerned before the event.

To show how this is so, I have taken examples from the nine critical cases which involved long-extended disruptions over several months, bringing contact with specialists or notable changes in daily activity. And I have marshalled these firstly according to whether the change was a deterioration or an improvement, and secondly according to the initial view of illness expressed before the event occurred.

To begin with, then, I consider events which signalled a marked deterioration.

The belief that illness could be controlled by normal living (1.1) was related to two kinds of subsequent contradiction when things got worse. The first was when the sick person set a value at the outset on obedience to doctor's orders, and a doctor later prescribed behaviour which was seen as abnormal. Given an antecedent belief both in living normally and in obeying the doctor, a medical intervention of this kind automatially generated contradictions. Even without medical intervention, though, a second type of contradiction occurred when the sick person recognized that trying to live normally had not contained the symptoms, but made them worse. This problem was commonest with those who not only believed that normal living controlled illness (1.1), but also kept struggling to act as if all was in fact normal against the odds (1.2)—the combination of views which, in Chapter 1, I labelled 'illness as a test of achievement'.

An example of the way in which somebody with this combination of ideas reacted to deterioration can be seen in the case of Benjamin Teakman, who suffered from severe back pain and sciatica after the failure of a back operation. He regarded his trouble as partly 'psychological', and was accordingly determined to maintain his normal activity in the garden in spite of the attacks of pain and disability it cost him. Normality thus controlled the psychological element (1.1). As for the medical treatment of his condition, when I first met him he presented himself as a man who had learnt from previous emergencies that doctors could do wonders and should always be trusted and obeyed; and he enumerated the restrictions in diet and smoking which he was observing on their advice.

Seven months after this meeting, his wife said he had admitted to her that he was having greater difficulty in keeping the garden going. She said he would not be satisfied just to sit and see it go to ruin, and she talked of moving. He was present at this conversation, but I noted:

His contributions to this didn't contradict but didn't assent either—they were all occasional interjections like 'Oh I did half an hour's digging this afternoon', or 'I did all the pruning the other day.' I said something about taking it in short stages, and she said 'Of course. The trouble with him is he won't stop after half an hour, he just goes on and on, and won't come in for a coffee.' He rose to this, and said she was aye rapping on the pane five minutes after he'd gone out.

This conversation testifies to his attempts to normalize the situation and to admit but at the same time minimize his difficulties (1.2), in spite of his wife's attempts to limit his efforts.

Four months later, his wife told me that the doctor had just come, and he had told them that the garden was too much for her husband now, and they must move. Thus the doctor had prescribed something which to Mr Teakman was a breakdown in his prized regimen of normal living, and a surrender of his principle of struggling to maintain the appearance of it as far as possible—and yet he believed in obeying the doctor; a clear contradiction. However although his wife reported this occurrence, Mr Teakman, when he came in later, was silent about it and continued to speak as if his gardening was going virtually as usual.

It was only after six more months that he actually avowed the contradiction. On this occasion he began with a disgusted comment characteristic of all his previous positions; today was his laziest day this winter—he had not been out at all. In thus describing himself as 'lazy', he was consistent with his earlier view that with the right psychology his pain and disability could be controlled. But later in this conversation his wife went out, and at this point he admitted that he was no longer managing the garden, and that the doctor had told him not to start again this spring. So, having had a year of increasing difficulties, he was considering giving it up. Thus he finally acknowledged, though he still had not resolved, the contradiction between his worsening symptoms, together with the doctor's warnings, on the one hand, and his principle of struggling to maintain the appearance of normal activity on the other.

In other instances, though, the meaning of deterioration was very different. I have mentioned the common view that normal activity was not only beneficial (1.1*a*), but also indispensable (1.1*b*), and to fall short of this norm thus led to a spiral of decline, after which one was 'finished' and cut off from past interests (1.4). In Chapter 1 I called this combination of beliefs 'illness as exile', and it proved a self-fulfilling prophecy in several cases where consistency was nevertheless maintained. Hugh Kidd, for example, had angina, and when I first met him, he explained that his doctor recommended three things to control his condition: gentle exercise, dieting, and no stress. Up till now, the exercise had been provided by his ordinary activities of walking and swimming, and he had been eating moderately, so his normal pattern of living had helped to control the illness (1.1). Should this fail, however, he saw the consequences as dire:

"I would say it's a worry getting ill as you get older. Well, and nobody ever wants to be a nuisance to anyone, you know—it's not on. So to a certain extent I think everybody is *somewhat* troubled about having . . . Oh I was sure I was going to have a heart attack, [and be] brought round with my wits half gone or my limbs paralysed."

The alternative to control was thus to become a paralytic and a nuisance (1.4), and this threat was much in his mind, with the result that this control was beginning to slip. The exercise and the dieting were in anyone's power, but how could one avoid stress? Stress was involved in trying to control stress, and this depressed him, with the result that now he was doing no swimming, and was walking only to the corner shop; and, because he slept badly, he had begun eating more than he should. This breakdown in his normal living pattern, a pattern which was essential for controlling his condition, thus itself implied a spiral of deterioration.

Nine months after the last of these conversations, hospital confirmation was given of his heightened level of risk, and he accidentally overheard a doctor say that his results were 'unacceptable'. Hugh Kidd's reaction was only too consistent with his previous understandings. He felt that his condition was now entirely beyond his control, and must be dealt with by immediate admission to hospital; and accordingly he abandoned his doctor's recommendations and ceased to go out at all. He described his state thus:

I'm not me at the moment. It's not me. It's another person in my body.

And he concluded that he must 'drop out' of society as far as he could (1.4).

In both these two cases, then, a marked physical deterioration had to be coped with; and in both cases, the doctor's advice was disregarded, and pre-existing convictions followed in doing so. But Hugh Kidd's initial convictions were consistent with deterioration, and deterioration meant that activity became hopeless, although his condition was only intermittently disabling. By contrast, Benjamin Teakman's initial convictions were inconsistent with deterioration, and during the time that he was making a rational reappraisal of his situation, his initial beliefs long upheld him in a higher level of activity, though his condition was physically very disabling. Thus the essential difference lay in the initial convictions concerned.

One may of course ask whether a contradiction like that of Benjamin Teakman is eventually resolved only by accepting Hugh Kidd's pessimism. My prospective material did not cover a long enough period to answer questions about extended developments of this order. But retrospective accounts suggest that those who had adapted positively to severe illness as an alternative way of life (1.3) had begun from premises like those of Benjamin Teakman rather than those of Hugh Kidd. In this case the difference between their starting points would have been maintained to the end.

I turn now to events which signalled a marked improvement in health prospects.

The initial view of 'illness as exile' once more emerged as perfectly consistent in this situation. We have seen that those who from the beginning felt that normal living controlled illness (1.1), and that inactivity was abnormal and a loss that could only be endured (1.4), could be remorselessly consistent in accepting a pessimistic definition of their own situation. But they could equally accept a more optimistic assessment of their situation without disturbing either of their initial prémisses.

For two years after her husband's death and her own return to Aberdeen, Peggy Watt was worried to find herself, in her own cautious words, 'easily fatigued' and 'not content'. And as a consequence, she suddenly saw herself as old, and drew comparisons with a friend who had been incapacitated by a chronic chest condition, and had let her fine West End house go to pieces. To Mrs Watt this was the end of active life. And finding that her own energy too was not now up to what she used to do, she had stopped short in her plans to buy a similar house and had applied to a scheme running small retirement bungalows. Thus all this revealed a view of old age and illness as the end of activity (1.4), and showed her beginning to identify this as her own situation.

At the same time, though, Peggy Watt was from the outset a convinced advocate of a healthy mind in a healthy body, and commended both physical and mental exercise. This was important for health, and fundamental to man's constitution as a thinking animal. And so she believed in the salutary power of such balanced living in normal circumstances (1.1), though because of her continuing inexplicable fatigue she felt her present situation was already abnormal, and therefore deteriorating.

Not long after all this she went to her doctor and was referred to a specialist; and after extensive testing, no serious degenerative disease was revealed. Following this, she immediately restated her theory of the balanced life, having, she felt, successfully avoided going down the hill. A due proportion of mental and physical activity would in due course restore her. Unhappiness and inactivity could produce an illness to justify it, and she recalled occasions when she had remonstrated with others along these lines. Thus such illness was still controlled by normal living (1.1). But the friend's case was still, too, a symbol of the future. She was referred to as, metaphorically, 'dead', and Mrs Watt said that she would rather be dead before she came to that stage. This remained, therefore, as a graphic image of irreparable loss (1.4). Hence both these original premises remained intact and consistent when her condition was declared not to be degenerative; and the only thing that changed was her definition of her present situation in relation to them.

However, while improvement in this case met with a consistent response, such improvement could also produce a contradiction for those who saw illness as an alternative way of life. A suggestive, though marginal, instance of such a turnabout occurred in the case of Violet Dickie, who had a severely disabling heart condition. In answer to a question about how she managed she said:

"I'm cheery. I like to enjoy myself, and I go to an awfully nice club on a Thursday afternoon. A lady asked me, and paid my ticket. Lovely entertainment—dancing for them that's able (because there's wheel chairs). Lovely afternoon . . . it's for the people who are disabled and that."

Thus she made a positive alternative, at least initially, out of an association for fellow-sufferers (1.3). At the same time, though, as recognizing that she was disabled, she held, like most Aberdonians, to the maxim that activity was beneficial (1.1), and urged her sister to go out more for her health. And she reconciled this activism with her own situation by translating it into 'interests':

"It's better to have an interest in something. If you haven't anything you go down and down and down."

Seven months later she had learnt that an operation was feasible in her case, and had successfully undergone it. The new regime of recovery was highly compatible with her theory of activity, and she was proud of the success she had achieved by walking regularly (1.1). But she no longer saw herself as 'disabled', and when she was asked about her relations with the association for fellow-sufferers, she stressed that it was somebody else who had invited her to it, and that having been appointed to the committee, she did not like never to go again. A contradiction with her earlier statement is implicit here—for if she went because she felt obliged, did she no longer go because she enjoyed the entertainment? Thus obligation and enjoyment could be contrasted in this case, if the hearer chose to take it so; but the speaker could nevertheless in this way avoid downright disparagement of former associates. And subsequent corroboration of this interpretation came from an acquaintance in this case, who depicted Violet Dickie's new attitude to a disabled neighbour by tipping her nose.

The change brought about by a successful operation thus, it appeared, undermined the value given to this association which had provided an alternative in a period of considerable disability. But it has also to be noted that in spite of her recovery, Mrs Dickie also strove to maintain a degree of consistency by continuing to attend the association as a committee member. Thus both coherence and implicit contradiction continued in this case to be maintained in uneasy tension.

In both these cases, therefore, health prospects markedly improved, and in both the doctor was seen as an ally; yet the previous convictions held by each person led to different responses. Violet Dickie had experienced much greater disability, yet she remained much more positive about the situation of the disabled, and found herself struggling to avoid a contradiction between this attitude and her restored sense of normality. Peggy Watt had experienced little actual disability, yet she had some powerful negative stereotypes of what it meant, and was able, even while her perception of her own position changed radically, to maintain these premises with consistency. Thus again, consistency and contradiction arose not out of the event but out of its relation to these previous convictions.

Indeed the overall consistency of the view of illness as exile, which was maintained by both Peggy Watt and Hugh Kidd, and in both deterioration and improvement, is particularly striking. One may wonder, in fact, whether it is impervious to falsification, especially as it is not always very comforting to its adherents. Fortunately, retrospective accounts suggest that in the long term, the distinctive belief embedded in seeing illness as exile—that at a certain point inactivity means a loss of self and a spiral of decline—may itself be vulnerable to contradiction. Daniel Shirras, for instance, learned as a young man that he had TB, and had wanted to separate himself entirely from his wife and family and to have his body burnt so that the disease would be destroyed; but within a few years he became one of the first patients to be given streptomycin, and his emphatic sense of separation and inevitable decline was replaced by an equally emphatic endorsement of struggle in all his subsequent illnesses. This was necessarily a retrospective account, but it indicates that even the ordinarily self-fulfilling prophecy which views illness as exile is not immune to refutation.

From all the examples which have been given, then, we can see that physical changes are indeed partly associated with contradiction, yet not because they change ideas by changing behaviour, but by reason of their role in confirming or refuting preconceptions. And it remains to remark only that in all the events that have been analysed, the changes in attitude, when they occurred, came before the changes seen in behaviour. These observations can now be taken together with the results discussed earlier in order to see their overall implications.

Conclusion

In this chapter I have attempted to chart two of the most immediate influences which Aberdonians feel in forming their thoughts about coping with illness, ageing, and death—the public face of moral opinion, and the private experience of their own physical events. Health is the focal point where these two influences meet, for health, unlike ageing and death, reflects physical change in the short term as well as the long term, and of all these topics it is subjected to the closest moral scrutiny by Aberdonians. What has emerged in this chapter in regard to health and to ideas about coping with illness is the critical importance, not of intrusive physical events by themselves, but of the relation between such events and the antecedent ideas of the person experiencing them; and the relation is made the more critical by the fact that people are committed to their ideas about coping with illness by being part of the continuous round of moral evaluation which takes place in ordinary gossip.

Taking first the temporal sequences of attitudes, behaviour, and events which have been analysed, a general conclusion can be drawn: that in all but one of these 62 comparisons of coping responses over time, the processes involved were essentially rational. Later attitudes and behaviour were either consistent with an earlier attitude, or followed logically from the invalidation of an earlier attitude by an intervening event. Putting it another way, changes in attitude did not follow changes in voluntary behaviour, and only in one instance did an event apparently act directly, despite countervailing attitudes, to create a pattern of behaviour which became habitual. This conclusion has three aspects: first, the trend to consistency between earlier and later ideas; second, the trend to consistency between earlier ideas and later behaviour in the absence of intrusive events; and third, the rational role of events in later contradictions.

The first aspect of this conclusion, the trend to consistency in ideas, has been revealed by prospective recording of attitudes. This shows what can be expected when attitudes are recorded over periods of months rather than years, and when they are expressed by people of mature years, speaking spontaneously about matters of direct autobiographical relevance which are often well known to friends and neighbours. I explored the possibility that the consistency of these attitudes was reinforced by my presence, but the indications available suggest that my part was insignificant.

The second aspect of the conclusion, the consistency of later behaviour with earlier ideas in the absence of intrusive events, has been revealed by a mixture of prospective recording of attitudes and retrospective recording of the later behaviour. Again I have noted the reservations which are appropriate in interpreting this result. Its most interesting substantive aspect was that, with the one exception which has already been mentioned, all behaviour which contradicted one earlier attitude was consistent with another earlier attitude—for the two attitudes were in conflict from the start.

Finally, the third aspect of the conclusion, that later contradictions flowed logically from the invalidation of earlier attitudes by intervening events, is again necessarily based on the same mixture of prospective and retrospective recording, though in this case fewer cautionary implications are involved. The evidence has shown that it was not the disruptiveness of the event, nor its threatening character, that created the contradictions, for similar types of event occasioned contradictory and consistent responses in different people. Rather, events occasioned contradiction only in the course of a rational process in which they refuted a preconception; and the change in attitudes thus begun preceded, and generated, the changes in voluntary behaviour.

All this evidence, therefore, underlines the importance of conceptions for behaviour in this matter of coping with illness; and it also indicates the significance of how open they are to contradiction by events. Perhaps paradoxically, it was the relatively dismal view of illness as exile which was most impervious to contradiction, whether by events marking a deterioration or by events marking an improvement in health. Those conceptions of illness which tried for greater rewards, on the other hand, involved a struggle to resolve contradictions afresh as each deterioration or improvement took place.

Health changes, then, were constantly testing Aberdonian ideas about coping with illness, and exposing them to contradiction and a choice of alternatives; but at the same time this choice was constrained by public comment, and by personal commitments which were publicly witnessed. I have shown that on the subject of health, the great majority of the judgements made by these Aberdonians about one another were accurate in their facts and broadly agreed in their standards. Moreover where criticism was made, the subject of it frequently felt it necessary to show recognition of it. And although the time span of the study did not permit me to observe any instances of persuasion alone changing behaviour, independently of intervening events, cases such as that of Benjamin Teakman show persuasion going on alongside these events, and negotiating joint responses to the situation. Further, the histories of failed persuasion which I have described, while they had not altered behaviour, had certainly made the people being persuaded think and talk about, and sometimes accept, the judgements of the persuader alongside their own. And in any case, public opinion is probably most effective not with those it punishes or tries to convert from acknowledged deviancy, but with the majority who reap its praises, having taken its sanctions into account in advance of acting. Thus in spite of the disorienting effects of physical changes, all this criticism helped to maintain the consistency of Aberdonian views about coping with illness.

Yet for all that, Aberdonian public opinion was a far from total form of social control in the present context, since, representing as it did a coalition of somewhat differing perspectives, its points of agreement could be seen as somewhat arbitrary and debatable. One example of this was the difficulties which the agreed endorsement of normality placed in the way of the positive, if unconventional, manœuvres of those sufferers who sought to make an alternative way of life. And another example was the endorsement tacitly given by the same concordat to the negative, segregative view of the severely ill which some people held as part of their advocacy of the norm. These crudities created a number of disaffected sufferers who were not always persuaded even when strategies of persuasion were fully exerted upon them. And in any case persuasion, praise, and blame were dispensed unevenly, both according to the topic—attitudes to health attracting the most, and attitudes to death the least comment—and according to how close each person was to the chief social entrepreneurs in their network of acquaintanceship.

Thus there remained considerable room for manœuvre in the way Aberdonians thought about coping. In these respects, their responses were related more to the moral and material resources which they had built up in the course of their lives; and I now turn to these.

Notes and References

1. S. H. Matthews, *The social world of old women*, London: Sage, 1979; C. Russell, *The ageing experience*, Sydney: Allen and Unwin, 1981; A. M. Rose, 'The subculture of the ageing', in A. M. Rose and W. A. Peterson, *Older people and their social world*, Philadelphia: Davis, 1965; I. Rosow, *Social integration of the aged*, New York: Free Press, 1967; A. Hochschild, *The unexpected community: portrait of an old age subculture*, Berkeley: University of California Press, 1973.
2. J. Scott, 'Social network analysis', *Sociology*, 22 (1988). 109–27; J. C. Mitchell, 'Social network data', in R. F. Ellen (ed.), *Ethnographic research*, London; Academic Press, 1984; J. C. Mitchell, 'Social networks', *Ann. Rev. Anthropol.* 3 (1974), 279–99; id. (ed.), *Social networks in urban situations*, Manchester University Press, 1969.
3. A. Finlayson and J. McEwen, *Coronary heart disease and patterns of living*, London: Croom Helm, 1977; J. B. McKinlay, 'Social networks, lay consultation and help-seeking behaviour', *Social Forces*, 51 (1973), 275–92.
4. D. M. Boswell, 'Personal crises and the mobilisation of the social network', in J. C. Mitchell (ed.), *Social networks in urban situations*, Manchester University Press, 1969.
5. I. Rosow, *Socialisation to old age*, University of California Press, 1974.
6. J. T. Tedeschi and S. Lindskold, *Social psychology*, London: Wiley, 1976, ch. 5.
7. I. Ajzen and M. Fishbein, *Understanding attitudes and predicting social behaviour*, Englewood Cliffs: Prentice-Hall, 1980.
8. M. Calnan and D. R. Rutter, 'Do health beliefs predict health behaviour? An analysis of breast self-examination', *Sco. Sci. and Med.* 22 (1986), 673–8; eid., 'Do health beliefs predict health behaviour? A follow-up analysis of breast self-examination', *Soc. Sci. and Med.* 26 (1988), 463–5; see also Ajzen and Fishbein, *Understanding attitudes*; M. Fishbein, 'Persuasive communication', in A. E. Bennett (ed.), *Communication*

between doctors and patients, Oxford University Press, 1976; and the reviews in I. Sutherland, *Health education: perspectives and choices*, London: Allen and Unwin, 1979.

9. D. J. Bem, 'Self-perception theory', in L. Berkowitz (ed.), *Advances in experimental social psychology* vol. 6, London: Academic Press, 1972; id. 'Self-perception: an alternative interpretation of cognitive dissonance phenomena', *Psychol. Rev.* 74 (1967), 188–200.

10. For example the control group in Calnan and Rutter, 'Do health beliefs predict health behaviour?' (1986, 1988).

11. P. White, 'Limitations on verbal reports of internal events: a refutation of Nisbett and Wilson and of Bem', *Psychol. Rev.* 87 (1980), 105–12; Tedeschi and Lindskold, *Social psychology*, ch. 5.

12. D. Mechanic, 'The stability of health and illness behaviour: results from a 16-year follow-up', *Amer. J. Publ. Health*, 69 (1979), 1142–5.

13. H. Schuman and M. P. Johnson, 'Attitudes and behaviour', *Ann. Rev. Sociol.* 2 (1976), 161–207; H. C. Kelman, 'Attitudes are alive and well and gainfully employed in the sphere of action', *Amer. Psychologist*, 29 (1974), 310–24; A. W. Wicker, 'Attitudes versus actions: the relationship of verbal and overt behavioural responses to attitude objects', *J. Soc. Issues*, 25 (1969), 41–78.

14. N. D. Richards, 'Methods and effectiveness of health education', *Soc. Sci. and Med.* 9 (1975), 141–56.

15. I. Ajzen and M. Fishbein, 'Attitude-behaviour relations: a theoretical analysis and review of empirical research', *Psychol. Bull.* 84 (1977), 888–918.

16. Schuman and Johnson, 'Attitudes and behaviour'.

17. L. Festinger, H. W. Riecken, and S. Schachter, *When prophecy fails*, University of Minnesota Press, 1956.

18. B. R. Bewley and J. M. Bland, 'Academic performance and social factors related to cigarette smoking by schoolchildren', *Brit. J. Prev. Soc. Med.* 31 (1977), 18–24.

19. P. M. Bentler and G. Speckart, 'Models of attitude–behaviour relations', *Psychol. Rev.* 86 (1979), 452–64.

20. Whereas a representative third of those appraised belonged to these organizations, a little over half of the appraisers belonged to them.

21. B. Wellman, 'Domestic work, paid work and network', in S. Duck and D. Perlman (eds.), *Personal relations*, London: Sage, 1985.
22. Again about half were members, as against about a third overall—see Appendix 1.
23. In a few cases conversations at revisits yielded only factual descriptions of symptoms or illness which had no particular relevance to present attitudes, or else issues concerned with old age or death were so prominent as to thrust illness into the background.
24. For a discussion of an analogous problem see G. H. von Wright, *Explanation and understanding*, Ithaca: Cornell University Press, 1971.

7

Work

Ask of his country, which so long will miss
That sturdy form with its honest heart,
True Scotch, all rugged, without art
Of fashion's sheen or glossy city smirk,
His was the impress of a *life of work*!

Anon., *In Memoriam, William McCombie
of Tillyfour*, 1880

Introduction

Among the biographical experiences that shaped Aberdonians'
ideas about coping, one of the most prominent was the meaning
which they had found in their working life. Some aspects of this
meaning were class-specific, and I deal with these in the next
chapter. But, as earlier chapters have already intimated, much
was more generally concerned with work as a moral value and as
a generational experience.

It is often argued today that the work ethic suffered a decline
during the prosperity of the 1960s, a decline which some say is
bound to continue as automation increases,[1] while others see signs
of its reversal with the recession in the 1980s.[2] These phases of
industrial growth and decline are likewise thought to have affected
the work ideology of different generations, and if so, we ought to
ask whether this has changed their ideas about illness or ageing.

Consideration of this issue requires careful discrimination
between different cultural versions of the work ethic before
aspects of change can be discussed. What the different versions
have in common is a focus on the rewards felt to be intrinsic
to hard work, and an unwillingness to treat jobs as merely instrumental—as a necessary evil. But the list of the attributes which are
intrinsic to work varies. Social relationships with employers and
fellow workers, for instance, are intrinsic to most jobs, but

these are not always a necessary part of a work ethic, especially in Britain.[3] The classic case where such involvements are supposed to generate diligence is the large company in Japan, where the need for 'self-sacrificing devotion' to tasks is argued from the idea of the firm as the extension of the family.[4] But in the West, certainly, strong working allegiances do not necessarily seem to mean greater zeal. Apart from the loyalty to fellow-workers which forbids rate-busting, there is a loyalty to the organization which, we are told, actually detracts from the ambition for achievement.[5] Hence the intrinsic features of tasks to which the British work ethic relates are usually found elsewhere.

Again, the possibility of promotion or some similar recognition of success is intrinsic to many kinds or work, but it is not always linked to production or achievement, and is thus not always essential to a work ethic. This link has been strongest in the United States;[6] but in Britain collective pressures have always been strong, and even in the individualistic middle class productive effort has arguably not been the sole, or even the most important, criterion for recognition.[7] Thus, again, it cannot be expected that striving for recognition would necessarily play a major part in a British work ethic.

Both recognition and social integration, as spurs to zeal, depend heavily on the co-operative setting of paid employment; but the other intrinsic aspects of work which can form the basis of a work ethic are less tied to such employment. Amongst these aspects, the emphasis is usually on at least three things: first there may be a value on work as some kind of self-discipline, as the ability to defer gratification, to pursue duty as opposed to pleasure, to follow a punctual and orderly routine; second, there may be a notion of work as effort, diligence, skill, or high standards; and third, there is usually some concept of work as a source of basic personal worth in the eyes not so much of others at work as of others anywhere in the web of common relationships.[8] These are basic elements, to which others may be added. A commitment to work in terms such as these may be quite distinct from a commitment to employment;[9] and with the retired, as with the unemployed,[10] there is an opportunity to explore what range of activities this notion of work and its equivalents can cover.

The question whether the work ethic has declined is complicated by these problems of definition and by these cultural variations on the basic theme. The conviction of decline rests initially on the emergence of highly visible protest amongst politically active youth in the late 1960s, who certainly touched new extremes of scepticism about work as about much else. However, there is also more prosaic evidence from the wider population to suggest that, certainly during the 1970s, some of the values previously placed on work had indeed been somewhat eroded amongst the young, and especially in the middle class.[11] But the evidence is both weak and complex and can still be read many ways: it remains possible to argue that on the one hand work remains a more or less universal psychological need,[12] and on the other hand that the British working class has never had anything other than an instrumental use for its labour.[13]

Suggestions that earlier generations were more attached to the work ethic are likewise complicated by variations in what the work ethic is supposed to include. Certainly if it is made to include loyalty to employers there must be considerable doubt whether much of the British working class—often taking their cue from their employers—ever had any other than an instrumental view of that relationship. But the struggle for control in the workplace has not precluded other values from being placed on work. While the historical evidence necessarily relates to the literate labour aristocracy, and only by inference to other members of the working class, the late nineteenth-century emphases on respectability and improvement, with their corollaries of thrift, self-help, independence, and diligence, were as prominent in the labour aristocracy as in the middle class.[14] What is less clear is how these virtues fared in the early twentieth century; and it is of some interest to see what they mean to Aberdonians who grew up in this period.

The most long-standing debate, however, about the place of the work ethic in historical change, has been that surrounding its supposed genesis in Protestantism. Recently the place of Scotland in this pattern of change has been much discussed. Long seen as a case which disproved the connection between Protestantism and capitalism,[15] Scotland has now been argued to prove the connection at least between Protestantism and the ethical attitudes of capitalists, including their work ethic.[16] The argument has been criticized;[17] but perhaps more to the point is the limitation, recognized by all parties, that there still is little evidence in the era of the first capitalists of a work ethic being generally accepted by much of the working population of Scotland.[18] Indeed later evidence from the mid-nineteenth century in Aberdeen suggests rather, along the lines of Thompson's well-known essay on the earlier developments in England,[19] that the task of establishing new work disciplines was one which employers were then undertaking afresh.

The impact of secular or cultural variation in the work ethic on ideas about health has received surprisingly little attention. Yet the morality of work may be clearly expressed in stoical attitudes to health,[20] and a critique of work and of the coercive aspects of a way of life may likewise be embodied in theories of stress and of liberation through illness.[21] Work may be seen as a stress that engenders illness or as a fortifier that protects against illness, and careful consideration is needed to tease out the relation of such ideas to one another. Although much writing of the 1970s viewed work as stress, recent studies suggest that, with the recession, stoical attitudes to health may be on the increase.[22]

These themes of growth and recession, of healthy and stressful work, of historical change and cultural context in the definition of the work ethic, all underlie what Aberdonians had to say about work in its relationship to health.

Conceptions of work in Aberdeen

I described earlier how in Aberdeen a shared history had been made the basis for a generational consciousness, in which war and economic depression, experienced in a youth long past, were felt to have given rise to an ethos quite different from that of contemporary youth, based on the experience of prosperity. There was embedded in this view a lay theory about the decline of the work ethic, and a sense that the older generation had been its latest guardians. But whether or not this generational claim was urged, it was common practice, in the context of health and ageing, to invoke a work ethic of a specific and distinctive kind—one which, even without unfavourable generational comparisons, was supported in part by reference to the economic exigencies of the period between the wars and to a sense of rational necessity deriving from those experiences.

In this perspective, work was valued for those of its attributes which transcended both the struggle for control and the struggle for recognition in the workplace, and which focused on the individual conscience: it was something done hard, by 'keeping going', by 'having your heart in it'; it was done properly, with tools and vehicles washed down and cleaned each day; and it was useful to others—something which gave a cachet to work in hospitals (even in a minor role in the kitchen), to the nursing of relatives, to teaching, to any activity which could be construed as 'producing', or as expressing a 'commitment to the community'. Not surprisingly, in the light of the seriousness thus accorded to work, to take days off even for illness, sometimes even to do no part-time work after retirement, was inherently a dubious decision.

It was consistent with these intrinsic attributes that activities could be seen as work even when they were unpaid. Most obvious and frequent amongst these activities was that of housekeeping, appropriated by many women of this generation as very much their work; but other activities given this seriousness by men and women alike included those which could be viewed as helping others outside the household in some organized way, through membership of, or still more through office in, voluntary associations. Besides the church groups, the Pensioners, and the Masons whom I mentioned in Chapter 1, these included groups concerned with hospital visiting and the disabled, and public bodies of various kinds. Similarly, the idea of work could be applied to the continued practice of special skills learnt in an occupational setting; and another skill which carried a universal symbolism, relating to the farm life of the immediate past, was that of running a garden. Gardens were something one could get 'lost' in, possessing the discipline of a 'military manœuvre'; but they also fed the household, in kind rather than in cash, and some gardens had involved traditional skills in shifting great granite blocks bedded in the soil and resetting them in dry-stone dykes, in the manner of the forbears who made the North-East landscape. All these activities, then, could be felt to deserve the title 'work', and all could partake in its moral nature, one in which strenuousness, diligence, and usefulness were woven together.

While work thus had an intrinsic virtue and did not have to be for pay, its essentially moral character was also underlined in another and complementary way, by dwelling on the notion that pay had to be for work. Acknowledgement of the justice of the better incomes obtained in the present was accompanied by a sharp eye for the delinquencies of workers who, like the council 'scaffy' or street cleaner, or the road gangs, were publicly visible: to have more was one thing, but to have it for less work was another, and tempted the observer to report malfeasances to the appropriate authority. Similarly, to receive more than the due rate for the effort expended could be uncomfortable, and result in, for instance, a housekeeper refusing a bequest from a former employer on the grounds that she had already had her wages. And it followed, from the precision thus given to the law of exchange, that to receive without having given, or being able to give, was the most demeaning situation of all. To be beholden, whether to kin, to neighbours, or to the state, was regarded with distaste, even in appalling poverty, and strenuous efforts had been made in the past to survive without help, and without even revealing to those likely to be concerned the straits which were being experienced. Indeed one man was thoroughly alarmed at having revealed such a situation even to the interviewer, although it was already more than twenty years ago. Hence inevitably, with so rigorous an ethic of reciprocity, there was a horror of debt. Two sisters occasionally tided each other over till the end of the week, but as for other borrowing:

That would be debt. I hate debt. If somebody wants to lend me I say you'll have to lend me for good, because if I can't keep inside my money this week why should I next week?

Neither a borrower nor a lender be?

That's . . . I was just going to say that myself. Mrs Allan has a pound from me for the hairdresser. I've asked her, but she's never returned it. If she'd given it me, could I have forgotten that?

The spendthrift, accordingly, was a figure who stimulated disapproval and awe in almost equal measures:

Wife : "I once said to him [an acquaintance], 'Why didn't you get a divorce? Then you might have married somebody, steadied up and had a nice home, might have had more family.' 'No, no,' he said, 'I've got one daughter, I don't want anybody else; I want to be a free man,' he says, 'and if [my mother] is giving me money, the more she gives me the more I enjoy myself.' He says, 'There's not a more beautiful way you can go.' Didn't he? He says, 'What a beautiful way to go.'"

Husband : "I didn't scarcely agree with him, but . . ."

Wife : "That's as true as I sit here. He was amazing, mind."

To avoid debt, then, to pay your way, and to deserve the pay by the due amount of work, were things assumed in the observance and astonishing in the breach; and this was so even at an age when pension arrangements meant that the relation between work and present income became inherently open to question. Although people were aware that pension levels were to some extent a political decision, in which pensions competed with (in 1980) 'the bobbies and the soldiers' for government largesse, the main law governing their right to their pension remained, and justly so as they perceived it, in the exchange between present pension and past contributions. One implication of this relation between past work and present income was that where the pinch of an income reduced by retirement was felt, as it was fairly evenly across social classes, blame was laid at the door of those who raised prices, or on the lack of work opportunities in the past, more than on the political settlement of pension levels; and blame could be eliminated by reducing wants—something familiar from the past, and positively acceptable compared with the severity of the past, not to speak of its being a valuable exorcism of the contemporary sin of greed, and appropriate when growing older anyway. Cuts were made by selling the car—a selfish novelty—by burning (against by-laws) coal rather than smokeless fuel, by sweeping the chimney oneself, by ceasing to have a bottle of whisky in the house or to buy butter; while at the same time certain things were fiercely protected—the money for burial, or a small bequest.

Nevertheless, this strict exchange of money for work was not part of an unrestrained creed of self-reliance: for just as the usefulness of work to the community helped to give it an axiomatic dignity, so the debt of the community to the worker elicited a reciprocal axiom—that of welfare provision. The welfare state commanded general support, and while the National Health Service and the state pension were the central focus of this conception, war pensions, invalidity pensions, and rebates or allowances under specific heads such as housing and heating shared in the respect accorded it. Past history had provided convincing evidence that there was no substitute for these things: old parents and their carers in winter had run out of coal, refused gifts from equally impoverished neighbours, and lacking more than one or two blankets had sat out the days wrapped in such coats and scarves as they could get on; and, as I noted earlier, there were memories of holding out as long as possible against going to the doctor, and of trying the home cures of knowledgeable-seeming neighbours, not out of any lively hope in their efficacy, but as a way of delaying medical bills whose payment would require everyone to go without for some time. The disappearance of these things with the welfare state gave it an unassailable legitimacy in principle; and it was only when supplementary benefits were considered that doubts began to be expressed. A few of these doubts related to the folly or immorality of some clients of social security, who were felt to cause their own problems by drunkenness, addiction, extravagance, or hypochondria. But underlying these suspicions was a fundamental and more powerful theme which exposed the hidden link between the duty of the community and the work ethic—the belief that supplementary benefits were money for nothing, money without work and without a corresponding contribution:

"I'll meet people in the bar haein' a pint, you know, and they're on social security, and they get everything, they're gettin' a' this specs, teeth, the lot. They hinna even contributed towards it, but idle. Nivver worked. This is fit [what] needles me, you know. No, ye fought a war, and because ye get war pension they include this intae yer allowance, you know, fit ye're earning. I suppose it's maybe—I dinna wint tae be greedy, but fin [when] I see ither people gettin' it, that's the thing that maks me [annoyed] . . . . Aye. Ye can go out and just squander 't like 'at, you know. They won't work. They boast, 'Oh, I don't need to go to work now,' you know."

It followed that supplementary benefits were avoided where possible, though there was one notable exception which itself confirmed the rule—women who had forgone a wage to nurse sick relatives could say with honour that they received their money from this source:

"I gave up work to look after my mother . . . . I went on to social security, and I hardly got anything. I would have been a changed person, I think, if I'd got what they get today, but I don't regret it. I was a happy person, and I had a happy mother, so I've no regrets . . . . I haven't a full pension as it is because I had to give up my stamp in the end because I hardly got anything to keep me. However I'm still on Social Security, but eh, I'm not ashamed to say it because I had to pay for it for years."

There were several such women, and all concurred in emphasizing the hidden contribution which they had made in nursing the sick.

These, then, were the central themes of the Aberdonian work ethic as it related to health and the other topics treated here; but in assessing its force, it is important to consider also whether other views of work were expressed at the same time, and whether these other views imposed some qualifications. In particular, it is important to consider instrumental views of work as a necessary evil, which were voiced much less frequently than ideas of work as duty, but which formed an undercurrent in Aberdonian attitudes. Two things were noticeable about such instrumental conceptions. First, while some comments along these lines praised enjoyment at the expense of work, other comments devalued one kind of work only in order to prefer another kind as real work. The activity most commonly devalued was housework, this being a middle-class view. As a married woman remarked:

"You always felt you had done something worthwhile when you were nursing . . . . [after retirement] I cleaned and cleaned the house—I don't do anything useful."

But in addition to these instances in which one kind of work was treated sceptically only in comparison with another, there were also instances in which the same work was viewed both as a necessary evil and also as conferring dignity. In these instances the contradiction undermined objections to work more than it undermined allegiance to work; for while the contradiction usually arose when work had become particularly burdensome for special reasons such as age or illness, these special reasons were felt to provide only flimsy justification for neglecting the more general claims of duty.

Overall, then, a work ethic held virtually uncontested sway in this Aberdonian generation, emphasizing the duty and usefulness of work, the necessity of work for pay though not of pay for work, and the necessity of prior work for welfare benefits. This was an economic theme which united these Aberdonians across divisions of class, and formed a common cultural ethos.

The work ethic and beliefs about health and ageing

In the present context, this work ethic was related mainly to views of illness and of the process of ageing. Few connections were made between work and views on dying or death; and those connections made with medical care were nearly all indirect, depending on the views of illness and ageing here discussed.

The work ethic was intimately related both to retirement and to health in old age, because in so far as work was felt to be necessary to health, health in old age depended on how work could transcend retirement. There were two sides to this possibility of transcendence. First, there was the question whether unpaid activities were at hand which could take, for the person concerned, the character of work. The usual range of such activities in Aberdeen has been outlined already. Then secondly there was the question whether the paid work done before retirement itself measured up to the expectations of the work ethic. Often it did not. And thus for those who felt this work ethic strongly there was no overall tendency for retirement to be a death knell to work or a threat to health. Rather there were two opposed patterns, just as there were for retired people in general. Where employment had failed to satisfy pride in diligence, skill, honesty, or usefulness, and—more critically—where skills and associations in retirement satisfied these aspirations better, retirement became either a liberation or a continuation of work's essential aspect. A nurse commented, looking back:

"Well, I was very, very tired, and it wasn't all that easy running a team, not nowadays. The young married ones were unreliable, and it came back on me when they stayed off . . . . Some stayed off who shouldn't, by rights. It depends on the boss. Three times late—to the office: that was the discipline. Now they're too inclined to take the easy way out."

Her profession having thus ceased to satisfy her, hospital visiting in retirement came to supply a preferable setting for conscientious endeavour. Hence it was only when these conscientious aspirations were fulfilled in employment, and when other ways of fulfilling them were not developed outside employment, that the work ethic made retirement a disaster.

These two opposed ways in which the work ethic was related to retirement by Aberdonians were connected, in turn, with the way in which the work ethic was related to health. The healthiness of work was a fundamental tenet: indeed the common belief of Aberdonians that their way of life itself generated health, and their conformity to its norms, depended, where it depended on any wider assumption, on this assumption that work was health-giving. Activity which had the character of work was felt to be essential first and foremost in helping people to prevent illness, to ignore minor illness, and to stop minor illness from sliding into something serious (1.1); and failing that when a condition became irredeemably serious, it was felt to be an equally essential incentive to maintaining the struggle (1.2). But just as an insistence on normality could lead to an abrupt reversal—a sense of exile from society—when serious illness was entrenched, so the sanctity of work could damn those whose illness finally made work impossible. For these people, to be in such a situation was, we have seen, to be 'lost', 'finished', even 'dead' (1.4), and likewise it was by the same token to become truly old (2.5). In this respect the struggle against illness and against late age was the same struggle.

It was between this work which gave health, and this loss of work which meant hopeless illness and true old age, that there intervened the biographical continuities which permitted work to transcend retirement. The particular limitations and idiosyncracies of· these continuities in each biography hold the key to the strengths and vulnerabilities of Aberdonians who thought in this way; and in order to see all these elements operating in their combined logic I present two case studies, one from Mannoch and one from the West End. In this way the pattern that cuts across social class can be made clear, while the individuality of each context is preserved.

James Esslemont had never been, he said, 'one for reading—I was always for making.' His father had been a sawyer at a local firm; and he became a box maker at another similar firm, tending a machine which nailed the boxes. For a period in his youth he had attempted to 'better himself' through emigration, taking work as a carpenter in New Zealand; but his wife had become homesick, and for her sake and the sake of his children's education he had come back. He was disappointed to return from carpentry to minding the machine, and commented that this kind of work was now over to female labour, though he emphasized that he in fact retrieved his job because of his specialized knowledge of how the mechanism worked: the younger lads were, he said, 'nae fly for the machine'. From this time on, however, he had engaged in carpentry proper only in his spare time. On this, as on all subjects, he was a man of actions rather than of words. As he went about his room, he rapped the chest of drawers: 'This is my make'; and as he opened his bureau to find photographs he commented 'This is my masterpiece,' and pulled the drawers further out to show the dovetailing. These pieces had been made in a shed on a piece of disused land several streets away from his old house; but eventually the land was reclaimed, and the shed—since he had no garden, and since his wife would never have allowed him to put his wood in her cupboards—had to be moved to his daughter's house at the other side of the city. He was still, at 75, working at the sawyer's, but now his wife fell ill and he retired to look after her until she died, after which, since he did not wish to impose on his daughter, he turned to making models in his sitting room. He started with precut patterns, but he was able to point to later patterns and say with satisfaction: 'My own design.'

Thus a pride in a skill inherited from his father—and expressed only imperfectly in his semi-skilled job—was the chief element in James Esslemont's attachment to his work; but this was only part of a wider significance which it had for him. The absence of this kind of application was, he felt, one factor in the mischief into which boys on the estate were drawn. As he demonstrated the plan of a model, he commented:

"Now the boys have nae time for this. Years ago there used to be a lot of crafts. That's dying out now."

Their dying was connected too with the disappearance of a moral discipline:

"You see, when we was young, we'd be in the Boys' Brigade. Ye canna blame the kids. As you come down here through that door, one of them panes was broken in three places—it was a drunk man."

But stronger yet than his sense that moral discipline and craft discipline went together was the connection he saw between what he made and what he received. His models formed one currency in this exchange. When he attended a Christmas dinner for pensioners, he presented the organizers with a model. When he went on a free outing for pensioners given by the local school, again he presented the organizers with a model; and he remarked, 'It was worth it. But some of the people who went', he added, his voice becoming contemptuous, 'were having it for nothing.' Perhaps most astonishingly (at any rate to the recipient), when he ended his first interview, he presented me with a model, and added, 'You see, you hinna come here for nothing.' And this was a refrain which was likewise echoed again and again in the exchanges he made in his other currency—money. While he accepted as his due the rebate for his rent, he emphasized that he had paid for his spectacles and his teeth:

"Some people get something for nothing. I'm nae on social security. Them on social security—that hoose—they were sayin' they didna pay onything for their TV . . . . They had coloured." [His own was black and white]. "They didna pay it. Coloured: 'Oh well, we're a' coloured now'. Of course they didna pay it."

And while he attended a local club for old people, he added,

"Ah, but we pay an' a'."

Even with the dinner which he took on a Saturday with his daughter, his coda was:

"But it was nae for nothing."

This stern reciprocity, then, and its accompanying self-discipline were expressed in the products of a quite specific skill—one sufficiently flexible to evolve with changing circumstances, yet tightly limited nevertheless to what could be done with saw and fretsaw; and it was this skill which dominated his assumptions about his health—assumptions which were again acted out as much as spoken. Their central theme was 'If I hadna had this a','— the wood-work—'I think I'd ha' gane crackers.' Through the increasing onset of two- or three-week periods in which he 'felt bad' and stayed in the house with an unexplained malady, the woodwork sustained him. Gesturing to it, he demanded, 'So I'm nae—I'm nae a spent force, am I?' And like others, he felt, 'If I didna do that a', I'd be lost.' The exact nature of what was wrong during these periods was difficult to elicit: it was a subject on which he did not focus his attention, always switching rapidly away from it; and although he took the problem to the doctor, he neither knew what diseases were responsible for his condition, nor what the tablets he was given were intended to do. On one occasion, he mentioned arthritis as a factor, but otherwise he explained his own illness, and the preceding illness of his wife, in the same way: 'It's age that's doing it, I suppose.' The illness was thus kept out of his mind, and, at the same time, its threats were neutralized by his work (1.1); but, at the same time, it was only his work that stood between him and it—between him and the threat of 'going crackers', becoming a 'spent force', being 'lost' (1.4).

For most of the last year of his life, James Esslemont sustained this view of his illness, though it was increasingly undermined as, in the last six months, three prolonged spells of trouble followed one another. These were periods when, he felt with dissatisfaction, he was 'doing nothing much', 'couldna be bothered', was getting up late and going to bed early, and making very little. For modelling, he explained, 'Ye've got to be in the . . .'—but he could find no word for what was missing. Perhaps it was the capacity for concentrated attention, for he rallied on the subject of the more routine work of housekeeping:

Some of the elderly people round here get a home help. I dinna want a home help. I can dae my jobs.

A month after this conversation, he died. It emerged at certification that the disease he did not know he had was arteriosclerotic heart disease, which had given him the 'turns' which neighbours had noted, and which finally precipitated a fatal heart attack. At this point his character, too, became, unusually, and briefly, a subject of conversation among the neighbours who knew him. His habit of walking two miles to church was noted; and the other comment was the approving one that he was 'aye working', for although his dedication to the work ethic was undoubtedly stricter than many, it was felt to be of a piece with common values which were taken for granted. He was, in fact, recognized only for his work and activity, and his own account confirmed that he was a man whose work—a lifelong moral resource as much as a technical skill—was essential to his well-being. It enabled him to cope with the early stages of his final illness, and to treat it as incidental to his normal life. But the character of work was invested in a highly specific skill which was vulnerable in the end to something akin to loss of concentration, and he was perhaps fortunate that he died before he could experience this reversal fully.

James Esslemont was prototypical of an old working-class generation: however, there were also middle-class interpretations of the same values, of their continuity in a certain range of skills, and of their relationship to health.

Andrew Donaldson was an Aberdeen burgess by virtue of his schooling at the Grammar, his lifelong career with a local finance company, and his involvement with a number of charitable committees. His occupational career was one which he looked back on in the following terms:

"With the type of experience I had, I used to enjoy problems. In fact, I've been a very active man. I'm one of those who've lived with pressures, accepted pressures in the normal way. In fact, it's true to say, I think, that I thrive on pressure, because I've so many commitments."

But in his last few years in the finance company, the type of pressure placed on him had changed with the advent of oil, become less honourable in a way he disliked. 'Professional etiquette' had 'gone out of the window'; bad debts had increased; the manipulative attitudes of 'management by objective' had taken hold. In this respect, he was glad to retire; but he made sure that his 'involvements' were retained. He remained on the committee of a professional association in which he had served, in various capacities, since the war. Similarly, 'activist that I am', he was shortly appointed to the governing bodies of two major charities— 'closely related, of course, because of my long experience of finance'. Thus, in these ways, skills specific to his past career were adapted to voluntary work, and sustained his underlying commitment; and again the essential qualities of this work were its 'activism', and in addition, its usefulness to others:

"As I said, I've lived with pressures; I think I've thrived on them. And—I hope I don't sound too cynical—one of the things that bugs me a bit is the lack of interest shown by the majority of the community in their fellow beings. This was why I found my spell in the [charity] so interesting. In my own little way, unofficially, I've been involved in voluntary social service work."

But this concern for the community was at the same time tempered by the usual rider about the proper relationship between giving and receiving:

"The concept of the National Health Service is first class—unfortunately, it's being abused in so many ways. I think one of the things the NHS has done is it's encouraged a breed of hypochondriacs . . . . The few times I've been to my own doctor—waiting room packed to capacity. You know, it makes me wonder. And there's me—eight years or something like that before my previous essential visit."

A respect for independence, then, combined with an 'interest in the community', expressed in 'activism' and an acceptance of 'pressures', had been enshrined in all Andrew Donaldson's 'involvements', whether those of his occupational career or of his present voluntary work; and the same ideas were related to health:

RW: "What's your prescription for being fit, particularly as you get older? Do you have any particular rules that you follow?"
AD: "Not essentially. I'm one of those who's taken an active interest in life. I never was, never could be, in hibernation. I've never regarded myself as a 9 to 5 man."—and after a digression—"If I can complete your

question: you said to me, the remedy or recipe for good health? I think one of the things I've seen, so many people who have retired, and because they have no—never had any—outside interests, I think this is the beginning of the end.''

This recipe reflected also his explanation of his health in the past:

''I think because of my own interest, and indeed, because of my sense of application, I trained very hard: I would think there were few fitter men than myself up to the age of 35.''

And again, earnest attention to these health-giving interests corresponded to a plan of deliberate inattention to illness—in this case asthma:

''I try to forget about it as much as I can. [Mother] again was inclined to play it down. Inclined to play it down. I think if you start—mention hypochondriacs—if you start thinking about it, you'll . . . I do, honestly.''

Thus hypochondria was suppressed, fitness achieved, and senescence postponed by the application, interest, and activism which had motivated his financial career and voluntary commitments (1.1). Nevertheless, one specific threat remained which could overthrow this control of health by application:

''I would relish (longevity) so long as I kept myself fairly fit. But more particularly, I think senility is a sad thing in so many ways. I would like, having been, I hope, a clear-thinking person, that if I were to live for a very ripe old age, I'd like to have all my faculties, including my mental faculties. I think this is, yes, this is the—yes, you know, senility in all its—you know—various stages.''

There was, therefore, for Andrew Donaldson, as for James Esslemont, one Achilles heel in a conviction otherwise firmly held about the health-giving powers of work. His activism had defined the nature of his involvements both in his job and in his leisure alike, and had given him a sense of contributing to the community, and of taking from it, in use of services, rather less than he gave; but because both sorts of involvement depended on his power of clear thinking in organizational and financial matters, it was the loss of this mental faculty which represented for him the one 'sad thing' to which he was vulnerable (1.4). Against other assaults on his health, his habit of applying himself and doing something useful left him, he felt, well armoured.

The other cases in which the health-giving powers of the work ethic were invoked varied, naturally, in detail from these two examples. For one thing, these were men; but women who were similarly involved in voluntary associations, or similarly possessed of occupationally related skills, had moral views of the same kind, except in so far as they were complicated by a dislike of housework. For other women, such household tasks presented no problem—on the contrary, they were a direct expression of the work ethic and its health-giving properties. Mrs. Stone was a case in point. In her emphasis on the healthiness of 'doing work', on helping and not being helped, she connected her lifelong cleaning and washing and baking, and her membership of the organizations for which she baked, with the suppression of illness (1.1); and the threat to these activities which she subsequently experienced, when she feared she had a fatal illness, meant for her 'sitting', 'moaning', becoming a 'poor thing', the equivalent of death (1.4).

All in all, there was less variation in these statements about the salutary effects of the work ethic than in the kind of hazard to which the chosen work was vulnerable. I have noted that retirement was the hazard for those who identified work with employment. For committed members of voluntary organizations, on the other hand, the threat was not only in failing mental powers, as with Andrew Donaldson, but also, if no car was available, in restrictions on walking. Occupation-based skills were vulnerable not only to loss of concentration, as with James Esslemont, but also, with manual skills, to loss of strength or dexterity. Gardens were vulnerable to the inflexible demands of the seasons—to the fact that, if strength failed at the wrong moment, a piece of ground could not be 'rolled up' and 'thrown over the dyke'. And housework was vulnerable, in the absence of labour-saving devices, to gross losses of mobility.

All these activities, then, could take the name or character of work, and each had its particular vulnerability to illness; but the essential implication of all these kinds of work was the positive one, that they were health-giving. However, this work ethic also had some equally significant negative implications, in the approaches to illness which it excluded.

Resistance to the work ethic and beliefs about health

Not surprisingly, a strong emphasis on the value of work conflicted with viewing illness as a release from duty (1.5). For women housework was, as we have seen, particularly rigorous in this way, and the few who felt their infirmities qualified them for a rest did so in the teeth of assumptions that doing their duty would keep them going. True, one or two men were more successful in opting out, arguing that their retirement had been hard won, and that illness prevented them from doing much now. But the rest of the men who valued work felt a continued obligation to be useful and so keep their health up, and, like the women, could not countenance giving up thankfully.

More frequent, therefore, and more sustained than this resistance to work based on the right to exemption, was the resistance based on the more creative response which viewed illness as an alternative way of life. This, it will be remembered, was a response to relatively disabling conditions, involving the development of alternative interests which had rewards which could in some degree compensate for what had been lost (1.3). I gave an example earlier (Chapter 1) of one of a number of people who, in developing this approach, retained an uncomfortable suspicion that they were 'lazy', and who met, or feared they might meet, explicit reproaches from others about giving up their 'work'. It helped, in fact, when adopting this response, to have a vigorous scepticism about the merits of work, to be able to say forthrightly that one was 'mad', or, at least, mildly eccentric, in conventional terms—that one hated housekeeping, or liked to enjoy oneself, or believed in the value of meditation and prayer on their own. But, in Aberdeen, such scepticism about work was only occasionally well sustained.

Even if these links between the work ethic and health had an overriding force, though, they still need to be considered against recognitions of a link between work and illness. The monitoring of this linkage is an important aspect of the work of trade unions, but there was only a small proportion of spontaneous references to trade union views on health. It was not that Aberdonians were blind to the fact that many of the health problems they referred to had arisen in the course of work; but the most striking aspect in their accounts of such instances was the virtual absence of any general critique of work in terms of risks to health.

To see why the risks of work were felt to be only marginally relevant, we have to look at the structure of the explanations given for illness arising in occupational contexts. To begin with, while work was often a contributory factor in the causation of illness, the pathogenic property concerned was one which was felt, in each case, to belong only to a particular type of work. In some cases it was assumed to belong to that type of work necessarily, as exposure to weather belonged necessarily to the building trade, and to the farming system in which many men had begun their working lives; but in other cases the pathogenic property was one which belonged to the work concerned only in special circumstances. Such special circumstances might be those of the worker: exposure to the weather might be deemed harmless except to a susceptible person with an inherited weakness of the chest. Or the special circumstances might be those of the work, due to a change in technology, in the organization of work, in the attitude of clients and so forth, which rendered a hitherto harmless exposure to risk or stress too acute. And in either case a wide range of explanations was available for these special circumstances arising in conjunction with that type of work. The conjunction could occur, for example, through choices for which the worker felt responsible, as in the case of men who had thrown up steady jobs only to find themselves subject to casualized and risk-prone occupations; or it could occur through the fault of other workers whose laziness or dishonesty increased the stresses on the industrious and honest; or it could occur because the individual was powerless in the face of poor education, technological or social change, or the authority of superiors. Nearly all of these explanations were felt to be compatible with adherence to the work ethic. It was only in the last instance, when the authority of superiors was held responsible for stressful or dangerous changes in work organization—an account offered by less than a fifth of those I spoke to—that a definite contradiction was felt between devotion to work and its recompense in risks of illness. And this contradiction pointed to a breach of the proper relation between work and reward, which to this extent was embedded in the work ethic itself.

Thus although nearly a third of these Aberdonians made references to illness generated in the course of work, the structure of explanation used seldom impinged on or qualified the health-giving properties of diligence; and in the few cases where a contradiction was felt, it was because the relation between effort and reward assumed in the Aberdonian work ethic had been seen to be breached. In these instances the employer was seen as wilfully acting to increase risks for the worker in response to honest service. But aside from these cases, explanations involved quite complicated appraisals of the conjunction of occupational circumstances which produced illness, and canvassed many factors not regarded as relevant to the essential beneficence of conscientious effort.

Ideas about work as a source of illness did not, therefore, significantly limit the Aberdonian emphasis on work as a source of health; and with this question answered it is possible to draw together what has been said about these local values and set it in the wider national and international context.

Conclusion

This Aberdonian generation has emerged as relatively united across sexes and social classes in their particular version of the work ethic. They were united, that is, about the importance of useful activity, performed as a duty, whether for pay or otherwise; and about the strict dependence both of pay and of benefits on work. In part, this conception was taken for granted as natural and rational; in part, it was seen as having corresponded to particular historical necessities in times of war and economic depression; and in part it was seen as a value which distinguished this generation from those which had followed it. It was not that Aberdonians were uncritical about the jobs they had held or about the social relationships attached to those jobs: low pay, sweated labour, the decline of skills, the increase of sharp practice, the loss of autonomy, and other features of their occupational life all came in for disapproval, and in these circumstances the job had some-times been given up with relief. But such criticisms (with some exceptions concerned with housework) left their commitment to the ideal of work still largely untouched—indeed the criticisms sometimes sprang precisely from the failure of the job to measure up to the ideal.

Because of this highly conditional relation between the work ethic of Aberdonians and their commitment to the jobs they had held, their view of retirement was not often as bleak as their enthusiasm for work might superficially lead one to expect. There were indeed those for whom loss of a job deeply and uniquely invested with this morality was loss of their moral self; but there were as many for whom skills and associations developed outside the job, or founded in it but now independent of it, provided a basis for the ethic which was equivalent to, sometimes even more satisfactory than, the job itself.

Thus it was health rather than employment which was unequivocally related to the work ethic. Work—including those unpaid activities to which the ethic was transferred in retirement—had the capacity to sustain normality and thereby to control illness and postpone late old age. This morality reinforced both the optimism of Aberdonians about their way of life and their conformity to it; and when serious illness came, the same ideal promoted the dichotomy noted earlier between continued unremitting struggle on the one hand, and if this failed, a sense of total loss on the other. It was the work ethic, in fact, which restricted the possibility of viewing illness coherently as an alternative way of life, and which virtually eliminated the possibility of seeing it coherently as a release from effort.

This Aberdonian idea of work as something health-giving, indeed at times as something indispensable to health, was, as I have said, referred in part to the experience of recession between the wars. And this raises the question whether phases of growth and recession have in fact affected, first, the strength of this work ethic on its own, and second, the kind of relation it assumes between work and health.

The Aberdonian belief that recession has been linked with the work ethic, and prosperity with the ethic's decline, is, according to the evidence cited in the introduction to this chapter, a view quite widely shared by management (and of course by Conservative politicians). But there is also a difference. These Aberdonians were not talking about work as the product of ambition or incentives in the marketplace, and they were suspicious of industrial practices based on personal gain rather than public usefulness and conscientious practice. The historical evidence does not indicate whether this commitment to conscientious usefulness declined in the prosperous 1960s and early 1970s; it only suggests that there was a decline in the commitment to paid employment. And similarly, while recession and sharpening inequalities can doubtless stimulate greater commitment to employment, it is far less certain that they can reawaken the conscientious spirit which older Aberdonians applied to paid and unpaid activities alike.

However, even if only part of the link between the economic cycle and commitment to work can be sustained, I have already quoted evidence which suggests that the economic cycle affects the sort of link Aberdonians made between work and health. There is indeed only an ambiguous indication in the fact that economic austerity can reduce sickness absence; but recession and casualized labour in inner London have also been found alongside a morality of 'working through' illness and thus proving oneself a good person. From this, it is a short—though significant—step to the contention of Aberdonians who grew up in the recession between the wars that work actually sustains health, controls illness, and postpones late old age. By contrast, evidence from before and after 1968 shows Parisians in prosperity increasingly viewing their work and way of life as coercive and as injurious to their health, and increasingly viewing illness as an expression of political protest.

These opposing notions about the health implications of work may well, therefore, be reflecting phases of growth or recession; but they may also be reflecting differences in cultural inheritance, as the French case reminds us. In France, the sort of work ethic which depends on loyalty to the firm seems to be still less evident than it is in Britain,[23] and in defining French views of work the long tradition of hostility to capitalism in both Socialist and Catholic thought needs to be considered. Much remains to be explored here, but I cited in the introduction to this chapter a few indications that the work ethic has evolved differently in different cultural settings; and to this can now be added—though the evidence is still more fragmentary—indications of related attitudes to health and ageing which help to place those found in Aberdeen.

I begin with comparisons between settings which have had a substantial Protestant history. First, some social commentators have detected a regional variation in the British work ethic. They have contrasted the industrial spirit with the gentlemanly ideal, and associated these with the North and South respectively;[24] and there is a little recent evidence that the Scots at any rate live up to this image of the North.[25] From this perspective it is not surprising that Aberdonians said so much in praise of labour and diligence, and made such explicit links between work and health: they were merely living up to these 'northern' attributes, long associated, amongst other things, with Methodism and Presbyterianism.

Societies with a strong Protestant bias may, however, go different ways. There are some indications that different health attitudes follow from the American stress on individual success and recognition through achievement. This was not an Aberdonian emphasis. Certainly recognition of effort was considered fair, but the virtue of hard work was very much the collective and self-sacrificing virtue of usefulness to the community, and the community rewarded it with rights to benefits. Incapacity might unavoidably exclude one from normal membership of this community, but this loss of self was endured stoically, in a way which acknowledged, even in this, the appropriateness of sacrifice: 'You have to content yourself.' A distinction like this between the collective loyalties and self-control of British society, and the emphasis on individual achievement of American society, was made speculatively by Parsons a long time ago,[26] and it helped to explain the observation of a cross-national study in 1962 that apparently equivalent levels of incapacity were less tolerable to Americans than to Britons.[27] In the light of this comparison, then, the individualistic aspect of the American ideal of achievement has to be seen as one development of a work ethic which in Scotland has rather evolved in a collective direction.

Yet the collective element in the Scottish conscience still differs from the collective work ethic fostered by Confucian tradition.[28] The Aberdonian work ethic was one in which duty to the employer played little part, unlike the diligence based on social loyalties at work for which the Japanese are reputed. It has been argued that this latter corporate version of the work ethic creates a distinctive view of ageing. One can see, for example, that Japanese loyalties to those at work should be a powerful spur to older people seeking, not useful and diligent voluntary pursuits, but continued employment in the marketplace. And in fact in Japan a much higher proportion of men and women remain employed after the age of 65 than in Britain. It seems that the duty to work plays a part in this, alongside other incentives, and although the corporate loyalties of the work ethic are supposed to be those of large firms, and these retire their workers very early by Western standards, many people continue to work part-time for these firms up to an advanced age.[29]

These differences between cultures with different histories raise issues about the historical ancestry of Aberdonian conceptions of work. The debt of the community to hard workers fallen on evil days, and the collective element which distinguishes the British from the American work ethic, are features which obviously owe much to the post-war consensus which created the British welfare state. But the emphasis on industry, thrift, and independence goes back to the values of respectability and improvement characteristic of the late Victorian labour aristocracy and to their equivalents in the late Victorian middle class. The creation of these disciplines have in Aberdeen been traced back at least to the mid-nineteenth century, when industrial change and Protestant enthusiasm were closely interwoven in the Disruption of the Church of Scotland and the growth of the Free Church.[30] And this connection brings us to the margins of the distinctively Scottish issues concerning the development of the Protestant ethic. Before Aberdonian culture can be placed in this context, however, we have to consider the role in it of religion; and before this we have to understand the other side of economic life—the divisions of wealth and class that counterbalance the unity about the value of work.

Notes and References

1. A. Gorz, *Paths to paradise: on the liberation from work*, tr. M. Imrie, London: Pluto Press, 1985.
2. M. Rose, *Reworking the work ethic*, London: Batsford, 1985, ch. 1.
3. For evidence that the work ethic flourishes in Britain in spite of wide-spread scepticism about the possibility of co-operation between workers and management see M. Mann, 'Work and the work ethic', in R. Jowell, S. Witherspoon, and L. Brook (eds.), *British social attitudes: the 1986 report*, London: Gower, 1987.
4. Phrase quoted from a Japanese minister in R. Dore, *British factory, Japanese factory*, London: Allen and Unwin, 1973, p. 396; the family symbolism of large Japanese enterprises has received repeated comment since the early work of J. Abegglen, *The Japanese factory*, London: Asia Publishing House, 1958.
5. W. H. Whyte, *The organisation man*, London: Cape, 1957.
6. The extraordinary influence in America of research on the 'achievement' motive illustrates this. See D. C. McLelland, *The achieving society*, London: Van Nostrand, 1961, ch. 2, where numerous international comparisons are made on this basis (the Japanese, ironically, scoring low and the USA high). Some of the complex realities behind the American myth of achievement are pointed out by D. T. Rodgers, *The work ethic in industrial America 1850–1920*, University of Chicago Press, 1978, and by H. G. Gutman, *Work, culture and society in industrialising America*, New York: Random House, 1966.
7. M. Wiener, *English culture and the decline of the industrial spirit 1850–1980*, Cambridge University Press, 1981.
8. Compare work as temporal structure, raised activity levels, and personal identity in P. Warr, 'Job loss, unemployment and psychological well-being', in E. van de Vliert and V. Allen (eds.), *Role transitions*, New York: Praeger, 1983. Similarly work as deferred gratification, diligence, and personal worth in Rose, *Reworking the work ethic*, p. 12, and as duty, diligence, and usefulness in early 19th century American versions (Rodgers, *The work ethic*, ch. 1).

9. M. Jahoda, *Employment and unemployment,* Cambridge University Press, 1982, ch. 2.

10. D. Fryer and R. L. Payne, 'Proactive behaviour in unemployment: findings and implications', *Leisure Studies,* 3 (1984), 273–95.

11. R. Kanter, 'Work in a new America', *Daedalus,* 107 (Winter 1978), 47–78; Rose, *Reworking the work ethic,* chs. 4 and 5. Contemporary cross-sectional data also show the work ethic being more sceptically regarded among the young: Mann, 'Work and the work ethic'.

12. Jahoda, *Employment and unemployment,* pp. 59 f.

13. Rose, *Reworking the work ethic,* ch. 6.

14. T. R. Tholfsen, *Working class radicalism in mid-Victorian England,* London: Croom Helm, 1976, chs. 7 and 8.

15. R. H. Tawney, *Religion and the rise of capitalism,* London: Pelican, 1938, pp. 134–5; H. R. Trevor-Roper, 'Religion, the reformation and social change', *Historical Studies,* 4 (1963), 18–44.

16. G. Marshall, *Presbyteries and profits,* Oxford University Press, 1980.

17. M. Lessnoff, 'Protestant ethic and profit motive in the Weber thesis', *Int. J. Sociol. and Soc. Pol.* 1 (1981), 1–18; T. Dickson and H. McLachlan, 'Scottish capitalism and Weber's Protestant ethic theses', *Sociology,* 17 (1983), 560–8, and Marshall's reply, ibid. 569–73.

18. T. C. Smout, *A history of the Scottish people 1560–1830,* London: Fontana, 1972, pp. 72 f.; Marshall, *Presbyteries and profits,* ch. 7.

19. E. P. Thompson, 'Time, work discipline and industrial capitalism', *Past and Present,* 38 (1967), 56–97.

20. J. Cornwell, *Hard-earned lives: accounts of health and illness from East London,* London: Tavistock, 1984.

21. C. Herzlich, *Health and illness,* tr. H. D. Graham, London: Academic Press, 1973.

22. P. Bellaby, S. J. Cleverly, and J. S. Sidaway, 'The recession and the effort bargain', Dept. Sociology and Soc. Anth., University of Keele.

23. D. Gallie, *Social inequality and class radicalism in France and Britain,* Cambridge University Press, 1983, pt. 2.

24. See references to the Northern and Southern metaphors of English society in Wiener, *English culture*.
25. T. Forester, 'Do the British sincerely want to be rich?', *New Society*, 40 (1977), 158–61. Unfortunately the key question confounds hard work and acquisitiveness, and it is not clear which of these two the Scots were approving. I have indicated that acquisition did not feature in the accounts of older Aberdonians.
26. T. Parsons, 'Definition of health and illness in the light of American values and social structure', in E. G. Jaco (ed.), *Patients, physicians and illness*, Glencoe: Free Press, 1958, ch. 20.
27. E. Shanas, P. Townsend, D. Wedderburn, H. Fries, P. Milhøj, and J. Stehouwer, *Old people in three industrial societies*, London: Routledge, 1968, ch. 3.
28. M. Morishima, *Why has Japan 'succeeded'? Western technology and the Japanese ethos*, Cambridge University Press, 1982.
29. E. Palmore, *The honourable elders: a cross-cultural analysis of ageing in Japan*, Duke University Press, 1975, ch. 5; but compare D. Maeda, 'Ageing in eastern society', in D. Hobman (ed.), *The social challenge of ageing*, London: Croom Helm, 1978.
30. A. A. Maclaren, *Religion and social class*, London: Routledge, 1974, ch. 7.

8

Wealth

I climbed the steep ascent towards a morning coat and an
English accent, and managed to wear both with distinction . . .
But it was no good . . . We were lost in a world of words and
pretensions. We had no reality. So I said goodbye to the
morning coat—I sold it for exactly half of what it cost
me—and returned in all humility to the place where I began.

J. R. Allan, *Farmer's Boy,* 1935

Introduction

That there is a structure of social classes in Aberdeen, and that this
affects the way people cope with physical limitations, is evident to
the most unobservant eye. These classes arise out of differences
between rich and poor, perpetuated by inheritance, and associated
with particular cultural characteristics; but their structure, as elsewhere, is not definable in any simple way, and much remains
perplexing. Not least of these perplexities is the ever-intriguing
relation between the material aspects of class divisions (themselves
many-sided) and the cultural constructions which trade upon them.

Analyses of the economic base of social class in Britain have
mostly emphasized differences in the market situation of occupational groups as the key to the diversity. But there have also been
powerful arguments for regarding property and its inheritance as
central: and although the largest aggregations of property are
confined within so small a circle as to be virtually invisible in the
daily life of the population, close study of some of the assets which
are more widely distributed, and of the various means of access to
them, has led some investigators to see wealth and poverty as
essential discriminators in ordinary life as well; and access to
housing in particular has occasionally emerged as an important,
though much disputed, principle of class division.

Whatever aspect of people's material circumstances is emphasized, however, a still more complex task lies in tracing those of
their cultural attributes which are related to those circumstances.
The chief problem lies in the extent to which cultural attributes are
determined by the economic base. On the one hand are examples
like the deferential or antagonistic images of society held by
different groups of manual workers, which may appear to be directly
determined by their situation at work and at home.[1] And on the
other hand are those aspects of 'cultural capital', exemplified in
command of information, which enable its possessors continually
to reproduce both their material circumstances and their cultural
position.[2] Either way, command over the market for goods and
reputation can be assumed to reveal itself in friendship choices,
and in various forms of exclusive closure which protect the monopoly of goods and reputation established.[3] But while all these facets
of class cultures have received separate attention, the way in
which they fit together has remained obscure; and concrete topics
like those of this book provide an opportunity for tracing some of
their interconnections.

Although social class has been considered for decades in relation to health, it has not for so long been considered in relation to
popular ideas, whether about health or about the other topics of
this book, and in Britain it is only recently that any attempts have
been made to understand some of these relations in terms of the
material and cultural explanations of the class system just discussed.
The Registrar-General's definition of social classes—the usual
index in medical research—was constructed with an eye mainly to
problems of fertility,[4] and later amended with an eye to mortality.[5]
In assessing social differences in these medical outcomes, it grouped
the occupations of householders into five classes, ordering them by
the public standing of the skills they required; and it also later
divided them more broadly into manual and non-manual categories,
these being commonly interpreted as the occupations of the 'working class' and the 'middle class' respectively. But in contemporary
terms, while it continues to have an intuitive usefulness, it has little
in the way of a clear explanatory underpinning. Thus it is remarkable that, in spite of the deficiencies of this index, the empirical
material which has emerged from its use is suggestive of several
explanatory accounts which might be appropriate to present topics.

Probably the best-evidenced class difference in research on these topics, and one reflected already in the present Aberdeen material, is in relationships with the doctor. The material basis for such a difference is obvious where private fees are a major element in medical remuneration, and it has been suggested that fee-paying patients have more control in the relationship and receive a fuller discussion of their problems.[6] However, in many parts of Britain, Scotland included, private practice is a rarity, and yet still, under the NHS, it has long been said that the middle classes 'know how to make better use of the service',[7] and there is evidence that they are more frequently referred (at older ages) to hospital,[8] and more critical of their doctors,[9] or at least more inclined to ask questions and obtain information about diagnosis and prognosis.[10] The resources used in this critical knowledge and questioning remain unclear, however. Cultural resources such as education and confidence may be a decisive factor,[11] but the class basis of these resources needs further exploration.

Social class explanations have also been worked out, as I mentioned in Chapter 2, for variation in ideas about ageing. Optimism about ageing depends in part, it is argued, on skills acquired in working life; and the capitalist mode of production, by separating the conception of tasks from their execution, progressively degrades the skills of those who merely execute tasks, while continuing to diversify the knowledge of the increasingly narrow band who give these tasks their design.[12] However, while the first part of this thesis—the necessity of skills for optimism about ageing—may well be true, and has already been reflected in the Aberdeen material, the second part—the degrading effect on skills of capitalist production—remains uncertain: managerial distinctions between those who design work and those who perform it are not now the monopoly of capitalism, and in any case conventional classifications continue to suggest that, overall, levels of skill are still rising.[13] Thus while a lifetime of designing work may indeed give greater scope for acquiring skills which last into old age, it is necessary also to look elsewhere for reasons why people lack such skills, or lack the conception of old age as a time for the expansion of skills in the first place.

New as are these attempts to explain ideas about ageing in terms of social class, explanations of ideas about health in such terms are still more recent and tentative. One possibility is that positive notions of health are a mainly middle-class phenomenon, associated with a middle-class emphasis on control over the causation of illness and on preventive behaviour.[14] Similarly, ideas about coping actively with established illness may be commoner in the middle class,[15] though the evidence is fragmentary.

Class explanations for such differences in health ideas have been attempted along several lines. One such account again uses the distinction just referred to between professional or managerial occupations, which are framed around the conception and control of tasks, and subordinate occupations, which are framed around their execution. In this view, control is associated with perceptions of health as personal property and as an end in itself, while execution is associated with perceptions of health as a collective obligation and as subject to the requirements of others.[16] Alternatively, class differences in health may themselves affect perceptions. They may, for example, disguise standards of comparison so much that the worst-affected groups, using their own fellow members for comparison, come to regard serious conditions as normal.[17] Implicit in this suggestion, of course, is the assumption that class differences in health are in turn caused by true class-related conditions founded in work, wealth, and power. These explanations emphasize material factors; but it has also been argued that cultural attributes, such as education, religion, and the willingness to defer gratification, may not only favour the accumulation of assets, but also help people to assimilate official views on health promotion, and to accept an element of personal responsibility for health.[18]

In ideas about health, ageing, and the doctor, then, class differences may well be important, but it is still not clear which of a number of varying explanations, implicating both material and cultural aspects of class, deserves the greatest attention. The design of the present study, tracing social networks in Mannoch and the West End, was one which gave prominence to class differences, and in particular to those elusive cultural aspects of such differences which cluster around house and neighbourhood. At the same time the Aberdeen Survey permits a representative picture to be drawn both of these cultural aspects and of the material basis for local class divisions.

Social class in Aberdeen

In the Aberdeen Survey, income, savings, and home ownership all reflected, as would be expected, the main occupational position which had been held by the respondent, or, failing that, by the head of the household, during working life, as represented in the Registrar-General's social classes; and combinations of these assets reflected that position still more strongly (Table 4).

Table 4. *Aberdeen survey of the elderly, 1980: social class by number of economic advantages (house ownership, net household income over £60 per week or £40 per week living alone, and savings, investments, or money put by over £1,000)*

Number of economic advantages	Social class %			Total	
	I – III non-manual	III manual	IV – V	%	No.
None	17.1	46.4	36.5	100	315
One	39.0	39.6	21.4	100	159
Two	54.3	34.6	11.1	100	81
All three	76.6	14.9	8.5	100	47

The occupational class of respondents, in turn, reflected that of their fathers, and although there are no exactly comparable figures from elsewhere, this aspect of inheritance appears, in the men of this generation, as unusually strict (Table 5). In particular, the intergenerational continuity of skilled manual work had been as high as that of other work, and had not reflected, as it has with other generations and in other areas, the expansion of opportunities to move into the urban middle class.

Table 5. *Aberdeen survey of the elderly, 1980: class of men by class of father*

Father's class	Respondent's class (men) (%)			Total	
	I – III non-manual	III manual	IV – V	%	No.
I – III non-manual	63.0	27.4	9.6	100	90
III manual	20.0	52.1	27.9	100	113
IV – V	21.3	26.7	52.0	100	85
No.	73	140	75		288

However, the impression of continuity is in some ways too complete: for these figures mask a different sort of discontinuity—

one between modes of production. The breakup of the North-East peasantry was nearing completion as this generation succeeded its predecessor. The urban middle class did indeed expand at this time in Aberdeen, as elsewhere; but the opportunities were seized rather by men and women whose fathers had been on the land. Now the numerous crofters and small tenant farmers of the turn of the century in the North-East comprise a large part of the fathers included, in Table 5, in the Registrar-General's social class II: and in so far as they had some capital, were self-employed, and held their farms through leases which, if not secure, were usually extended over terms of a number of years, this comparison with the urban middle class gives a not unfair impression of the independent status and, in some cases, the financial backing which many were able to pass on to sons and daughters. But in so far as many of the farms were very small, and in so far as the occupational knowledge and skills of many of these farmers were primarily manual, and thus regarded as inferior by the educated, the comparison with the urban middle class is misleading.[19] Thus to the extent that the affinities of many of these farmers with urban manual work are ignored in Table 5, their sons and daughters who moved into the urban middle class give an enhanced impression of intergenerational continuity in the middle class, while those who moved into skilled manual trades give, for the same reason, an enhanced impression of downward social mobility.

However, even allowing for this uncertainty about the interpenetration of urban and agricultural classes in this period of North-East life, the inheritance of occupational advantages in the urban population seems to have been substantial;[20] and other forms of inheritance were also at work in producing differences in assets. The most important form of property was house ownership. Nobody in this age group who had savings or investments over £20,000 (the low end of the house price range in 1980) was renting; and amongst house owners nine-tenths did not have additional savings or investments of this order, reflecting the fact that the house had been the priority for investment. Now while the access to mortgages provided by, especially, middle-class occupations was obviously a major factor in house ownership, the part played by inheritance was surprisingly large in view of the small proportion of houses owned in the preceding generation. Data on inheritance were not available from the Aberdeen Survey, but in the qualitative study—admittedly conducted in the best residential sector of the city—over half of house owners had derived all or part of their title from inherited money or property; and it seems that this feature of property ownership in later life deserves wider investigation.

Inheritance, then, both of assets and of occupational position, was a prominent feature of this Aberdonian age group, with the proviso that the notion of inheritance included, in many cases, the translation of fathers' occupational positions in the agricultural marketplace into children's occupational positions in the urban marketplace—a process which, in the North-East of this period, is not sensitively reflected in the Registrar-General's national classification.

The broad fact of inheritance can be appreciated without being precise about class boundaries; and of course the continuous curve which marks the distribution of income and savings gives, in old age as at other ages, little basis for drawing boundaries of any more than an arbitrary kind. But just as the differing market position of occupational categories such as 'staff' and 'labour' has given a traditional justification for distinguishing those who have been in manual and non-manual work for the main part of their lives, so the differing market position of house owners and tenants in Aberdeen gives a justification for distinguishing those who have lived in owned or rented accommodation for the main part of their lives. And it is a notable feature of Scottish class formations that while private renting has shrunk, home ownership is still limited, and local authority tenancy is, compared with England, both extensive and much more nearly coincident with the traditional division between manual and non-manual occupations (Table 6). Thus while in English towns chances for security in work, housing, finance, and other economic dimensions have become more loosely linked,[21] and social mobility in the middle range has created relatively stable islands of inheritance only at the extremes,[22] in this Aberdonian generation economic advantages in these different areas have been relatively closely tied, and continuity in skilled manual work has been especially high. Accordingly, in the Aberdeen Survey, two fairly well-defined groups emerge, who had worked in middle-class and working-class occupations most of their lives, and who were by this stage typically owners and tenants respectively; while between them the mixed stratum which shows some characteristics of either appears, against English comparisons, relatively narrow.[23]

Table 6. *Aberdeen survey of the elderly, 1980: housing tenure by social class*

Housing tenure	Social class (%)			Total	
	I – III non-manual	III manual	IV – V	No.	%
Owner occupation	51.5	19.3	9.3	163	27.1
Local authority	31.6	61.1	72.8	329	54.6
Private renting	9.7	10.2	5.6	53	8.8
With family/other	7.2	9.4	12.3	57	9.5
TOTAL	100	100	100	602	100

This basic distribution of economic chances was reflected both directly and indirectly in the economic assumptions which Aberdonians took for granted in thinking about health, ageing, and death. It was reflected directly in references to property as an enabling factor, and in the degree of control which people felt they exercised over their housing; and it was reflected indirectly in references to the repertory of skills acquired during upbringing and working life, and in the social allegiances and distinctions which were based upon shared economic position.

Property made a number of things possible for people in the West End. The main asset was ownership of the house, and many had a lively awareness of what could be done in the property market of a city in which the office sector was rapidly expanding into traditional middle-class areas. The house was an investment, one which with a little luck would actually make one's fortune, and which at the least provided the means for a variety of manœuvres both financial and familial. Exchanging it for a smaller house could release money to be turned into investment income; buying into an up-and-coming area before retirement could help to ensure this surplus; letting rooms for a period could tide over a crisis in the current account; and selling the house could permit buying power to be made available to the younger generation from part of the proceeds, in exchange for their care and protection. By contrast, the limited instances of house ownership in Mannoch generated no such strategic schemes for exploiting ownership as an asset; the house was to be lived in, and the only transaction contemplated with it was the ultimate one of selling it to the council in exchange for a suitable tenancy. Houses tended in any case to be of awkward size or siting from the perspective of the owner-occupied market, and owners in this sector felt correspondingly powerless.

Aside from the use of housing as a financial asset, however, the sense of control over the house itself was differentiated by tenure. Council housing—perhaps partly because it is largely distributed by others' judgement rather than by an apparently impersonal market—created in tenants a sense of frustration and helplessness which was seldom alluded to amongst owner-occupiers. First, tenants had preferences which were not allowed to influence their choice. Whether wisely or unwisely, they sometimes wanted a kind of house which was not approved as suitable for their age and health—one with stairs, for instance, because it was in an area which had a view and caught the sun. In other cases, preferences were not felt to be actively discouraged by officials, but they could not enter into the choice because there was so little room for choice. Tenants expected a maximum of three offers, not together but in series, and there was no knowing, if the first offer was rejected, whether the second and third would not be worse. In these circumstances the less audacious felt a need to please the authorities by accepting the first offer because 'they dinna like it if you refuse'; and in this acceptance a number of criteria relating to the local area went by the board. Ownership also had occasional problems, but they were seldom felt to the extent of these limitations which tended to eliminate choice based on neighbourhood and locality.

Undoubtedly the council housing which dominates working-class Aberdeen, while it gave rise to this sense of powerlessness, had also made possible for this generation certain amenities which they had once lacked. And further opportunities which the council offered in late life were the 'low door' (ground floor accommodation), the chance to move into a smaller flat after the children had left, and perhaps (with a considerable wait) sheltered housing. All these possibilities were also open, however, to owners, either in the market or by selling to the council and entering its system at a strategic moment when, say, sheltered housing was preferred; and in addition, besides the financial manœuvres described earlier as a resource of house ownership, it was possible to adapt and renovate to save housework, and to choose one's locality both from a wider range (which included in particular the nearby valleys of Deeside and Donside), and with a greater precision about what was wanted in the neighbourhood.

Property and money, then, controlled some very different patterns of constraint and opportunity—patterns which were assumed as given in middle-class and working-class Aberdeen. Other such patterns, however, were less given, more the mixed result of both economic possessions and the use made of them. One such mixed product lay in the skills and knowledge practised in different social settings.

That the skills and interests of Aberdonians bore some relation to social class is evidenced by the connection between occupational categories and the number of interests and hobbies described by respondents in the Aberdeen Survey (Table 7)—a connection as evident among women as among men. And just as the middle class in the survey cited more interests, so skills which derived in some sense from their economic position formed a more frequent point of reference in conversations with people in the West End than with those in Mannoch. In fact West Enders were both more enthusiastic about skills which were rewarding, and more critical of those that were unrewarding. Middle-class enthusiasm more often dwelt affectionately on vocational skills, and in addition reached out to embrace arts of painting, calligraphy, interior decoration, and music, and the related occupations of collecting, buying, and selling; and where common household skills were not professed alongside these, it was because they were devalued as inferior.

Table 7. *Aberdeen survey of the elderly, 1980: sex and social class by number of interests or hobbies in spare time*

Social class	Number of interests							
	Men (%)				Women (%)			
	0 – 1	2 – 3	4 +	Total	0 – 1	2 – 3	4 +	Total
I – III non-manual	33.3	33.4	33.3	100	29.8	47.1	23.1	100
III manual	38.1	46.3	15.6	100	33.0	53.6	13.4	100
IV – V	48.8	41.7	9.5	100	38.5	53.8	7.7	100

Note: men, $P < .001$; women $P < .01$.

These skills were derived from the owner's economic position in a number of senses, direct and indirect. Some derived directly from the line of paid work which had dominated working life: the knowledge of the joiner, the mason, the nurse, the teacher, the doctor, the bank manager, and many others transcended their occupations in various ways, as I showed earlier, by being transferable to other situations. Some, though, of these abilities derived not so much from occupational specialization as from an inherited style of consumption—a pattern which was most marked in the arts of housekeeping. Other capacities, such as the range of games played, were traceable to the kind of school attended, with fee-paying schools having the advantage; and yet others had been acquired through institutions such as adult evening classes which were open to all, but which were best adapted to the purposes and values of people who made an art of decorating their own house or who already had extensive foundations of academic knowledge on which to build. And the middle-class focus on acquiring accomplishments had a further consequence: not only was a relatively wide range of distinctive skills assumed, but informal access to the distinctive skills of others, through the network of middle-class acquaintanceship, was easier.

In a number of ways, therefore, skills, or talk about skills, had a basis in class experience. How far this talk represented real differences in accomplishment, and how far it represented a special value on accomplishment, is hard to say. But it was noticeable that skills were a topic of greater interest to those who in general emphasized individual distinction rather than collective loyalties. And these emphases were themselves an indirect product of economic differences, being related to the way social allegiances and social divisions had been formed.

Many of the social loyalties of Aberdeen emphasized the collective. One of the most noticeable tendencies of these allegiances was a certain historical time-lag between the social world to which allegiance was felt and the economic divisions discernible in current experience. The oldest stratum of economic life which continued to animate present thinking was the communal life of the farm 'touns' and fishing villages of the North-East as they existed in the early part of the century. There is, indeed, a flourishing local literature on this subject; and it is accompanied by a stream of magazine, pamphlet, and newspaper articles which retrace and portray aspects of this rural past. An identification with the 'fisher folk' of the North Sea and Moray Firth coasts, with the Orkney, Shetland, or Hebridean colonies in Aberdeen, with the country and the 'auld tradition' had accordingly, in both middle- and working-class Aberdeen, a symbolic force which, even in those cases where the demise of that life was acknowledged, survived to influence thinking and behaviour.

Something of this historical aura also surrounded the other form of communal allegiance—that to the local urban neighbourhood. It was, for example, the old mill and fishing townships now encapsulated by the city which retained the strongest loyalty, even when the attachment could only be expressed in the form of an elegy for what had been swept away by the demolition squads of the Town, or by the impulses of new generations to 'get busy and mak better'. The conjunction of these enemies—municipal demolition and individual competition—was not accidental; for the keynotes of this conception were the local community and its reciprocal egalitarianism:

Wife: "I mean we've got wir neighbours, we've got good neighbours, and it makes an awfa' difference."

Husband: "I mean she was born and brought up in Woodside, born and brought up in Woodside, aye . . . ."

Wife: "I mean in this line here [of houses] there's a lot o' Woodside people; and there's one at the end I wis tae school with, and I said to her, 'Hello Violet.' And she said to me, 'Fit wye div [what way do] you ken my name?' I says, 'I wis tae school wi' ye.' But she couldna mind on me."

Husband: "Of course ye get them that disna wint tae mind. I mean I've spoken till [to]—oh he was at the school wi' me, oh he didna ken. He wis in the police, and we had a big conference you know, and I drove up, and the boy's there parkin' you see. And of course whenever I saw him I come oot o'er: 'Hallo Bert.' He says, 'Do I know you?' I says, 'Oh that's enough, cheerio, I'm away.' "

Wife: "One o' his schoolmates—Bucksburn neeps [turnips]."

Husband: "Aye so that wis, that wis the finish. 'Should I know you?' I just walked awa', just walked awa'. Couldna be deein' wi' that lot. The officers I wis wi' used to say [imitating], 'I don't know a word you're saying.' I says, 'Well I canna help bein' a countryman, I'm nae changin' my tongue for you or naebody else.' 'And [imitating] I still don't know what you're saying.' "

This conversation reflected well both the continuing local allegiance to urban villages now discernible only as outcrops of granite cottages among the dun estates—an allegiance built on neighbourly relations dating back to shared schools—and the corresponding rejection of attempts to claim a status above this common life, whether by former schoolmates or by national élites like the officer class. It was a combination of themes expressed even in apparently insignificant things: cups and saucers, for example, were uneasily felt to be 'fancy', and while hospitality demanded honouring the guest with them, egalitarianism required at the same time their disavowal, with the result that numerous conversations reaffirmed, at the appropriate moment, the solidarity of plain mugs. And in the same way, the social ranking of occupations was denied; promotion was to be avoided, and professions were trades like anyone else's.

Contrasted with this locally rooted egalitarian vision, however—one comparable with that of the classic 'proletarian' communities of the mining villages—was another interpretation of social membership based on economic categories: that of hierarchy. While this was fundamentally a middle-class vision, it did not lack working-class adherents who claimed, on the basis of suitable connections, a certain level of gentility. But the source of this conception lay in the nexus of fee-paying schools, professional and managerial occupations, West End residence and selective clubs, all bound together by links of kinship and friendship, which define the Aberdeen bourgeoisie. Signs of status were not necessarily used with exclusionary intent by this circle; it was rather assumed as a fact of life that members of it had been lucky enough to share most of the things which were in general demand—the best schools in the city, the positions of authority, the membership of clubs with long waiting lists and rigorous conditions for sponsorship. Indeed hierarchy was stated in the detached tone of an observer, noting for example that 'Aberdeen is a snobbish city' or that 'our taste of honey has been better than most', and it did not prevent the commentator expressing a personal dislike of signs of status:

"We travelled a lot, and lived it up and enjoyed it. I had my own car, I had a nanny for the kids, we had a gardener who was a Communist and who used to sit in the kitchen and indoctrinate the maids with the *Daily Worker*, and we were all one happy family. I mean we were very left-wing in our interests, you see, all of us actually, and so we didn't treat servants particularly as—we didn't adhere to the 'Sir and Madam' attitude, you know: more of a happy family."

And in fact the links which bind together the native middle class, being unusually strong in Aberdeen, did not require any additional formal emphasis. It had been unnecessary to send boys away to boarding schools, for Gordon's and the Grammar had gained a sufficient reputation for most Aberdeen burgesses to have been to school together in one or the other. And many then went through the city's university, and later joined private social clubs or sporting clubs based formally or informally on previous membership of these institutions. Thus irrespective of the further links created in the world of work, there existed unusually systematic local links which bound this élite together.

This local élite, then, formed a compact status group and dominated a hierarchy of prestige which, where it was accepted in the working class, led to a focus on genteel connections. But beside this model of society there coexisted two others which were fundamentally similar and egalitarian—the small and homogeneous world of the local working-class communities, recreating the ethos of the old mill and fishing townships of Aberdeen itself, and the wider farming and fishing society of the past. These two models gave some reflection—and also perhaps some historical distortion—of the present pattern of skills, resources, and economic power. Together, all these dimensions formed a background of knowledge about social classes in Aberdeen whose implications for health ideas must now be discussed.

Social class and views of health

Assumptions about resources in terms of occupation, income, and property, and about the personal accomplishments and social allegiances based on these things, all of which helped to reflect and replicate the structure of classes in Aberdeen, were related primarily to ideas about health, ageing, and medical care, and only occasionally by extension to ideas about death.

As regards health, the data of the Aberdeen Survey suggest that, in this age group, class was more closely related to the way people coped with illness than to the amount of illness they experienced and expected. No relationship emerged here between class and poor health, nor between poor health and stoic norms. It is common, indeed, to find that in the sixties and at older ages class differences in health are partially resolved, though this may only be because death has prematurely removed the sickest and the poorest. Certainly working-class Aberdonians of this age group no longer had a disproportionate share of illness, and they did not assess serious illness as normal. It is likely that they are more apt to do so in younger age groups, where class differences in health are sharper.[24]

However, if class was not here involved in self-assessments of health, it was nevertheless involved to some degree in ways of coping with illness. The Aberdeen Survey gives an indication that working-class Aberdonians were especially likely to rely on normal activity to control illness, while at the same being especially pessimistic about the degree of control they had (Table 8). These, though, are only hints, and to understand their meaning it is necessary to turn to the qualitative study.

Table 8. *Aberdeen survey of the elderly, 1980: social class by percentage disagreeing with two statements about illness*

Statement	Social class (% disagreeing)			P (whole table)
	I–III non-manual	III manual	IV–V	
I'm not really ill as long as I'm able to go out.	23.4	17.2	10.5	P<.001
There's not much you can do about your health because it's mainly a matter of luck.	55.6	42.6	30.2	P<.001

In Mannoch, when class factors were related to coping with illness, the main constraints were those imposed by council tenancies on neighbourhood preferences. There was a complex and delicate relationship between the position of the house and the web of neighbourly relationships which, while local in character, was yet astonishingly varied in its geography, depending on the biography of individuals and the social allegiances of their past. In the same square mile of council houses, for instance, where for many there was a thriving local community, there were several people who were cut off from their own web of relationships partly because of the location of the house assigned to them; and for these their location was part of the burden of their illness which they either were struggling against, or more usually, were compelled to endure with a sense of helplessness (1.4). Eleanor Fordyce, for example, had grown up in one of the old mill villages engulfed by the city after the First World War; and she had lived there all her life until, three years previously, her street was knocked down and she was moved to an estate a mile away. As she understood it, she had no choice about where she should move; the people of the street, where she had spent her childhood and where she in her turn had had her own children, had been scattered to different areas. These neighbours from her old street, and her position among them, formed an idealized point of contrast with her present situation:

We had good neighbours. They aye came round to me if they were ill and I aye helped them, you see? We had good times together. They should never have knocked it doon. This is a nice enough hoose, has a good low door [i.e. ground floor] but it's nae the same. I know some of the neighbours here. I'm very pleasant, careful fit [what] I say and fit I dae. But you dinna ken fa [where] ye are. I canna make up with them. They've different ways.

The contrast was accentuated by her own present need of help on a daily basis, which a home help once a week could not sustain. In addition, her family situation obviously increased her vulnerability: one child, a son, was on the far side of Aberdeen, and was seldom seen; the others were elsewhere. This helps to explain her emphasis on her previous long-standing reciprocal relationships with her neighbours, in which she felt that she herself had helped others, and thus accumulated a credit which she could have drawn on. Failing these, she turned instead to paying the small boys of the vicinity to run errands. But with them her relationship was at best ambiguous: not only did they want 'a good handful' afterwards, but their noise aggravated her tendency to 'nerves' and she was divided about 'checking' them; also, more sinisterly,

There was a young man who was awfa' friendly. He was aye talking to me through the window and brought his little girl for me to admire, and she was a lovely little girl really, but something held me back just the same. Now he's doing time—for thieving.

Ambiguity and a sense of vulnerability in regard to neighbours, then, had replaced trust—a familiar result of local authority clearances, but one which, taking place in the context of disabling illness, was critical. Suffering from vertigo and the associated risk of falling, and from the 'nerves' already mentioned, she stayed indoors, and on a daily basis saw only the small boys who came to the door. Of her condition in these circumstances she simply said 'It gets you down—I've naebody to talk to,' and repeated such phrases as 'Ye've no choice,' and 'I dinna ken how I keep going, but I do.' And this stoicism went with a general suppression of the whole subject:

That's my health. You see I've told you about my health. I never tell anyone about my health except the doctor.

Eleanor Fordyce was, then, one of seven cases in which a stoic helplessness—illness as a loss to be endured (1.4)—was explicitly referred to local authority moves which had broken the web of a neighbourhood network of support built up in the absence of a strong Aberdeen-based family. And a few others, too, had experienced the same combination of circumstances, and expressed the same view of illness, without explicitly connecting the two. Forced to move by the lack of 'low doors' or sheltered housing in their long-accustomed neighbourhood, or by the demolition of old streets, and sometimes grouped with other invalids in 'health houses' where little life was visible, all but one of these people viewed their situation as intractable because of the falling off of relationships which had formerly given them help and encouragement. This, then, was a severe difficulty when it occurred, but it was experienced only by an unlucky minority of working-class Aberdonians.

Social class and attitudes to the doctor

While the approaches to illness just discussed were affected by class differences only where control of housing was concerned, approaches to the doctor were affected as much by the social hierarchy and social connections within which doctoring takes place, as by control over money and property; and I now turn to explore this more complex pattern.

That class had something to do with the search for information and control by the patient is attested not only by the qualitative study but also by the Aberdeen Survey, in the critical issue of knowledge about a fatal prognosis. Even in this matter, where Aberdonians were relatively disinclined for the truth, it was the middle class who more commonly wished to know it (Table 9). What it was about class that thus affected demands on doctors emerges from various aspects of the qualitative study.

The first aspect of relationships with the doctor that was affected by class was, as I noted in Chapter 5, compliance. Although Aber-donians maintained, as I argued earlier, a stout, if secretive, independence of thought in regard to medical advice and medical values, there was nevertheless a rule enunciated of obedience to medical orders (5.4), and it was, as I noted earlier, virtually only in Mannoch—the council estate—that this rule was invoked. The rule had to coexist with plenty of actual disagreement with the doctor, which greatly weakened its hold on behaviour. But, in so far as the rule was taken seriously, one argument for compliance related to the doctor's social status and the possibility of privileged access to medicine.

Table 9. *Aberdeen survey of the elderly, 1980: social class by whether respondents would want to be told if they were going to die.*

Response	Social class (%)		
	I–III non-manual	III manual	IV–V
Certainly/probably	64.7	54.5	50.0
Might or might not	14.2	11.9	18.5
Probably/definitely not	21.1	33.6	31.5
TOTAL	100	100	100

Note: $P < .003$.

In the hierarchical picture of society held by some working-class Aberdonians, doctors commanded respect by their education, their manners, and their experience of other places, as well as by doctoring *per se*. Indeed these social qualities overlapped with, and could be inferred from, the doctor's professional qualities: professional knowledge suggested education and travel, and a good bedside manner suggested 'niceness'. Thus a personal connection with doctors had, in these circumstances, not only a medical but also a social value; and the forms of access to such a connection were various. One obvious way was through having sufficient money to pay fees for private medicine. Even though private practice is relatively rare in Scotland, one crucial treatment is not necessarily beyond the range of working-class savings. Other ways, too, of getting privileged access to doctors were open to the paramedical worker and the interesting case. Naturally many in these privileged positions of access were unconcerned with such possibilities, their philosophy being as vigorously egalitarian as any in the local community; but a few who had a suitably hierarchical view of the world could use their position to derive certain social benefits. For example it could be felt that the doctor in this context acquired a greater personal 'regard' for the patient—a distinction of status sometimes deliberately contrasted with material advantage:

At the end he said to come back *any* time, and I thanked him very much. He said that to show his regard for me; but of course I wouldn't, I'm not that sort of person, I don't want to receive unfair treatment; I want it to be just the same as other people.

In this context, every act of the doctor which was not purely technical could acquire personal significance: moments of joking, taking the patient's hand, admiring the patient's performance, were all treasured as examples of personal esteem. And this reinforced pride in being a 'good patient'. Then again the claims of medical authority when receiving orders could also be used to back claims to give orders, and in relevant charitable endeavours this enabled snubs to be delivered to others who tried to take the lead. Thus obedience had a positive pay-off in this hierarchical view of the world, since it both expressed the deservedly high status of doctors, and thus, through a privileged personal connection with them, raised one's own. At times this social value became not merely implicit in a consciousness of being distinguished by the doctor, but quite explicit in a thoroughly practical way such as in taking a job:

They didn't ask for my character, but I mentioned that I knew Dr Shirrefs in Mill Loaning—Oh, you know Dr Shirrefs?—And it was quite all right.

Thus in the hierarchical vision of things, a personal connection with doctors—sometimes deriving from a command of the necessary fees—made it possible to exploit, through a strategy of obedience, the reflected glory of the doctor's admired cultural attributes. This was not a common conjunction of ideas, but it accounted for some of the similarly infrequent seriousness given to the working-class rule of obeying doctor's orders.

This compliance of working-class deference contrasted, in turn, with the control sought by middle-class consumerism (5.3)—the second way in which relationships with the doctor were affected by class. If the middle classes expected to choose their doctors, and to debate with them about the diagnosis and treatment, it was because they had command both of necessary material resources and of appropriate social connections. The material resources which helped were again the ability to pay fees for private attention, or, more usually, the ability to follow one's preferences in the housing market—for to get access to the right doctors, it may be necessary, under a state health service, to live in the right place. It is only at the margin, naturally, that such housing choices, and their necessary resources, become explicit. The threat of illness and the alleviatory value of good care have to acquire the same salience as, for example, good schooling at an earlier phase; and this only happens to a few at any one time, some of whom are already, as it happens, in the right place. Thus although in Aberdeen control of housing only occasionally became an explicit resource in getting access to good doctors, it signalled an underlying structural condition which, over many years, would continuously favour middle-class choice. To these material conditions, then, were added the social links of the medical profession with other professions and with middle-class families. Children, brothers, sisters, neighbours, and fellow members of societies who were doctors found themselves applied to for a friendly opinion about the person to see, diagnoses to explore, questions to ask, treatments to suggest, and treatments to avoid:

"I have another friend, quite a good fishing friend I knew at school, and he is a haematologist—not a surgeon, but a consultant. He's retired too . . . . Very ponderous. He says, 'Angus,' he says, 'you know the surgeon's philosophy?'—But I said no. I said no. He said [the speaker here imitates a lugubrious bass)—'The knife. Have nothing to do with it.' I said that's good enough for me. He's a consultant."

In extreme instances, even the dosage might be checked with a medical relative through an international call: one man said that he did not like to take up doctor's time, and 'there are always questions you leave unasked', so to find out the best way of taking the various pills he had been given he rang his doctor daughter at her pharmaceutical laboratory in Switzerland. Thus by checking and cross-checking through social connections, middle-class Aberdonians elicited the divergences of opinion within the medical profession itself; and this both forced on their attention the necessity of choice, suggested to them the desirability of making it according to their own preferences, and gave them a lever which they might at times be able to use to achieve more control. Such cross-checking was not of course confined to the middle class, but in Mannoch the resources were nurses and other patients, and these were not highly rated against the doctors themselves. In the West End, in addition to their social connections with doctors at the highest level, people could turn to knowledge picked up in medical units during the war, or in serving on public bodies connected with the health service, or even, in the last resort, by joining appropriate societies and thus finding out, and reading, the research published on their condition. In this way knowledge became expected for the sake of choice; and it followed from the circumstances which favoured these expectations that, in facing death as in facing illness, it tended to be middle-class Aberdonians who wished to know the truth, or who, if they hesitated about whether they wished it, nevertheless felt that they ought to have it.

Views of the doctor, then, in so far as they divided along class lines, were clearly traceable, in both Mannoch and the West End, to cultural as well as to material aspects of class divisions; and the significance of such cultural aspects was still more evident when we consider, finally, class differences in views of ageing.

Social class and views of ageing

Class differences related mainly to ideas about early old age, and in particular it was nearly always in the middle class, as I mentioned in Chapter 2, that early old age was viewed as a liberation (2.1). It is now possible to be more precise; for in the first place these middle-class Aberdonians referred such views to the institutions of their class—to skills and interests learnt or developed, in ways which I have already illustrated, in their characteristic education or occupations. And in the second place, while they were not of course, as I have indicated, alone in applying at leisure a skill developed at work, they also put their skills to use in feeding their notions of marriage and of friendship in a way which was rare among working-class Aberdonians of their generation. The historical origins of these notions—marriage as being together and doing things together, and friendship as an individualistic relationship involving couples in sharing varied activities including hospitality in the home—are complex, as are the reasons for their association, especially in this generation, with the middle class; but one factor which helped to sustain these Aberdonian marriages and friendships was the sharing of specialized skills which derived in part from their economic background.

To separate what in these skills and values was dependent on this economic background from what was not is a difficult task. Some of its complexities can be illustrated by the example of a couple who show the pattern I have described quite clearly, without at the same time having inherited it.

Paul and Ava Baxter had both been trained as language teachers. They had in fact met at their first school, and as well as speaking, between them, French and Spanish, they had travelled to France and Spain, and had learnt about their art and music. Retirement had freed the Baxters from the routine aspects of teaching, and enabled them to cultivate these acquirements more intensively (2.1):

"And we have other interests. We both like painting; I like collecting records, and he does translations, and—we've no trouble, and we never become bored that we hear so much about. And I like gardening, and we're hoping to get some fruit trees, and we'll both like that."

The extent to which these things were joint interests, and thus underpinned their marriage, is already apparent. But the same activities also formed an important strand in individual friendships, varying according to the friend's speciality. Paul Baxter was currently engaged in writing a historical guide for a friend in a tourist organization who was setting up an exhibition of French impressionists; and for another who was a theatrical producer he had recently completed a translation of a French one-act play. Ava Baxter was thinking about learning the guitar, and had friends who collected recordings of Spanish guitar music to which she had been listening. These specialized skills and interests, therefore, ran in a connecting thread through both their marriage and their acquaintanceships, while at the same time continually differentiating the basis of relationship according to the skill involved.

Now many of the vitalizing interests in this couple's relationships branched from a single parent tree—their training and subsequent careers in teaching. In the husband's career, posts and interests were seen as a sequential line of development:

"Well we were both trained as linguists, you see, and of course with languages you can be interested in all sorts of aspects—the language lab, the literature, the art, the theatre. And then when I taught I was appointed to the school that I first went to in order to build up the language lab. And then I went on to the Academy, and I was appointed to that post for the same reason, but they also wanted me to produce plays, and that involved painting sets and so on. So that I've always found myself developing the oral and dramatic side of it rather than the literary side of it."

In the wife's case the continuity had been of a different kind. The division of household labour and wage-earning between husband and wife, often assumed in this generation, had been preserved; but in the wife's part cleaning and cooking were not the focus of attention, although they were taken for granted:

"I didn't really want to do a full-time thing because we had a son, and I enjoyed using what skills I had in educating him—and still did a little part-time tuition, or temporary work at the school if somebody was off."

It was the application at home of her specialized skills, not of the common or garden domestic skills, which she emphasized; and these skills were more a source of pride than either the earning or the housekeeping role.

In this example, then, joint skills shared in marriage and friendship were the key to liberated old age, and the skills originated substantially in the training and working practices of the teaching profession. Plainly teachers acquire such skills both by their command of information and by designing the tasks which make up school activity; and as I noted at the beginning of this chapter these characteristics have been seen as defining attributes of the whole class which dominates the division of labour. Furthermore this couple actually met in the course of work, and this in itself ensured that they would share joint skills in their marriage. And the teaching profession was also one source of friends.

Thus far, then, their pattern of life was dependent on their position in the division of labour; but more complex factors were at work too. The state education system in which they grew up and worked was not dependent on parental fee-paying and economic capital. And the occupations and background of this couple's parents had not provided them with any educational capital either. To this extent they began from scratch, and although the teacher's income which was their only asset was secure and better than many, it was small enough to compel significant choices. For example they did without a car until their children had grown up in order to enable them to buy a house, and to allow the wife to do only part-time work—standards which were expected of their profession at that time. These choices then themselves had consequences: they had a garden which could become an interest in itself (something virtually unavailable in Aberdeen Council schemes); they made friends with other neighbours who were house owners and in professional or managerial occupations; and the wife's use of her spare time created, as we have seen, an element of educational capital for the next generation, though the result was not entirely the expected one:

"When he went to school, as soon as they found out who he was, they said, 'Now you'll be good at languages.' Which absolutely overpowered the child, you know, put him off completely . . . . But he's good at painting, you see, so—it probably came out that way."

Thus in their start in life, their choice of an occupational training, their financial priorities during adulthood, and the wife's use of her leisure, they had made decisions which did not follow routinely from economic opportunities inherited in childhood, and which drew creatively on the cultural forms available to them.

One sees here, therefore, in the assumptions which underpin one couple's liberated retirement, an aspiring adoption of a cultural paradigm and a corresponding use and development of material advantages in working life. Of course there were other routes to acquiring this style of life than the occupational one illustrated. Merely by owning the house, or a cottage in the country, some couples developed skills of decoration or improvement for the twin purposes of pleasure and investment. And it could be enough, especially for women, to have the appropriate cultural capital. One woman, who had no occupational advantages, looked forward to retirement partly because she came from a well-known family of Aberdeenshire fiddlers, and had an acquaintance in the world of Scottish fiddle music which included members of the local gentry. Thus all these were assets which could be used to develop the skills, and thereby the pattern of marriage or friendship, for a liberated retirement.

However, while a few people aspired to the cultural ideal and partly by these means acquired the assets, there were three larger groups of people who also have to be accounted for. First were the native Aberdonian burgesses who had been at fee-paying schools together, and who inherited skills, marriages, and friendships as one complex. Second were those—no less numerous—who inherited the economic basis for this pattern, but who nevertheless did not adopt the whole view of marriage, friendship, and skills involved, or did not adopt the view of retirement which was related to it. And third was the large working-class constituency which had neither the economic basis nor the cultural inclination for this pattern.

When we compare two of these groups, the native burgesses who had all the cultural accomplishments for a liberated retirement, and the solidly working-class Aberdonians, it seems at first that economic determinism will take us a long way in explaining the difference. I have suggested that the entirely ordinary processes of making friends at work and at home imply that marriages and friendships would often have been made selectively between Aberdonians who had high levels of control over their work and their housing, and who thereby had high levels of related skills. To this may be added the equally ordinary process of making friends at school, where the school was largely funded by fee-paying parents who also had this kind of economic control, and these kinds of skills, and who passed some of these skills on to their children as a form of educational capital. No doubt acquaintanceships formed at school, at work, or at home, or through institutions like the university and the social clubs which depended to some extent on school career, and acquaintanceships formed through these acquaintanceships, would account for a high proportion of Aberdeen marriages and friendships.

But although these processes alone would explain much of the way in which liberating skills became implicated in the marriages and friendships of established middle-class Aberdonians, they do not explain the equally substantial number of their social peers who did not adopt this lifestyle, nor those who had come fresh into the kind of work and housing involved here, and who had, as we have seen, faced harder choices and made more of an entrepreneurial effort in adopting this pattern of life.

To explain these discrepant groups, it is necessary to see the place of marriage, friendship, and skills in different cultural conceptions of society. I have described how one Aberdonian image of society emphasized a hierarchy of distinction, while those images based on the old urban villages and on the farm life of the past emphasized localism and equality. The latter images were invoked in the present context only by people in Mannoch, several of whom, when describing the difficulties facing those newly retired, appealed to the idea of the 'community' and to 'community centres' where people of all ages could meet on a level and engage in different activities together. By contrast, the quotations from West Enders who found retirement a liberation, given in Chapter 2, emphasized personal distinctiveness, from which a selective, individualistic approach to friendship flowed naturally. Thus the idea of distinction, with its accompanying values in regard to skills, marriage, friendship, and retirement, could, as we have seen, be taken up and made effective by an entrepreneurial effort even where economic and cultural circumstances did not at first favour it. And correspondingly, merely inheriting the economic basis for these values could not make retirement a liberation, for this could only be done by the adoption of the values themselves. Those who had a command of information in their job but had developed no skills which transcended their workplace, or who owned a house but had learnt no skills of improvement, and those who had done these things but who did not do things together with friends, or did not construct joint interests in their marriage, made up the substantial number who, though they had the economic basis of middle-class life, saw retirement only as a setback, or, if they saw it ideally as a liberation, could not make the ideal work.

The material advantages were necessary, therefore, to this view of retirement as a liberation; but so too was the detailed adoption of the appropriate cultural conception. With these observations, it is now possible to draw together into one perspective the various ways in which class differences work in the formation of Aberdonian views about all these subjects.

Conclusion

The influence of social class has emerged as being strongest, and at the same time most involved with cultural values, in ideas about retirement and about medical care. In ideas about health (though the emphasis here has been on conceptions of health and ideas of coping more than on ideas of causation and prevention) class differences mainly reflected material constraints, and seemed to have an influence only when, through lack of control over their housing, working-class Aberdonians with few family members left in the city were taken from their accustomed milieu, and thus lost the neighbourhood resources on which they relied for the struggle against illness. Such lack of control is a normal feature for people in the Scottish working class, where council tenancy is the norm, and it only takes these few additional structural conditions—serious illness, a dispersed family, and a forced move in the wrong direction —to impose a crushing constraint on their capacity to cope actively. But because this combination of circumstances was not common in Aberdeen, attitudes to illness were, overall, only weakly related to class.

Above all, therefore, class is constituted, in its influence on the ideas discussed here, by one particular kind of structure in which material and cultural elements are closely wedded. This structure can be described as a web of acquaintances who relate to one another in companionate marriages and individual friendships, sharing in this way varied aspects of their specialized knowledge and accomplishments. They try to pass on the same way of life as a form of cultural capital to their children, and they move into occupations which control information and design work, and into house owner-ship, trading on both financial resources and skills. Their control of these things then feeds back again to augment the knowledge and skills which they exchange in their personal relationships. And by these means members of such circles enlarge their opportunities in retirement, while at the same time drawing on stocks of know-ledgeable opinion about medical care.

These relationships form networks which are partially closed and partially open to people of other classes. The element of closure derives to some extent from exclusive institutions in which acquaintanceships have been formed in the past—fee-paying schools, clubs based on recommendations and high subscriptions, occupations demanding high qualifications. To a greater extent, closure occurs simply because people prefer to form relationships with those who have similar tastes and skills. But there is often no intention to exclude; indeed, many members of these circles emphasize their dislike of social distinctions, and have some close relationships which cross classes.

That such social webs, with their characteristic values, can quickly be characterized by the sobriquet 'middle class' helps to identify them, but does not necessarily add to our understanding of their genesis. For they do not penetrate through all the members of that conventional occupational category, nor yet through all of its members who are in occupations which control information and design work. Nor do they do penetrate through all members of the category of owner-occupiers. They are fluid structures created by the active efforts of people who are following a particular set of cultural conceptions, though these people necessarily require and develop a high level of control over their work and housing in achieving their purposes. Certainly, the absence of that economic basis by the time old age is reached is decisive; for no council tenants in Mannoch saw retirement as a liberation, and even when people living there adopted an image of society as a hierarchy of distinction, it acted not to make them critical about their medical care, but only to suggest a deferential rule of obedience to the doctor which, in a limited way, could be exploited socially. So too, in the absence of economic control, the egalitarian localism that appealed to neighbours and to the 'community' in Mannoch was helpless against both ageing and illness. But as decisive as economic control is the decision not to adopt or enact one of the constituent values of the 'middle-class' cultural conception—the friendships, the type of marriage, or the implicit hierarchy of skills, knowledge, and distinction which underlies them. For the absence of these, even when the economic basis is present, makes ineligible, or ineffective, the particular pattern of understandings which, in Aberdeen, asserts control over old age and medicine.

These 'middle-class' structures are thus defined not merely by their economic position but also by a particular pattern of ideas; and it is worth speculating on the source of this pattern. Companionate marriage is one element whose origin has been located in the eighteenth-century squirearchy and urban boureoisie.[25] Similarly, although historical accounts have not so far given much inkling of how views of retirement as a liberation grew up, it is interesting that this element of the pattern can be found in an early nineteenth-century source, the essay of Charles Lamb on his superannuation.[26] Notwithstanding some ambivalence, Lamb expresses what is in many ways the paradigmatic liberated view; and significantly he sums up this view by describing it as 'Retired Leisure', with fore-shortened allusion to the classical '*otium cum dignitate*', a phrase which had long come to denote the financial security of the leisured class, with inevitable connotations of the competitive intellectual and cultural pursuits which made up that leisure. By linking his pensioned retirement from that classic capitalist enterprise, the East India Company, with the kind of retirement from political or urban life to which the leisured class periodically withdrew, Lamb thus expressed a potent mixture of ideas whose connotations included financial security, companionate marriage, retirement, leisure, and cultural accomplishment; and just as this gentlemanly ideal long survived in education, so it seems to have survived to define for a range of modern middle-class families some of the aspirations with which they seek to shape old age.

Notes and References

1. D. Lockwood, 'Sources of variation in working class images of society', *Sociol. Rev.* 14 (1966), 249–67. However, later studies have been more sceptical about the determination of these images by work and home circumstances. See H. Newby, *The deferential worker: a study of farm workers in East Anglia,* London: Allen Lane, 1977; R. Scase, 'Conceptions of the class structure and political ideology: some observations on attitudes in England and Sweden', in F. Parkin (ed.), *The social analysis of class structure,* London: Tavistock, 1974.
2. M. Douglas and Baron Isherwood, *The world of goods: towards an anthropology of consumption,* London: Allen Lane, 1979; P. Bourdieu, *Distinction: a social critique of the judgement of taste,* tr. R. Nice, London: Routledge, 1984.
3. A. Stewart, K. Prandy, and R. M. Blackburn, *Social stratification and occupations,* London: Macmillan, 1980; F. Parkin, 'Strategies of social closure in class formation', in id. (ed.), *The social analysis of class structure,* London: Tavistock, 1979.
4. S. R. S. Szreter, 'The genesis of the Registrar-General's social classification of occupations', *Brit. J. Sociol.* 35 (1984), 522–46.
5. I. G. Jones and D. Cameron, 'Social class analysis—an embarrassment to epidemiology', *Community Medicine,* 6 (1984), 37–46.
6. D. Silverman, 'Going private: ceremonial forms in a private oncology clinic', *Sociology,* 18 (1984), 191–204.
7. R. M. Titmuss, *Commitment to welfare,* London: Allen and Unwin, 1968, p. 196.
8. Royal College of General Practitioners, Office of Population Censuses and Surveys, and Dept. of Health and Social Security, *Morbidity statistics from general practice 1970–71; socioeconomic analyses,* Studies on Med. and Pop. Subjects no. 46, London: HMSO, 1982.
9. A. Cartwright, *Human relations and hospital care,* London: Routledge, 1964, ch. 15; A. Cartwright and R. Anderson, *General practice revisited,* London: Tavistock, 1981, pp. 175–8; M. Jefferys and H. Sachs, *Rethinking general practice,* London: Tavistock, 1983, pp. 318–21.

10. M. L. M. Gilhooly, J. S. Berkeley, K. McCann, F. Gibling, and K. Murray, 'Truth telling with dying cancer patients', *Palliative Medicine,* 2 (1988), 64–71; B. Earthrowl and M. Stacey, 'Social class and children in hospital', *Soc. Sci. and Med.* 11 (1977), 83–8.

11. A. Cartwright and M. O'Brien, 'Social class variations in health care', in M. Stacey (ed.), *The sociology of the NHS,* Sociol. Rev. Monograph no. 22, 1976.

12. C. Phillipson, *Capitalism and the construction of old age,* London: Macmillan, 1982.

13. J. H. Goldthorpe and C. Payne, 'Trends in intergenerational class mobility in England and Wales 1972–1983', *Sociology,* 20 (1986), 1–24.

14. M. Calnan, *Health and illness,* London: Tavistock, 1987; M. Blaxter, 'Self-definition of health status and consulting rates in primary care', *Quarterly J. Social Affairs,* 1 (1985), 131–71.

15. G. Gordon, *Role theory and illness,* New Haven: College and University Press, 1966.

16. A. d'Houtaud·and M. G. Field, 'The image of health: variations in perceptions by social class in a French population', *Sociol. of Health and Illness,* 6 (1984), 30–60.

17. The suggestion made by M. Blaxter and E. Paterson, *Mothers and daughters: a three-generational study of health attitudes and behaviour,* London: Heinemann, 1982, ch. 4.

18. R. Pill and N. C. H. Stott, 'Choice or chance: further evidence on ideas of illness and responsibility for health', *Soc. Sci. and Med.* 20 (1985), 981–91; eid., 'Concepts of illness causation and responsibility: some preliminary data from a sample of working class mothers', *Soc. Sci. and Med.* 16 (1982), 43–52. Their 1982 results are amended and elaborated in the 1985 paper.

19. I. R. Carter, *Farm life in north-east Scotland 1840–1914,* Edinburgh: Donald, 1979.

20. For example the Scottish Mobility Study quotes percentages of men continuing in the same category as 37% for skilled manual workers and 43% for semi-skilled and unskilled (G. Payne, G. Ford, and C. Robertson, 'Changes in occupational mobility in Scotland: some preliminary findings of the 1975 Scottish Mobility Study', *Scottish J. Sociol.* 1 (1976), p. 65. Note however that there are differences in the age at which father's

class is measured, and in occupational classification, as well as in age range and cohort, between the surveys.

21. M. Stacey, E. Batstone, C. Bell, and A. Murcott, *Power, persistence and change: a second study of Banbury,* London: Routledge, 1975; R. E. Pahl, *Divisions of labour,* Oxford: Blackwell, 1984, ch. 12.

22. See Goldthorpe and Payne, 'Trends in intergenerational class mobility'.

23. For example in the Aberdeen Survey the mixed stratum was 26% of the sample, while in the General Household Survey for 1980, a calculation on Table 3.10 shows this stratum as 41% of the (economically active) sample. British pensioners would fall somewhere in between these figures.

24. See Blaxter, 'Self-definition of health status'.

25. L. Stone, *The family, sex and marriage in England 1500–1800,* London: Weidenfeld and Nicolson, 1977.

26. Charles Lamb, 'The superannuated man', in *Prose works,* vol. 3, London: Edward Moxon, 1836.

9

Religion

(The minister) may, from consideration of the present sickness, instruct him out of scripture, that . . . whether it be laid upon him out of displeasure for sin, for his correction and amendment, or for trial and exercise of his graces, or for other special and excellent ends, all his sufferings shall turn to his profit.

> *The Directory for the Public Worship of God* (established and put in execution by Act of the General Assembly, 1645)

Introduction

Ultimately, illness, ageing, and death present moral questions about the explanation of suffering, the power to cope, the sources of healing, and the meaning of death, to which answers are given by religion. But religion in this broad sense is not necessarily easy to identify, for it covers a number of alternatives which may or may not be religious in a narrower sense. In Europe, in the past, the cultural dominance of the church meant that religious answers were effectively Christian answers, though there were always alternatives in magic or philosophy. But the decline of formal church Christianity in Britain[1] has now underlined the importance of looking both at the church and at its alternatives.

At the extreme, of course, the alternative to church religion is in fact the absence of religion. By this I do not mean something carefully considered—a secularist philosophy—but simply indifference. The resurgence of this attitude reflects a long secularizing process in which, it is said, moral interpretation has been steadily replaced by a technical approach,[2] of which medicine is, with regard to present topics, the most prominent exemplar. Technology seems to have triumphed, not so much because of its philosophical underpinnings, but because it has allowed society to become progressively insulated from insecurity; and thus the churches have been undermined, not by a rationalist or materialist cosmology, but by a loss of interest in all cosmologies.[3]

Indifference, then, is the extreme alternative; but this trend to the 'disenchantment' of the world is not necessarily ineluctable. The trend is variable, and depends on the historical context. Church religion may be reinforced, for example, where one church has held a historical monopoly, or where the threat of external domination has been high. And Scotland is cited as an instance of both conditions.[4]

Again, religion has reappeared in the contemporary Western world in a number of altered forms. Amongst these are the much-debated new religious movements, chiefly relevant to the younger generation, but there are also a number of other, more latent, alternatives, some far from religious in a narrow sense, which are common everywhere. At the beginning of the century Troeltsch argued that mystical individualism constituted a third mode, other than church and sect, for the evolution of Christianity;[5] and more recently others have suggested that 'invisible', 'common', or 'customary' religion persists in many Western ways of thinking. Similarly a religious role, in a broad sense, can be performed by many of the positive aspects of secularist thought. All of these ways of thinking offer universal themes which people can use to give integration and continuity to their world view.[6]

Finally, there is also the brute sense of moral identity which dispenses with all such intellectual constructions, and yet can perform a broadly religious function. It may not always be necessary, in order to live in an advanced capitalist society, to embrace any very developed world view, and some have suggested that the interest of intellectuals in such matters is not matched by that of other members of society.[7] But another way of stating a religious or ethical world view is to state a personal commitment; and any conception of identity, whether formally religious or otherwise, may influence a person's thinking if it is given a similarly axiomatic status.[8] For this reason such self-concepts are compared, in what follows, both with cosmological beliefs, and with ways of speaking and thinking which are truly indifferent—which do not apparently use any fixed moral or metaphysical assumptions about oneself or the world.

Some indications suggest that, in harmony with the secularizing trend previously noted, the more religious of these alternatives—church membership, world views, possibly also the sense of moral identity—may have become increasingly irrelevant to how illness and death are coped with today, and that this is reflected in the way indifference has grown in this context too. Some of the literature on illness, for example, draws an inexplicit parallel between the decline of religion and our growing dependence on medicine. Nineteenth-century medical cosmology turned away from the person as a microcosm uniting physical and spiritual natures, to focus on the body as an object containing diseases and cellular processes.[9] Correspondingly the modern medical profession partly destroyed the functions of the minister, the healer, and the diviner, and partly converted them into the mysterious and embarrassing placebo effect.[10] At the same time, as a result of this ever-increasing dependence on medicine, so it is said, industrial populations gradually lost not only these curing powers, but also the cultural and religious resources to cope with the incurable.[11] Similarly, on the subject of coping with death, many detect a process in which the technical aspirations of hospital medicine have entirely ousted the moral aspirations of religion—in which the sick die 'covered with tubes' rather than alert and prepared, and the bereaved remain as an embarrassment to a society otherwise assured of its invincibility.[12]

On the other hand, there are also opposing developments in the way illness and death are now understood, which suggest that the relevance of religion to these topics may be substantial and increasing. Theories which presuppose a psychosomatic equilibrium have reappeared.[13] Forms of Pentecostal healing have been reintroduced; and religious commitment has re-emerged as a possible factor in adopting a healthy lifestyle,[14] and in maintaining higher levels of physical and mental health.[15] Similarly, while chronic illness is often experienced as a profound loss of self,[16] tantalizing indications have also emerged of the way in which people who experience these biographical disruptions look for explanations of suffering,[17] and construe their situation as a personal destiny with reference to teleological ideas.[18] And in confronting death, a new medical discourse is replacing the old, eliciting the feelings of those concerned, and seeking to guide them to an acceptance of their situation.[19]

Whether religion is now irrelevant to coping, as suggested by the former argument, or on the contrary especially relevant to coping, as in the latter argument, is the first question that can be addressed in the Aberdonian material which follows. A second question, though, relates to an interesting hypothesis which may help to suggest how both arguments could be true. This hypothesis holds that while the secularizing process is undeniably at work, there are inherent limits to it; and these limits exist precisely in experiences of death and suffering such as those that form the subject of this book, which no technical order can, beyond a certain point, eliminate.[20] Beyond these technical frontiers, where we are no longer insulated from the world around us, religious issues have once again to be confronted. In this chapter, I consider whether, and in what way, these issues are confronted when Aberdonians experience suffering.

This second question leads in turn to a third, the final question which this chapter will address: if religion is indeed relevant to suffering, what is it that it offers people in this situation, and how does contemporary Scottish religion compare in what it offers with the wider tradition from which it comes?

Of the emphases which have characterized historical Scottish Calvinism, one of the most important here is its activism in trying to overcome evil. This emphasis has of course been tied up with Calvinist views on predestination and lay asceticism; and it has also been related to the methodical form taken by Calvinist concern for those in need,[21] and to the work ethic. The last theme has already featured strongly in Aberdonian efforts to control illness.

Still more relevant, however, is the Calvinist interpretation of suffering. Among relevant themes in the wider Christian tradition, three in particular may be compared. The first is the interpretation of suffering as the consequence of sin. In understanding this idea, there is an important distinction to be made between the conception that the general sin of humanity is a cause of general suffering, which is ubiquitous in the tradition, and the notion that particular sins of individuals are punished by particular sufferings—a theme especially evident in the 'particular providences' of the seventeenth century. Also critical, though, is the extent to which suffering is regarded as exclusively the result of sin. This is a position to which seventeenth-century Calvinists often seem to have come very close.[22]

There are, however, at least two themes which have been as important, or more important, in the tradition generally. One is the notion of suffering as a trial, one which permits sufferers, or others close to them, to learn lessons of faith or grace.[23] And the other is a complex of ideas which can loosely be encapsulated in the idea of suffering as a sacrifice or offering.

Probably the most fundamental theme in these ideas of sacrifice, which appears in the piety of both the Eastern and the Western churches, is the notion that the members of the church who suffer re-enact and in some sense 'complete' the suffering of Christ.[24] This idea has been as relevant to illness and other misfortunes as to persecution, and this is strikingly illustrated in the medieval phrase 'Our Lords the sick'.[25] It is a theme which acquired a number of elaborations in Western Catholicism; and in particular it became connected with the concept of merit. For Thomas More, suffering, whether deserved or undeserved, was made fruitful by patience, for patience lays up merit, and 'we in this world sow that we may in the other world reap'.[26] So too a Frenchwoman in 1972 could imagine her mother saying of her handicaps, 'This is something where there are merits that you can acquire for yourself or for others.'[27]

These three interpretations of suffering, therefore, as punishment, as trial, and as sacrifice, may give very different meanings to both illness and death. The question of how they are used in Scottish religion, together with the question of how far that religion is relevant to coping today, and the question whether the experience of suffering raises inherently religious issues and marks the final limit of the secularizing tendency, are the ultimate topics of this chapter. With this background in mind, I now consider the part played by religion in Aberdeen.

Church membership in Aberdeen

The Aberdeen Survey shows the denominational allegiances of Aberdonians in this age group and the frequency of members' attendance at church (Table 10). When these figures are broken down by social class, familiar tendencies emerge emphasizing the prominence of the middle class among churchgoers and church members (Table 11). Class divisions, then, are a factor in Aberdonian church membership and attendance, but careful examination of the evidence reveals that they were far less significant in the religious ideas discussed in the remainder of this chapter, and so for reasons of space I do not refer to them again.

Table 10. *Aberdeen survey of the elderly, 1980: church member-ship and attendance (weighted to estimate population)*

Denomination	Membership (%)	Attendance (%)		
		Weekly or more	Monthly or more [a]	Within the year [b]
Church of Scotland	56.3	10.2	18.9	36.3
Episcopalian	4.1	0.7	1.6	2.3
Roman Catholic	3.3	1.1	1.1	2.1
Other sects and denominations	7.2	3.1	3.6	4.4
TOTAL AFFILIATED	70.9	15.1	25.2	45.1
Non-members	29.1	0.2	0.2	0.5
TOTAL	100	15.3	25.4	45.6

[a] Includes weekly or more.
[b] Any frequency of attendance within the year.

Table 11. *Aberdeen survey of the elderly, 1980: church member-ship and attendance by social class*

Church membership and attendance	Social class (%)		
	I – III non-manual	III manual	IV – V
Church members Attending monthly or more	39	20	15
Attending less than monthly	41	48	46
Non-members	20	32	39
TOTALS %	100	100	100
No.	196	244	162

Note: P < .0001.

Other comparisons emphasize the generational and ethnic aspects of Aberdonian church loyalties. Compared with other parts of Britain, as I noted earlier, and with other age groups, this was a local generation still quite strongly church-oriented;[28] and it was also one in which a single locally established church, the Presbyterian Church of Scotland, was heavily dominant.

The qualitative study showed a similar overall level of membership and practice, and it helped in addition to reveal the way in which different kinds of commitment to membership of the church were conceived. Despite the democratic forms of Presbyterianism, membership was usually a hierarchical relationship of exchange with the minister. The ideal of the Church of Scotland, that the local congregation should support its own church and minister, was evident here. In this ideal relationship, as older Aberdonians saw it, the chief returns made by the minister were to call on the sick and the bereaved. And the strength of this contract was underlined, too, by the reluctance of people who had moved to break their connection with churches which, in some cases, required a longer journey than any otherwise undertaken during the week; and by the fact that the change of connection, when it occurred, was accomplished by obtaining 'lines' from the old to the new minister, just as a general practitioner gave people 'lines' in referring them to hospital.

Apart from this dominant conception of the church as a contract between membership and minister, there was also both a much stronger and a much weaker form of commitment to membership. In the stronger form—expressed by only a few people—membership was both an intense involvement and much more of an equal brotherhood, being related not merely to the minister but to 'the community', a conception in which the lay members of a local church contributed to a wide range of overlapping activities, including communal meals, musical dramas on sacred themes, fund-raising schemes, and informal help. The weaker form of church commitment, on the other hand—also that of a minority—was one which is aptly described as mystical individualism. Here church services were seen as 'trappings' essentially superfluous to the individual's relationship with God. In such cases it was axiomatic that 'you can get through to God without going to church', and characteristically, the setting in which this communion was most possible was when alone in the hills or by the sea.

It was, interestingly, those who showed either the strongest or the weakest church commitment in these terms who most readily referred to some sort of world view; and I now turn to consider ideas which fell into this category.

World views

There is a sense in which everyone has a world view, but in what follows I use the term to denote only those ethical or metaphysical aspects of such a view that are universalized and treated as valid in all circumstances, forming an overarching structure, or 'symbolic universe'[29] A world view in this latter sense is something which individuals may or may not build in to their own thinking. In the present case, a little over half of these Aberdonians referred in the present context to such universal themes, irrespective of whether they were church attenders or not.

For the most part, it was to their Protestant inheritance that Aberdonians turned in selecting their themes; and foremost amongst these topics, attracting references from a third of the people I met, was the meaning given to suffering by faith.

I referred earlier to the Old Testament explanations of suffering adopted by Scottish Calvinists in the seventeenth century, in which misfortune is the consequence—almost exclusively the consequence—of sin. It follows that misfortune is something which the virtuous can almost always expect to avoid. This syllogism still haunted some of the Aberdonians I met. The suffering of Christ was not seen as a relevant consideration, and though it was once referred to, in a quotation already given in Chapter 3, the intention was only to assume its irrelevance: there was no point in being 'Jesus Christ all over again'. Thus the suffering of the good was not merely emotionally difficult—it was also doctrinally absurd, and only two resolutions were offered. One resolution was to doubt either the absolute power or the absolute goodness of God:

When you look at this world, it must have been made by someone—I don't know, God, Christ, say the Creator . . . . the only thing is, whoever had the makkin' o' this world, he could have mak it better.

The other resolution was that of the authentic Puritan, which was rather to doubt, in misfortune, the sufficiency of the antecedent virtue, a doctrine stated in another case in something approaching its former majesty. Here the starting point was illness:

"Some of them say, I don't know why God allows this, that and the other thing. I says, it's nae God that allows it, it's people that does it. It's nae God's blame. I say, I widna blame God for anything like 'at [illness]. I says, when good things come, do you thank him?"

Then, without a break, the theme of human ingratitude was extrapolated to the winter of discontent in 1979:

"You canna blame God for everything. The country's in an awfa' state. We canna blame God for that, it's man's own stupidity: Give me, give me, give me—I'm needin', needin', needin'. Ach!"

"Yes—it's come to a fine pass now, hasn't it?"

"Well, I dinna ken, if they *did* work eight hours a day . . . ."

Then after a good deal more along the same lines:

"Now they're wantin' to work thirty-five hours a week. God help them, that's what I say."

In this view, then, neither illness nor social disorder was to be laid at God's door. The causes lay rather in laziness and overindulgence— the great Puritan vices—and in failing to notice the good things already received.

However, given these alternatives of imputing sin or doubting God that bedevilled this interpretation of suffering, it is understandable that most religious Aberdonians turned to other interpretations which treated suffering rather as an occasion for learning lessons of faith. They sought, not to explain the cause, but to give meaning to the process of suffering. The faith they learnt was that suffering would pass, that whatever the cause it was a period of trial, and that in the mean time the 'good things' of the previous quotation—divine provisions, consolations, and answers to prayer—could be seen by the noticing eye to be occurring in the course of it, so that further explanation was not absolutely required. This was the view which permitted the recognition of 'miracles' in response to prayer, and of something 'fated' or 'meant' in the unexpected resolution of practical difficulties. It was not a matter of reading or planning the future; rather, it was by this kind of faith that anxiety about the future was laid aside, because in a world where the flow of divine gifts was carefully noted, it could be held that 'one day at a time' was 'all we're meant to live.'

Faith in these instances thus took its meaning from the sense of providential help in active struggle; and there was little emphasis on the sense of sin and punishment which played so important a historical part in Calvinism, and which defined faith primarily as a countervailing sense of the grace and forgiveness of God. In contemporary Aberdeen this theme of forgiveness was not entirely eliminated, for it remained in several accounts as a consummation to be desired in ths life; but a less than constant sense of it was not felt to be damning in the next.

The idea of faith, therefore, was a frequent resource. However, ethical axioms were referred to with similar frequency, and they constitute the second major aspect of Aberdonian world views in the present context. These ethical principles had a complex basis both in religious values and, at times, in themes from socialist, communist, Unitarian, or even sociobiological thought which were sometimes opposed to Protestant religion, and sometimes felt to expand on its essential truths. The prescriptions most often felt to be relevant to present issues were the traditional ones of self-discipline and helping those in need; but the work ethic also received a few mentions which set it a similar background of wider beliefs. Self-discipline or 'moderation' was defined as care with diet or was illustrated by several lists of prohibitions which still bore the stamp of working-class movements for temperance and self-improvement which originated in the nineteenth century. The occasion for such lists could as well be medical as moral:

"He examined my chest again and said, 'You don't smoke?' I said, 'Dr Drummond, I neither drink nor smoke, and for good measure I dinna tak up wi' men'. Well he laughed and laughed.

These negative, ascetic rules were one side of the coin. The other was the positive requirement of care for others, active involvement with them, concern for their dignity, reverence for life. This too was often a rule, a set practice relating especially to neighbours, friends, the old, the ill:

"I mean, you have to work at friendships, and give as much as you get, and you usually get. I've had so much from friendships."

It was a short step, therefore, from individuals 'working at' giving to others in this way, to ideals of social organization in which need was systematically met; and within this matrix of ideas the work ethic proper entered harmoniously, adding its connotations of daily duty, vocational skills, and strict exchange. But the work ethic was merely one possibility compatible with the central moral conception, and despite its historic affinities with the Calvinist state of grace, and the implied use of this affinity by the person quoted earlier who attributed suffering to laziness, the connections made between these ideas were, in fact, surprisingly few.

In general, therefore, the world view drawn on by Aberdonians in making sense of illness, ageing, and death was that of a much modified Calvinism—shorn of predestined wrath, and somewhat detached from its work ethic. But the Calvinist inheritance was still recognizable in Aberdonian explanations of suffering, their activist faith, and their emphasis on self-discipline and meeting need. However, not everybody expressed a world view in the sense I have defined here, and many of those who did not were not church members either. To understand the morality of these pragmatists one must consider their images of themselves.

Self-conceptions

Autobiographical accounts are naturally peppered with self-characterizations, but a few of these are, from time to time, marked out by various verbal formulae as essential properties of the person the speaker is, or would like to be. Not everyone uses such formulae, but in discussing present topics the majority did so.

The first and commonest sort of formula drew on the theme of a constant self. Most commonly, they were direct claims about what 'I have always been' or 'I have never been'; but these permanent qualities were also frequently introduced by phrases referring to the 'kind of person I am', to 'my nature', and their numerous equivalents, or by more complicated phrases referring to qualities which were 'part of me', 'my own', or which 'I am in myself' and so on.

Less frequent than references to this apparently objective self, but still frequent, was an acknowledgement by the speaker of qualities which had been characterized, or indeed created, by other people. The family of origin was naturally the main source of such assumed influences, with present qualities being seen as implanted by an often unspecific mixture of heredity and upbringing. But simple recognition of such qualities by others—by a husband, a neighbour, an employer, a doctor—could also reinforce them. Such formulae, then, reflected aspects of the self which were felt to be socially moulded.

Finally, the third, least common, way in which essential properties of the person were introduced was by the sort of formula which is used for an act of profession. The commonest such formula was credal, indicating an acceptance—or a rejection—of the Christian way.

Self-professions chiefly occurred, then, as a way of stating a religious world view; but among those who expressed no world view at all the key formulae were those implying a constant or socially moulded self. In the rest of this chapter, therefore, I refer to both these latter ways of speaking under a single heading. Not surprisingly, the qualities identified with these latter self-images were those on which public opinion insisted most strongly: hard work, activity, determination, and the health which flowed from these. Such self-conceptions supplied an axiomatic framework for dealing with health-related topics which either supplemented world views, or, in their absence, and in the absence of church membership, could stand alone.

The relevance of religious assumptions

I have argued that church membership, world views, and self-images all play a religious or quasi-religious role in Aberdeen, and in fact few of the Aberdonians I spoke to (less than a fifth) considered present topics without referring to one or more of these sets of assumptions. Particularly important in what follows are the differences between those who expressed a world view (a little over half) and those who referred only to their church membership, or to their self-image (a little over a quarter). Also important, though, are the differences between world views based on faith and those that were purely ethical or rationalist—both perspectives being represented with fairly similar frequency. The way in which these religious resources were related to coping can now be seen in more detail.

Religion and ideas about health and ageing

Illness and ageing are conveniently taken together, because religious references to ageing mostly concerned late old age with its implications of chronic ill health. These were subjects in which the majority of those I spoke to drew sooner or later on some kind of quasi-religious assumption.

As long as there was hope of resisting old age (2.4) and of controlling or fighting illness (1.1, 1.2), all these religious assumptions implied the possibility of moral control though the range of such implications grew progressively wider as first ethical and then theological assumptions were drawn in. The weakest assumptions were those of people who expressed no world view, but referred only to their membership of a church, or to their image of themselves as healthy, active, determined, or hard-working. The church in such cases was merely one among many voluntary associations whose demands kept people active and therefore healthy; and this activism was seen simply as a habitual, socially moulded capacity for control of health. Purely ethical world views added to this an implication of personal moral commitment. Here control of health was not just by habitual powers of character, but by personal rules of good living: not drinking, not smoking, being actively involved in helping people. And finally, when faith was invoked in addition, habitual powers and personal commitments were supplemented by the power of prayer, which had on occasions achieved a 'miracle' where these other resources had failed. Margaret McKinlay, for example, prided herself on 'never letting things get her down', and never touched drink or cigarettes; but she was defeated, and so was the hospital, by a 'turn' which immobilized her for six weeks. Then something extraordinary happened:

"I couldna move. I was jist sittin' here. And I had friends in the afternoon, and they made a cup of tea—I could hardly make a cup of tea to myself. And eh, a halo came over me. And I thanked God where I was sittin'. And I jist got up and made a cup of tea to myself . . . . I went and told my two neighbours, and they jist looked in amazement: 'She's a miracle, so she is.' I said, your prayers and mine—my friends have had their prayers answered. God has something for me to do. I don't know what it is, but I'll do it."

Such experiences were celebrated as a proof that prayer was a vital extra weapon in the moral armoury which defeated illness. Thus the widest range of possibilities for overcoming illness was defined by notions of faith, and a progressively narrower range was defined by purely ethical views and by church membership or self-images on their own; but they all agreed on the basic premiss, that illness was to some extent subject to moral control.

However, when moral control failed, and the possibility of irreducible dependency emerged, so differences in kind were revealed between these religious and quasi-religious assumptions. The first difference lay in whether illness was simply a negative or dependent state—a loss to be endured (1.4), or at best a release from burdensome tasks (1.5)—or whether it was possible to develop an alternative way of life with new interests and activities, accompanied if necessary by a shift in values which permitted the new interests to be seen, amid the hardships otherwise accepted, as a positive gain (1.3). And if the latter course was chosen, a further difference emerged between those who felt this alternative way of life to be in contradiction with the Aberdonian ethic of work and activity, and those who found ways of reconciling the contradiction. The religious assumptions which lay behind these differences in attitudes to serious illness were fairly evenly divided into three groups.

First, serious disabling illness was solely a negative or dependent state (1.4, 1.5) for nearly all those (marginally the largest group) who spoke of themselves only as church members, or as having the personal qualities which were generally commended. These were people who had not worked out (or did not express) an organized world view. Those of them who were church members made no reference to their membership in making sense of serious illness. Rather, as in all cases where no world view was elaborated, it was their self-image as a person deserving social approval which dominated their discussion of illness, and serious illness typically undermined and negated such self-images:

I've hardly been out at all this winter—lackadaisical, just not the person I was.

There were only two people who appeared to be exceptions, who in some ways reinforced the point. Both attempted spontaneously to develop positive alternative interests, without any particular rationale for so doing, but the conventional church membership of the one, and the conventional self-image of the other, either did not help, or else actively counteracted, this adjustment. In these respects, people with these conventional moral allegiances were if anything possibly worse off even than those who were wholly indifferent to religion or to moral identity.

Secondly, serious disabling illness was also a solely negative or dependent state to those who expressed world views of a rationalist type, or who invoked only the social ethic of Christianity. Ethical and rationalist world views were, like contractual church membership on its own, at best only marginally relevant to serious illness; and again, in the absence of any such relevance, the destruction of the sick person's self-image emerged as the central issue. Once more there were exceptions which in some ways proved the rule. In three instances attempts were made to see serious illness positively as an alternative way of life; but, as before, these attempts were made in spite of, and in tension with, an otherwise activist self-conception, and they apparently derived no support from the world view expressed.

Finally, by contrast, such illness was rarely a solely negative or dependent state for those whose world view emphasized notions of faith (marginally the smallest group). Those who centred their world view on ideas of faith, or their self-conception on an act of religious profession, and who related these notions to the experience of serious illness, were able to derive from their beliefs a continuing sense of their own value:

"I've come through a lot, but God always comes with me and guides me, and I've kind friends helping me . . . . The caretaker says, 'I wish I had your faith,' and I says, 'If you ask God he'll help you.'"

Similarly their faith gave them a conviction that, however abnormal their life was, however far outside the compelling respectability of conventional standards, a positive alternative way of life with its own activities, interests, and society was available to them (1.3). And through the same beliefs, they were also often able to treat this alternative way as an expression of the same ultimate principles which gave meaning to conventional living, so that the opposition between normal and abnormal behaviour, which others found so constraining, was resolved. Again there were exceptions, but again the limits of these exceptions were revealing. For one person faith was merely a speculative possibility; and two others who were firm believers had not thought about serious disabling illness. Thus it was in confronting disabling illness, and with a convinced belief, that the link was made. However, the further qualification must also be added that not everyone who made the link, arguing from notions of faith to the possibility of an alternative way of life, succeeded in reconcilling themselves to the abnormality of their position. This reconciliation was evidently the last and hardest task of interpretation—or perhaps of persuasion—for understandings of normality, or of worth, have to be negotiated with others, as well as achieved within oneself.

This necessarily simplified summary reveals, then, that purely ethical or rationalist world views on the one hand, and purely conventional church memberhip on the other, were not easily related to the experience of serious, disabling chronic illness. And in the absence of any other counsel, Aberdonians could only interpret their illness in terms of their approved active image of themselves—an image which serious illness tended to destroy. Examples of this negative view of illness, and its relation to active self-images, have been given earlier in Chapter 1 and Chapter 6.

Faith, on the other hand, did relate to serious illness, and to the ability to react positively and create an alternative way of life. True, a few struggled towards this outcome without faith, but they seemed to be acting instinctively and had no alternative world view which helped in this situation. An example was Christine Taylor, whose situation I described in Chapter 1; but I also showed there the tension which she felt from the pressure of the conventional activist view (1.1). Thus it remains in this section to analyse in further case studies how it is that faith can generate this alternative way of life, and how such notions succeed, when they do, in resolving the tension between the alternative and the conventional view.

The following two case studies represent extremes in the range of religious conceptions, and in the range of institutional supports, which are relevant here.

The first of these exemplifies the communal, highly committed form of church membership. Betty Thomson had, a few years earlier, had a serious car accident which left her paralysed from the waist down. She gave up her work, and remained confined to her chair; and she would also have been confined to her flat, but for her helpers from the church who carried her out to the street and drove her to meetings.

Since this accident, the church had involved her in a number of previously unaccustomed activities such as singing to the guitar, acting in plays, and helping in the Women's Guild. In this setting, the facts of her handicap were not overlooked. Typical of this aspect of her role was her part in a mime presented at a local school, in which she played the stranger who, in the parable, is taken in and given help. But in addition to having her handicaps clearly recognized, she also acquired a reputation for heroic effort. Forever practising new methods of extending her capacities, she continuously used the watchwords of expectant struggle: 'Always

look forward', 'You canna lie down to it', 'Everything's an achievement, and you want to speak about it'. Warm approval greeted
these well-loved themes, and Miss Thomson became in this way a
major asset of the church, exemplifying not only, as in the school
mime, the answer to the parable's question 'Lord, when did we see
you a stranger and took you in?', but also the life of active faith.

The church, therefore, could be an alternative way of life in
which, at the same time, Betty Thomson's incapacities were
acknowledged (1.3). But it was also a setting which validated her
as a normal person; and this was possible for two complementary
reasons. First, the church, in its attempt to act out the Christian
society, had a place for Miss Thomson in both her roles, both as
the stranger who must be helped and as the person of active faith.
In this respect the church was a setting somewhat similar to the
rehabilitation ward in which Miss Thomson had also shone. But
second (and here the church and the rehabilitation ward differed
crucially), the church was not itself an abnormal or segregated
society of disabled people, but rather was seen by Miss Thomson
and the most devoted of her fellow parishioners as synonymous
with 'the area' and 'the community'—an assembly representative
of local people. Because of this she was determined, against offers
of ground floor accommodation elsewhere which would resolve
many of her needs for help, to remain in the area, saying that the
people here had been very good to her, and she could not do
without them. Thus the church for her was the community, and
this resolved the potential contradiction between struggling to be
normal and accepting her incapacity and need for help.

The foundation for this positive way of coping was in this case
church membership, though church membership of an exceptionally
committed kind. This personal commitment was apparently the
outcome of a radical reconstitution of Betty Thomson's world view
after the accident. She had not belonged to any church before the
accident, and a church member who had spent a good deal of time
with her commented that as a result of it she had experienced 'a real
spiritual awakening'. She was thus a late convert, and it was this
commitment which restored her sense of worth and provided her with
a new society which was for her the local community in its essence.

The second example is at the opposite extreme in the sense that it
represents the kind of mystical individualism which had little to
do with church membership, though it had much to do with an

organized network of support from like-minded devotees. Kenneth Napier was still technically a member of a church on the other side of the city, but had not attended there for years. He occasionaly attended a local church (though not at the communions, for which membership was necessary); but his main religious activity had become the practice of Christian meditation, following a meeting with the teacher of a correspondence course.

Kenneth Napier's main illness was a long-standing paraplegia which held almost no hope—in his doctor's opinion no hope at all—of improvement; and this was associated with other circulatory problems which had required a number of medical interventions. He had had to stop work twenty years previously, while still in middle life, and had considerable and obvious difficulty in managing buses, crossing streets, shopping, and so on, although he was able to live on his own with the services of a home help. In place of his former occupation, however, he had invented an alternative occupation of his own (1.3)—voluntary work, invclving fund-raising for technical aids to help fellow-sufferers extend their activity. There was, he felt, something active and positive in this, which contrasted with the segregated social groups in which other unfortunates passed the time:

"It's the Technical Aids Association, but we have a local branch in Aberdeen. So I work; I work on my own, but I still work through them too . . . ."

"And are there clubs, organizations, or group meetings of any other kind that you're involved in?"

"No, not really. I could go to the Friendship Club, but I'm not interested really . . . I'm really not interested in that kind of affairs at all."

"Yes. Yes, some people like all this socializing in a group, and mostly—?"

"Well, this is it, you see: I don't see anything in it, for me. I'd rather do something I can see an end product to—this is it."

In this way, too, although his abnormal handicaps were immediately visible to anyone, he continued to feel that he had some-thing to give. This conviction emerged, for example, in a passing comment:

"Once a fortnight I go into town to a deaf friend to spend an evening there. You know, that is a heavy evening because he's deaf and you've got to sit and speak on the fingers to him. But it's a worthwhile evening, because, eh, you're giving joy to him, kind o' style."

This extending of other people's possibilities, so giving them 'joy', was thus the thing that was worth while, the 'end product' of his skill in technical aids. And similarly he admired the capacity to lift others out of depression, as possessed by an old friend of his family, who remained a model for him. This capacity he traced to her serenity:

"She was a darling—and you never saw her ruffled. Never saw her ruffled . . . . She was a darling—everybody used to say that about her, if you ever feel depressed, go up and see Granny Lumsden . . . . She coped very well, you know, with her [condition]."

His aims, then, were in terms of coping and being unruffled, so banishing others' depression, or of using special skills, and training them in others, so doing something worth-while, with the end product of giving joy; but he worked towards these aims through his practice of meditation. He linked meditation with two intermediary states. The first was a sense of trust in God; and the second was the ability, which he saw as flowing from this trust, to surmount his illness:

"I just sit now and again. I have a few sentences that, if I'm in doubt of anything-now I mean, one of my sentences which I often use: 'O taste and see that the Lord is good: blessed is the man that trusts in him,'—now that just calms me immediately. If I went forward for an operation or anything like that, that's the prayer I would use. And that would calm me immediately."

Thus Kenneth Napier's faith took the form of a meditation by which he achieved trust in God; by this trust he achieved a calm unruffled state; by this calm he was able to cope with his illness; and by coping in this way he could, by using his skills or just by being himself, give others joy or banish their depression. This matrix of ideas defined the end product of the work which he had found as an alternative to the loss of his occupation; and thus the positive content of his alternative way of life, and his sense that he had something to give, were bound up in numerous ways with his concept of faith.

Other people who achieved this Christian version of the resolution between activism and an alternative way of life mixed elements from both these examples. They were generally more articulate about theological aspects of their faith than Betty Thomson, and more involved in church or sect than Kenneth Napier. They stressed the ideas which were described earlier, of trust, of living for the day, of prayer, and of counting and looking

out for blessings and 'miracles'; and they also took part in congrega-
tional meetings, services, and communions. But none of these
things was absolutely necessary, and it was also possible, though
rare, to make use of similar themes without any church affiliation
or religious network, and indeed without any creed other than a
very general and entirely individualistic mysticism.

How far were these religious responses new, evoked by the
challenge of the illness itself? Some indications can be gleaned
from the accounts I was given, although they were necessarily
retrospective. It was clear that a few people, like Betty Thomson,
had indeed acquired a new faith in the course of their experience,
though many others in similar situations had not, but had held to
ethical views or self-images of a more conventional kind. Why
some shifted towards faith and some did not is not certain from the
material I was given. There was no sign amongst those who did not
shift in this way that faith had actually been lost in the course of
illness, as there was with some of those who had experienced a
premature bereavement; and it seemed merely that antecedent
assumptions had carried over into the illness, and had not been
discarded even when their implications in this situation were
entirely negative. An example of this process has been given in the
case of Hugh Kidd in Chapter 6. Perhaps part of the difference lay,
as some of the converts' comments suggested, in the people who
had influenced them after their illness; but the present material
does not allow us to test this possibility adequately.

These, then, were the ways in which religious assumptions
related to illness. It now remains to see how they were involved in
attitudes to death.

Religion and ideas about death

In coping with death, the religious assumptions drawn on again fell
into three groups. First, as before, was the large group of people
who expressed no world view, and who referred at most to church
membership or to a conventional self-image. With exceptions
which are noted later, these were assumptions which tended
to leave a vacuum on the subject of death, and which led to
attempts to disregard it, relying on the hope of a speedy death, in
ignorance, and after a natural term, with deviations from this

norm consigned to the medical profession as arbiters of life and death.

The remaining religious—or quasi-religious—assumptions relevant to death, on which the rest of this section is focused, comprised world views of varying provenance. These were expressed by a large (and diverse) group with Christian views, and by a small group with secularist views.

Among those expressing Christian views, more than half referred to theological ideas which encompassed elements of what I called 'ritual dying' and of the old pattern of mourning. These were ideas which endorsed the sanctity of life and the prohibition against taking life (3.8), the need to be spiritually prepared for the destined time of death (3.2), and the appropriateness of knowing that the time was approaching (3.5). And they also supported the notion of the dead being with kin in a better place (4.1), the emphasis on remembering the dead (4.5), and—though with qualifications given below—the sanctity of the body or the grave (4.3).

Where these conservative ideas rested on a broader religious world view, the key assumption in that world view was a traditional, transcendent faith—faith in a God beyond this world who was both provident and forgiving. The idea of providence was relevant because the age when death occurred (3.2), the process of dying (3.8), and what lay beyond death (4.1) were all subject to the overruling, benevolent, and foreknowing power of God; and the idea of forgiveness was relevant because awareness of approaching death (3.5), and preparation for it (3.2) were part of a reconciliation with God, or with other people, which ought to occur before death as it ought to occur, for the properly prepared, throughout life. Similarly, that family members who had died had been properly prepared for their death, by faith or honest life, and were now awaiting reunion in a better place with those still living, were themes essential to the way in which believers kept their memory (4.5). Thus all these themes were linked to faith in the providence and forgiveness of a transcendent God. Only one conservative idea remained whose governing principle was, to Aberdonians, deeply obscure, and thus to some extent optional: the sanctity of the body. Those who felt the body to be sacred could only define this attitude as somehow religious, and I indicated in Chapter 4 the way in which it represents a materialized recasting of an original spiritual symbolism which disappeard in Calvinist areas after the Reformation.

The vulnerability of these 'religious' attitudes to the body, which rested only on inertia, and the coherence of the more interconnected conceptions, which rested on ideas of providence and reconciliation, can be illustrated in the comments of Isobel Morrison. The need to be aware of approaching death (3.5), so as to be prepared (3.2), emerged following a question about what doctors should tell the dying:

"Well, my mother, she knew."

"Your mother knew?"

"Oh aye. My dad knew 'n' all that he was goin'—in the end, he went real quick—he knew he was goin'."

"Yes. And would you want to know the same?"

"Oh yes."

"You would?"

"Oh aye."

"It wouldn't trouble you?"

"No, it wouldn't trouble me at all. I'd be ready to go and that's the main thing."

This readiness, in turn, was achieved, in her accounts of other deaths, by reconciliation with God. Typical was a Dickensian scene from her stay in one of the isolation wards in the typhoid epidemic some years previously. A girl lying *in extremis* asked her neighbour, a well-known Salvation Army Officer, to sing 'The Old Rugged Cross'. The officer, also very weak, could manage only the first verse, after which a nurse stopped her and finished the remaining verses herself. Tears poured down the girl's cheeks and she died shortly afterwards. The reconciliatory moral and providential timing dramatized in these Evangelical colours needed no underlining; but providential timing was in any case explicitly stated in the conclusion to another of her narratives:

"If it's God's will she has to go, well she'll go whenever she's ready."

Finally this emphasis on the time of death being subject to God's will also forbade intervention to hasten its coming (3.8).

There's always—life . . . . They're not meant to take life, you see.

At the same time Isobel Morrison had personal knowledge of many of the troublesome situations where others turned to the thought of euthanasia:

Of course, you can have the body there, and the life there, but so little of it . . . If they're suffering, sometimes you wish the Lord would take them.

Then, after a pause, a firm rejection of complaint:

But there's a lot of suffering in the world.

These various attitudes to death, therefore, hung together within a single theological perspective; and they were connected in their turn with rememberance of the dead and with hopes of reunion after death. Father was ready because he had known not just that he was going, but that he was going to join mother; and though the new life where this happened was 'difficult to think of', Mrs Morrison firmly believed that she would join them too (4.1). They had died long before, and she did not say explicitly that she missed them (4.5), but she reminisced long and affectionately about their idiosyncrasies, interweaving assurances of their present grace, such as their hymn singing on Sunday nights.

It was only, in fact, when it came to attitudes to the body that Mrs Morrison switched to a different starting point. As a good theologian, she discarded those traditional ideas of the body's sanctity which had no theological basis in Evangelicalism; and she left her body to medical research, on the simple argument that, as doctors had helped her, so she had decided to help them—an argument consistent with the ethical aspect of her belief.

This conservative pattern was the main Christian view; and the remaining Christian alternatives were fairly evenly divided between two variants. The first of these variants regarded death from a perspective solidly rooted in this world. Here the destiny of good people had become a natural term of life (3.1); and preparation for death being by then accomplished by a lifetime of decent living, there was no need to know if one was dying (3.6). It is true that this expectation of a natural term was often accompanied by the idea of the dead being in a better place, but there was no connection made between the two ideas.

This form of popular belief was, in the present instance, identifiable by a particular idea of good people—one in which the reciprocal contract of church membership was dominant. The grief and conflict of Jessie Thomson, Mary Gilbert, and Maureen Baikie, already quoted in Chapter 4, and of one or two others too, were clearly centred on claims relating to the church, on what members contributed to the church, or what the minister should give them by way of consolation in return; and James Dearness too, in words immediately preceding those quoted in that chapter, likewise related the 'goodness' of his wife to church membership:

"She was quite enthusiastic about going to church, which we did a lot, and *she* was keen, just as her mother was."

Minister and membership seemed to represent, in fact, a local community which had something of the Old Testament relationship with its God, and which took for granted the Old Testament assumption referred to earlier, according to which suffering—here including premature death—was expected only as the consequence of sin. Hence members of this godly community could expect a natural term of earthly life (3.1). As for the next life, it might or might not exist, and the possibility that it did not could actually reinforce, as in Judaism, expectations of this present world. Hence James Dearness (and also, in an unquoted passage, Mary Gilbert) did not believe in a life beyond (4.2), and yet they remained haunted by what they felt as the broken promises of providence in this life.

Again it followed, both from this expectation of living a long and godly life, and from the uncertainity of another life after death, that preparation for death was unnecessary, and that death should therefore come unannounced and unawares (3.6):

"Die in your sleep or have a stroke, and not know anything about it—you know, something quick—that would be ideal."

In this latter respect, conventional conceptions of church membership did not so much exert an influence, as leave a vacuum in which, as before, the assumptions of 'disregarded dying' took over.

If this first variant from the conservative pattern was this-worldly rather than other-worldly, proponents of the second variant struggled, with varying success, to resolve both worlds, taking ethical responsibility for controlling death, while keeping faith with transcendental themes. People who thought along these lines grappled with the question of taking life, either recognizing it as a matter for complex distinctions between killing and letting die, or shifting quite definitely towards taking life in certain circumstances (3.7), even while at the same time they felt helplessly in tension with a continued belief in not taking life at all (3.8). They might have a strong notion of preparing for death (3.2*b*), but they could only consistency accept a weak notion of the destined time of death (3.2*a*), in which meaning could be ascribed to the point when death occurred in the biographical sequence, but not to the precise 'time' in hours, days, or weeks.

It was a strong emphasis on the social ethic of Christianity, or on developments of that ethic in modern systems of thought, which, even when the idea of providence was retained in a relatively conservative and other-worldly form, thus raised the issue of controlling death. The notion of providence was in this context partly helpful and, in so far as it was awkward, partly adaptable. It was helpful in that the shortening of life was not so important for those who believed firmly in a better place to come and in their preparedness for the passage. And it was adaptable in that, by the same token, the time was for these people already ripe; hence, should anything happen to make death a possibility, medical decisions which hastened or delayed the precise moment could be governed by the other, ethical considerations. These considerations were either argued as the Christian ethic of mercy, or as a supplementary value, felt to be consistent with the Christian ethic, of 'dignity', or a 'quality of life' defined by, for example, Socialism.

For the Socialist in this instance, Leonard Yule, ethical considerations were indeed virtually free of any notion of providence, and although he also had a mystical outlook this did not have clear implications for his view of death. This view was relatively coherent on how far control should be exerted:

"If it's a heart thing, and it's only the heart, and there's no brain damage or anything, I think they should make the effort. I think they should try because there are so many people who have had a stroke and everything else that have led quite useful lives afterwards. But when it's something where they would be a vegetable and utterly useless, I don,t think so . . .''

"What do you think about the thing some people ask for, that people should actually get a shot of something in some circumstances?"

"I wouldn't like to be the one to have to do that, and I wouldn't *ask* anyone else to do it. I would rather say not give them what keeps them alive, rather than that. Though I'm quite sure it's quite often done in cases of cancer or something like that—they give them a little more than they should have of morphine or something. But I wouldn't say, and I wouldn't ask anybody to do it."

This view thus attempted a resolution between the sanctity of life (3.8) and the ethical considerations argued in demands for euthanasia (3.7), along the usual lines of the distinction between acts and omissions. Asked then if the religious ideas he had discussed earlier influenced these questions, he hesitated:

"I think probably my philosophy of life rather than my Christian philosophy, although the two are together I suppose."

It was a 'fuzzy' area:

"My outlook is Socialism. Now I know there's an awful lot of different kinds, just like (there's) an awful lot of different kinds of Christianity, or the belief of Christ. I don't believe in the Virgin Birth, but I'm still a Christian—I still think that Christ lived and left something with us, a way of life. That's where they get muddled up and entangled. You can't say I think that way because I'm a Christian or I think that way because I'm a Socialist. Probably more because I'm a Socialist than because I'm Christian . . . Probably more because I am a Socialist—the quality of life means a great deal to me. The quality of people's lives."

In so far, then, as Christianity was a 'way of life'—and it also had another, mystical element which he discussed elsewhere—it was 'together', 'entangled' with Socialism; and Socialism in turn centred on safeguarding 'the quality of people's lives'. The final connections of considering the quality of people's lives remained implicit: first, when life ceased to be 'useful', not striving to keep alive; and second, not asking others to do what one would not like to do oneself.

These conclusions, arising out of ethical concern with a Christian background, were in Leonard Yule's case not referred to any view of providence; but in other cases a strong faith in providence could be felt consistent with similar or, in regard to taking life, still more radical arguments. Thus a woman who believed firmly in the rectification of suffering in a life to come, argued for outright euthanasia (3.7):

"Well, I would be for a pill. I'm sorry, I would be—to finish it off while they still have dignity . . . . From the point of view of the people who are suffering, it's a crime just keeping people alive. I would rather go. Now I would be quite happy to go now."

In this way her own preparedness (3.2), itself based on her faith in a providential redress in the next life (4.1), persuaded her to see the timing of death after that point as a purely ethical assessment of dignity and suffering.

Finally, and perhaps paradoxically, this Christian version of controlled dying was paralleled by an otherwise antagonistic secularist version, which included four types of statement about death; first, and most obviously, a denial of any life after death (4.2); second, an advocacy of suicide rather than continuing to live indefinitely at a low level of consciousness, in pain, or at excessive cost to others (3.7); third, a preference for knowing a fatal diagnosis and prognosis (3.5); and fourth, an insistence on dealing with the dead solely in accordance with the interests of the living (4.4), practising cremation, and minimizing funerary ritual except in so far as it could be supposed to benefit the bereaved.

Secularist assumptions in Aberdeen often reflected a stage marked merely by a selective scepticism about supernatural Christian beliefs. But alongside these negative starting points, there was also a positive principle which animated the practical consequences of this world view—that of individual autonomy. This preference for individual control was sometimes universalized into a principle which unbelievers opposed to the faith of the Kirk, and it was sometimes adopted merely as a constant attribute of the person concerned.

Iona Mackie was one of these who saw the wish for autonomy as a constant personal attribute, but she contrasted this with what she felt was the religious attitude. The victim of a cancer which had gone into remission, she was unequivocal about what she would do if it recurred and the pain could not be controlled: she would take an overdose (3.7). She recognized that this meant having full information about her situation (3.5), and believed that not everyone would wish for this, that it depended on personal make-up. About her own make-up she was not in doubt: she had discussed her case fully with her brother, who was an oncologist, and felt that with the right treatment her chances were good. But in all these matters, she would make up her own mind. It was at the end of this conversation that she took this self-definition further into the religious realm. Standing up at its conclusion, she remarked:

"Well, the Lord won't look after me—that's certain. I'm not a religious person."

And asked if she was referring to the idea of a reward after death, she merely said:

"Oh, that!—But he won't look after me in this life either".

Thus life after death was dismissed (4.2), and death was to be planned for. And in planning it, finally, Iona Mackie's criterion was, logically enough, whatever would minimize trouble for the bereaved (4.4).

In defining herself, therefore, as a person who made up her own mind, she was defining herself in opposition to religion, which she equated with being 'looked after'. And she also had a stronger definition than many of a positive alternative to religion—an alternative expressed in tapping her brother's scientific knowledge, and in the determination to make up her own mind freely on that basis: an implicit statement, in fact, of the rationalist position.

These varying world views thus pictured death in very different ways, but all agreed in refusing merely to disregard it, in the way adopted when people were sustained by nothing other than formal membership of a church or a sense of personal identity. This picture can now be compared with the picture drawn earlier of religious responses to illness and ageing, so as to see something of the overall significance of Aberdonian religion in this sphere of life.

Conclusion

I began this chapter by sketching the range of religious alternatives which has emerged as church religion has been fragmented and transformed. In this Scottish generation churchgoing has not declined as far as it has in other generations and other areas of Britain; but a decline has nevertheless occurred. In Aberdeen the pattern of transformation was one in which two other religious resources had become prominent—as prominent, in fact, as church membership. One was an 'invisible' or 'customary' religion or world view which, often selective in doctrine and uncommitted to the church, nevertheless drew on historic themes of Scottish Protestantism to make sense of experience. And the other resource was the notion of a constant self—one which sometimes went with commitment to a world view, but which more often merely affirmed an identity formed on the culturally accepted model. Although both these ways of thinking could be united with church religion, world views and self-conceptions were also treated by Aberdonians as alternative resources.

These alternative sets of axioms which Aberdonians brought to their everyday life were related to very different ways of approaching illness, ageing, and death. Simplifying, it can be said that on its own, a self-image tied to the usual approved qualities—those of being a healthy, active, determined, or hard-working person—was an inflexible ideal which excluded severe illness and late old age from normal society and easily implied, for the irremediably disabled, a disastrous loss of self. Death, too, by default of any more general understanding relevant to coping with it, was something to be excluded, and attitudes to death, correspondingly, were summed up in the wish for a quick dispatch which, for the most part, should take place unawares, and hastened on, if necessary, by the doctor who, in this situation, was ceded absolute authority.

Similarly, conventional church membership on its own, which was also based on quite narrow assumptions, also went with a limited activist approach to illness. Death was shut out by default here too, and the doctor was again to determine when it occurred. There was little need to be prepared for death, for the emphasis was rather on this-worldly expectations of a natural term of life—an outlook fostered by the sense of a contract between minister and membership, and between both and a somewhat Old Testament God. These expectations were as vulnerable to premature death as activism was to illness.

In comparison with these identities based solely on church membership, or on personal qualities which were socially approved, the world views drawn on by Aberdonians supplied a wider and more flexible repertoire. Purely ethical or rationalist philosophies extended the active responses to controllable illness, and added demands both for medical information about a fatal prognosis and for personal control of the timing of death. But when illness was irreducible, yet not fatal, this approach left a vacuum, in which the negative side of the approved Aberdonian self-image again became prominent. By contrast, world views which centred on some conception of faith not only offered the widest repertoire for coping positively with controllable illness, but also offered resources for dealing positively with irreducible illness. And they also had a wide application in coping with dying, where they either affirmed traditional ritual conceptions or attempted to innovate in order to resolve the problems of painfully delayed deaths.

We can thus summarize all these religious and quasi-religious resources in terms of their range of relevance for coping, and so answer the first question raised in the introduction to this chapter. In Aberdeen, the widest range of relevance was found in ideas of faith. A more limited, though still substantial, range was found in purely ethical or rationalist world views. And it was those who did not draw on such world views at all, whether they belonged to a church, or relied solely on an image of themselves as decent, hard-working people, whose ideas had the narrowest range of relevance.

Yet in spite of the fact that world views, and in particular theistic world views, were seen to have the widest range of relevance in coping, some Aberdonians seemed to be indifferent to religion in this sphere. How far was this the case? How far, too, was indifference tied up with a tendency to relegate authority to the technical judgements of medicine? And how far was it experience of the limits to technical control that set limits to this indifference? This was the second set of questions raised in the introduction to this chapter.

Indifference to religion *tout court* was an attitude most clearly exemplified in those Aberdonians who just described how they coped without referring to any axiomatic assumptions about the world or themselves at all; but these were a minority of less than a fifth. However, a more limited indifference, expressed in a neglect of, or diffidence about, universal questions, was also evident, both in those who merely tried to live up to the approved self-image, and in those who declared a loyalty to their church but who expressed no world view. I have shown that, taken together, these pragmatic approaches characterized the way of thinking adopted by nearly half of these Aberdonians.

While such pragmatism involved, as we have seen, rather repressive attitudes to illness, it did not necessarily involve a dependent attitude to medicine, until the illness became terminal. But at that point those who shrank from universal questions certainly relegated death to medical control. The prospect of dying was, for practical purposes, something to be ignored as far as possible, and medicine was relied upon to do all that was necessary.

There were, however, limits to this indifference, for the majority of Aberdonians had built up and sustained a world view which did confront troubling topics. Many of these views no doubt derived from upbringing; but certain marked changes in them which were recounted do seem to have been a response to experiencing the limits of technical control. The failure of technology was of course felt less with remediable illness and with good 'natural' deaths than with irremediable illness and premature deaths; and while it has to be borne in mind that we are relying here on retrospective accounts, these two issues certainly seem to have evoked new questions and fresh attempts to grapple with universal themes.

Nevertheless, these uncontrolled medical situations only made a few people think afresh, for many retained their previous beliefs even where these had entirely negative implications; and in any case the response of the few was not only towards but also away from faith. The change was towards faith among those who had sought ways of coping positively with disabling illness. But in coping with premature bereavement, those who were prompted to new questions were chiefly church members or disillusioned former church members who seemed not to have thought much about these subjects before the death of the person concerned, and who subsequently ran into difficulties from previously unexamined assumptions about the justice of living a natural term of life.

All in all, therefore, it appears that in those areas where the limits of technical control by medicine had been reached, the response of faith was in the end dependent on two things. First, people did not *hold* to faith, unless the faith involved realistic expectations about suffering—about the limits to technical control over premature death, for example—and offered an understanding of the way in which suffering could be interpreted and overcome. And secondly, people did not *come* to faith just by experiencing the limits of technical control. Those who acquired a new belief were probably right in pointing to the counsellors and helpers who were available to help construct a new understanding after the crisis of control had occurred. Belief, therefore, was not dictated by suffering; it depended on the quality of the vision offered—its ability to match and transcend the suffering—and on the presence of people who could offer it.

How then does the vision which is offered today compare with the Calvinist past? This, the last question raised in this chapter, had particular reference to two relevant emphases of historic Calvinism—its ascetic activism, and its characteristic explanation of suffering.

The ascetic activism of the past was still strong in Aberdeen, and, as we have seen, it was effective where illness and death were controllable, though it was inflexible and negative in its results where they were not. Some of this inflexibility derived from the way in which this activism had lost touch with its theological roots—a link which only a few were able to reconstruct when things went wrong. Activism had sometimes become tied to socialist or rationalist ideals instead, or, more usually, had become an unquestioned assumption which needed no deeper justification. This was most obvious in endorsements of the powerful Aberdonian work ethic. It is true that the emphasis on work continued to fit harmoniously both with the Calvinist ethic of self-discipline and helping others, and with the active conception of faith; and a few Aberdonians did in passing make an explicit link between some of these ideas. But overall the extrapolation from faith to work ethic was in fact seldom made. Indeed, the moral quality of work seemed more frequently to be tied to unconsidered self-images than to a definite world view. Thus when work in its many senses became impossible, there was often no way left to hand for reinterpreting the situation in a positive fashion.

Nevertheless, in certain cases the need to find a positive meaning was eventually met by adopting religious interpretations of suffering; and these had changed from those which seem to have been characteristic of the Calvinist past. They had moved away from reading illness and death as punishments for sin, as the 'particular providences' of seventeenth-century Calvinists tended to do, and towards the task of overcoming suffering, by means of a notion of providences that reward and encourage active struggle and sustain a sense of worth. It is true that the old logic was still in the air, and dogged the less committed in unexpected ways when they met trouble. But in the move away from it, one can perhaps see ways in which the optimistic approach of Victorian Evangelicalism has been at work on the stern predestinarian stuff of the Calvinist inheritance.[30]

This shift from suffering as punishment to suffering as a trial has continued, though, to bypass the third of the Christian themes outlined in the introduction to this chapter—suffering as a sacrifice or offering, which in some sense helps to 'complete' the suffering of Christ, or, in its specifically Catholic form, to gain 'merit' in the next world for oneself or for others. The barriers placed before such interpretations of suffering by the Reformed tradition were already recognized by Thomas More, who quoted the Lutheran objection:

'They that would do penance for their own sins, look to be their own Christs.'[31] The critical position of this argument in Reformed theology seems to have established an obstacle to both the versions of the sacrificial theme which have been quoted—certainly to the Catholic version which relates present sacrifice to future merit, and maybe also to the more traditional version in which the sufferer simply shares in the work of Christ. If this is so, it is perhaps no surprise that the possibility of these interpretations remained unrecognized in Aberdeen; and while Aberdonians did not put the full Reformist argument in this context, the one occasion on which a religious reason was given for avoiding suffering could be heard to echo its essential assumption: 'That's Jesus Christ all over again.'

With these reflections on the changing tradition, my survey of the religious and economic resources which are available in contemporary Aberdonian culture is complete; and I leave it to the concluding chapter to attempt a perspective on the historical relationship between these religious and economic aspects of the culture as a whole.

Notes and References

1. R. Currie, A. Gilbert, and L. Horsley, *Churches and church-goers: patterns of church growth in the British Isles since 1700*, Oxford University Press, 1977.
2. B. Wilson, *Religion in sociological perspective*, Oxford University Press, 1982.
3. A.D. Gilbert, *The making of post-Christian Britain*, London: Longman, 1980, ch. 3.
4. D. Martin, *A general history of secularisation*, Oxford: Blackwell, 1978; for the figures see Currie *et al.*, *Churches and churchgoers*.
5. E. Troeltsch, *The social teaching of the Christian churches*, tr. O. Wyon, London: Allen and Unwin, 1931, vol. 2, 'Conclusion'.
6. T. Luckmann, *The invisible religion*, London: Macmillan, 1967; P. L. Berger and T. Luckmann, *The social construction of reality*, London: Allen Lane, 1967; R. Towler, *Homo religiosus*, London: Constable, 1974; M. P. Hornsby-Smith, R. M. Lee, and P. A. Reilly, 'Common religion and customary religion: a critique and a proposal', *Rev. Relig. Research* 26 (1985), 244–52.
7. B. S. Turner, *Religion and social theory*, London: Heinemann, 1983, pp. 244–6.
8. Berger and Luckmann, *The social construction of reality*, pt. 3.
9. N. D. Jewson, 'The disappearance of the sick man from medical cosmology 1770–1870', *Sociology*, 10 (1976), 225–44.
10. R. Porter (ed.), *Patients and practitioners: lay perceptions of medicine in pre-industrial society*, Cambridge University Press, 1985; C. Herzlich and J. Pierret, *Malades d'hier, malades d'aujourd'hui*, Paris: Payot, 1984, ch. 11; L. Price, 'Art, science, faith and medicine: the implications of the placebo effect', *Sociology of Health and Illness*, 6 (1984), 61–73.
11. I. Illich, *Limits to medicine*, London; Penguin, 1977.
12. P. Aries, *The hour of our death*, tr. H. Weaver, London: Allen Lane, 1981, pt. 5 and p. 614; Gilbert, *The making of post-Christian Britain,* ch. 3.
13. R. Totman, *Social causes of illness*, London: Souvenir Press, 1980; E. T. Cassell, *The healer's art*, London: Pelican, 1978.

14. R. Pill and N. C. H. Stott, 'Choice or chance: further evidence on ideas of illness and responsibility for health', *Soc. Sci. and Med.* 20 (1985), 981 – 91.

15. D.R. Hannay, *The symptom iceberg*, London: Routledge, 1979.

16. K. Charmaz, 'Loss of self: a fundamental form of suffering in the chronically ill', *Sociol. of Health and Illness*, 5 (1983), 168–95.

17. M. Bury, 'Chronic illness as biographical disruption', *Sociol. of Health and Illness*, 4 (1982), 167–82.

18. G. Williams, 'The genesis of chronic illness: narrative reconstruction', *Sociol. of Health and Illness*, 6 (1984), 175–200.

19. D. Armstrong, 'Silence and truth in death and dying', *Soc. Sci. and Med.* 24 (1987), 651–7.

20. Gilbert, *The making of post-Christian Britain*.

21. T. C. Smout, *A history of the Scottish people 1560–1830*, London: Fontana, 1972, ch. 3.

22. L. Stone, *The family, sex and marriage in England 1500–1800*, London: Weidenfeld and Nicolson, 1977, ch. 5; C. Larner, *Enemies of God: the witch hunt in Scotland*, London: Chatto and Windus, 1981, pp. 171–2; K. Thomas, *Religion and the decline of magic*, London: Penguin, 1971, ch. 4. Larner has suggested that witches provided the only alternative explanation—hence the enthusiasm with which they were hunted. Similar tendencies also appeared in Catholicism around this time: Herzlich and Pierret, *Malades d'hier*, p. 179.

23. Herzlich and Pierret, *Malades d'heir,* pp. 189, 191.

24. For a recent reaffirmation of this theme in the Western tradition see John Paul II, *Salvifici doloris*, Apostolic letter of the supreme pontiff on suffering, Catholic Truth Society, 1984; for the Eastern tradition see Iulia de Beausobre, *Creative suffering*, SLG Press, 1984.

25. Herzlich and Pierret, *Malades d'hier*, p. 180.

26. Thomas More, *A dialogue of comfort*, London: Everyman, 1951, p. 178.

27. Herzlich and Pierret, *Malades d'hier*, p. 190. Compare peasant understandings of penance in Catholic pilgrimages: W. A. Christian, *Person and God in a Spanish valley*, London: Seminar Press, 1972.

28. All-Britain surveys in 1983–4 put those claiming membership of Christian churches at 62–3% of the voting population, and

those attending weekly at 12–13%—R. Jowell and C. Airey (eds.), *British social attitudes: the 1984 report*, London: Gower, 1984, p. 195, and R. Jowell and S. Witherspoon, *British social attitudes: the 1985 report*, London: Gower, 1985, p. 233: Other measures show clearly that membership and attendance have been higher in Scotland than in England for some decades: P. Brierley (ed.), *The UK Christian handbook: 1983 edition*, London: The Evangelical Alliance, The Bible Society, and MARC Europe, 1982; id. (ed.), *Prospects for the eighties*, London: Bible Society, 1980; P. Brierley and F. Macdonald, *Prospects for Scotland*, National Bible Society of Scotland and MARC Europe, 1985; J. Highet, 'Great Britain: Scotland', in H. Mol (ed.), *Western religion: a country by country sociological enquiry*, The Hague: Mouton, 1972; Currie *et al., Churches and churchgoers.* Note that on these measures, while only 10% of the adult population attended church in Aberdeen on an average March Sunday in 1984, it can be calculated that 17% of those over 65 did so.

29. For the concepts of 'world view' and 'symbolic universe' see Luckmann, *The invisible religion,* and Berger and Luckmann, *The social construction of reality.*
30. C. G. Brown, *The social history of religion in Scotland since 1730,* London: Methuen, 1987.
31. More, *A dialogue of comfort,* p. 226.

10

A Protestant legacy

Throughout this book, the concern has been with the way in which practical ideas about coping with illness, old age, and death are bound up with the economic and religious conceptions of one place and period. Thus the decisions and dilemmas which engaged Aberdonians in these matters were for nearly all of them shaped at some point by a work ethic which strongly endorsed the welfare capitalism of the post-war period, or by class cultures which were built on marked differences in control over houses and occupational skills. And they were also nearly always further shaped either by a typically activist self-image or by ethical or religious convictions deriving mainly from the Protestant tradition. These were diverse influences, and they originated, not in the medical sphere, but in the heart of Aberdeen life; and this prompts the first question with which this conclusion is concerned. How far did these vital and wide-ranging influences cohere in a single, mutually reinforcing system, whose key lay in certain ruling beliefs which were secure and stable? And how far had they generated competing systems, which have to be understood with reference to the historical pathway which they have travelled?

Again, while these conceptions of coping had deep roots in Aberdonian culture, they also fed extensively into the practical, co-operative business of dealing with physical change. Aberdonians might construct their ideas to make sense of their working life and religious biography, but on this basis they also, as I described in Chapter 6, formed coalitions of opinion, discussed, with fair accuracy, the reactions of others to physical limitation and loss, and dealt out praise and blame accordingly. Hence their ideas about coping, founded in biographical experience, and tested by this criticism, were sustained over time and expressed in their behaviour; and events which contradicted these ideas were not easily rationalized, and left a legacy of conflicts and dilemmas which took time to be worked over and, where possible, resolved.

Finally, in resolving such dilemmas, as we saw in the last chapter, the flexibility and creativity of their responses depended on the range and relevance of their overarching world view. Thus the creative role of these ideas has emerged in many places, and this prompts the second question addressed in this conclusion. How far is it sufficient merely to understand the material constraints which have shaped these patterns of coping, and how far is it necessary to grasp the intellectual and religious developments from which they were conceived?

Thus the first of these questions asks how far there is a single ruling system of beliefs which dominates ideas about coping in Aberdeen, and how far there are competing systems. And the second question asks how far these conceptions of coping can be understood merely by looking at the material development of the society, and how far they have to be understood in terms of its cultural inheritance. These are large questions, and this limited enquiry can do no more than suggest, with varying degrees of uncertainty, those answers that seem most valid for one historical generation, in one place and time, and in one partial domain of their view of things.

First, then, do the Aberdonian ideas which have been discussed form a strong and unitary cultural pattern, either one which is consensual, or one which successfully controls and suppresses alternatives, whatever the fragmentation and disagreement apparent on the surface? If such a unitary cultural pattern can be discerned, it is, first of all, plain already from every chapter of this book that the unity concerned is not one of universal agreement. In every department of Aberdonian thinking which has been considered there is disagreement, debate, opposition, and contradiction in continual ferment. But the question then is how much of this conflict can be explained as a problem simply of individual deviance, itself constantly reordered by processes of negotiation, segregation, or rehabilitation? And certainly a number of the contradictions recorded can be explained in this way. In Chapter 1, for example the loss of self felt by some Aberdonians when they could no longer make a show of carrying on normally was the mirror image of the conventional idea that normal activity controlled illness; and similarly the idea of illness as a release from effort, and the surrender of late age described in Chapter 2, were marginal and stigmatized, though tolerated, conditions. In Chapter 5, avoidance of, and hostility to, the doctor was a response which stimulated efforts to bring the person in question into line, or marked them as irredeemably 'cussed'. And in Chapter 7, disagreements with the work ethic, too, were sporadic and disorganized, and were often expressed by people who at the same time reaffirmed allegiance to the norm. Thus the antitheses in this whole complex of ideas merely represented reaffirmations of its central themes, bargaining about their interpretation, and segregation of those who failed to exemplify them.

At the same time, however, the identification of such processes of social control is not the end of the story; for there are also irreducible divisions in Aberdonian culture such as that between Christianity and secularism, and between various Christian views themselves, on the subject of death. In these respects there was little unitary pattern in the sense of a common denominator or 'civil religion'. But if these were competing systems, they showed at the same time a remarkably precise and determinate interrelationship, in which certain key terms were inverted, while remaining terms were still shared. The patterns of Aberdonian thinking about dying, for instance, which were described in Chapter 3, can, with a certain amount of crudity, be simplified as shown in Table 12.

Table 12. *Attitudes to dying*

Attitude	Ritual dying	Transitional pattern	Disregarded dying	Controlled dying
Prepared death (+) vs. natural death (−)	+	(+)	−	(+)
Death after reunion (+) vs. quick death (−)	+	−	−	+
Death aware (+) vs. unaware (−)	+	−	−	+
Sanctity of life (+) vs. euthanasia (−)	+	(+)	(+)	−

In this table bracketed entries represent mixed or equivocal attitudes. The table begins in the left-hand column with the

Calvinist model of ritual dying, with its carefully defined notion of lifelong preparation; and reading from left to right it shows next, in the transitional pattern, how preparedness comes to be associated with 'natural' death in old age, and how lifelong preparedness makes it acceptable if death occurs quickly and unawares. Then, in the third column, preparedness is rejected altogether, and the notion of a natural age for death takes over entirely. And finally, in the fourth column, comes the reversal of most of these notions in the arguments of those who seek control over painfully prolonged deaths.

In the same way, the patterns of thinking about the dead elicited in Chapter 4 can be rendered as shown in Table 13.

Table 13. *Attitudes to the dead*

Attitude	Old style	New style religious	New style non-religious
Reunion (+) vs. annihilation (−)	+	+	−
Sanctity of the body (+) vs. interests of the living (−)	+	−	−
Uniqueness of loss (+) vs. need for replacement (−)	+	+	+

Here the old style of mourning in the first column gives way to two more or less contemporaneous alternatives in the second and third columns, both rejecting the sanctity of the body, while one rejects also the idea of reunion with kin in an afterlife.

In Tables 12 and 13, therefore, each column represents a distinct system of thought, yet the patterns are not self-contained or separate from one another. The systems are related, in fact, through 'family resemblances',[1] each system resembling each of the others in a different set of terms. Correspondingly, each also contradicts each of the others in a different set of terms. Moreover the linkages thus depicted represent dynamic reactions of one system of thought to another, as the historical perspectives discussed in Chapters 3 and 4 make clear. For the columns of these tables have been arranged from left to right in a broad historical sequence, such that each pattern at its inception inverts certain terms of its predecessor, while retaining the rest. At the same time, though, the predecessor is seldom banished, but continues to coexist—and to compete—with the new pattern. And also a subsequent pattern, such as that labelled 'controlled dying', by inverting certain terms of its immediate predecessor, may actually restore certain terms of the first pattern of the sequence, negating its negations. The contemporary culture, therefore, is a web of sequential theses and antitheses, and its constitution is in this respect (though not necessarily in any deterministic sense) dialectical.

Thus the divisions between religious or philosophical patterns of thought about death in Aberdeen are unitary only in the sense that they are dialectical variations on the same themes: and the same seems to be true also of the second type of fission which has been apparent in Aberdonian thinking on these subjects—that between the class cultures which are especially evident in issues of ageing and medical care, described in Chapter 8.

Even if attitudes to the last stage of ageing reflect pressures towards social conformity, other attitudes to ageing, and the pattern of these attitudes as a whole, again reflect dialectical competition and change. A tabular summary of some of the chief results from Chapter 2 would be as shown in Table 14.

Table 14. *Attitudes to ageing*

Attitude	Ageing as delayed capitulation	Ageing as siege	Ageing as resurgence
Retirement as liberation (+) vs. retirement as setback (−)	−	−	+
Late age as resistable (+) vs. late age as surrender (−)	−	+	+

Here the left-hand column is the pattern closest to the medieval and early modern schemes of the Ages of Man, though it is in fact more active and optimistic about early old age. The second column represents the spread across class divisions of belief in moral control of late old age. And the third column picks out the liberated view which depends on the economic resources and cultural capital of sections of the contemporary middle class.

Similarly, attitudes to medical care only achieve a degree of consensus in disapproving extreme cases where the doctor is treated as an enemy; and the overall picture in Chapter 5 is again one of dialectical variation between patterns which have family resemblances (see Table 15).

Table 15. *Attitudes to medical care*

Attitude	Doctor as enemy	Doctor as authority	Doctor as collaborator
Realism in con-sulting (+) vs. delay in consulting (−)	−	+	+
Control of decisions (+) vs. obedience to orders (−)	( )	−	+

In this table the brackets in the first column indicate avoidance of the doctor because disagreement is expected, and believed to be irresolvable. The historical background to this pattern of thinking has not been discussed, and it is complicated by historical change in the medical profession, in the treatments it offers, and in the alternatives to it. But it is probably significant that the fear of hospitals and of 'experiments' expressed here corresponds quite closely to attitudes already evident among the poor during the early development of the modern medical profession in the nineteenth century.[2] Then, in the second column, comes the stoical and paternalistic pattern which is probably founded, I suggested, in pre-war experience of limited insurance and charity among the poor. And the third column represents middle-class assumptions about consumer choice carried over into the NHS from private medicine. A degree of historical progression from left to right is suggested, first, by the fact that views of the doctor as enemy have been forced into the position of being odd and deviant, and second, by literature cited in Chapter 5 which suggests that the consumerist view is spreading.

In all these different aspects of Aberdonian culture, therefore, there is historical debate and competition between patterns of thought which are both related and opposed, and which stem from religious and economic divisions which have been evolving for a long time. And in attitudes to illness too, elements of a similar dialectical pattern are discernible, though their historical sequence is less clear, being subject to a more complex interaction of moral and economic issues. The literature cited in Chapter 1 suggests, amongst other things, that there has been an important historical development from excluding to protecting the chronic sick; and that there has been a recurring tension between the pressure to try and go on living normally, and attempts to develop positive alternative ways of living. The present evidence suggests that in this latter tension two different moral imperatives are involved. One is the work ethic, which emphasizes the norm; and the other is the religious approach to suffering, where the emphasis may favour either the norm or the alternatives. Historically, suffering—of which irremediable illness is a primary example—has sometimes been seen as punishment for sin, again emphasizing the norm; but it has also been seen as a form of sacrifice or a trial of faith, which emphasizes the possibility of positive alternatives. Thus there is some evidence in the literature discussed in Chapters 1 and 7 that positive views of illness have been easier when the work ethic is relaxed. And there is evidence in Chapter 9 that positive views are easier for the religious who see illness as a trial of faith. But these are historical questions which have only just begun to be explored.

Even in these universal predicaments of illness, old age, and death, then, Aberdonian culture was not primarily consensual or conformist, but was shaped around religious and economic themes which continued a series of historical debates; and in these important respects it was a unitary culture only in the family resemblances of what each religious or economic conception affirmed and denied in its competitors. This does not of course mean that the society was falling apart—far from it: precisely because the agreements and disagreements criss-crossed, rather than joining to form a single religious, social, and economic cleavage, the society held firmly together.[3] Thus the undoubted solidity of Aberdonian culture in this medical sphere was based for the most part on something which at first sight seems relatively fragile and unstable—on the evolution of social and religious discourses deriving from a long history, in such a way that, at any one time, opponents in any one discourse were not forced to be opponents in all the other discourses as well.

This brings me to the second and last question to be discussed in this conclusion: how far have these debated economic and religious conceptions concerned with health, ageing, and death, which are found in contemporary Aberdeen, to be understood not just in terms of material factors, but also in terms of their intellectual origins? Once again a preliminary reservation is in order: the historical explanations for present patterns which have been put forward in this book are necessarily partial, and have relied on connecting them with past patterns in areas where historical research is relatively new, sometimes speculative, and geographically patchy. With such counsels for caution, the suggestions made are inevitably provisional.

In the historical background sketched during previous chapters a few typical sequences of events can sometimes be dimly discerned among the enveloping historical complexities. All these sequences involve an interplay between creative thought and natural or deterministic connection, and consequently represent possible examples of Weber's ambiguous term 'elective affinities'.[4] First, there is the process whereby ideas are disseminated and selected, even possibly in some degree conceived, in accordance with material conditions or changes therein. Secondly, there is the process whereby ideas themselves generate challenges and counter-challenges, which alter the ensuing pattern of thought and conduce to changes in material conditions. And thirdly, there are varying combinations of these two patterns. In what remains, I explore the origins of Aberdonian ideas with special reference to these typical sequences, bearing in mind that they cannot represent more than a part of the whole.

Plainly the first of these processes—the selective influence of material conditions on ideas—is closely connected with the way class cultures develop. In Chapter 8 I showed that the economic control and cultural paradigms of certain middle-class Aberdonians gave them a marked optimism about ageing, and a wish for control of decisions about medical care. The historical processes that lie behind these cultural features can most clearly be illustrated in ideas about ageing.

In Chapter 2, I started from existing arguments that current optimistic views of ageing have been generated by certain features of capitalism. I suggested that some aspects of this analysis fit well, as far as they go, with the present Aberdeen material, but that positive images of old age can be traced back well before capitalism. We can certainly accept that negative images were predominant in the past, as recent efforts to debunk the nostalgic view have correctly suggested; but age was also approached more optimistically, by a minority of the well-to-do, as a final opportunity to reveal moral character. Thus it is necessary to begin from this initial divergence of ideas in explaining the present situation.

Even when we accept, though, that this conflict of ideas about ageing predates capitalism, it is still apparent that the subsequent experience of increasing longevity—something undoubtedly based on advances in material conditions during the capitalist period— has acted selectively on these ideas. When the state pension was introduced at the beginning of this century, retirement was generally seen as coinciding with the last phase in a fatalistic paradigm of ageing, and meant no more than rest from labour. But by the end of the Second World War, as longevity increased and pension age fell, and as pensions at that age became automatic, retirement came to be seen as coinciding with a penultimate active stage of life. Even in terms of fatalistic paradigms, it became a still 'green' old age; but it was also increasingly seen in terms of moral paradigms, as a time of building defences against any final collapse.

Thus far, then, the story is a simple one of the selective dissemination of pre-existing ideas according to changes in material conditions. However, the full story is obviously not so simple, for these ideas took conscious account of material conditions even in their conception. In pre-industrial Europe, moral prescriptions for fending off ignominious old age were explicitly premissed on the possession of property. The poor could not hope for moral victories. And something similar was involved in the early nineteenth-century idea of retirement as a liberation. I suggested in Chapter 8 that this idea was formed by a creative analogy—by assimilating superannuated retirement on a pension from a capitalist enterprise to the seasonal retirement of the gentry from urban business. In this way the gentlemanly leisure of the landed classes became the image of retirement for the pensioners of commerce. Thus all these optimistic ideas about ageing were creatively conceived; yet they also declared themselves from the outset as partly dependent either on wealth or on a previous class culture. Thus in their conception, as well as in their dissemination, these ideas of ageing have been quite highly dependent on material conditions.

Nevertheless, other conceptions have developed according to their own internal dynamic, and some have also themselves helped to form material possibilities. In the present study, these processes can be illustrated by ideas about mourning.

Chapter 4 began with the insight of Hertz, that after a death ideas about the body, the soul, and the mourner tend to be symmetrical. But it emerged that this symmetry is only a moment in the internal dynamic of such ideas. Again the recapitulation is necessarily simplified. The symmetrical pattern is most discernible in correspondences between the gradual decay of the body, the slow transition of the soul, and the extended period of mourning in medieval Catholicism, and in contemporary Catholic and Orthodox cultures in Europe. In the late Middle Ages, though, this conception began to be exploited financially through the sale of indulgences, creating an intensely felt contradiction, which the more thoroughgoing Reformers resolved by denying wholesale the doctrine relating to the gradual purgation of sins after death, and by replacing it with a doctrine of the immediate transition of the soul either to heaven or to hell.

Among Puritan zealots, as a consequence, the extended pattern of mourning and concern for the body were both rejected, creating a new symmetry and confirming Hertz's thesis. But in the more conservative mass of the population, forms of extended mourning hung on, despite their conflict with beliefs about the soul. A partial resolution was indeed achieved, but only by refocusing mourning ritual on the body, and by using it to symbolize, not the purgation of sins, but the soul's immediate bliss. Cemeteries acquired the trappings of a family home, picturing the soul's reunion with kin. This however was a precarious symbolism which was incompatible with the facts of bodily decay, and it was increasingly shaken by a series of urban grave scandals, and by the death scenes of the First World War. The collapse of this bodily symbolism was irrelevant to Catholic and Orthodox mourning, which still corresponded to the progressive purification of the soul; but Protestant Europe, with its picture of the soul's immediate translation, was compelled to reassert its original attitude both to mourning and to the body. Mourning ritual, which had survived on the compromise of body-centred symbolism, began to collapse; and the body was again seen, after the departure of the soul, as being finished with, and as needing to be disposed of as efficiently as possible in the interests of the living. In Protestant countries, cremation spread, with all its consequences for land use and environmental sanitation. And in this way there emerges the present situation in Aberdeen, in which the newest patterns of thinking reveal a rapid transition of soul, body, and public mourning, in conflict with a private grief which changes only slowly.

In this sequence, the material facts of bodily decay are a constant, though one dramatized by the material changes of urban growth and modern warfare; and the dynamic at work, including the changes in land use and so on brought about by the technology of cremation, is the slow unfolding, in Protestant countries as a whole, of the original logic of the Puritan vision.

I have now illustrated, in these necessarily simplified stories, two very different types of historical development which can account for the dialectical patterns or strata to be found in Aberdonian thinking about health, ageing, and death. Both sorts of development have acknowledged an autonomous, creative element in the genesis of these ideas, and have recognized their capacity to be handed down over very long periods of time; but one emphasizes the additional role of material factors in their conception and dissemination, while the other emphasizes the continuing internal dynamic of ideas, as well as their capacity to form new technical or material possibilities. From these illustrations I now turn to a central historical process, combining features of both types of development, which seems to be reflected in several aspects of Aberdonian thinking on these subjects—the long and turbulent relationship of Scottish society with the Protestant ethic. Hints of the importance of this influence have appeared in several chapters already, but it is now possible to draw these threads together.

The history of the Protestant ethic in Scotland is one in which the formative power of ideas, their internal dynamic, and the selective constraints of material factors are all entangled. Only by carefully disentangling them can one account for the oddly self-sufficient role of the work ethic in Aberdonian ideas about health and ageing, and for the historical strata visible in Aberdonian ideas about dying.

I referred in Chapter 7 to discussions on the Scottish dimension of the Protestant work ethic. Much of this debate deals with problems which need not concern us here; but there is one clear respect in which the link between Calvinism and the 'serious-minded strain in the Scottish character'[5] has been confirmed. Work, honest reward, and care for the welfare of the industrious in misfortune were as tightly linked to salvation by many Scottish capitalists and divines of the seventeenth century, as they are to health by many Aberdonians of all classes in the present study. In this respect, Calvinism certainly had a formative influence in the lives and projects of seventeenth-century Scottish capitalists, and that influence was carried down at least to the Aberdonian burgers of the nineteenth century, who believed that religious conversions were a prerequisite for diligence.[6]

However, the assimilation of the work ethic by Scottish working people of the seventeenth century, rather than by capitalists and divines, remains in doubt. Moreover the large vagrant population of the time was certainly outside the Kirk,[7] and a similar population was still present in nineteenth-century Aberdeen, swelled by the breakup of the old farming system, when the churches made a vigorous onslaught on the task of educating the poor to godly and industrious habits. It is probably the success of this nineteenth-century effort, apparent among the labour aristocracy of the time,[8] which is reflected in the attachment to the work ethic of Aberdonians of all classes in the older generation depicted here. But it is reflected in a significant way, for, as I have noted, this generation of Aberdonians, although they frequently linked industriousness with health, very seldom linked it with godliness. And the explanation for this is probably to be found in the fact that the education of the preceding generation or two in industry was accomplished more by middle-class control of a complex system of material rewards and punishments, than by the religious conversions from which better-off citizens explicitly hoped such virtues would flow. Thus, in espousing the work ethic, working-class Aberdonians learnt from this system of social control not a Protestant ethic, but an ethic of capitalism; and that ethic—one which the evidence of this book has shown is not merely a pragmatic assessment of economic interest, but a morality generalized to health and old age—has proved, as Weber suggested it would, to be self-sustaining.

In accounting for the contemporary Aberdonian view of work and health, therefore, we find a complex sequence from the Calvinist genesis of the work ethic, through its formative influence over those who created the foundations for Scottish capitalism, to its selective reconstitution in the experience of those who were disciplined and rewarded by that same capitalism. Finally, much the same sequence can be brought out also in accounting for contemporary Aberdonian ideas about dying. Here I recapitulate themes combined from both Chapter 3 on dying and Chapter 9 on religion.

The internal dynamic in ideas about dying again springs from the Reformation reconstruction of the last things. Just as death, in the Puritan view, was followed by the immediate passage of the elect to glory, so the preparation of the elect in life was dependent not on sacraments, and particularly not on deathbed repentance and final absolution, but on the continuous demonstration of grace in well doing following conversion. The necessity for specific preparations by the dying was thus removed. True, in the absence of any other developments, such preparation remained appropriate, and this is one view which continues to be reflected in contemporary Aberdeen. But it also became possible for a decent Protestant to die unawares, though still with the blessing of providence and at the time appointed. Moreover, the idea of providence too was capable of further extension. Why should not the time appointed for the death of a decent Protestant be in old age? The germ of this idea already lay in the Old Testament emphases of some Calvinist theology, and in Old Testament promises that a blameless life would be a long one.

Despite these developments, though, a strong version of this claim to long life could not easily flourish with the number of contradicting examples available up to late Victorian times, and for it to acquire plausibility the twentieth-century decline in mortality at earlier ages was probably a necessary condition. Thus a major material factor began to act selectively on these religious ideas, encouraging the early spread in Protestant countries of a new ideal which in Aberdeen became the commonest contemporary conception of a good death—one unaware, swift, and in old age.

This sequence too, then, can be simplified to bring out a by now familiar logic in the way the strata of contemporary Aberdonian thought have developed: a logic of new ideas originating in Reformation debates, which evolve by their own dynamic, and are then eventually sifted by experience of contradicting or confirming material conditions. This and the other sequences I have illustrated do not cover all the historical material which has emerged as being relevant to the topics of this book. I drew attention earlier to the legacy of the past in the relationship between doctor and patient, and in the way illness is coped with and suffering understood; but good explanations for these things must await further explorations by historians. I have discussed, too, the new dynamic at work in ideas about dying. Here the very success of medicine has compelled many deaths not to be quick and unconscious, but to be slow and at least half-aware; and attempts to resolve this contradiction are drawing on both Christian and secularist themes from the past in a fresh way. But in these examples which I have passed over, the picture looks to be much the same as in the examples I have picked out. In this medical side of living, creative thought has played as vital a role as material conditions in the development of contemporary attitudes.

With these historical perspectives, this analysis of Aberdonian culture, and the way in which it has taught its older generation to cope with illness, ageing, and death, can be brought to a close. The Aberdonians depicted here are members of a united and self-confident community; but this is not because their world lacks debate and contradiction. There are areas of strong conformity, but also many areas where conflict is the rule. The culture is united not because it does not contain these contradictions, but because the same people take different sides in different debates. To understand the contradictions, it is necessary to see the contemporary city as a moment in a historical process, and to see that as Aberdonians ponder on illness, old age, and the prospect of death, they are drawing not only on the present stock of knowledge, but on the past which is buried in it. And that past, in turn, derives both from the internal springs of European thought and from the subsequent collision of this thought with material constraints. In Scotland—and not in Scotland alone—understanding demands not only a grasp of the material constraints, but also a recognition of these inner springs, many of which are here retraceable to the Reformation; and it is in this sense that, in contemplating physical limitation and loss, Aberdonians draw on a Protestant legacy.

Notes and References

1. L. Wittgenstein, *Philosophical investigations*, tr. G. E. M. Anscombe, Oxford: Blackwell, 1953, pt.1, sec. 66 f.
2. I. Waddington, 'The role of the hospital in the development of modern medicine', *Sociology*, 7 (1973), 211–24.
3. This is merely a variation on the old point about social cohesion which goes back to G. Simmel, *The web of group affiliations*, tr. R. Bendix, Glencoe: Free Press, 1955.
4. For a recent review of the interpretations of this enigmatic Weberian phrase see J. Thomas, 'Ideology and elective affinity', *Sociology*, 19 (1985), 39–54.
5. T. C. Smout, *A history of the Scottish people 1560–1830*, London: Fontana, 1972, p. 90
6. A. A. Maclaren, *Religion and social class*, London: Routledge, 1974, ch. 7.
7. Smout, *A history of the Scottish people,* pp. 72 f.
8. Maclaren, *Religion and social class*, ch. 7; compare R. Q. Gray, *The labour aristocracy in Victorian Edinburgh*, Oxford University Press, 1976; however, this interpretation is disputed in favour of an indigenous artisan origin for these ideas in N. Abercrombie, S. Hill, and B. S. Turner, *The dominant ideology thesis*, London: Allen and Unwin, 1980, ch. 4

APPENDIX 1

Methods

I noted in the introduction that the evidence used in this book comes chiefly from a qualitative study of two social circles comprising 70 men and women aged 60 and over, and that additional reference is made to random sample data for 619 people of the same age group. Both studies were conducted in the city of Aberdeen in 1978–80. In what follows, the methods of these two studies are outlined in turn, beginning with the Aberdeen Survey, which can be dealt with quite briefly.

The Aberdeen Survey

The sample was drawn from the population of the relevant age group living in their own homes, and was based on GP patient records held in the Primary Care Register. This Register had already been compared with a house-to-house check of residents and their reported GPs at a random sample of addresses in Aberdeen, and had been established as highly reliable. Sampling proceeded in two stages, random sampling of GPs preceding selection of patients. At the second stage patients were stratified into twelve age/sex strata, in five-year age bands, with an open band from age 85 on, each containing 65 people. Interviewing was completed in the first three months of 1980 and resulted in an achieved sample of 619 (79%). This achieved sample, containing almost equal numbers of men and women in each of the five-year cohorts, has been weighted by the appropriate fractions on the few occasions where population estimates of percentages are given. A few tables are also weighted (and marked as such). But for most cross-tabulations unweighted figures have been used in assessing statistical significance (weighted figures differ only trivially).

The questionnaire covered various aspects of health, disability, and psychological functioning, as well as work and retirement, family and social support, daily activities, housing, and finance. The social class measure—the main explanatory variable called upon here—followed the Registrar-General's classification, and related to the main occupation during most of adult life. Where women answered this question by giving the name of a paid occupation, rather than by describing themselves as housewives, they were classified according to their own occupation, not their husband's. Other details of the measures used are noted where relevant in the chapter concerned.

Sampling in the qualitative study

The basis for selecting the sample for the qualitative study rested on two main principles: first, the need, in studying ideas about illness, ageing, and death, to choose people who shared a communication network in which such ideas might be traded; and second, the need to do this while controlling other major variables affecting the experience of health, such as age and social class.

Although ideas about health and ageing can usefully be explored by questioning randomly chosen individuals, there are certain advantages to be hoped for in talking to connected networks of acquaintances. One of these advantages lies in the way in which consistencies and contradictions between the ideas of different people may be pointed and emphasized. Disagreements may be expounded; the story of one person may be used to illustrate another's argument; or stock phrases of their social circle may be picked up and placed in the individual context. Evidence of this kind is valuable in making sure that the contextual implications of an account, which make its meaning much more precise, are fully grasped, and that the contradictions and consistencies which underlie behaviour are clearly brought out.

A second advantage of studying connected networks of acquaintances is the possibility which this implies of picking up some of the processes of persuasion, criticism, and discussion by which conceptions of health and illness are adapted to physical experience and the views of others. These processes can best, of course, be observed over time, and some pattern of revisiting is easily built into a design of this kind.

The design as realized in this study involved two separate social networks, that in the West End comprising 28 individuals in 22 households and that in the Mannoch estate comprising 42 individuals in 31 households. The networks were built up by seeking further introductions from those already interviewed, starting with two or three volunteers each from a retirement club (in the West End) and from a pensioners' association (in the Mannoch estate).

In general, each network consisted, by the end, in three to four 'rings' of growth—(1) the original volunteers, (2) their introductions, (3) the introductions from these introductions, and (4) a scattering of additional people introduced by some members of the third group before the decision was made to halt sampling. Not everyone, naturally, offered an introduction, and when it appeared that enough prospective addresses had already been obtained, introductions were in any case no longer required; hence the introducers formed about a third of each network, and in the remaining two-thirds introductions were not obtained, not sought, or not acted upon. Nevertheless each of the two samples thus obtained satisfied the conditions aimed at, that every member would be directly acquainted with at least one other, and that all the members should be 'reachable'[1] through a minimal number of links of acquaintanceship.

Nearly half of the members of each of these networks were revisited— some, who were pivotal, being visited several times because they provided the main access to news about others. The aims of this pattern of revisiting were twofold. First, it was possible in this way to assess the stability and the behavioural expression of the ideas mentioned, and to pick up the occurrence of new events affecting health, leading to a fresh interview of the person concerned where possible. And second, it was possible to learn something of how sample members saw one another. Further detail on this aspect of the study is provided in Chapter 6.

Control of bias in the qualitative study

To control the possibility of bias implicit in this non-random design, intro-ductions were occasionally steered so that critical variables were represen-ted proportionally to population. Two types of variable were critical in relation to the design outlined: those descriptive of network structure (since channels of introduction were presumably highly dependent on these), and those relating to health, ageing, and the experience of bereavement. The primary factors which influence or reflect the distribution of these latter experiences were assumed to be age, sex, marital status, and social class. Medical resources, in two urban areas which had rapid access to the same teaching hospital, were not regarded as a variable of comparable significance.

The network of acquaintanceship between elderly people in one locality, being dense among the most sociable, sparse among the most isolated, is not easy to represent adequately. In the present case the chief danger was that introductions would tend to be deflected towards members of clubs, and towards elderly people who were regularly involved in social contact, rather than towards those who were isolated. Hence at an early stage introductions were requested to people who were not connected with clubs, and this method of control proved reasonably effective. Thereafter it proved unnecessary to seek introductions to the relatively isolated, for the busy elderly spontaneously made such introductions where cases were known to them, since these cases were a source of anxiety. Comparison can be made with the Aberdeen Survey (Table 16), which matches well. These proportions for the combined networks were approximately reproduced in both the working-class and the middle-class network.

These guidelines, representing the typical structure of social networks in the elderly population, were paralleled, as I have said, by guidelines

Table 16. *Representativeness of the network sample by degree of sociability*

Sociability	Aberdeen Survey (weighted) (%)	Aberdeen networks (%)
Members of clubs	33	36
Not club members, seen by relatives during the week	55	52
Neither club members nor seen by relatives during the week	12	12

designed to represent experience of health, ageing, and bereavement. Health experience has been found repeatedly to be associated most strongly with a conventional distinction between the 'young' elderly (under 75) and the 'old' elderly (75 and over).[2] The match obtained on these age divisions was within 1% of the 1981 Census data for Aberdeen City. This overall match was good, but it was less good in the working-class network, where the 'old' elderly reached 36%, against 25% in the middle-class network. The origin of the bias is worth noting—it arose from the fact that volunteers from the middle-class club for the retired tended to be 'young' elderly, while volunteers from the working-class pensioners' club tended to be 'old' elderly; and from the associated fact that while the 'young' middle-class elderly were often benefactors of a few unrelated older people and would, if their protective instincts were allayed, introduce them, the 'young' working-class elderly seldom knew unrelated people from the generation immediately ahead of them, and were similarly not often known by them. These constraints delayed, rather than prevented, the balancing of the age groups in each network, and further interviewing would have corrected the bias; however I felt the imbalance was insufficiently serious to justify holding up the timetable of analysis.

The other variables considered were sex, marital status, and social class. Sex and marital status have been found to be amongst the measures correlating most strongly with need for community services,[3] and the match obtained with 1981 Census data for those aged 60 and over in Aberdeen City was within 1% on both measures. These overall proportions in the Aberdeen sample were closely similar to those achieved in the middle-class and the working-class network taken separately.

Finally, representation by social class can be compared with the Aberdeen survey, as shown in Table 17.

Experience in analysis, which included a number of additional comparisons with the Aberdeen Survey, suggests that the guidelines used were

Table 17. *Representativeness of the network sample by social class*

	Aberdeen Survey (weighted) (%)	Aberdeen networks (%)
Middle class	35	40
Working class	65	60

quite successful in controlling bias arising from the design of this qualitative study.

Interviews in the qualitative study

Apart from a number of observations made in casual encounters or in social events in which I took part, my chief qualitative material came from interviews. Questions in the initial interview followed an aide-memoire, and the sequence of introduction and initial questioning was relatively standardized. Having mentioned the person introducing me, I said where I came from; that I was interested in the health history of older people and how it affected their life; and that I was gathering material through conversations rather than by questionnaire because this enabled people to raise the issues which were important to them. I then explained that I usually began with where people had lived in their life, as this gave me an idea of the background to the conversation; and in the course of this opening residential history I tried to make sure that I had acquired the usual data on household composition, siblings and children and parents (if alive), occupational history, church or associational membership, and current patterns of sociability. The next step was to introduce health history, in which the initial task was to define the chronology of past conditions, and the nature of current conditions, with their associated disabilities, and services or treatment received. As I listened to this descriptive material, I also paid careful attention to the form of the description and its evaluative overtones, and thus the third stage, involving the exploration of these evaluative notions, began, partially overlapping with the preceding descriptive stage. The chief evaluative topics which I had prepared myself to attend to were relations with the doctor, attitudes to illness, the alternative activities envisaged in the event of falling sick, ways of keeping healthy, expectations of the future (especially with regard to getting older, moving house, institutionalization, and so forth), and attitudes to death—attitudes to one's own death, experience of others dying, whether the dying person should know about it, the appropriate setting for it (not discussed in this book), and views on prolonging or taking life. Where necessary, direct questions were asked on these topics; but from this stage onward the

unpredictable element of the conversation—the progressive unfolding
of the lines of thought already implicit in the initial autobiographical
accounts—was the governing factor.

Interviews lasted on average for two hours, and the initial interview was
tape-recorded unless the person concerned did not wish this. Field-notes
were also written up immediately after the interview (often including,
as usually happens, important material which only emerged when the
tape recorder was stopped); and second and subsequent interviews were
recorded entirely in field-notes.

Analysis in the qualitative study

The first part of the analysis was straightforward, and is represented in the
description of the range of Aberdonian understandings in the early part of
each chapter. This description relied simply on indexing passages of transcripts or field-notes as relevant to the topic of a chapter, after which the
task was one of grouping similar passages together for illustration and
précis until the material was exhausted. The similarities a researcher
perceives are of course responsive to the existing literature, but a good
description situates and qualifies the more general terms of the literature,
and points to limiting cases where the similarity becomes rather marginal;
and this was the aim of this part of the analysis.

There is nothing novel in these descriptive procedures; in so far as there
is a novel aspect of the analysis, it lies in what followed—in the procedures
for locating the statements in the material whose logical patterns were of
interest, and for revealing their relation to assumptions about work, social
class, and religion. An account of some of these procedures has appeared
elsewhere,[4] and in what follows I refer only summarily to issues which are
illustrated and discussed at length in that account, and I expand on some
other matters which reflect analyses performed since.

The statements of interest in the present study were those that were
autobiographical, relating to the coping beliefs, attitudes, and behaviour
of the person speaking, or of 'we' groups which necessarily included that
person. They were statements which bore not solely on the past, but also
on the present or future, and many of them were repeated in varying contexts. Hence for the most part they were generalizing statements, easily
identifiable by such features as verbs in the generalizing present. But statements of intention or expectation were also included, together with the
occasional occurrence of general statements about the past which, while
not applicable to the present situation, were sufficiently endorsed to act as
a resource if similar situations recurred in the future. Purely narrative
statements, however—those concerning a single event, or a sequence of

single events in the past—were excluded, except in a few cases where close similarities in the description of several such events suggested a generalized pattern. Narratives were indeed common, but they were usually tied to some form of generalized conclusion, so their import was not ignored; and pure narratives, without any such conclusion, were not common enough to need special consideration.

These procedures isolated statements which had present personal relevance for coping; and patterns at once began to emerge, because many of these statements were logically connected to another statement, forming a premiss. For example, a narrative of illness included the following linked statement:

"People have said, oh well this [the illness] is what comes with you retiring early—which indeed has got nothing to do with it at all."

For the sake of simplicity, such connections can be reformulated and noted in a standardized summary form; and with autobiographical statements of the kind concerned here it is ordinarily possible to use the simplest form: two clauses of the structure 'If A, then B'. At the same time, any contradictions which seem to arise between such statements can be noted. Thus in the example given, it is said that others connect the speaker's illness with early retirement, suggesting the reformulation:

'If I retire early, then I am more likely to be ill.'

—which can be noted as (retire early > ill). But the speaker at the same time denies this premiss, so contradiction, and the possibility of a personal dilemma, can be noted by adding NOT (retire early > ill), and by flagging the passage for future reference. People may express no premiss or varying numbers of premisses on a given topic, as I noted in the introduction to this book, and when there are two premisses one may imply the other, or one may contradict the other, or the two may merely be contingent. The business of interpreting these relationships is further discussed in Appendix 2.

This part of the analysis done, it is then possible to classify all these premisses into groups, and to represent each group by a typical premiss, or by a longer description, according to the needs of the argument at that point. Thus in the example given, the premiss (retire early > ill) is akin to premisses from other people's transcripts which argued that work was a precondition of health, and all these premisses form a group which is described in part of Chapter 7. And at the same time this group is itself a subclass of a larger group which is represented by the typical premiss which appears in Chapter 1:

1.1 (b)   If I do not keep up my normal activity, I make my condition worse.

And finally, connections and contradictions between one typified group of premisses and another can be explored to reveal the relationships between major aspects of the culture. So, in the example given, the group of premisses about work and health already outlined is opposed to another group of premisses about alternative ways of living, one of which (quoted in Chapter 1) was used by the speaker in defending the decision to retire early.

The form of this analysis is therefore logical; but logic is helpful not because the interpretation is mechanical—nothing could be further from the truth—but because logical procedures help to make the hermeneutic process as systematic and precise as possible. The analysis still rests ultimately on the ability of the one who questions and the one who responds, as also of the writer and the reader, to negotiate shared meanings. And so one question which arises is how much agreement about these analytical operations can be achieved. This raises complex issues which are still under exploration in both quantitative and qualitative research. One way of outlining some of the issues is to compare typical survey procedures. The following table presents some suggestive correspondences:

Levels of analysis

	Logical analysis	Quantitative analysis
Level 1	Describing the range of responses obtained.	Coding variables and obtaining frequency distributions.
Level 2	Identifying and classifying pairs of statements linked into a premiss.	Cross-tabulating/correlating pairs of variables.
Level 3	Identifying and classifying relations between groups of premisses.	Operations on correlation matrices and other multivariate techniques.

Critiques of survey research have in the past focused on the element of judgement in coding decisions at level 1. Judgement is frequently used at this point, but the reasoning involved in its use generally remains unrecorded. Instead, the tests of reliability and validity which are made assess the level of agreement between the coded measure and other indicators. Agreement between the respondent and other observers, agreement with other evidence from the same respondent, and agreement between coders or raters are among the principal tests used.

The element of judgement in survey research at level 2 has not proved to be so measurable. The principal debate has been about the extent to which the interpretation of a relationship can and should be pre-specified (the hypothesis-testing approach). But while this, when it is feasible, clearly helps to prevent the interpretation being biased by chance findings, judgement remains in the interpretation which is chosen for a correlation, and in the alternative interpretations canvassed. This element of judgement is usually assessed by readers for themselves from the text of the analysis.

Finally, at level 3, various forms of statistical modelling abound, but there are usually elements of judgement in the assumptions about causal priority which are made whenever any particular version of a model is run. Again these are assessed directly from the argument of the text.

Analogous problems of judgement arise at the corresponding levels of the qualitative analysis conducted here, and there are similar problems in measuring them. To some extent, certainly, one can follow the approach which measures agreement with other indicators. In Chapter 6 I have discussed evidence of agreement between responses made to me and to other observers, and throughout this book I have been concerned with the internal consistency of each person's responses. But I also made some tests of agreement between coders or assessors. For example, I tested agreement in indexing a random sample of transcript and fieldnote pages as relevant to the key topics of illness and death. The passages were indexed by myself and either of two colleagues, working in pairs on three separate occasions, following a brief initial trial. All passages indexed by either member of the pair were pooled, and over 85% of the pooled passages were agreed on each occasion. This is not in itself a particularly remarkable finding, but it at least suggests that potential levels of agreement at level 1, and the problems of judgement, are of a similar order in quantitative and qualitative research. One could proceed further to test agreement about selected sub-categories in a given topic, but this is an essentially similar task, and I have thought it more useful to explore what might be measurable in the element of judgement at level 2.

In interpreting linkages between statements at level 2, one measurable task is that of identifying passages of text in which relevant premises—here autobiographical premises about coping—are located. The element of judgement thus measured necessarily includes and reflects some of the disagreement involved in indexing already discussed (though much of that disagreement was over references which for present purposes are trivial); but it adds to it any variability in identifying relevant logical connections. In the same exercise already referred to, out of passages of text identified by either assessor as containing relevant logical connections, over 70% were agreed on each occasion.[5]

At such points, therefore, some of the judgemental elements involved in the present method are measurable; but, as with all social science methods, there remain many such elements which can only be assessed by the reader directly from the text of the analysis. At level 3 in particular, as I have argued in the introduction to this book, many of the judgements involved in interpreting larger structures of ideas can be exposed by analysis of case studies.

A final question which often arises from the comparison of qualitative and quantitative methods is how far qualitative categories should be treated in a statistical fashion, with numbers of cases under each category being counted and cross-tabulated. In the present method, as I have said, the search is for logical rather than probabilistic relationships between categories; but counting can still be useful. I have in fact counted cases for every classification made, but after several experiments at ways of presenting such counts in a summary, I have concluded that they are more tedious and confusing than broad textual indications like 'some', 'most', 'a few', or proportional indications of only a slightly more definite kind. This is appropriate because a qualitative sample like the present one is not designed to estimate proportions in anything other than the grossest possible way—where better estimates are needed I turn to the Aberdeen Survey. And it is also appropriate because in the present study I have tried, as I said in the introduction to this book, to avoid equating structures of ideas with types of people—an equation which becomes insidious in proportion as the analysis identifies ideas solely by the groups who hold them. Thus while counting is a useful discipline, compelling precision in description and classification, it is a part of the analytic machinery which I have left in the background.

These are the forms of analysis which underpin the greater part of the text. However, other supplementary forms of analysis have also been used. Apart from the areas where the Aberdeen Survey is referred to, there are some circumstances in which the comparative method known as analytic induction[6] helps to consolidate the conclusions drawn. The chief circumstance is where one reaches the margins of people's awareness about their own culture. In these marginal areas, a minority may argue for ways of responding which large numbers of others have not even thought about; and while this minority may give strong indications, in the resources which they assume, of the reason why the difference occurs, one must check by comparison that these resources are lacking amongst the majority, and it is necessary to account fully for deviant cases. These supplementary procedures have been especially useful in the chapters on social class and religion.

Notes and References

1. J. C. Mitchell, *Social networks in urban situations*, Manchester University Press, 1969.
2. See, e.g. M. Abrams, *Beyond three score and ten*, London: Age Concern, 1978.
3. R. G. A. Williams, 'Rationing: how it is done with community services for the disabled', *Int. Rehab. Med.* 2 (1980), 160–6.
4. R. G. A. Williams, 'Logical analysis as a qualitative method', *Sociol. of Health and Illness*, 3 (1981), 141–87.
5. 'Passages of text' are units of sense which are not easily standardized, but in the present context they usually comprise sentences, or sequences of two or three sentences on the same topic, only occasionally rising to paragraph or page length when a moral is drawn from a piece of narrative.
6. This method is amongst those reviewed in J. C. Mitchell, 'Case and situation analysis', *Sociol. Rev.* 31 (1983), 187–211, and in J. Katz, 'A theory of qualitative methodology: the social system of analytic field-work', in R. M. Emerson (ed.), *Contemporary field research,* Toronto: Little Brown, 1983.

APPENDIX 2

Assessing consistency and contradiction over time

A prospective record of natural verbal behaviour reveals, unsurprisingly, that there is always an irreducible element of discrepancy in the phraseology of somebody who, at two different times, expresses what is recognizably the 'same' attitude. These discrepancies mean that later formulations have to be seen not as identical with, but as evolved from earlier formulations in the context of changing circumstances—some of these circumstances being related merely to the order of the conversation, and some to intervening processes of thought and experience. Thus a measure of the distance of this evolution, in logical terms, is necessary.

This logical bridge between two utterances is, in fixed-choice attitude questions, constructed by the respondents, who may be supposed to determine their relation to the attitude statement provided by the questionnaire in steps such as the following:

1. P (the attitude statement)
2. Q (my attitude)
3. If Q then P

I agree with P

These reasoning processes, using the interpolation of (one hopes) trite shared premises, are often spoken aloud to interviewers and are part of their normal experience. Correspondingly, at least two such processes may be supposed to take place when attitudes are measured at two points of time. Thus, with fixed-choice items used prospectively, a minimum of two premises will be interpolated between the questionnaire statement and the respondent's natural statement, to which the researcher has no access.

In the present method, the aim is to transfer the onus of interpolation from the respondent to the researcher. Ideally, of course, both should co-operate in the task; and in the present material some clarifications were obtained at interview where apparent later contradictions could safely be queried without 'leading' the person concerned. But in order to avoid forcing consistency on people, such help had to be limited, and some interpretation had necessarily to be done by the researcher alone. What matters is that interpretation is based on the original words and context, and that the premiss interpolated in assessing contradiction or consistency can thus be retrieved.

In what follows, I give four varied examples of 'adequate' and 'marginal' interpolations. 'Marginal' interpolations are included because even an ambiguous disconfirming instance needs examination—but such instances need to be clearly marked as ambiguous.

Adequate interpolations

The examples which follow examine consistency over time, defining this, in the way already sketched, as a relation of implication between two statements obtained by interpolating other assumptions which are shared. Contradiction over time is assessed in an exactly corresponding way; and statements which do not meet the criteria for either consistency or contradiction are regarded as contingent. I should note that I use the word 'consistency' in this strong sense chiefly for continuity over time in Chapter 6 (elsewhere I use terms like 'implication'), and otherwise, where the interest is primarily in contradiction, I generally use 'consistency' in its weak sense to include any relation, implied or contingent, which is not contradictory.

Taking the example already used in Appendix 1, we can first compare the following two tape-recorded statements, which were separated by eleven months:

(1) 'People have said, oh well this [bad health] is what comes with you retiring early—which indeed has got nothing to do with it at all.'
(2) 'People say oh you shouldn't have retired so young. But that had nothing to do with the fact that I had this [bad health].'

The correspondence here is remarkably close, and to say that these two comments are consistent is to rely mainly on the correct identification of 'this' as the same, or virtually the same, bout of bad health, and to interpolate the uninteresting premiss: when I retired so young, I retired early.

If the example just given represents one of the safest attributions of consistency, the example which follows represents a more usual case. The following statements, both recorded in field-notes, were separated by seven months:

(1) These houses are for invalids—they never show themselves. It used to be mill cottages. It was really friendly in those days.
(2) These next door houses are invalid houses. It's depressing living down here—they've never a good word to say for themselves.

The connection here is the behaviour expected of invalids; and to say that the expectations expressed on each occasion are consistent is to interpolate a premiss such as the following:

If the place is not friendly, it is depressing.

The conclusion then follows on both occasions that if people are invalids, to live near them is depressing; and thus the statements are consistent.

Sometimes not one but two premises may be interpolated in order to argue consistency. The following two statements, the first taped, the second recorded in field-notes, were separated by three months:

(1) (after description of walking habits)
  (Q): You get out and about quite a bit, do you?
  (A): Oh yes, now, oh yes, as long as I'm able and I'm going. The doctor said to keep on the move, keep my legs from stiffening, you see.

(2) She commented that people die early these days—they don't walk enough, even the policemen. We had no cars, we *had* to walk.

The element of consistency here lies in the powers attributed to walking or keeping on the move, but in order to secure the implication in a more formal fashion two premises are required such as the following:

If my legs don't stiffen, my health is good.
If their health is good, people are less likely to die early.

The implication then follows on both occasions that if people keep walking, they are less likely to die early.

Marginal interpolations

The examples given so far are all regarded here as legitimate imputations of consistency for present purposes; finally, I give an example of a marginal case where there is more doubt about imputing consistency for the present purpose, though the imputation could easily be made by way of a hypothesis aimed at guiding further questioning. The following two statements, both recorded in field-notes, were separated by a little over one month:

(1) (in view of his hip problem)
  (Q): Is there anything you used to do that you don't do now?
  (A): Well I have a large garden out there and I dug that all over last summer and put tatties in. I took my own time.

(2) [Since he can't bend for bowls] I raised the garden. He doesn't dung it—you don't need that now, and the last lot they had was all straw. He uses Growmore, and gets neeps [turnips], leeks, and other vegetables as well as tatties, some of which are the envy of Mr P. [neighbour].

In both these notes, the person answering is recorded as resisting any implication in the questions asked that because of his hip he does not do the garden as well as ever; and in each case he offers grounds for this conclusion by citing the special tactics which he adopts—taking his time, using Growmore instead of dung. But there are two difficulties: first his method of resisting the question's implication is indirect—on each separate occasion one might have asked, perhaps he did not catch the question properly?—and thus the premiss 'It is not the case that if I have a hip problem, I do not do the garden well' is very much 'understood' on both occasions; and second, consistency can only be secured by two further premisses being 'understood', such as these:

If I take my time, I use a special tactic.
If I use Growmore, I use a special tactic.

With these additional assumptions, it may finally be concluded that, on both occasions, so long as I use special tactics, it is not the case that if I have a hip problem I do not do the garden well. However, in arriving at this demonstration of consistency, premisses have been four times 'understood', or interpolated, by the researcher; and for the present purpose this seems too liberal.

The small number of premisses 'understood' is thus one factor in the judgement of consistency; the other, clearly, is the assessment of these understandings as platitudinous. This latter judgement appeals to understandings shared with the speaker and with the reader, and is perhaps best exposed by citing examples, as I have done.

APPENDIX 3

Typical premisses identified in Part I

1.1 *Illness as controlled by normal living*

(a) If I keep up my normal activity, I help myself to prevent or cope with illness, and/or

(b) If I do not keep up my normal activity, I make my condition worse.

1.2 *Illness as a continuous struggle*

Even if I am partly restricted, I do not stop struggling to perform my normal activities.

1.3 *Illness as an alternative way of life*

If I am seriously restricted by illness, I develop alternative interests which offer positive rewards

1.4 *Illness as a loss to be endured*

(a) If I am seriously restricted by illness, I am finished, and/or

(b) If I am seriously restricted by illness, I forget about my past interests, and/or

(c) If I am seriously restricted by illness, I pass the time with distasteful alternatives.

1.5 *Illness as a release from effort*

If I am restricted by illness, I give some things up with relief.

2.1 *Early old age as a liberation*

As I am (we are) retired, I am free to follow my interests.

2.2 *Early old age as a setback*

(a) As I am (we are) retired, my interests and social connections are reduced, and/or

(b) If I encounter the younger generation, I may have trouble.

2.3 *Early old age as a repairing of defences*

(a) As I am (we are) retired, I keep my interests going, and/or

(b) As I am (we are) retired, I keep up my social connections.

2.4 *Late old age as resistable*

If I keep active, I will always keep real old age at bay.

2.5 *Late old age as a surrender*

If I become really old, I may legitimately give up my activities.

3.1 *Natural death*

We ought to die when, and only when, we are old and not too old.

3.2 *Prepared death*
(*a*) We only die when our time has come, and/or
(*b*) We ought to be ready when we die.
3.3 *A quick death*
If we die quickly, we die the proper way.
3.4 *Death after reunion*
When people are dying, those close to them must spend time with them before they die.
3.5 *Death aware*
If I am dying, I wish to know it.
3.6 *Silence about death*
(*a*) If I am dying, I do not wish to know it, and/or
(*b*) One should not tell people if they are dying
3.7 *Euthanasia*
If I am a burden, or if I am in pain or virtually unconscious, and have no pleasure, I wish to be helped to die.
3.8 *The sanctity of life*
Nobody should take a person's life.

4.1 *Reunion*
When we die, we are at once united with our family in the next world.
4.2 *Annihilation*
When we die, nothing of us lives on except in others' memories.
4.3 *The sanctity of the body*
It is a religious act to visit the grave and keep it up.
4.4 *The interests of the living*
The body should be disposed of so as to minimize problems for the living.
4.5 *The uniqueness of loss*
The person who has died is unique and irreplaceable.
4.6 *The need for replacement*
Grief must be got over and a new life begun.

5.1 *Obligatory delay in consulting*
If I have symptoms, I don't go easily to the doctor
5.2 *Realism in consulting*
If I have symptoms, I am not afraid to know the truth.
5.3 *Control of decisions*
When I consult the doctor, I want to make my own decisions.
5.4 *Obedience to orders*
When I consult, I ought to take the doctor's advice.
5.5 *Expectation of disagreement*
When I consult, I don't always agree with the doctor's opinion.

Bibliography

Abegglen, J., *The Japanese factory*, London: Asia Publishing House, 1958.

Abercrombie, N., Hill, S., and Turner, B. S., *The dominant ideology thesis*, London: Allen and Unwin, 1980.

Abrams, M., *Beyond three score and ten*, London: Age Concern, 1978.

Abrams, P., *Historical sociology*, Shepton Mallet: Open Books, 1982.

Ajzen, I. and Fishbein, M., Attitude-behaviour relations: a theoretical analysis and review of empirical research, *Psychol. Bull.* 84 (1977), 888–918.

—— and —— *Understanding attitudes and predicting social behaviour*, Englewood Cliffs: Prentice-Hall, 1980.

Alexander, W., *Johnny Gibb of Gushetneuk*, Edinburgh: David Douglas, 1884.

Allan, J. R., *Farmer's boy*, London: Longman, 1975, orig. Methuen, 1935.

Amoss, P. T., and Harrell, S. (eds.), *Other ways of growing old*, Stanford University Press, 1981.

Anon., *In memoriam, William McCombie of Tillyfour*, Aberdeen: privately printed, 1880.

Antonovsky, A., *Unravelling the mystery of health: how people manage stress and stay well*, London: Jossey-Bass, 1987.

Arensberg, C. M., and Kimball, S. T., *Family and community in Ireland*, Harvard University Press, 1940.

Ariès, P., *The hour of our death*, tr. Weaver, H., London: Allen Lane, 1981.

Armstrong, D., *The political anatomy of the body*, Cambridge University Press, 1983.

—— 'Silence and truth in death and dying', *Soc. Sci. and Med.* 24 (1987), 651–7.

Askham, J., *Report of a pilot study on the choice of place of care for patients in the later stages of cancer*, Institute of Medical Sociology, Aberdeen, 1981.

Beatty, N. L., *The craft of dying*, New Haven: Yale University Press, 1970.

de Beausobre, I., *Creative suffering*, SLG Press, 1984.

Becon, T., *The sicke man's salve*, Edinburgh: Thomas Vautroullier, 1584.

Bellaby, P., Cleverly, S. J., and Sidaway, J. S., 'The recession and the effort bargain', Dept. Sociology and Soc. Anth., University of Keele.

Bem, D. J., 'Self-perception: an alternative interpretation of cognitive dissonance phenomena, *Psychol. Rev.* 74 (1967), 188–200.

Bem, D. J., 'Self-perception theory', in Berkowitz, L. (ed.), *Advances in experimental social psychology* vol. 6, London: Academic Press, 1972.

Bengtson, V. L., and Cutler, N. E., 'Generations and intergenerational relations', in Binstock, R. H., and Shanas, E. (eds.), *Handbook of ageing and the social sciences*, New York: Van Nostrand Rheinhold, 1976.

Bentler, P. M., and Speckart, G., 'Models of attitude-behaviour relations', *Psychol. Rev.* 86 (1979), 452–64.

Berger, P. L., and Luckmann, T., *The social construction of reality*, London: Allen Lane, 1967.

Bewley, B. R., and Bland, J. M., 'Academic performance and social factors related to cigarette smoking by schoolchildren', *Brit. J. Prev. Soc. Med.* 31 (1977), 18–24.

Blaxter, M., 'Self-definition of health status and consulting rates in primary care', *Quarterly J. Social Affairs*, 1 (1985), 131–71.

—— and Paterson, E., *Mothers and daughters: a three-generational study of health attitudes and behaviour*, London: Heinemann, 1982.

Bloor, M. J., 'Professional autonomy and client exclusion: a study in ENT clinics', in Wadsworth, M., and Robinson, D. (eds.), *Studies in everyday medical life*, London: Martin Robertson, 1976.

—— and Horobin, G. W., 'Conflict and conflict resolution in doctor/patient interactions', in Cox, C., and Mead, A. (eds.), *A sociology of medical practice*, London: Collier-Macmillan, 1975.

Boswell, D. M., 'Personal crises and the mobilisation of the social network', in Mitchell, J. C. (ed.), *Social networks in urban situations*, Manchester University Press, 1969.

du Boulay, S., *Cicely Saunders: the founder of the modern hospice movement*, London: Hodder and Stoughton, 1984.

Bourdieu, P., *Distinction: a social critique of the judgement of taste*, tr. Nice, R., London: Routledge, 1984.

Brierley, P. (ed.), *Prospects for the eighties*, London: Bible Society, 1980.

—— (ed.), *The UK Christian handbook: 1983 edition*, London: The Evangelical Alliance, The Bible Society, and MARC Europe, 1982.

—— and Macdonald, F., *Prospects for Scotland*, National Bible Society of Scotland and MARC Europe, 1985.

Brown, C. G., *The social history of religion in Scotland since 1730*, London: Methuen, 1987.

Bury, M., 'Chronic illness as biographical disruption', *Sociol. of Health and Illness*, 4 (1982), 167–82.

Buxton, J., *Religion and healing in Mandari*, Oxford University Press, 1973.

Calnan, M., 'Clinical uncertainty: is it a problem in the doctor–patient relationship', *Sociol. of Health and Illness*, 6 (1984), 74–85.

Bibliography

Calnan, M., *Health and illness*, London: Tavistock, 1987.

—— and Rutter, D.R., Do health beliefs predict health behaviour? An analysis of breast self-examination', *Soc. Sci. and Med.* 22 (1986), 673–8.

—— and —— 'Do health beliefs predict health behaviour? A follow-up analysis of breast self-examination', *Soc. Sci. and Med.* 26 (1988), 463–5.

Cameron, D. K., *Willie Gavin, crofter man*, London: Gollancz, 1980.

Cannadine, D., 'War and death, grief and mourning in modern Britain', in Whaley J. (ed.), *Mirrors of mortality: studies in the social history of death*, London: Europa, 1981.

Carter, I. R., *Farm life in north-east Scotland 1840–1914*, Edinburgh: Donald, 1979.

Cartwright, A., *Human relations and hospital care*, London: Routledge, 1964.

—— *Patients and their doctors*, London: Routledge, 1967.

—— and O'Brien, M., 'Social class variations in health care', in Stacey, M. (ed.), *The sociology of the NHS*, Sociol. Rev. Monograph no. 22, 1976.

—— and Anderson, R., *General practice revisited*, London: Tavistock, 1981.

Cassell, E. T., *The healer's art*, London: Pelican, 1978.

Census 1981, *Key statistics for local authorities,* London: HMSO, 1984.

Charmaz, K., 'Loss of self: a fundamental form of suffering in the chronically ill', *Sociology of Health and Illness*, 5 (1983), 168–95.

Christian, W. A., *Person and God in a Spanish valley*, London: Seminar Press, 1972.

Church Information Office, *On dying well: an Anglican contribution to the debate on euthanasia*, 1974.

Cicero, Marcus Tullius, *Cato major, or, a treatise on old age*, tr. Logan, Glasgow: R. Urie, 1751.

—— 'On old age', in *Selected Works*, tr. Michael Grant, London: Penguin, 1960.

Converse, P., 'The nature of belief systems in mass publics', in Apter, D.(ed.), *Ideology and discontent*, New York: Free Press, 1964.

Cornwell, J., *Hard-earned lives: accounts of health and illness from East London,* London: Tavistock, 1984.

Currer, C., 'Concepts of mental well- and ill-being: the case of Pathan mothers in Britain', in Currer, C. and Stacey, M. (eds.), *Concepts of health, illness and disease*, Leamington: Berg, 1986.

Currie, R., Gilbert, A., and Horsley, L., *Churches and churchgoers: patterns of church growth in the British Isles since 1700*, Oxford University Press, 1977.

Danforth, L. M., *The death rituals of rural Greece*, Princeton University Press, 1982.

Davis, F., *Passage through crisis*, Indianapolis: Bobbs-Merrill, 1963.

Dickson, T., and McLachlan, H., 'Scottish capitalism and Weber's Protestant ethic theses', *Sociology*, 17 (1983), 560–8.

Department of Health and Social Security, *Health and personal social services statistics for England*, London: HMSO, 1982.

Directory for the public worship of God, in *Westminster confession of faith*, Edinburgh: Blackwood, 1928.

Dore, R., *British factory, Japanese factory*, London: Allen and Unwin, 1973.

Douglas, M., *Natural symbols*, London: Pelican, 1973.

—— and Baron Isherwood, *The world of goods: towards an anthropology of consumption*, London: Allen Lane, 1979.

Douglas, W. A., *Death in Murelaga*, London: University of Washington Press, 1969.

Earthrowl, B., and Stacey, M., 'Social class and children in hospital', *Soc. Sci. and Med.* 11 (1977), 83–8.

Elias, N., *The loneliness of the dying*, tr. Jephcott, E., Oxford: Blackwell, 1985.

Festinger, L., Riecken, H. W., and Schachter, S., *When prophecy fails*, University of Minnesota Press, 1956.

Field, D., 'The social definition of illness', in Tuckett, D. (ed.), *An introduction to medical sociology*, London: Tavistock, 1976.

Finlayson, A., and McEwen, J., *Coronary heart disease and patterns of living*, London: Croom Helm, 1977.

Fishbein, M., 'Persuasive communication', in Bennett, A. E. (ed.), *Communication between doctors and patients*, Oxford University Press, 1976.

Foner, A., 'Age stratification and conflict in political life', *Amer. Sociol. Rev.* 39 (1974), 187–96.

Fontana, A., *The last frontier*, London: Sage, 1977.

Forester, T., 'Do the British sincerely want to be rich?' *New Society*, 40 (1977), 158–61.

Foucault, M., *The birth of the clinic*, London: Tavistock, 1973.

Freidson, E., *Professional dominance*, New York: Atherton, 1970.

—— *Profession of medicine*, New York: Dodd, Mead and Co., 1971.

Fryer, D., and Payne, R. L., 'Proactive behaviour in unemployment: findings and implications', *Leisure Studies*, 3 (1984), 273–95.

Gallie, D., *Social inequality and class radicalism in France and Britain*, Cambridge University Press, 1983.

Gaullier, X., 'Economic crisis and old age policies in France', *Ageing and Society*, 2 (1982), 165–82.

van Gennep, A., *Rites of passage*, tr. Vizedom, M. B., and Caffee, G. L., Chicago University Press, 1960.

Geyer-Kordesch, J., Cultural habits of illness: the Enlightened and Pious in eighteenth century Germany', in Porter, R. (ed.), *Patients and practitioners*, Cambridge University Press, 1985.

Gilbert, A. D., *The making of post-Christian Britain*, London: Longman, 1980.

Gilhooly, M. L. M., Berkeley, J. S., McCann, K., Gibling, F., and Murray, K., 'Truth telling with dying cancer patients', *Palliative Medicine*, 2 (1988), 64–71.

Gittings, C., *Death, burial and the individual in early modern England*, London: Croom Helm, 1984.

Glaser, B. G., and Strauss, A. L., *Awareness of dying*, Chicago: Aldine, 1965.

Goffman, E., *The presentation of self in everyday life*, New York: Doubleday, 1959.

—— *Frame analysis*, London: Penguin, 1975.

Goldthorpe, J. H., and Payne, C., 'Trends in intergenerational class mobility in England and Wales 1972–1983, *Sociology*, 20 (1986), 1–24.

Goody, J. (ed.), *Family and inheritance: rural society in Western Europe 1200–1800*, Cambridge University Press, 1978.

Gordon, G., *Role theory and illness*, New Haven: College and University Press, 1966.

Gorer, G., *Death, grief and mourning in contemporary Britain*, London: Cresset Press, 1965.

Gorz, A., *Paths to paradise: on the liberation from work*, tr. Imrie, M., London: Pluto Press, 1985.

Grassic Gibbon, Lewis, *A Scots quair*, London: Pan Books, 1973.

Gray, R. Q., *The labour aristocracy in Victorian Edinburgh*, Oxford University Press, 1976.

Gutman, H. G., *Work, culture and society in industrialising America*, New York: Random House, 1966.

Habermas, J., *Knowledge and human interests*, tr. Shapiro, J. J., London: Heinemann, 1972.

Halpern, S., 'What the public thinks of the NHS', *Health and Soc. Servs. J.* (6 June 1985), 703–4.

Hannay, D. R., *The symptom iceberg*, London: Routledge, 1979.

Herlihy, D., 'Growing old in the Quattrocento', in Stearns, P. N. (ed.), *Old age in pre-industrial society*, New York: Holmes and Meier, 1982.

Hertz, R., *Death and the right hand*, tr. Needham, R. & C., Aberdeen University Press, 1960.

Herzlich, C., *Health and illness*, tr. Graham, H. D., London: Academic Press, 1973.

—— and Pierret, J., *Malades d'hier, malades d'aujourd'hui*, Paris: Payot, 1984.

Highet, J., 'Great Britain: Scotland', in Mol, H. (ed.), *Western religion: a country by country sociological enquiry*, The Hague: Mouton, 1972.

Hill, M., *A sociology of religion*, London: Heinemann, 1973.

Hindess, B., ' "Interests" in political analysis', in Law, J. (ed.), *Power, action and belief: a new sociology of knowledge?*, Sociol. Rev. Monographs no. 32, London: Routledge, 1986.

Hochschild, A., *The unexpected community: portrait of an old age subculture*, Berkeley: University of California Press, 1973.

Hornsby-Smith, M. P., Lee, R. M., and Reilly, P. A., 'Common religion and customary religion: a critique and a proposal', *Rev. Relig. Research*, 26 (1985), 244–52.

d'Houtaud, A. and Field, M. G., 'The image of health: variations in perceptions by social class in a French population', *Sociol. of Health and Illness*, 6 (1984), 30–60.

Huntington, R., and Metcalf, P., *Celebrations of death: the anthropology of mortuary rituals*, Cambridge University Press, 1979.

Illich, I., *Limits to medicine*, London: Penguin, 1977.

Information Services Division, *Scottish health statistics 1980*, Edinburgh: HMSO, 1982.

Inglis, B., *The book of the back*, London: Ebury Press, 1978.

Jahoda, M., *Employment and unemployment*, Cambridge University Press, 1982.

Jefferys, M., and Sachs, H., *Rethinking general practice*, London: Tavistock, 1983.

Jewson, N. D., 'The disappearance of the sick man from medical cosmology 1770–1870', *Sociology*, 10 (1976), 225–44.

John Paul II, *Salvifici doloris*, Apostolic letter of the supreme pontiff on suffering, Catholic Truth Society, 1984.

Jones, I. G., and Cameron, D., 'Social class analysis—an embarrassment to epidemiology', *Community Medicine*, 6 (1984), 37–46.

Jowell R., and Airey, C. (eds.), *British social attitudes: the 1984 report*, London: Gower, 1984.

—— and Witherspoon, S., *British social attitudes: the 1985 report*, London: Gower, 1985.

Kanter, R., 'Work in a new America', *Daedalus*, 107 (Winter 1978), 47–78.

Katz, J., 'A theory of qualitative methodology: the social system of analytic fieldwork', in Emerson, R. M. (ed.), *Contemporary field research*, Toronto: Little Brown, 1983.

Keith-Ross, J., *Old people, new lives: community creation in a retirement residence*, University of Chicago Press, 1977.

Kelman, H. C., 'Attitudes are alive and well and gainfully employed in the sphere of action', *Amer. Psychologist*, 29 (1974), 310–24.

Kleinman, A., *Patients and healers in the context of culture*, London: University of California Press, 1980.

Lamb, Charles, 'The superannuated man', in *Prose works*, vol. 3, London: Edward Moxon, 1836.

Lamerton, R., review of Veatch, R., 'Death, dying and the biological revolution', in *J. Med. Ethics* (1977), 3, 194–5.

Larner, C., *Enemies of God: the witch hunt in Scotland*, London: Chatto and Windus, 1981.

Lazarus, R. S., and Folkman, S., *Stress, appraisal and coping*, New York: Springer, 1984.

Lessnoff, M., 'Protestant ethic and profit motive in the Weber thesis', *Int. J. Sociol. and Soc. Pol.* 1 (1981), 1–18.

Lewis, G., *Illness in a Sepik society*, London: Athlone Press, 1975.

Lloyd-George, D., Speech at the Second Reading of the Old Age Pensions Bill, *Hansard* (15th June 1908).

Locker, D., *Symptoms and illness*, London: Tavistock, 1981.

Lockwood, D., 'Sources of variation in working class images of society', *Sociol. Rev.* 14 (1966), 249–67.

Lofland, L. H., *The craft of dying: the modern face of death*, London: Sage, 1978.

Lucas, F. L. (ed.), *Tennyson: poetry and prose*, 'Introduction', Oxford University Press, 1947.

Luckmann, T., *The invisible religion*, London: Macmillan, 1967.

McIntosh, J., *Communication and awareness in a cancer ward*, London: Croom Helm, 1977.

Macintyre, S., 'Old age as a social problem', in Dingwall, R., and Heath, C. (eds.), *Health care and health knowledge*, London: Croom Helm, 1977.

Mackenzie, H., *The city of Aberdeen*, Third Statistical Account of Scotland, London: Oliver and Boyd, 1953.

McKinlay, J. B., 'Social networks, lay consultation and help-seeking behaviour', *Social Forces*, 51 (1973), 275–92.

Maclaren, A. A., *Religion and social class*, London: Routledge, 1974.

McLelland, D. C., *The achieving society*, London: Van Nostrand, 1961.

McManners, J., *Death and the Enlightenment*, Oxford University Press, 1981.

Maeda, D., 'Ageing in eastern society', in Hobman, D. (ed.), *The social challenge of ageing*, London: Croom Helm, 1978.

Mann, M., 'The social cohesion of liberal democracy', *Amer. Sociol. Rev.* 35 (1970), 423–31.

—— 'Work and the work ethic', in Jowell, R., Witherspoon, S., and Brook, L. (eds.), *British social attitudes: the 1986 report*, London: Gower, 1987.

Mannheim, K., 'The problem of generations', in Mannheim, K., and Kecskemeti, D., *Essays on the sociology of knowledge*, London: Routledge, 1952.

Marris, P., *Loss and change*, London: Routledge, 1974.

Marshall, G., *Presbyteries and profits*, Oxford University Press, 1980.

—— 'Mad Max true?', *Sociology*, 17 (1983), 569–73.

Martin, D., *A general history of secularisation*, Oxford: Blackwell, 1978.

Matthews, S. H., *The social world of old women*, London: Sage, 1979.

Mechanic, D., 'The stability of health and illness behaviour: results from a 16-year follow-up', *Amer. J. Publ. Health*, 69 (1979), 1142–5.

Mitchell, J. C. (ed.), *Social networks in urban situations*, Manchester University Press, 1969.

—— 'Social networks', *Ann. Rev. Anthropol.* 3 (1974), 279–99.

—— 'Case and situation analysis', *Sociol. Rev.* 31 (1983), 187–211.

—— 'Social network data', in Ellen, R. F. (ed.), *Ethnographic research*, London: Academic Press, 1984.

More, Thomas, *A dialogue of comfort*, London: Everyman, 1951.

Morishima, M., *Why has Japan 'succeeded'? Western technology and the Japanese ethos*, Cambridge University Press, 1982.

Morley, J., *Death, heaven and the Victorians*, London: Studio Vista, 1971.

Newby, H., *The deferential worker: a study of farm workers in East Anglia*, London: Allen Lane, 1977.

Office of Population Censuses and Surveys, *General household survey 1980*, London: HMSO, 1982.

—— *Population and vital statistics 1984*, London: HMSO, 1986.

—— *Mortality statistics 1980*, London: HMSO, 1983.

Ogston, D., *White stone country: growing up in Buchan*, Edinburgh: Ramsay Head Press, 1986.

O'Neill, B. J., *Social inequality in a Portuguese hamlet*, Cambridge University Press, 1987.

Ott, S., *The circle of mountains*, Oxford University Press, 1981.

Pahl, R. E., *Divisions of labour*, Oxford: Blackwell, 1984.

Palmore, E., *The honourable elders: a cross-cultural analysis of ageing in Japan*, Duke University Press, 1975.

Parkes, C. M., 'Psychosocial transitions', *Soc. Sci. & Med.* 5 (1971), 101–15.

Parkin, F., 'Strategies of social closure in class formation', in Parkin, F. (ed.), *The social analysis of class structure*, London: Tavistock, 1979.

Parsons, T., *The social system*, London: Routledge, 1951.

—— 'Definition of health and illness in the light of American values and social structure', in Jaco, E. G. (ed.), *Patients, physicians and illness*, Glencoe: Free Press, 1958.

Parsons, T., Fox, R. C., and Lidz, V. M., 'The "gift of life", and its reciprocation', *Social Research*, 39 (1972), 367–415.

Payne, G., Ford, G., and Robertson, C., 'Changes in occupational mobility
in Scotland: some preliminary findings of the 1975 Scottish Mobility
Study, *Scottish J. Sociol.* 1 (1976), 57–79.

Pharos International (Summer 1986).

Phillipson, C., *Capitalism and the construction of old age*, London:
Macmillan, 1982.

Pill, R., and Stott, N. C. H., 'Concepts of illness causation and responsibility:
some preliminary data from a sample of working-class mothers', *Soc.
Sci. and Med.* 16 (1982), 43–52.

—— and —— 'Choice or chance: further evidence on ideas of illness and
responsibility for health', *Soc. Sci. and Med.* 20 (1985), 981–91.

de Pina Cabral, J., *Sons of Adam, daughters of Eve*, Oxford University
Press, 1986.

Pincus, L., *Death and the family*, London: Faber, 1976.

Pius XII, 'Religious and moral aspects of pain prevention in medical
practice', Address of 24 February 1957, *Irish Ecclesiastical Record*,
88 (1957), 193–209.

—— 'Allocution on ordinary and extraordinary means', *Acta Apostolicae
Sedis*, 24 November 1957.

Porter, R. (ed.), *Patients and practitioners: lay perceptions of medicine in
pre-industrial society*, Cambridge University Press, 1985.

Price, L., 'Art, science, faith and medicine; the implications of the placebo
effect,' *Sociol. of Health and Illness*, 6 (1984), 61–73.

Quiller-Couch, A. (ed.), *The Oxford book of English verse*, 2nd. edn.,
Oxford University Press, 1939.

Registrar-General (Scotland), *Annual Report 1984,* Edinburgh: HMSO, 1985.

Richards, N. D., 'Methods and effectiveness of health education, *Soc.
Sci. and Med.* 9 (1975), 141–56.

Riddle, S., 'Age, obsolescence and unemployment—older men in the
British industrial system 1920–1939: a research note', *Ageing and
Society*, 4 (1984), 517–24.

Robinson, D., *The process of becoming ill*, London: Routledge, 1971.

Rodgers, D. T., *The work ethic in industrial America 1850–1920*, University of Chicago Press, 1978.

Rose, A. M., 'The subculture of the ageing', in Rose, A. M., and Peterson,
W. A., *Older people and their social world*, Philadelphia: Davis, 1965.

Rose, M., *Reworking the work ethic*, London: Batsford, 1985.

Rosenblatt, P. C., Walsh, R. P., and Jackson, D. A., *Grief and mourning in
cross-cultural perspective*, New Haven: Human Relations Area Files
Press, 1976.

Rosow, I., *Social integration of the aged*, New York, Free Press, 1967.

—— *Socialisation to old age*, University of California Press, 1974.

Royal College of General Practitioners, Office of Population Censuses and Surveys, and Dept. Health and Social Security, *Morbidity statistics from general practice 1970–71: socio-economic analyses*, Studies on Med. and Pop. Subjects no. 46, London: HMSO, 1982.

Russell, C., *The ageing experience*, Sydney: Allen and Unwin, 1981.

Scase, R., 'Conceptions of the class structure and political ideology: some observations on attitudes in England and Sweden', in Parkin, F. (ed.), *The social analysis of class structure*, London: Tavistock, 1974.

Schuman, H., and Johnson, M. P., 'Attitudes and behaviour', *Ann. Rev. Sociol.* 2 (1976), 161–207.

Scott, J., 'Social network analysis', *Sociology,* 22 (1988), 109–27.

Scottish Education Department, *Home care services, day care establishments and day services 1980, Scotland*, Statistical Bulletin, Social Work Services Group, 1981.

—— *Residential accommodation for the elderly, Scotland 1980*, Statistical Bulletin, Social Work Services Group, 1981.

Shanas, E., Townsend, P., Wedderburn, D., Fries, H., Milhøj, P., and Stehouwer, J., *Old people in three industrial societies*, London: Routledge, 1968.

Silverman, D., 'Going private: ceremonial forms in a private oncology clinic', *Sociology*, 18 (1984), 191–204.

—— *Communication and medical practice*, London: Sage, 1987.

Simmel, G., *The web of group affiliations*, tr. Bendix, R., Glencoe: Free Press, 1955.

Smith, S. R., 'Growing old in an age of transition', in Stearns, P. N. (ed.), *Old age in pre-industrial society*, New York: Holmes and Meier, 1982.

Smout, T. C., *A history of the Scottish people 1560–1830*, London: Fontana, 1972.

Stacey, M., Batstone, E., Bell, C., and Murcott, A., *Power, persistence and change: a second study of Banbury*, London: Routledge, 1975.

Stainton-Rogers, W., 'Accounting for health and illness: a social psychological investigation', Ph.D. thesis, Open University, 1987.

Stannard, D. E., *The Puritan way of death*, Oxford University Press, 1977.

Stearns, P. N., *Old age in European society*, London: Croom Helm, 1976.

Stewart, A., Prandy, K., and Blackburn, R. M., *Social stratification and occupations*, London: Macmillan, 1980.

Stimson, G., and Webb, B., *Going to see the doctor*, London: Routledge, 1975.

Stone, L., *The family, sex and marriage in England 1500–1800*, London: Weidenfeld and Nicolson, 1977.

Strong, P. M., *The ceremonial order of the clinic*, London: Routledge, 1979.

Sudnow, D., *Passing on: the social organisation of dying*, Englewood Cliffs: Prentice Hall, 1967.

Sutherland, I., *Health education: perspectives and choices*, London: Allen and Unwin, 1979.

Szasz, T., and Hollender, M. H., 'A contribution to the philosophy of medicine', *Arch. Intern. Med.* 97 (1956), 585–92.

Szreter, S. R. S., 'The genesis of the Registrar-General's social classification of occupations', *Brit. J. Sociol.* 35 (1984), 522–46.

Tawney, R. H., *Religion and the rise of capitalism*, London: Pelican, 1938.

Tedeschi, J. T., and Lindskold, S., *Social psychology*, London: Wiley, 1976.

Tholfsen, T. R., *Working class radicalism in mid-Victorian England*, London: Croom Helm, 1976.

Thomas, J., 'Ideology and elective affinity', *Sociology*, 19 (1985), 39–54.

Thomas, K., *Religion and the decline of magic*, London: Penguin, 1971.

Thomson, D., 'The decline of social welfare: falling state support for the elderly since Victorian times', *Ageing and Society*, 4 (1984), 451–82.

Thompson, E. P., 'Time, work discipline and industrial capitalism', *Past and Present*, 38 (1967), 56–97.

Titmuss, R. M., *Commitment to welfare*, London: Allen and Unwin, 1968.

Totman, R., *Social causes of illness*, London: Souvenir Press, 1980.

Towler, R., *Homo religiosus*, London: Constable, 1974.

Trevor-Roper, H. R., 'Religion, the reformation and social change', *Historical Studies*, 4 (1963), 18–44.

Troeltsch, E., *The social teaching of the Christian churches*, tr. Wyon, O., London: Allen and Unwin, 1931.

Troyansky, D. G., 'Old age in the rural family of enlightened Provence', in Stearns, P. N. (ed.), *Old age in pre-industrial society*, New York: Holmes and Meier, 1982.

Tuckett, D., Boulton, M., Olson, C., and Williams A., *Meetings between experts: an approach to sharing ideas in medical consultations*, London: Tavistock, 1985.

Turner, B. S., *Religion and social theory*, London: Heinemann, 1983.

Veatch, R. M., and Tai, E., 'Talking about death: patterns of lay and professional change', in Fox, R. C. (ed.), *The social meaning of death*, Annals of the American Academy of Political and Social Science, 1980.

Vovelle, M., *La mort et l'Occident de 1300 à nos jours*, Paris: Gallimard, 1983.

Waddell, G., Main, C. J., Morris, E. W., and Gray, I. C. M., 'Chronic low back pain, psychologic distress, and illness behaviour', *Spine*, 9 (1984), 209–13.

Waddington, I., 'The role of the hospital in the development of modern medicine', *Sociology*, 7 (1973), 211–24.

Waitzkin, H., 'Medicine, superstructure and micropolitics', *Soc. Sci. and Med.* 13A (1979), 601–9

Warr, P., 'Job loss, unemployment and psychological well-being', in van de Vliert, E., and Allen, V. (eds.), *Role transitions*, New York: Praeger, 1983.

Weber, M., 'The social psychology of the world religions', in Gerth, H. H., and Mills, C. W., *From Max Weber*, London: Kegan Paul, 1947.

Wellman, B., 'Domestic work, paid work and network', in Duck, S., and Perlman, D. (eds.), *Personal relations*, London: Sage, 1985.

Westminster confession of faith, Edinburgh, Blackwood, 1928.

White, G. M., 'The role of cultural explanations in "somatisation" and "psychologisation"', *Soc. Sci. and Med.* 16 (1982), 1519–30.

White, P., 'Limitations on verbal reports of internal events: a refutation of Nisbett and Wilson and of Bem', *Psychol. Rev.* 87 (1980), 105–12.

Whyte, W. H., *The organisation man*, London: Cape, 1957.

Wicker, A. W., 'Attitudes versus actions: the relationship of verbal and overt behavioural responses to attitude objects', *J. Soc. Issues*, 25 (1969), 41–78.

Wiener, M., *English culture and the decline of the industrial spirit 1850–1980*, Cambridge University Press, 1981.

Williams, G., 'The genesis of chronic illness: narrative reconstruction', *Sociol. of Health and Illness*, 6 (1984), 175–200.

Williams, G., *The sanctity of life and the criminal law*, London: Faber, 1958.

Williams, R. G. A., 'Theories and measurement in disability', *Epidemiol. and Community Health*, 33 (1979), 32–47.

—— 'Rationing: how it is done with community services for the disabled', *Int. Rehab. Med.* 2 (1980), 160–6.

—— 'Logical analysis as a qualitative method', *Sociol. of Health and Illness*, 3 (1981), 141–87.

—— 'The salt of the earth: ideas linking diet, exercise and virtue among elderly Aberdonians', in Murcott, A. (ed.), *The sociology of food and eating*, London: Gower, 1983.

—— 'Concepts of health: an analysis of lay logic', *Sociology*, 17 (1983), 185–204.

—— 'Awareness and control of dying: some paradoxical trends in public opinion', *Sociol. of Health and Illness*, 11.3 (1989), 202–12.

Wilson, B., *Religion in sociological perspective*, Oxford University Press, 1982.

Wittgenstein, L., *Philosophical investigations*, tr. Anscombe, G. E. M., Oxford: Blackwell, 1953.

von Wright, G. H., *Explanation and understanding*, Ithaca: Cornell University Press, 1971.

Index

The index includes a general index of authors and subject-matter, and also, under each chapter topic treated in Part I, a detailed index of the ideas and combinations of ideas there discussed.